SECOND EDITION

NELSON MOSES | HARRIET B. KLEIN

Long Island University   New York University

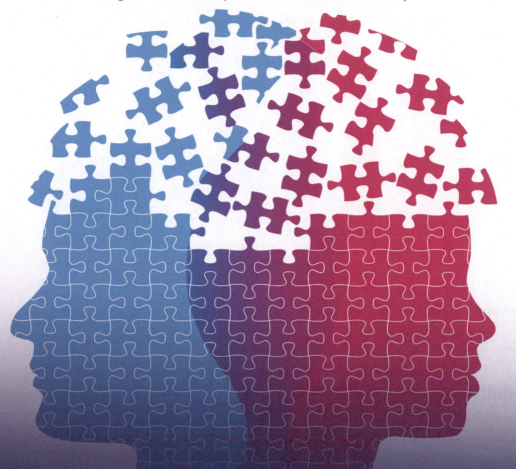

INTERVENTION PLANNING
for Communication Problems
Across the Lifespan

STRIVING FOR EVIDENCE-BASED PRACTICE

Kendall Hunt
publishing company

Cover image: © Shutterstock.com

Figures within book by Nelson Moses unless otherwise noted.

Kendall Hunt
publishing company

www.kendallhunt.com
Send all inquiries to:
4050 Westmark Drive
Dubuque, IA 52004-1840

contents

PART 1: FOUNDATIONS OF INTERVENTION PLANNING 1

PART 2: SELECTED CASES OF SPEECH AND LANGUAGE INTERVENTION IN CHILDREN AND ADULTS 159

PART 1

Foundations of Intervention Planning

Introduction to Evidence-Based Intervention Planning

READER WILL:

- Become familiar with the process of intervention planning
- Describe the nature of language
- Define evidence-based practice
- Describe categories of evidence

The practice of speech-language pathology involves affecting change in the functional communication of individuals who are experiencing problems communicating effectively. Functional communication has been defined as "the ability to receive and convey messages regardless of the mode, to communicate effectively and independently in natural environments" (ASHA FACS, Frattali, Thompson, Holland, Wohl, & Ferketic, 1995, p.42). The emphasis here is on effective communication, which involves the expression of the speaker's intent to a communicative partner, as well as comprehension by the speaker of a partner's intent. The emphasis is also on communication expressed in *natural* contexts (and not restricted to therapeutically contrived settings).

Promoting communicative independence and effectiveness in individuals who have been diagnosed as having a speech or language problem involves systematic and careful intervention planning. The essence of "intervention planning" is the determination of intervention goals and the development of procedures. An intervention goal is a potential achievement by an individual with speech/language dysfunction directed toward the improvement of speech/language performance. An intervention procedure represents the clinician's plan of action, that is, conceptualizing and implementing interactions and contexts to facilitate the achievement of desired linguistic goals (Klein & Moses, 1999a). As one can well imagine, intervention planning in speech-language pathology is a challenging decision-making process.

Intervention planning is challenging because the behavioral system targeted for change—speech and language—is complex. Language is a multimodal, nonlinear behavioral system. *Multimodal* signifies that language comprises multiple interactive yet unique subsystems; these subsystems have traditionally been grouped within a "content/form/use" rubric, with "content" signifying ideation and semantic relations represented by form (phonology, morphology, syntax, and story grammar) and use referring to the adaptive functions that language serves and the pragmatic devices employed to achieve functionally effective communication (Bloom & Lahey, 1978).

Nonlinear signifies that each component of language has its own organizational characteristics. These characteristics on one hand exist independently of the organizational characteristics of the other subsystems of language; on the other, all components of language interact with one another. Thus, the structure of semantics is not the same as phonologic organization, which is distinct from the rules of syntax, and so on; nevertheless, each influences the others. Any and all subsystems of language, therefore, have the potential to influence any speech-language problem and may need to be addressed in the course of intervention planning.

Still further, language interacts with nonlinguistic behavioral systems, namely, cognition, sensorimotor, and psychosocial. Typical language development is supported by intact behavioral systems. A problem in any one of the nonlinguistic behavioral systems may contribute to the maintenance of a speech-language problem. These potential maintaining factors will need to be considered in intervention planning (Klein & Moses, 1999).

Figure 1.1 depicts the interaction between language, its subsystems, and nonlinguistic behavioral systems.

It must also be noted that language receives influence from two sources: the environment that each individual finds himself or herself in, and the

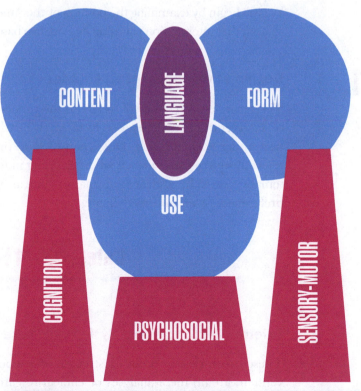

FIGURE 1.1: Sensorimotor

universal, linguistically generative, properties of the human mind. The term *universal* signifies that a common set of relational (i.e., organizational) processes influence all human languages. *Generative* signifies that these organizational processes are creative and underlie the production and comprehension of an unlimited variety of utterances that incorporate the organizational properties of the language system and enable functional communication. These two source of influence—the environment and the mind—have to be taken into consideration in the course of intervention planning.

When we think about procedure planning, two additional bodies of information must be considered: theoretical premises of learning and rehabilitation and the clinically relevant research that tests the utility of these premises as guides to speech-language interventions. These premises and the related clinical research have implications for designing procedures that will be effective in achieving goals established for particular clients.

It is into this complex world of speech and language that both client and clinician enter in the process of intervention planning. It is our intention to help the speech-language clinician navigate intervention planning by explicating decision-making that defines the process and sources of information and underlying principles that guide the process. Along the way, we provide exercises intended to concretize our description of the process and principles of intervention planning. We believe this text will provide useful guidelines for making decisions about intervention goals and procedures, applicable to the variety of clients and range of presenting problems the clinician may encounter in practicum or professional practice. We will begin by examining the position of the American Speech-Language-Hearing Association; that intervention planning be evidence based (Klein & Moses, 1999a).

Defining Evidence-Based Practice

The term "evidence-based" refers to the process of developing goals and procedures of intervention with reference to research bearing upon the efficacy of the intervention under consideration. Dollaghan (2007a) proposes that clinicians integrate three relevant sources of evidence when planning interventions: external evidence from systematic research, evidence internal to clinical practice, and evidence concerning the preferences of an informed client.

Categories of Evidence

External Evidence from Systematic Research

These categories, in order of strength of support for a particular approach to intervention, are (a) meta-analyses of clinical research addressing the treatment of a particular speech-language impairment, (b) randomized controlled experiments assessing particular treatment procedures, (c) case study examinations of an intervention protocol, and (d) clinical experiences of respected authorities (American Speech- Language-Hearing Association, 2004). Each of these categories of information plays an important role in the process of planning goals and procedures (see, also, Galloway, Blikman, Omaivboje, & O'Rourke, 2009; Phillips, Ball, Sackett, Badenoch, Straus, Haynes, & Dawes, 1998; 2009).

META-ANALYSES. There are published studies that reanalyze all of the research conducted over the years that has focused on specific intervention procedures for specific disorder categories. This research design is termed "meta-analysis." ASHA's task force on evidence-based practice considers meta-analyses of clinical research *the strongest* (Level 1) source of evidence for intervention planning. Such studies provide critical methodological and statistic assessments of the research available to clinicians.

TRUE EXPERIMENTS. True experiments that evaluate specific intervention programs represent Level 2 evidence. Such studies involve large numbers of participants randomly assigned to experimental groups (which received the treatment under study) and control groups (who did not). Such research has the potential to provide clear evidence of the efficacy of a specific intervention procedure. An experiment may demonstrate that a particular intervention procedure is an effective way to achieve a behavior that was targeted in the study.

The question may arise, however, whether the behavior acquired by the client contributes to the achievement of functional communication. In other words, was there a change in the individual's spontaneous speech and language in everyday situations? For example, there are a number of studies that support prioritizing more complex over less complex sounds in the treatment of phonological disorders. Results describing success of the treatment are reported with reference to successful trials on testing probes. These results of treatment have not yet advanced to follow-up in conversational speech settings (e.g., Gierut, Morrisette, Hughes, & Rowland, 1996). A similar situation obtains with the research supporting the "Fast Forward" approach to the treatment of language disorders. Here too, positive results are measured by improvement in responses on tasks that are similar to those in the treatment protocol rather than in conversational speech settings (Gillam, Loeb, Hoffman, Bohman, Champlin, Thibodeau, Widen, Brandel. Friel-Patti, 2008).

Evidence Internal to Clinical Practice

CLINICAL OUTCOMES. In the course of clinical practice, clinicians write goals, which include criteria for their achievement (e.g., Client will produce /k/ in initial position of CVC words in 8/10 trials). Clinicians then collect data during the clinical session to determine whether the stated criterion for goal achievement (e.g., /k/ produced in the word's initial context 8/10 trials) has been met. Clinical intervention comprises, in essence, mini studies yielding evidence about how effective the clinician's procedures were in helping the client achieve goals. Clinicians may refer to various facets of this self-generated evidence internal to clinical practice in planning future interventions.

THEORETIC PERSPECTIVES. Related both to evidence derived from outcomes of clinical practice and published research is "theory." Clinicians typically reflect upon their work; specifically, goals successfully achieved or unsuccessfully attempted, and procedures employed. In the process, clinicians may try to understand better how to think about language in general or the specific behavior targeted. Clinicians may try to explain why the procedures they have employed were effective or not in facilitating outcomes, and whether outcomes will truly affect the client's functional communication. Ideas about the nature of language and language learning represent personal theories about what language is and how language is acquired and functional communication achieved. Theories of language and language learning, personally constructed or drawn from the research literature, guide the development of specific goals and procedures (Fey & Justice, 2004; Lonsbury-Martin, 2006). Such explanations aid in the evaluation and interpretation of published research. Theoretic considerations are especially important in assessing whether specific clinical achievements obtained in a research study contribute to functional communication in real-world settings. Theoretic premises also help clinicians address gaps in evidence on best practices available in the literature.

It is helpful for the clinician to be cognizant of the various perspectives on speech and language that have evolved over the years. That is because different lines of thinking offer potentially important and unique information relevant to the achievement of functional communication given a particular communication problem. Consider, for example, three perspectives on language that contribute to intervention planning in cases of language delay and language disorders: operant, information processing, and psycholinguistic.

Skinner's classic 1957 work, *Verbal Behavior*, drew the field's attention to observable behavior (operants) and features of the observable context (discriminative and reinforcing stimuli) as fundamental to our understanding of language and its acquisition. The influence of Skinner' work in areas such as treatment of individuals with autistic spectrum disorder continues to be strong; this influence is pervasive and exemplified in popular programs such as applied behavior analysis (Lovaas, 1987) and picture exchange system (PECS; Frost & Bondy, 1994).

Skinner's position was in contradistinction to information processing models of the day (e.g., Osgood, 1957). These models focused on mental processes, such as memory, retrieval, discrimination, and closure. Information processing models have continued to evolve, however, especially in the domain of executive functions (i.e., the reflective use of language for acquiring information and problem-solving; Singer & Bashir, 1999). Witness contemporary assessment instruments, such as the clinical evaluation of language fundamentals (CELF-5; Wiig, Semel, Secord, 2013), and treatment programs for children and adults with language-learning disabilities and language disorders (e.g., strategy training—Council for Exceptional Children, 2011; Fast ForWord—Tallal,1997; phonological awareness programs—Gillam, 2012).

Meanwhile, another voice emerged that drew our attention to the genetic bases of language ignored by Skinner; the voice also challenged the mechanistic bent of information processing models of the day. That voice was Chomsky's, who introduced a generative and minimalist approach to our understanding of language and language acquisition. This approach, which focused primarily on syntax, has had a powerful influence on language assessment and intervention (e.g., Bloom & Lahey, 1978; Lee,1974; Tyack & Gottsleben, l974).

In the early1970s, given Chomsky's influence, the presumption was that training in aspects of form (morphology, syntax) would lead to improvement in overall *expressive language*. After the publication of the book *Language Development and Disorders* (Bloom & Lahey, 1978) the focus in the area of child language shifted to a consideration of three interactive components: content, form, and use. This change in perspective redirected the clinician to evaluate and treat children with language delays in naturalistic contexts. Such contexts integrating play and familiar caregiver–child interactions were believed to facilitate a child's integration of content, form, and use as a means of promoting functional communication. Contemporary programs, influenced by the Bloom and Lahey orientation, address intent, affect, and the act of communication itself to promote language learning (e.g., Bloom, 1995; Greenspan & Weider, 2006).

The application of these contrastive theories of language and language learning to intervention planning will be explicated in subsequent chapters.

MAINTAINING FACTORS. The evidence we seek as speech-language pathologists is first and foremost about the linguistic system itself (i.e., form, content, and use). In working with clients with various communication problems, however, one becomes aware that behavioral systems other than the speech and language system may be affecting communication. Cognition, sensorymotor functioning, and psychosocial status are factors that can affect speech and language function. In the course of clinical practice, the clinician may attempt to address suspect nonlinguistic factors, for example, hypotonicity and cognitive impairment in a child with Down's syndrome manifesting an articulation disorder Recognition of such factors as potentially maintaining a speech or language problem may lead the clinician to seek evidence from clinical research relevant to addressing such factors in the course of intervention. Behavioral systems implicated in intervention planning will be addressed in subsequent chapters.

Preferences of an Informed Client

COLLABORATION. As noted above, Dollaghan identifies the *informed client* as a source of evidence to guide intervention planning. Clinical intervention must be viewed as collaboration between client and clinician. The term *collaboration* signifies active participation of all parties, each contributing to and guiding the process. An informed client participates in establishing goals of treatment and procedures; this process involves communication by the client of personal knowledge, beliefs, and experiences—information that is taken into consideration by the clinician in the course of intervention planning. Critical information also includes contexts in which the client performs optimally, and contexts that pose special challenges. Information about cultural norms, which may influence communication and performance, constitutes an additional client-based factor.

CULTURAL AND LINGUISTIC DIVERSITY. Our profession is more than ever aware that cultural and linguistic diversity represents the norm in this country. Culture is about the behavior, beliefs, and values of a group of people who are brought together by their commonality (Battle, 2002). Culture interacts with ethnicity and socioeconomic status to influence language content, form, and use across the lifespan. In addition to language-specific differences among cultures, there are also differences in practices that are not strictly linguistic but that can have a significant influence upon clinical intervention. Such practices include childrearing procedures and families' approaches to clinical interventions.

Cultural practices can affect how a client responds to specific intervention procedures, such as listening to and then being queried about literature. The outcome may be a function of a related cultural practice. For example, a child accustomed to being read stories by parents and then questioned about the stories (as is typical in some cultures) might respond comfortably on standardized assessments given literature-based questioning procedures. Contrastively, a child entering therapy without the experience of being read to by parents but instead entertained with stories about personal experiences might respond very differently to direct questioning about a story (see Heath, 1983; Reese & Cox, 1999). It is, therefore, necessary to consider culture-related variables to establish appropriate intervention goals and procedures. Such variables include routines, foods, toys, games, technology, and norms of parenting, social interaction, and celebration (ASHA, 2009).

Based on the 2010 census, the U.S. Census Bureau reported that at least 25% of the American population comprises people of color: 13% are African American, 13% Hispanic, 6% Asian/Pacific American, and 2% native American and Eskimo. As many as 125 different languages are represented in New York City alone! There is a sizable literature that has described patterns of language acquisition in bilingual children and adults. Different patterns have been observed in those who achieved bilingualism simultaneously (two languages acquired together as young children), sequentially (a second language acquired after the first), and who experienced loss of a first language while acquiring a new language (Paradis, Genesee, & Crago, 2011) Typical patterns of language use, acquisition, and loss in such cases influence assessment and goal planning. Similar considerations apply to individuals who are bidialectal (use more than one dialect, or find themselves in situations where a dialect different from their own prevails; Khamis-Dakwar & Froud, 2007).

Evidence of Change with Development and Aging

Research that provides insights about development and change across the lifespan is foundational for intervention planning across the lifespan. For the purpose of intervention planning, it is useful to identify three periods of development and change: preschool, school age, and adult. Normative data across the lifespan provide an empirical basis for intervention planning. These data will be examined in subsequent chapters.

Behavioral change across the lifespan has been viewed within the frameworks of rehabilitation, habilitation, and intervention. Behavioral change as *rehabilitation* involves the recovery of former speech-language skills lost due to accident or illness. Behavioral change as *habilitation* involves the acquisition of novel skills. Behavioral change as a product of *intervention* is the shift in behavior as a consequence of some clinical interaction.

Conclusion

One might expect that clinical research provides program guides offering failsafe therapeutic recipes for resolving specified speech-language problems. Clinical research does not, however, work that way. The value of clinical research is realized as the clinician engages in the complex decision-making, problem-solving process that is "intervention planning." In the course of this process, consideration is given to all factors that might be contributing to a speech/language disorder, and processes that could affect change in communication performance. As the clinician considers these variables, he or she turns to corresponding research that could provide insight into the derivation of effective intervention goals and procedures.

In this chapter, we introduced an evidence-based model of intervention planning. This model incorporates essential categories of evidence derived from external clinical research, internal clinical practice, and preferences of an informed client. In the next chapter, we will address the idea that intervention planning proceeds in phases, and we will turn to the first phase of intervention planning—the long-term phase.

CHAPTER EXERCISES

1. Gillam et al. (2008) found that children with language-learning disabilities scored significantly higher on a test of phonologic awareness after six weeks of intervention following the Fast ForWord program than children following more traditional language programs. Participants receiving Fast ForWord intervention, however, did not fare better on assessments of general language performance (comprehension and production) than children receiving more traditional interventions, and some actually performed more poorly on such assessments. Given a child with learning disabilities, how might this information contribute to intervention planning? What cautions do these findings raise about their applicability to intervention?

2. In some Salvadoran families, children's ability to correctly respond to instructions containing nonspecific vocabulary (e.g., nonreferenced pronouns "it", "thing") is a sign of intelligence. The need for specific vocabulary is a sign of stupidity. How might such information inform intervention planning for a child whose performance on the Concepts and Following Directions subtest of the CELF-4 was problematic: The child refused to follow instructions, such as "Point to the last black car and the first white car."

RECOMMENDED TERM PROJECT

Choose one of the following articles, providing a systematic meta-analysis of intervention procedures in speech and/or language. Identify the following elements of this type of evidence.

1. Criteria for studies entering review

2. Number of studies identified

3. Basis of elimination

4. Overall findings

5. Effect on clinical treatment

RECOMMENDED TERM PROJECT REFERENCES

Ballard, K. J., Wambaugh, J. L., Duffy, J. R., Layfield, C., Mass, E., Mauszycki, S., & McNeil, M. R. (2015). Treatment for acquired apraxia of speech: A systematic review of intervention research between 2004 and 2012. *American Journal of Speech Language Pathology, 24*, 316–337.

Cherney L. R., Patterson, J. P., Raymer, A., Frymark, T., & Schooling, T. (2008). Evidence-based systematic review: Effects of intensity of treatment and constraint-induced language therapy for individuals with stroke-induced aphasia. *Journal of Speech, Language, and Hearing Research, 51*, 1282–1299.

Coleman, J. J., Frymark, T., Franceschini, N. M., & Theodoros, D. G. (2015). Assessment and treatment of cognition and communication skills in adults with acquired brain injury via telepractice: a systematic review. *American Journal of Speech-Language Pathology, 24*, 295–315.

Cleave, P. L., Becker, S. D., Curran, M. K., Owen Van Horne, A. J., & Fey, M. E. (2015). The efficacy of recasts in language intervention: A systematic review and meta-analysis. *American Journal of Speech Language Pathology, 24*, 237–255.

Fey, M. E., Richard, G. J., Geffner, D., Kamhi, A. G., Medwetsky, L., Paul, D., Ross-Swain, D., Wallach, G. P., Frymark, T., & Schooling, T. (2011). Auditory Processing Disorder and auditory/language interventions: An evidence-based systematic review. *Language, Speech & Hearing Services in Schools, 42*, 246–264.

Gillam, R., Loeb, D., Hoffman, L., Bohman, T., Champlin, C., Thibodeau, L., Widen, J., Brandel, J., & Friel-Patti, S. (2008). The efficacy of FastForWord language intervention for school age children with language impairment: A randomized control trial. *Journal of Speech, Language, and Hearing Research, 51*, 97–119.

Latoszek, B. B. V, Maryn, Y., Gerrits, E., & De Bodt, M. (2018). A Meta-Analysis: Acoustic Measurement of Roughness and Breathiness. Journal of Speech, Language, and Hearing Research, 61, 298–323.

Kurland, J., Stanek, III, E. J., Stokes, P., Li, M., & Andrianopoulos, M. (2016). Intensive language action therapy in chronic Aphasia: A randomized clinical trial examining guidance by constraint. *American Journal of Speech Language Pathology, 25*, S798–S781

Krock, W. C., & Leonard, L. B. (2015). Past tense production in children with and without specific language impairment across Germanic languages: A meta-analysis. *Journal of Speech, Language, and Hearing Research, 58*, 1326–1340.

Law, J., Garrett, Z., & Nye, C. (2004). The efficacy of treatment for children with developmental speech and language delay/disorder: a meta-analysis. *Journal of Speech, Language, and Hearing Research, 47*, 924–943.

Leung, Y., Oates, J., & Chan, S. P. (2018). Voice, articulation, and prosody contribute to listener perceptions of speaker gender: A systematic review and meta-analysis. *Journal of Speech, Language, and Hearing Research, 61*, 266–297.

Lof, G. L., & Watson, M. M. (2008). A nationwide survey of nonspeech oral motor exercise use: Implications for evidence-based practice. *Language, Speech, and Hearing Services in Schools, 39*(3), 392–407.

Melby-Lervåg, M., & Hulme, C. (2013). Is working memory training effective? A meta-analytic review. *Developmental Psychology, 49*(2), 270–291.

Murray, E., McCab, F., & Ballard, K. J. (2014). A systematic review of treatment outcomes for children with Apraxia of speech. *American Journal of Speech Language Pathology, 23*, 1–19.

Ntourou, K., Conture, E. G., & Lipsey, M. W. (2011). Language Abilities of Children Who Stutter: A Meta-Analytical Review. *AJ S LP*, 20, 163–179.

Robey, R. R. (1998). A meta-analysis of clinical outcomes in the treatment of Aphasia. *JSLHR, 41*, 172–187.

Salis C, Hwang F, Howard D, & Lallini N. (2017). Short-term and working memory treatments for improving sentence comprehension in Aphasia: A review and a replication study. *Seminars in Speech and Language, 38*, 29–39.

Scott, K., A., Roberts, J. A., & Glennen, S. (2011). How well do children who are internationally adopted acquire language? A Meta-Analysis. *JSLHR, 54*, 1153–1169.

Sirtori, C. D., Moja, V, Gatti L., & Eur, R. (2010). Constraint-induced movement therapy in stroke patients: systematic review and meta-analysis. *European Journal of Physical Rebalitative Medicine 46*, 537–544.

2

Long-Term Planning: Establishing a Foundation for All Subsequent Planning Phases

READER WILL:

- Define long-term goals across the lifespan and across disorder types in terms of functional communication
- Distinguish subordinate long-term goals as intrinsic to long-term goal planning
- Identify baseline data in speech and language and maintaining factors as foundational to long-term goal planning
- Identify developmental and complexity taxonomies as foundational to long-term goal planning

Planning Phases

We will now examine the basics of intervention planning—the determination of intervention goals and procedures. In the course of intervention planning, the clinician envisions three types of goals: long term, short term, and session. The clinician also derives a procedural approach to goal achievement.

It is our view that given the complexity inherent in goal and procedure planning, developing these different types of goals and procedures involves three phases of decision-making. The term "phases" denotes a developmental process. In the course of planning, the clinician himself or herself undergoes a developmental process in which he or she establishes a relationship with the client and engages with diagnostic information concerning the client. As he or she engages, the clinician achieves greater and greater insight about the client's strengths and difficulties, and variables that will need to be addressed, manipulated, and modified in the course of intervention; the clinician makes discoveries and relationships relevant to the establishment of long-term goals and a procedural approach (planning phase 1), short-term goals and an operationalized procedural approach (planning phase 2), and finally session goals and procedures (planning phase 3).

As we delve into the planning phases, we will exemplify decision-making by following three clients: two children (Amahl and Darryl) and an adult (Mr. B). A diagnostic profile of each appears in Appendix 2. We turn now to the initial long-term planning phase, within which a foundation is established for the entire intervention planning process.

Long-Term Planning Phase

Our conceptualization of long-term planning is, admittedly, nontraditional. Tradition in the field of communication disorders is to approach long-term planning as a kind of nuisance or atavistic appendage to what is perceived as the real job of planning, generating a lesson plan for today's session. Thus, clinicians typically write very general, all-encompassing, nonspecific long-term goals: We are all too familiar with the iconic long-term goal in cases of language delay: "to improve receptive and expressive language."

Our approach to long-term goal planning is different. Long-term planning serves as a guide for all subsequent goal and procedure planning. The long-term goal and procedural approach serve as the basis for short term through session goals and procedures. Far from being a nuisance, long-term planning is arguably the most critical planning phase.

The Long-Term Goal as Functional Communication

The long-term goal represents the ultimate outcome of speech-language intervention—the prognosis. As such, the long-term outcome of speech-language intervention is by necessity the client's achievement of an optimal level of functional communication, optimal being dictated by the client's potential in interaction with the clinician's skill. It bears repeating that functional communication involves the expression of the speaker's intent to a communicative partner, as well as comprehension by the speaker of a partner's intent. Functional communication is expressed in *natural* contexts (and not restricted to therapeutically contrived settings). Regardless of the specific area of speech and language being addressed in intervention, from the client's perspective, the ability to communicate effectively and functionally across the vicissitudes of daily experience is the desired outcome of intervention. As clinicians, we will, therefore, devise long-term goals that specify an optimal level of functional communication that will be achieved within natural (as opposed to therapeutic) contexts and within the specified long-term time frame. Since a functional communication goal will be specific to a client and speech/language disorder, it would not be appropriate for an LTG to be expressed as "The client will achieve functional communication."

Language As an Organizing Property of the Mind—The Foundation of Functional Communication

Our approach to long-term goal writing is influenced by Noam Chomsky (2004, 2013, 2014). Chomsky has described Language (capital "L") as a biologic property of the mind. This definition of *Language* as property of mind stands in contrast to more traditional definitions, such as Bloom and Lahey's, which stipulates language (written here with a lowercase "l") as the specific codes (i.e., English, Spanish, Urdu, etc.) that represent ideas about the world. To Chomsky, *Language* as property of mind interacts with the sensorimotor system and perception to generate and comprehend the varieties of linguistic codes that represent the languages of the world.

Language as property of mind is genetically based and biologic; as such, language has universal, generative, organizing properties. The term *universal* signifies that there are a common set organizational processes that influence all human languages. *Generative* signifies that these organizational processes are creative and underlie the production and comprehension of an unlimited variety of utterances in the course of daily experiences; generativity enables functional communication. Envisioning long-term goals of speech and language intervention involves describing achievable linguistic behavior in terms of the communicative, functional, and organizational features of the behavior—these are the necessary properties of functional communication.

Developmental Research That Guides Long-Term Goal Planning

With our focus on functionality and generativity as long-term outcomes of intervention, we have established the principle that long-term goals (and short-term goals) across the lifespan be conceptualized as either developmental or complexity based. The behavioral categories that are central to long-term goals represent organizing and relationship-making characteristics expressed in the comprehension and production of language, and ultimately influence language behavior—both expressive and receptive—across multiple contexts. These behavioral categories are found within pub-lished developmental taxonomies. Developmental (and complexity) taxonomies are our guides for long-term and short-term goal planning.

DEVELOPMENTAL TAXONOMIES. Developmental taxonomies provide us with three sets of information: (a) components of speech and language that may be targeted in the course of intervention, (b) the organization of the components, and (c) the typical se-quences in development of these components.

For example, Bloom and Lahey (1978; Lahey, 1988) identify content/form/use com-ponents of language; specific components described in their taxonomy include content categories, subject-verb-complement constituents of syntax, and language functions. Their taxonomy describes phases in the development of object-relation and event-relation content categories, syntax, morphology, and functions of language in children. The acquisition or rehabilitation of components of language such as these are poten-tial long-term and short-term goals.

Other examples of developmental taxonomies that can provide direction in long-term and then short-term goal planning are Dore's seminal (1975) taxonomy that identi-fies functions of intentional communication, phonologic processes identified by Klein (1981a, b), Hodson and Paden (1991), Shriberg and Kwiatkowski (1982), and others (e.g., Ingram, 1981); nonlinear phonological features (Bernhardt & Stemberger, 2000); and Greenspan's (2005) six essential stages of development (Greenspan & Lewis, 2005).

Examples of the influence on goal planning of taxonomies identified within clinical research can be identified within interventions (Weider, 2008), and similar developmen-tal, relationship-based programs (e.g., Social Communication/Emotional Regulation/Transactional Support—SCERTS; Prizant, Wetherby, Ruben, & Laurent, 2006) are examples, as is Carbone's (2007) operant verbal behavior program. Each of these pro-grams establishes goals of intervention based upon features of language as property of mind, such as content–form interactions, and functions of discourse between care-givers and children. The context for expression of such competencies is client directed (e.g., play, spontaneous conversation).

"Life participation approaches" (Chapey et al, 2000) to the treatment of language in adults with aphasia also target acts of functional communication in naturalistic contexts. Here, taxonomies of functional communication (i.e., content/form/use), derived from the developmental literature, lend themselves to the sequencing of short-term goals.

Long-term and short-term goals are written in terms of these kinds of behavioral cat-egories; for example, client will

- eliminate all developmental *phonological processes* that are no longer age expectant.

- produce interevent content–form interactions (complex sentences) in discourse.

- respond to request for information when given procedural and causal questions.

- coordinate respiration, phonation, and resonation to produce adequate volume for a range of pragmatic functions.

Session goals, on the other hand, may reflect a variety of targets, both developmental and skill oriented. The contrast between a behavioral category and a skill can be illustrated with reference to helping a nonverbal six-year-old make requests using an augmentative device. A long-term or short-term goal would be written in terms of the behavioral category, for example, "'requesting objects and actions' using an augmentative device." A session goal might be "'to request bathroom' using a Dynavox." The communication function "request" and the content categories of the request, "objects and actions," are developmental in nature; according to Dore (1978), requesting appears universally after one year of age, and applies to multiple possible objects and actions. "Objects and actions" are types of content that corresponds to Bloom and Lahey's (1978; Lahey, 1988) content categories "existence" and "action." Requesting "bathroom" is a skill; the specific request "bathroom" refers to only one target object. There is no developmental taxonomy that indicates when the specific things referenced appear in a child's repertoire. This principle will be elaborated as this chapter and this book progresses.

Subordinate Long-Term Goals and Related Taxonomies of Behavior

After identifying the broad area of communication to be targeted, it is necessary to consider whether this broad area of communication interacts with subsystems of speech and language that would be involved in improving communication in the targeted area. The identification of such subsystems of language may lead the clinician to consider targeting, simultaneously, a number of subordinate long-term goals, within his or her respective taxonomies.

For example, a five-year-old child with a language delay and favorable prognosis is expected to achieve language typical of his or her age group (i.e., narrative and conversational discourse). To address this ultimate achievement, it would make sense to identify the subsystems of language that are intrinsic to narrative and conversational discourse. These include narrative forms and story grammars (e.g., Labov & Waletsky, 1997; McCabe & Rollins, 1994; Lahey, 1988; Champion, 2003; also see Klein & Moses, 1999a), developmental morphemes, complex sentences, and pragmatic skills. Each of these areas contributes to the production and comprehension of discourse and may need to be addressed throughout the course of intervention; as such, any or all of these areas could be targeted at the long-term planning phase. Any related additional goals may be targeted as subordinate LTGs if they may be located within a separate hierarchy.

Another example comes from phonology. For a client with a moderate developmental delay in the area of phonology, an ultimate goal may be to acquire all segmental and prosodic features of the ambient language or to eliminate all phonological processes no longer age expectant; to this end, potential subordinate goals may address segmental features, syllable/word shapes, and stress contours (or syllable processes, substitution processes, and assimilation processes). Each of these areas may be embedded within its own developmental hierarchies. Figure 2.1 illustrates the relationship between ultimate behavioral achievements and subsidiary achievements that may be established as a set of subordinate long-term goals.

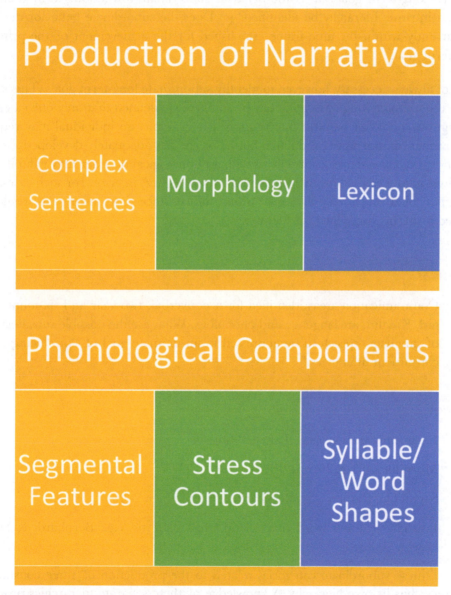

FIGURE 2.1: Long-Term Goal and Possible Subordinate Goal Areas: Language and Phonology

As indicated in Figure 2.1, the primary long-term goal, "the production of narratives," has an intrinsic hierarchy: narrative development from additive to causal content categories; similarly, other simultaneously occurring linguistic categories (e.g., complex sentences, morphemes) have their own intrinsic hierarchies.

When individual hierarchies, associated with the primary long-term goal, can be determined we consider each behavioral category as a separate (although simultaneously occurring) long-term goal. There are three factors to be considered in establishing subordinate long-term goals: (a) Is the behavior subordinate to the long-term goal? (b) Can an intrinsic hierarchy be identified? (c) Does the subordinate behavior develop concurrently within the time frame established for the achievement of the primary long-term goal.

It is not always necessary, however, to identify subordinate long-term goals. This is because the ultimate long-term goal may be so narrowly defined that only one category of linguistic behavior requires intervention. For example, an individual may require improvement in narrative production but he or she has adequately developed lexicon and morphology systems. Some clients with a phonological disorder may exhibit only substitution processes, or even a single phoneme (e.g., /r/) in error. For such cases, the projection of a single long-term goal would suffice, since short-term goals would be derived from this single intrinsic hierarchy.

Exercises

Communication areas identified for a nonverbal, two-year and six-month-old girl, Kaytlin, are language and phonology. What are the possible subcategories of language/speech to be addressed in an ultimate goal of "producing three constituent utterances."

Answer

Language functions (e.g., Lahey, 1988)

Morphology (e.g., Brown, 1973)

Segmental features (e.g., Bernhardt & Stemberger, 2000)

Prosodic features: word shapes and stress patterns (e.g., Bernhardt & Stemberger, 2000)

Each of these subordinate categories related to the production of three constituent utterances has its own hierarchy. A knowledge of these separate hierarchies provides guidance for the formulation of short-term goals in each category.

Maintaining Factors

Our model of intervention planning directs us to identify, at the outset of long-term goal planning, those behavioral systems other than language itself that may be maintaining the speech and language problem under consideration. Three behavioral systems known to influence language learning and performance are the cognitive, sensorimotor, and psychosocial systems. An impairment in one or more of these behavioral systems may contribute to a communication problem.

In general, knowledge of the number and severity of maintaining factors at the long-term planning phase is a consideration in making a prognosis—how much can be expected of a client in the long-term. The more behavioral systems involved in a disability and the greater their involvement, the poorer the prognosis. Beyond prognosis, nonlinguistic maintaining factors have implications for both goal and procedure planning. In this chapter, we will consider the influence of maintaining factors on long-term goal planning. Subsequent chapters examine how a consideration of maintaining factors guides procedural decisions across all planning phases, as well as the derivation of session goals.

COGNITION. A deficit in cognition will likely influence language content and both metalinguistics and executive functions that language serves. A cognitive delay may therefore be addressed in long-term goals for children at prelinguistic developmental levels that address developmental achievements that may contribute to the development of language content. Such goals may address pretend-play and prelinguistic functions of intentional communication.

We will return to cognition as a maintaining factor in our consideration of intervention procedures in Chapter 4.

SENSORIMOTOR SYSTEM. The sensorimotor system is a second behavioral system that supports speech-language function; if deficient, the sensorimotor system can maintain a speech-language problem. With our emphasis on intervention planning across the lifespan we are concerned with four interrelated areas of sensorimotor functioning; these are (a) speech-related perception, (b) maintenance of body stability and movement of the body through space, (c) the processing of sensory feedback, and (d) sensorimotor functioning of the peripheral speech mechanism. The individual's functional status in each of these areas has implications for the development of intervention procedures addressing language content, form, and use. The speech-language pathologist's cognition of the potential sensorimotor contribution to a speech-language disorder has additional implications for collaborative assessments and intervention planning (involving occupational and physical therapists).

In this chapter, we will discuss speech-related perception, since perception bears upon goal-setting considerations. We will return to sensorimotor behavior as a maintaining factor in Chapter 4 addressing the development of a procedural approach as well as in discussions of procedure planning in subsequent chapters.

SPEECH-RELATED PERCEPTION. Speech/language clinicians often address perceptual abilities in individuals with communication disorders. Children with articulation disorders are taught to attend to, compare, and distinguish among speech sounds. A review of the research in perception suggests that "A relationship between speech-sound perception and production in some children with speech disorders seems to exist, although the precise nature of that relationship has not been determined" (Bernthal, Bankson, & Flipsen, Jr., 2017, p. 151).

The evidence indicates that one must consider the source of speech production, that is, the discrimination target: speech of another person (external) or judgment of one's own speech (internal; Bernthal, et al.) The evidence indicates, further, that if perceptual testing is undertaken, the assessment should focus only on those sounds that the individual misarticulates (Lof, 2003). If training in speech perception is indicated, this intervention should be undertaken concurrently with exercises in speech production (Rvachew, 1994).

IMPLICATIONS FOR INTERVENTION PLANNING. Perception is a potential factor contributing to a communication disorder and the ability to engage in functional communication. A clinical activity targeting perception, such as discriminating contrasting sound pairs, however, does not represent functional communication. Therefore, perceptual skills cannot be long-term goals of intervention. Skills, such as discrimination of contrasting sound productions, can be session goals, and perceptual exercises can be session procedures.

Sensorimotor behaviors are not targeted as long-term goals of intervention. However, the severity of the sensorimotor problem and its identified influence on language bear upon the prognosis—the prediction of a client's ultimate achievements within the time frame established for achievement of the long-term goal.

Psychosocial

Given that language serves critical affective and social functions, difficulties in psychosocial functioning may contribute to a speech/language disorder. Psychosocial factors that affect speech/language functioning include (a) the individual's ability to engage in and benefit from social interactions; (b) the individual's typical affect and strategies for adapting to environmental demands, including reactions to communicative successes and failures; (c) the caregiver's or partner's efforts to facilitate communication development and their reactions to the individual's communicative attempts; and (d) the characteristic composition of the client's environment (caregivers, spouses, partners, friends, peers, siblings, culture, socioeconomic background, affect, languages spoken, etc.).

Social skills are reflected in the pragmatics of language. Language functions, pragmatic skills, discourse skills, and speech acts that reflect theory of mind (the child's ability to think about another's point of view) can be targeted as goals of intervention. Goals can be written for the caregiver or significant other as well as the child or the adult. We will return to relationship-based matters when deriving procedural approaches in Chapter 4 and in subsequent chapters addressing procedural planning.

Long-Term Planning as a Foundation for Short-Term and Session Planning

Planning for the long-term involves establishing a foundation for all subsequent phases of intervention planning (i.e., short-term and session goal planning). That foundation is established by identifying (a) the communication area to be targeted, (b) taxonomies of behavior intrinsic to the area of communication targeted, (c) additional communication areas intrinsic to the broad communication area targeted as the long-term goal and identification of related taxonomies (subordinate goals), (d) projection of a time period, (e) a description of performance expected of the client by the end of the projected time period.

One more point before we examine each of the steps necessary to formulate long-term goals. It is somewhat paradoxical that we begin intervention planning by thinking about its termination. Nevertheless, this is exactly what we do when we embark upon intervention planning with a new client. We predict outcomes (the long-term goal) and specify a likely time frame for intervention. Thinking about the end-results of treatment cannot be avoided when a parent asks, "Will my child sound like other children his age when therapy is over?" or when a spouse asks, "How long will my husband need therapy?" or "How will he communicate at the termination of treatment?" The finite resources of families and public agencies constitute another factor that makes consideration of the termination of treatment, in terms of time frame and likely outcome, a clinician's professional responsibility. Answering questions regarding clinical outcomes is a highly complex task, central to professional accountability.

Appendix 2: Diagnostic Reports

Appendix 2A—Amahl

Any Town

Speech-Language-Hearing Disorders Clinic

Address

City, State

Speech and Language Evaluation

Client Name: <u>AM</u>   Primary Disorder: <u>Language and Speech</u>

Date of Birth:_____ Date of Testing:_____ Chronological Age: <u>9:6</u>

Parent/Caregiver Name:_____   Language of Testing:_____

Clinician: _____   Supervisor: _____

_____

Statement of Problem:

Amahl is a nine-year and six-month-old English-speaking child of African American descent. He was referred to the Anytown Speech-Language Hearing Clinic for an evaluation of articulation and language by his grandmother, who served as the primary informant. Amahl is diagnosed with autism spectrum disorder and cognitive disability.

Background History

Amahl manifested typical infant sound production (cooing and babbling) and began to use single words at 15 months. Currently, he produces primarily unintelligible word approximations, coupled with eye gaze, distal gestures, approximations of several manual signs, and aggressive actions (hitting directed at self and others) to communicate his intent during play and standardized testing. Grandmother reported that Amahl does not like milk, green vegetables, candy, and hard-textured foods.

Grandmother reported that mother was diagnosed with RH Factor incompatibility and hypertension during her pregnancy. Subsequently, Amahl was delivered via caesarian section and required incubation for approximately one month after birth. Postnatal medical history is unremarkable except for allergies (i.e., peanuts and seasonal allergies). No history of ear infections was reported. According to grandmother, early sensorimotor milestones were age appropriate. He crawled approximately at nine months, walked approximately at one year, and began to feed himself at one year.

Amahl lives in Brooklyn, New York, with his parents, grandmother, and great-grandmother. His father is employed as a plumber, and his mother is a teacher assistant. According to grandmother, family history of speech, language, and hearing problems is unremarkable.

Amahl has been attending a special education program since preschool with a class ratio 8:1:1. He receives occupational and speech therapy, 2 × 30 each. The focus of speech therapy is use of an assistive communication device to communicate intentions and desires. Grandmother reported that Amahl enjoys many different activities, such as watching videos on his computer, or Dora, Scooby Doo, and Sesame Street DVDs, and looking at books. Amahl counts, solves simple arithmetic problems (single-digit addition and subtraction), and reads Level 1 books. Grandmother was critical of present school program, emphasizing that the school is not providing Amahl adequate support.

Assessment Information

Results of Communication Assessment

Language

Standardized assessment:

The Receptive One-Word Picture Vocabulary Test was administered to assess Amahl's receptive language skills. His raw score was 24, and standard score 55, which places him below the first percentile.

Results indicate that Amahl's receptive language skills are severely delayed. Amahl identified familiar items and attributes. He had difficulty identifying action words and words of low frequency.

Two subtests (Letter–Word Identification and Writing Sample) of the Woodcock Johnson Proficiency battery were administered (nonstandard procedure). Amahl identified rebus representations of familiar objects, graphemes, and single words (to, dog). He wrote his name, alphabet, and numbers (1 to 10, given verbal prompts). Writing was disgraphic.

Amahl's language sample collected during a play situation was analyzed for content/form/use interactions according to Lahey's taxonomy. Results were as follows:

Content/Form Interactions

Content Category	Form	Developmental Phase	Productivity
Existence (SW)	Single word	1	Strong
Action (SW)	Single word, 2 constituents	1	Emerging
Quantity (SW)	Single words	1	Emerging
Attribution (SW)	Single words	3	Emerging

Amahl's language was productive for existence (naming objects) at phase 1. The use of word combinations was restricted.

Language Use

Amahl uses language to comment, request, and to respond to directions. Any responses, within a single turn, were contingent on the speaker.

Phonology/Articulation:

Goldman–Fristoe Test of Articulation–2 (GFTA-2). This test was administered to assess accuracy of single-word productions.

Results indicate a severe articulation delay. Amahl's phonemic inventory consists of the stops /t/,/d/,/b/,/p/,/k/,/g/ and the fricative /v/. The Prompt for Restructuring Oral Muscular Phonetic Targets Technique (PROMPT) was attempted to assess Amahl's response to motokinesthetic feedback. Given moderate to maximum physical and visual models during the assessment, Amahl was stimulable for the production of *nasals* /m/ and /n/, *fricative* /f/, and the *liquid* /l/. Groping behavior across all his productions was observed. Amahl's production of syllable shapes consists primarily of CV combinations.

Phonological process analysis. Results of a phonological process analysis were as follows:

Syllable Structure Process	Percentage of Occurrence
Cluster reduction	100
Final consonant deletion	89
Weak syllable deletion	85
Substitution/Manner/Place Change Process	**Proportion**
Stopping of fricatives	100
Vowel alternation	100
Gliding	100

Nonlinear Analysis

Inventory of Syllable Shapes. Results of a syllable structure analysis revealed that the only match with attempts at words of a variety of syllables was the CVCV structure.

Adult Target	Child's Production (Unmatched)
CVC house /haus/	V [ə]
CVCV feather /fɛðɚ/	CVCV [fɛ.do]
CVCC girl /gɝl/	CV [gʌ]
CVCCV window /wɪndo/	CVCV [wi.do]
CVCCVC jumping / dʒʌmpɪŋ/	CV [pi]
CCV tree /tri/	CV /ti/
CCVC /brʌʃ/	CV [bʌ]

Segmental/feature analysis

Results of a segmental analysis revealed that Amahl presents with a predominance of the +dorsal feature across the majority of his productions (e.g., lamp→[ka], chair→[kei]). He has acquired the coronal place node only for the sounds that required tongue tip articulation ([+anterior]; for example, t, d). In addition, there was no evidence of Amahl's spontaneous production of sounds that required the tongue blade articulation ([-anterior]; for example, ʧ, ʃ, r). Amahl demonstrated vowel distortion across all his productions. His productions are highly variable.

Voice

Pitch is high relative to age and gender. Intensity is typically soft. Amahl manifests minimal variation in prosody.

Fluency

Appears typical for his age.

Associated Behavioral Systems (Factors maintaining or supporting Communication Behavior).

Sensorimotor

Oral Peripheral Examination/Feeding

An oral peripheral examination was performed to evaluate Amahl's oral-facial structure and function, symmetry, coordination, and range of motion of his articulators. Labial symmetry and labial range of motion were judged to be adequate. However, lingual range of motion was limited as evidenced by his difficulty elevating the tongue. There was symmetry of the soft palate and apparent adequate velopharyngeal closure during vowel production.

During snack time, Amahl self-fed four cookies and drank thin liquids from a bottle. He exhibited a munching pattern with occasional lateral movements of the jaw and a delayed oral transit to swallowing.

Gross and fine motor function

Impaired fine motor function exacerbated by compromised proprioceptive function.

Hearing

Amahl passed a bilateral hearing screening at 25 dB. Normal hearing was supported in communicative interactions.

Cognition

Play skills were analyzed according to Nicolich (1977). Amahl played with sensory materials, puppets, cars, and food. Spontaneously and given a model and verbal command, Amahl demonstrated single-scheme pretend-play (Nicolich, phase 2) with replica toys (e.g., cars, spoon, Ernie figure), In the context of a routine, such as cooking (making Play Doh), Amahl demonstrated combinatorial scheme sequences (e.g., pouring and stirring). It is notable that Amahl used one hand in an effort to resolve a problem requiring bilateral hand movement (attempting to join Hot Wheel race tracks). Amahl requested help from the clinician by guiding the clinician's hand over the tracks.

A Piagetian assessment of problem-solving skills was conducted. Amahl manifested multischeme action sequences and tool use to engage in causal problem-solving. He made a replica toy car jump off a ramp by manipulating a switch. He manipulated a string to operate a toy elevator (upon request). Amahl accurately counted a group of five objects (cookies) arranged in a circle, without overcounting. This indicates that conservation of number is emerging.

Psychocial

Amahl, an only child, lives with his extended family (three generations). Primary caretakers are grandmother and great-grandmother due to the difficulty the mother has in regulating his aggressive behavior. He frequently directs his aggression toward his mother by hitting, kicking, and scratching. He attends an 8:1:1 public school program, for children with severe and profound developmental disabilities. He appears obsessed with miniature animal toys.

Summary/Impressions

Amahl, a nine-year and six-month-old English-speaking child of African American descent, presents with a severe language and speech delay. His language is characterized by delays in content, form, and use. This judgment is supported by a severe delay in comprehension of vocabulary in the context of the Receptive One-Word Picture Vocabulary Test and by results of a nonstandard assessment of a language sample. Amahl's production consists primarily of single-word approximations.

Phonological assessment revealed a severe articulatory and phonological delay. Amahl exhibits apraxic speech characterized by excessive groping and pervasive sound/syllable deletions. His intelligibility is affected by vowel distortion as a result of reduced mandibular action. Amahl's phonemic inventory is restricted, consisting of stops and one fricative (/f/). Syllable structure consists primarily of CV constructions. Amahl's articulatory deficits appear to be limiting his language production.

In addition to his sensorimotor limitations Amahl's prognosis is guarded due to his cognitive impairment. Amahl's play skills are commensurate with Nicolich's symbolic stage I. He demonstrated single-scheme pretend-play and combinatorial scheme sequences of familiar events using replica toys. He has difficulty in executing planned symbolic games and engaging in extended problem-solving. Results indicate a moderate delay in symbolic play skills.

Favorable indicators for treatment success include signs of linguistic progress in his identification of familiar objects and attributes and the demonstration of academic language skills using simple arithmetic and reading Level 1 books. Amahl reads sight words with verbal prompts and can write the alphabet and familiar CVC words. He can produce two-constituent utterances when given prompts and has begun to use some action words and attributes.

Amahl willingly engaged in all tasks presented during this assessment.

Appendix 2B. Darryl

Any Town

Speech-Language-Hearing Disorders Clinic

Address

City, State

Speech and Language Evaluation

Client Name: <u>DS</u>   Primary Disorder: <u>Language</u>

Date of Birth:_____ Date of Testing:_____ Chronological Age: <u>5:1</u>

Parent/Caregiver Name:_____ Language of Testing:_____

Clinician: _____ Supervisor: _____

_____

Statement of Problem:

Darryl is a five-year and one-month-old boy who was referred for a speech-language evaluation by his mother and has been diagnosed as language-delayed. He receives speech service at Open House preschool (focus is pragmatics) where he also receives occupational therapy (primarily to facilitate eye–hand coordination and hand function.)

Background History

Darryl said his first words at 18 months, and first word combinations at 30 months. No feeding problems were reported.

Gestational and birth history were unremarkable. Darryl walked by 12 months,

Darryl lives with his mother, a television executive; father, a composer; and eight-year-old brother, Joshua. Joshua has been diagnosed with autistic spectrum disorder. He was treated for a language delay during his preschool years. Ms. X described Darryl as a social child.

Darryl presented as friendly and communicative and easily engaged in play activities. Darryl, like his brother, enjoys playing with trains. He is conversant about the New York Subway System (train numbers and routes). His mother describes his play as narrowly focused.

Assessment Information

Results of Communication Assessment

Language

Standardized Testing

Preschool Language Scale 5 (PLS 5)

The Preschool Language Scale assesses auditory comprehension and expressive communication in the context of adult-directed, symbolic activities.

Results were as follows:

Subtest	Standard Score (SS)	SS Confidence Band (90%)	Percentile Rank (PR)	PR for SS Confidence Band
Auditory comprehension	71	67–80	3	1–9
Expressive communication	70	66–77	2	1–6
Total language score	69	65–76	2	1–5

Results indicate a moderate delay in auditory comprehension and expressive communication.

Darryl manifested comprehension and expression of spatial, quantity, and qualitative (looks like a triangle, star) concepts, actions (gerund noun forms), attribution (single attribute), temporal directive (comprehension of two-verb action sequence), and possessive pronouns. Darryl made inferences in response to complex questions (two-verb) about pictured events; for example, "How do you think the little girl hurt her knee?" He did not respond to hypothetical questions about himself (what would you do if you were cold?) He did infer the identify of objects given complex verbal descriptions (conjunction form, coding temporal and conditional causal relations)—"What do you use when you take a bath? You dry off with it" (towel).

Darryl had difficulty, however, comprehending comparatives, complex sentential complements denoting object function (e.g., "show me what you use to drink water"); relative, embedded clauses (girl with the long hair); and queries involving more than one modifying adjective (big, brown dog). He did not mark possessives ('s).

Darryl's language sample collected during a play situation was analyzed for content/form/use interactions according to Lahey's taxonomy. Results were as follows:

Content/Form Interactions

In the context of play, Darryl's language was productive for Lahey's content/form interactions through phase 5 (content categories existence + copula + attribution; action; locative action + attribution + possession; state + possession; temporal; quantity.) Utterances were primarily single-verb three+ constituents. Two-verb sentences were emerging; Darryl was productive for mood (infinitival complement, for example, try *to make* Thomas go). Results indicate a mild-to-moderate delay in expressive language in context of play and spontaneous conversation.

Language use

Functions of Language	
Functions (Use)	Proportion (%)
Comment—label	42
Total comment	42
Regulate—focus attention	3
Regulate—direct action	18
Regulate—obtain object	6
Total regulate	27
Discourse—initiate	5
Discourse—respond	17
Discourse—routine	9
Total discourse	31

Darryl used language primarily to comment on objects and actions during play, and to initiate and extend routines. In the context of discourse, Darryl responded to requests for information and sought to obtain objects and responses from others.

Phonology/Articulation

Articulation was observed in continuous speech and found to be free of sound changes that were not age appropriate.

Voice

Appears typical for his age and gender.

Fluency

Appears typical for his age.

Associated Behavioral Systems (Factors maintaining or supporting Communication Behavior).

Sensorimotor

Oral Peripheral Speech Mechanism Examination/Feeding

An oral peripheral speech examination was attempted to evaluate oral-facial structure and function, symmetry, coordination, and range of motion of articulators. Darryl also was observed eating a snack consisting of a chicken sandwich, pudding, and juice. Structure of the articulators and their functions appeared adequate for speech and vegetative purposes. Darryl manifested lip closure adequate to remove pudding from a spoon, and to drink from a straw and a rotary chew when eating solid food.

Gross and Fine Motor Function

Darryl manifests mild hypotonia affecting fine motor function, especially involving eye–hand coordination and skills involving hand function.

Hearing

Darryl passed a bilateral hearing screening at 25 dB. Normal hearing was supported in communicative interactions.

Cognition

Symbolic Play

Pretend-play was analyzed according to the Nicolich (1977) scale. Darryl engaged in a planned game (combinatorial scheme play with Thomas Train set supplied by clinician). Play was narrowly focused on the train moving through tunnels.

Psychosocial

Darryl's parents reported that their attention is often directed toward Darryl's eight-year-old brother, Joshua, who has been diagnosed with autistic spectrum disorder (PDD-NOS). Parents explained that Joshua is very needy, and sometimes throws tantrums, especially when his routines are interrupted. Parents are concerned that the demands that Joshua makes on them (and the time those demands take away from interactions with Darryl) are contributing to Darryl's language delay.

Summary/Impressions

Darryl is a five-year and one-month-old boy who was referred for a speech-language evaluation by his mother. Results of standard (PLS-5) and nonstandard (Lahey analysis of language sample) assessment of language revealed a moderate language delay, affecting the form and content of language. Darryl produces primarily single-verb sentences. Multiverb utterances are emerging. Darryl, however, comprehends complex multiverb sentences (temporal sequences, causal relations, questions, and sentence complements coding epistemic content; for example, "How do you think the girl got hurt?"). Darryl's ability to comprehend complex sentences is indicative of good prognosis for the development of more advanced complex forms of expression (two- to three-verb sentences, narratives.) Darryl's symbolic play skills are complex (planned games) but restricted in theme. It is notable that the train theme was initially an interest of Darryl's brother. Parents' concern that attention demanded by Darryl's brother is contributing to Darryl's language delay appears to be unfounded.

Appendix 2C: Mr. B

Any Town

Speech-Language-Hearing Disorders Clinic

Address

City, State

Speech and Language Evaluation

Client Name: <u>Mr. Brown</u> Date of Birth: _____ Date of Testing: _____

Chronological Age: <u>45</u> Primary Disorder/ICD-9: <u>Aphasia/Dysarthria/Apraxia</u>

Parent/Caregiver Name: _____ Language of Testing: _____

Clinician: _____ Supervisor: _____

Statement of Problem

Mr. B, a 45-year-old, trilingual maître d' in a popular restaurant, was referred by himself and his neurologist after suffering a stroke resulting in aphasia and moderate right hemiparesis; he came for treatment approximately two months after the stroke, presenting with language consisting of one- and two-word utterances. His wife, who was provider of intake and case history information, reported that he communicates by using a combination of speech, written words, and gestures. Family members interpret his words and gestures and repeat back to him what they think he said. He smiles and nods when they make the correct interpretations and shakes his head when they guess incorrectly. Mr. B's wife reports that he understands most of what is said to him. However, he gestures or says "again" when asking her to repeat words and watches her mouth very closely when she repeats.

Background History

Family and living environment: Mr. B lives at home with his wife and two teenage daughters whom he hopes to send to college. His hobbies include jogging, music, food, and spending time with his family. Before the stroke, he had worked as a maître d' in a popular restaurant frequented by Broadway stars. He had enjoyed joking with his customers and had been a beloved personality at the restaurant. He had greeted many patrons by name and had made them feel comfortable by remembering their favorite table and drinks.

Medical history: Mr. B has a family history of coronary disease, high cholesterol, exertional angina, and heavy smoking. A coronary angiogram had shown stenosis and occlusion of the aorta. He had suffered recurrent angina when walking only one block and had episodes of angina at work. As a result, he had undergone a coronary bypass. He had progressed well and he had been discharged from the hospital.

Seven days later in his sleep he had an embolic stroke and a sudden onset of aphasia with right hemiparesis. Computed tomography (CT) scan revealed a new large lesion in the territory of the left middle cerebral artery and an old smaller lesion in the left posterior cerebral artery. He was discharged two weeks after hospitalization with severe mixed aphasia and mild right hemiplegia affecting his face and arm more than his leg. He is presently taking Coumadin to prevent further strokes and has qualified for total disability because of his aphasia.

He is reported to be depressed often because of his inability to communicate. He continues to attempt to talk but becomes frustrated when people do not understand what he is trying to say. Mr. B has begun to avoid speaking to friends.

Assessment Information

Results of Communication Assessment

Language

Standardized testing

Mr. B. was administered the Boston Diagnostic Aphasia Exam (BDAE). He achieved a severity level of 1. There were 10- to 20-second latencies on 25 of 60 pictures. Phonemic cues helped 50% of the time. His scores ranged from 0 to 80% across subtest items: word reading (80%) and word–picture matching (80%) earned the highest percentages; others ranged between 60% (writing mechanics) and 15% (repetition of words). Other scorable subtests tests were at 40% (symbol discrimination, word recognition, and singing), 30% (word discrimination), and 20% (body part identification, serial writing, rhythm, and primmer-level dictation).

Content/form

Language samples based on picture description and conversation, revealed the following: *Cookie Theft Picture* yielded one- and two-word utterances produced with much hesitation and phonetic groping, "Boy . . . co...co...co...cookie . . . ga...ga...girl. . . . ma . . . mama . . . water . . . sssinkie . . . window . . . nice . . . co...co...no...water... no...sinkie...eee...why......ok......I sorry."

In conversation he used a mixture of English, Spanish, and Italian words and gestures, writing, and drawing. Here too, he spoke in one- and two-word utterances coding primarily *existence* and *action*. He produced the words with pauses between them making them appear as separate utterances. When asked, "What do you do with a razor?" he said, "... all the time." When cued with "ʃ" he said, ...shshsh...shave." When asked, "What do you do with soap?" he said, "...wa...wa...water." When asked, "What do you do with a pencil?" he said, "...ssssometimes" but said "write" after the phonemic cue "ɝ."

Use

He uses language to comment, respond, and direct action. Although his responses are typically on topic they often appear to be noncontingent due to the nature of his word-finding difficulty. Mr. B has mild-to-moderate difficulty changing topics when topics are similar or if the change is abrupt. His difficulty shifting topic may be related to impaired auditory comprehension, but he attempts to repair language breakdowns by using gestures, writing, and drawing.

Literacy:

Mr. B. scored highest on the subtests of the BDAE that involved literacy.

Phonology/Articulation:

Mr. B's speech displays characteristics of his aphasia and apraxia, resulting in irregular articulatory breakdowns, distorted consonants and vowels, literal and verbal paraphasic errors, and neologisms. He makes groping movements with his articulators to find the correct articulatory positions and sequences, and some movements appear random. He occasionally adds sounds to words. The articulation of vowels is more precise than the articulation of consonants, and his articulation is more precise in connected speech than in isolation. Some single words are articulated precisely. A pattern of sound changes could not be discerned.

Fluency

Dysfluencies associated with aphasia and apraxia were observed: irregular pauses between sounds, syllables, and words. He matches rhythms with humming when doing

Melodic Intonation Therapy (Sparks & Holland, 1976). His singing is mildly impaired for familiar songs. No formal measures were taken

Voice

His pitch, loudness, and quality are appropriate. Prosodic features are distorted due to the short, slow speech and irregular pauses. He displays mono-pitch and mono-loudness with excess and equal stress on syllables. Nevertheless, he matches melodies when humming and singing.

Some vocal huskiness, possibly related to dysarthria, was observed. No formal measures were taken.

Associated Behavioral Systems (Factors Maintaining or Supporting Communication Behavior)

Sensorimotor

Oral Peripheral Examination

The following findings are based on results of the Frenchay Dysarthria Assessment and nonstandardized observation. Mr. B's articulators are mildly asymmetrical and quiet at rest. His respiration is rhythmical and appropriate during rest, speech, and swallowing. His spontaneous lip seal, smile, and pucker are appropriate at rest and during eating, but awkward and inaccurate when done volitionally. He attempted to move his mouth on command and then shook his head indicating that he couldn't do it. Spontaneous and volitional movements of the jaw and soft palate were judged to be normal. His tongue appeared normal at rest but he did not protrude, lateralize, or elevate his tongue on command. When asked to do a diadochokinesis task, he shook his head, laughed, and said, "no."

Mr. B did not sustain a vowel, change vocal loudness, or sing a scale upon request. He exhibited normal movements of his articulators during eating. During speech, he made moderately slow, labored movements. His spontaneous cough appeared normal, but he did not cough on command. When he performed facial movements on command, he had an overflow of movement from one structure to another. He did not pucker or smile on command but displayed both movements spontaneously.

Feeding and Swallowing

He swallowed his saliva and food spontaneously but did not swallow when directed.

Gross and Fine Motor Function

All volitional movements were done slowly. Mr. B walked briskly and sat upright without aid.

Hearing and Vision

Mr. B has passed a bilateral hearing screening at 25 dB. He frequently confused expressions that sounded similar. When asked "How are you?" He replied "45." He confused "card" and "car" and letter "t" and the word "key."

Based on Mr. B's responses to language-test visual stimuli, he appears to have normal vision, with no visual field cut.

Cognition

Mr. B exhibited symptoms of acoustic agnosia when he indicated that some words sounded similar to him. His auditory short-term memory appears to be impaired. He followed simple single-event directions but not two perceptually present temporal events. At times he appeared unaware of his errors in comprehension, but he frequently tried to self-correct his errors in production. Mr. B initiated conversation and topics. He exhibited planning and goal-directed behavior in scheduling his next treatment appointments by using his calendar to point to the days and times he was available. He appeared impulsive when standing up to act out ideas that he could not verbally communicate. He was enthusiastic about testing and responded to failures by attempting to communicate through gestures, acting out scenes, writing, and drawing. He did not exhibit emotional lability or perseverative behavior.

Psychosocial Behavior

Mr. B has been on long-term disability since experiencing the stroke. He lives at home with his wife and two teenage daughters. His family is supportive of his speech and are usually successful in understanding his communicative attempts. His wife accompanied him to the assessment. He is highly motivated to go back to work so that he can help his two daughters go to college. In addition, he is highly motivated to communicate. When he does not say a word, he gestures, writes, or draws pictures. His facial affect is appropriate.

Summary/Impressions

Mr. B., a 45-year-old man, was diagnosed with a severe speech and language disorder associated with aphasia and apraxia as a consequence of a stroke. His language is characterized by predominantly single- and two-word utterances representing a narrow range of content. His communicative attempts are further compromised by characteristics of apraxia. His use of language is not as impaired, as he exhibits the desire to communicate and makes every effort in that direction. While a prognosis is guarded due to the extent of the neurological damage, further advancement is expected due to his strong motivation to regain his ability to communicate and the commitment of his family.

Long-Term Planning: Formulating Long-Term Goals

READER WILL:

- Derive long-term goals with reference to baseline data from three clients: two children and one adult
- Derive subordinate long-term goals with reference to components of the behavioral system targeted by the long-term goals
- Become familiar with steps of decision-making and information that guides long-term goal planning
- Become familiar with the use of the M-K SLIP template as a tool for goal planning

Formulating Long-Term Goals

In this chapter, we discuss formulating long-term goals by introducing three clients who we will follow across the three planning phases: two children, Amahl and Darryl, and one adult, Mr. B. A summary of each client's diagnostic report appears in Appendix 2, A–C. The following is a summary of baseline data from the three clients.

Client 1. Amahl is an eight-year-old child who was diagnosed with autistic spectrum disorder and moderate cognitive impairment. Nonstandard assessments of play (Westby) and language (Lahey) revealed severe delays in symbolic functioning. Amahl displays repetitive, perseverative actions on objects (shaking, spinning, and gazing). He produces single-word utterances alternating with manual signs to request for water, food, bathroom, and to protest. Amahl was also diagnosed as apraxic. Single-word utterances are monosyllabic, CV structures, containing initial stops or nasals as onset-neutral vowel (e.g., gʌ, bʌ, mʌ).

CLIENT 2. Darryl is a five-year-old child with a language delay. Content/form interactions are productive at Lahey's Phases 2–4 (e.g., existence, action, locative action, attribution, and possession); productive language use functions include comment, direct, and respond to requests. Two-verb sentences are emerging (modals: gonna, wanna). Darryl has some difficulty identifying colors, letters, numbers, shapes, social emotional states, textures, quantity, and time sequences. He has difficulty with making inferences and interpreting complex sentences.

In the area of pretend play (Nicolich play scale), Darryl is functioning at or near expected levels expected for his chronological age but with a narrow focus (e.g., script play about trains). Darryl manifests a reticence to engage in interpersonal interactions with peers, mild hypotonicity, and delayed equilibrium reactions.

CLIENT 3. Mr. B is a 45-year-old, trilingual maître d' in a popular restaurant, who suffered a stroke, and consequently described by the neurologist as globally aphasic with total expressive aphasia, severe receptive aphasia, and moderate right hemiparesis affecting his face and arm more than his leg. He came for treatment approximately two months after the stroke, presenting with language consisting of one- and two-word utterances. He communicates by using a combination of speech, written words, and gestures. Family members interpret his words and gestures and say back to him what they think he said. He smiles and nods when they make the correct interpretations and shakes his head when they guess incorrectly. Mr. B's wife reports that he understands most of what is said to him. However, he gestures or says "again" when asking her to repeat words and watches her mouth very closely when she repeats.

Step 1: Identify the communication area to be targeted.

The first decision to be made when planning long-term goals is determining what communication area needs to be targeted.

INFORMATION SOURCE. Baseline data presented in a diagnostic report constitute the primary source of information used by the clinician to make this decision. Baseline data provide information about the current status of speech and language function. These data provide the basis for a comparison of the communication performance of the client suspected of having a speech/language disorder with the performance of typically achieving peers. Discrepancies in one area or multiple areas of communicative functioning would direct us to target the areas of deficiency in one or more long-term goal statements. Major communication disorder areas identified by the American

Speech-Language-Hearing Association that are potential targets of intervention are language, speech, fluency, voice, and literacy, and most recently added cognitive disorders are viewed in certain venues as potential targets.

Child 1. Amahl

Potential target areas: Language
Phonology/articulation

Rationale: Baseline data indicate severe delays in comprehension and expression of language, symbolic play, and speech-sound production.

Child 2: Darryl

Potential target area(s): Language

Rationale: Child manifests moderate language delay, but age-appropriate play. Phonology does not seem to be affected.

Adult. Mr. B

Potential target area(s): Language

Rationale: Mr. B is experiencing difficulty in "word retrieval," which implicates the expression of content/form interactions. Although comprehension is largely intact, understanding "most" of what is said (with family members emphasizing their articulation of words) also indicates that it would be useful to address content/form interactions, and, perhaps, perception.

Step 2: Select one or more developmental or complexity taxonomies relevant to the targeted areas that will guide goal planning.

INFORMATION SOURCE. As established in Chapter 2, any long-term goal must be situated within a description of observable, measurable, and generative language performance that represents functional communication. Since the long-term objective must be some form of generative language performance, we turn to research which has identified and described generative language performance in observable, measurable terms. Research on typical language acquisition and typical language structure is devoted to discovery of the linguistic bases of generative language performance. Such research provides us with developmentally and structurally oriented linguistic taxonomies.

Linguistic taxonomies describe generative components of language and how they are organized; examples include Bloom and Lahey's content/form/use taxonomy, which describes content categories and syntax (see Appendix 3A); Chomskian syntactic structures, which include phrases and case assignment relations, and so on; Brown's morphemes and semantic features; the narrative taxonomies of Stein and Glenn (1990), Slobin and Berman (2000), and Labov and Waletzky (1967); phonological processes and their developmental history identified by Klein (1981), Shriberg and Kwiatkowski (1982), Ingram (1981), and others (e.g., Hodson & Paden, 1991); and Bernhardt and Stemberger's (2000) phonologic features. Such taxonomies guide long-term goal planning across the lifespan, in both children and adults.

Among children, it is with reference to *current level of performance* within a recognized developmental hierarchy that goals may be planned and projected across the timeline of treatment. Among adults, the structural complexity of potential targets of intervention provides guidance for goal planning (see Appendix 3B for examples of component sentences of adult discourse analyzed with reference to the Bloom and Lahey taxonomy).

We have selected the Bloom and Lahey taxonomy as a guide for goal planning in the area of language for the two children we are following.

We considered both Bernhardt and Stemberger's nonlinear taxonomy of phonologic feature, word and syllable structure acquisition, and Shriberg's taxonomy of phonologic processes as taxonomies to guide phonologic intervention planning in the area of phonology for Amahl. On one hand, feature acquisition, within a nonlinear framework, was considered since Amahl has a very limited repertoire and needs to acquire new features to increase his repertoire of sounds. On the other, Amahl's production of stops when fricatives are obligated could also be seen as the process of stopping within a phonological process framework. Our decision is to approach articulation change through the addition of missing developmentally appropriate features; this approach has been found to facilitate expansion of the phonological system and in turn the lexicon (Bernhardt & Stemberger, 2000).

Mr. B

Working with an adult, the clinician can still describe the long-term goal with reference to developmental taxonomies. This is because developmental taxonomies translate into complexity hierarchies. So while an adult is viewed as having completed expected phases of language development we can still organize levels of performance with reference to linguistic complexity. For example, John will respond with additive and temporal utterances during conversational routines (Youmans & Youmans, 2010). This choice of target is with reference to a complexity hierarchy of complex sentences. By way of contrast, some aphasiologists follow a different conceptual framework, focusing on presumed processes underlying language production. Examples from Chapey (2008) are "will fix new information in memory in order to improve communication." This approach is inconsistent with our intervention planning model.

Step 3: Identify subordinate long-term goals and related taxonomies of behavior.

After identifying the broad area of communication to be targeted, it is necessary to consider whether this broad area of communication interacts with subsystems of speech and language that would be involved in improving communication in the targeted area. The identification of such subsystems of language may lead the clinician to consider targeting, simultaneously, a number of subordinate long-term goals, within their respective taxonomies.

Darryl, the child with a language disorder and favorable prognosis, is expected to achieve language typical of his age group (i.e., narrative and conversational discourse). To address this ultimate achievement we need to identify the subsystems of language that are intrinsic to narrative and conversational discourse. These include narrative forms and story grammars (e.g., Labov & Waletzky, 1967; McCabe & Rollins, 1994; Lahey, 1988; Champion, 2003; also see Klein & Moses, 1999a), lexicon, developmental morphemes, complex sentences, and pragmatic skills. Each of these areas contributes to the production and comprehension of discourse; as such, any or all of these areas could be targeted at the long-term planning phase.

For Amahl, a client with a delay in the area of phonology related to apraxia, an ultimate goal may be to acquire all segmental and prosodic features of the ambient language or to eliminate all phonological processes no longer age expectant; to this end, potential areas may include segmental features, syllable/word shapes, and stress contours (or syllable processes, substitution processes, and assimilation processes).

Step 4: Specify best performance, that is, how much improvement to expect.

Having identified an area of communication to target, and the linguistic subsystems intrinsic to this area, a clinician needs to decide how much the client can be reasonably expected to achieve at the end of the long-term intervention. This decision will be influenced by (a) age of the client (i.e., whether the client is a child or an adult), (b) the factors maintaining the disorder, and (c) the discrepancy between typical speech-language performance and performance of the client under consideration.

CHILDREN. In work with children, information about two interacting factors is fundamental to making predictions about the long-term outcome of treatment: (a) the discrepancy between the child's current functioning and what is expected given the child's age and (b) the number of maintaining factors implicated in the disorder and the degree to which each is impaired. The greater the difference between baseline performance and typical performance, the lower the probability that the child will eventually perform within the typical range.

Chances of achieving behavior typical for a client's age decrease as a greater number of behavioral systems are implicated in the disorder. The degree of disability associated with maintaining factors further decreases the child's potential for typical communication functioning.

Exercise 1. The school system has established three years (triennial period) as the time frame for long-term goals. Of the two sets of data presented in Appendices 2A and 2B in Chapter 2 (Amahl and Darryl), which child could be expected to catch up with his peers at the end of this long-term goal period? Why?

Answer. Darryl has the better prognosis. Darryl presents with a moderate language delay, symbolic play intact, and mild sensorimotor difficulty (hypotonicity). Amahl presents with severe language delay, characteristics of autism and cognitive impairment, and emotional and sensorimotor deficits.

Exercise 2.

1. What would be the ultimate achievements in the area of language for Darryl, a child with a mild language disorder and minimal impairments in the related behavioral systems?

2. Now, contrast Darryl's ultimate language achievements with what may be expected of Amahl, the child who manifests a severe language problem and multiple behavioral system impairments.

Answer. As discussed, Darryl has a relatively good prognosis (can be expected to reach age-expected levels of performance across the linguistic taxonomies identified). Therefore, we project that he will ultimately achieve narrative and conversational discourse.

Amahl, with a more limited prognosis, can be expected to ultimately produce simple (single-verb) sentences coding early developing content categories (existence, action, locative action, and state) for the basic functions of language (comment and request) in a variety of contexts.

In the area of phonology, we expect that Amahl will ultimately produce syllable/word structures of limited complexity (CVC, CVCVC), and consonants with features of limited complexity (stops, nasals, glides, and early fricatives).

Adults. In work with adults, it is important to be knowledgeable about the parameters of typical communication and language functioning in adults. This is because communication and language performance do not remain static across the lifespan. Performance changes as adults' physical and psychosocial status evolves with the aging process. It is necessary, therefore, to adjust expectations with reference to these changing parameters. Baseline data about both language and maintaining factors help us to make decisions about how much can be expected of the adult client within the long-term treatment period.

The severity of the language problem, the number and degree of involvement of maintaining factors, will determine (a) the ultimate level of performance realistically possible, and (b) a time frame for the accomplishment of this level of performance. For example, an individual with aphasia who is using only single words and who has severe sensorimotor involvement (dysarthria) and psychosocial stresses (no family support system) would be given a poorer prognosis than an individual producing sentences with mild sensorimotor and psychosocial involvements.

Knowledge of an individual's past communication performance will also influence ultimate expectations. At best, a client can only be expected to return to prior levels of behavior. Furthermore, the client's rate and degree of change over the course of prior treatment will affect the prognosis. Past goal achievement is often a reliable predictor of present treatment outcomes. If a prior course of treatment was slow and inconsistent, then a rapid change in a short period of time would not be expected.

When planning for adults, it is important to recognize that developmental data are useful as indices of complexity for establishing long-term goals and, subsequently, for sequencing short-term goals. Developmental hierarchies of content/form interactions in children present, in a systematic manner, levels of complexity of the semantics and syntax of word combinations, sentences, and sequences of sentences (narratives). A summary of Bloom and Lahey content/form interactions appears in Appendix 3A. An application of Bloom and Lahey's content/form interactions to adult language appears in Appendix 3B.

ALTERNATIVE TAXONOMIES AND REPRESENTATIVE LEVELS OF ACHIEVEMENT. There may be several taxonomies available in the literature appropriate for establishing long-term goals in the area of communication targeted for change. Consider Darryl, the school-age child who is producing simple sentences (three constituents). As noted previously, Darryl has a relatively good prognosis (can be expected to reach age-expected levels of performance). Since Darryl is producing three constituents, increasing complexity of sentence production would appear to be an appropriate long-term goal.

A clinician approaching the area of complex sentences may use a syntactic taxonomy proposed by Paul and Norbury (2012). This perspective emphasizes changes in syntactic structures. Within this framework a clinician is likely to write "Child will produce a range of later occurring sentence types in conversation." On the other hand, a second clinician who views language in school-age children and adults with reference to the interaction of content/form/use might write, "Child will produce complex sentences to code a range of content categories with their appropriate connectives in a variety of discourse contexts" (e.g., Lahey, 1988).

CAUTION: AVOID PSEUDODEVELOPMENTAL SEQUENCES. Some clinicians set goals that only *appear* to be hierarchical in nature. These goals, however, do not imply any identifiable, research-based developmental sequence. For example, two frequently set goals for children with language learning difficulties involve following multiple-step commands and sequencing. Such goals may read as "Jose will follow three-step commands" or "Miguel will correctly sequence activities represented in pictures." These goals seem to fall within a clear-cut sequence of objectives; following three-step commands precedes following four-step commands and sequencing five pictures follows sequencing four pictures. Sequences like these, however, are generated intuitively rather than on the basis of developmental evidence. Basing hierarchies on intuition is a ***"Don't"*** of intervention planning. In this case, the clinician might base a sequence of short-term goals on developmental evidence about complex semantic relations or story grammars, such as additive, temporal, and causal chains (e.g., see Lahey, 1988). See Wallace (2014) for a cogent argument against the traditional use of "step commands" and "sequencing" in the treatment of language disorders, specifically in the targeting of narrative production.

Within the domain of phonological disorders, a clinician using a traditional SODA (substitution, omission, distortion, addition) framework may, given a three-year-old presenting with multiple misarticulations, target specific age-appropriate speech sounds, for example, "Child will produce /k/, /g/, /s/, and /z/ in initial, medial, and final positions in words in conversation." Another clinician, utilizing a more linguistic framework, might specify "the elimination of fronting and stopping (phonological processes) as the long-term goal." The second goal recognizes the relationships among sounds and leads to a better understanding of the difficulty in producing them (e.g., which features cannot be maintained across sounds).

EXERCISE. Suppose that one of our clients with aphasia produces only single-word responses in conversational speech. One clinician wrote a long-term goal stating, "The client will increase sentence length in conversational speech on a variety of topics." The other clinician wrote, "Client will produce three-constituent utterances in conversation on a variety of topics." Which goal would better facilitate goal-writing at the next phase of intervention planning: the short-term phase?

ANSWER. The second goal references a universal structure and would better facilitate writing short-term goals because it is embedded within a linguistic hierarchy providing direction for the intervention trajectory; contrastively, the alternative goal does not provide the opportunity for identification of a taxonomy of subordinate achievements (the short-term phase). Research indicates that sentences do not increase in length on the basis of adding random words but rather on the merging of semantic/syntactic relations.

In sum, there are alternative ways in which long-term goals may be formulated. Alternative goals will reflect the clinician's theoretical framework (e.g., target only syntax or C/F/U interactions in a case of language delay; target specific sounds or work from a model of speech-sound features or phonological processes in an articulation case).

Step 5: Establish criteria for achievement of long-term goals (exit criteria).

The achievement of a long-term goal will eventually be equivalent to the termination of therapy. As such, the criteria that we set for such achievement is tantamount to "exit criteria" (Campbell & Bain, 1991). The determination of exit criteria is motivated in part by issues related to accountability such as the documentation of cost-effectiveness and treatment efficiency (Geirut, J.A. 1998; Olswang & Bain, 1994).

Exit criteria are generally described with reference to the degree of spontaneity or contextual support surrounding the target behavior(s) and an acceptable rate of performance. Context descriptions are usually expressed in general terms, such as "in context of discourse," "in spontaneous speech," "in obligatory contexts," and "as a contingent response." Rate of performance may be described in different ways. Rate may be stated as proportion of correct productions (e.g., Bloom & Lahey, 1978; Eger, 1988) or number of instances of a behavior within a particular time frame (frequency of occurrence; for example, Bloom & Lahey, 1978; Lahey, 1988).

Information relevant to establishing exit criteria may be available in published clinical research. Eger reviewed research (1988) on articulation therapy for school-age children; participating clinicians viewed sound mastery as 90%–100% proficiency in conversational speech. Contrastively, Hodson and Paden (1991) terminate therapy when school-age children's phonological process percentage-of-occurrence scores are below 40%. (This is another way of saying that the children are not applying phonological processes, that is, generating correct performance—60% of the time.) These authors present evidence that upon achieving this rate of acceptable performance, children can be expected to continue to improve spontaneously.

It has been suggested that performance criteria should be different for structured tasks from those occurring in spontaneous contexts. For example, Fey (1988) suggests that one might expect 80%–100% accuracy for targeted performance in clinician-directed contexts before the achievement of 50% correct usage in naturalistic contexts.

Degree of spontaneity or contextual support for a target behavior are included in the long-term goal statement. Rate of performance is not, however, typically included as part of the long-term goal. Instead, frequency criteria are incorporated in the short-term goal written during the semester in which the client's dismissal is anticipated (New York State Department of Education, 2005).

Long-Term Goals for Amahl, Darryl, and Mr. B

The following are long-term goals for Amahl, Darryl, and Mr. B.

Amahl: 9 years and 10 months old

Long-term goals:

1. Amahl will produce three-constituent utterances coding early content categories in conversational speech.

2. Amahl will produce segmental and prosodic features absent from and emerging in his repertoire (Bernhardt & Stemberger, 2000) in conversational speech.

Subordinate long-term goals:

Amahl will use a range of language functions in conversational speech (Lahey, 1988).

Darryl: Five years old

Long-term goal:

Darryl will produce conjoined/embedded causal chain narratives in a variety of conversational contexts (Lahey, 1988; Stein & Glenn, 1979).

Subordinate long-term goals:

1. Darryl will produce a range of complex sentences with appropriate connectives (Bloom, Lahey, Hood, Lifter, & Fleiss, 1980) a variety of conversational contexts.

2. Darryl will increase lexical variety across content categories (Lahey, 1988).

3. Darryl will produce a range of developmental morphemes (Brown, 1973; Lahey, 1988)

Mr. B.

Long-term goal: Mr. B will produce two- to three-constituent utterances as contingent responses within conversations

Subordinate long-term goals:

1. Mr. B. will produce context-appropriate words in conversations

2. Mr. B will express a variety of communicative functions in conversation (Lahey, 1988)

The MK-SLIP is an electronic device application designed to guide and assist clinicians through the planning of goals and procedures across the three phases of intervention planning. The app outlines steps in decision-making and directs the clinician to appropriate research-based sources of information useful for deriving goals and procedures at each planning phase. The app ensures that goals generated at each planning phase are consistent with higher-order goals established at previous phases (e.g., the long-term goal and the reference developmental taxonomy serve as the basis for deriving short-term goals; session goals and procedures are derived from the same clinical research and related theoretical paradigms established and operationalized at the long-term and short-term planning phase).

Figures 3.1a and 3.1b illustrate templates directed toward long-term goal planning. Figure 3.1a lists all long-term goals corresponding to discrete areas of speech and language. Figure 3.1b displays any subordinate long-term goals which have been derived from goals appearing in Figure 3.1a. If subordinate goals are identified, separate 3.1b templates should be completed for each corresponding 3.1a long-term goal.

Deriving the Long-Term Goal			
Decision	**Guiding Information**		
Areas of Speech/Language to be Targeted, Referent Taxonomy, and Current Level of Performance	**Area of Speech/ Language**	**Referent Taxonomy**	**Current Performance**
Projecting a Prognosis	**Maintaining Factors**	**Severity**	**Current Performance**
	Cognitive	Mild Mod. Sev.	
	Sensorimotor	Mild Mod. Sev.	
	Psychosocial	Mild Mod. Sev.	
	Medical	Mild Mod. Sev.	
	Caretaker Attendance	Frequently	Intermittently	Rarely
Time Frame	Time Allotted		
Long-Term Goals			

FIGURE 3.1a: MK-SLIP Long-term goal template

Deriving Subordinate Long-Term Goal(s)			
Long Term Goal:			
Decision	Guiding Information		
Areas of Speech/Language Intrinsic to the Long-Term Goal	Area of Speech/Language	Referent Taxonomy	Current Performance Level
Subordinate Long-Term Goals			

FIGURE 3.1b: MK-SLIP Subordinate long-term goal template

Figures 3.2a–3.4b represent long-term and subordinate long-term goal templates completed for Darryl, Amahl, and Mr. B.

Deriving the Long-Term Goal			
Decision	**Guiding Information**		
Areas of Speech/Language to be Targeted, Referent Taxonomy, and Current Level of Performance	**Area of Speech/ Language**	**Referent Taxonomy**	**Current Performance**
	Language	Language content/form/use Bloom & Lahey (1978) Lahey (1988)	Single-word utterances that code existence, to request or demand
	Phonology/articulation	Non-linear phonology Bernhardt & Stemberger (2000)	Apraxic, produces only single syllable CV words, anterior stop consonants
Projecting a Prognosis	**Maintaining Factors**	**Severity**	**Current Performance**
	Cognitive	Mild Mod. Sev.	Moderate delay
	Sensorimotor	Mild Mod. Sev.	Apraxic, perceptual problems, low-tone
	Psychosocial	Mild Mod. Sev.	Perseverates on routines; angers when routines are broken; aggressive towards mother
	Medical	Mild Mod. Sev.	
	Caretaker Attendance	Frequently (Grandmother)	Intermittently · Rarely
Time Frame	Time Allotted	Three years (DOE revaluation cycle)	
Long-Term Goals	Amahl will: Produce a range of syllable and word structures and segmental features absent from and emerging in his repertoire Produce three constituent utterances coding early content categories in conversational speech		

FIGURE 3.2a: MK-SLIP Long-Term Goal Template for Amahl

Deriving Subordinate Long-Term Goal(s): Language			
Long Term Goal: Produce three-constituent utterances coding early content categories in conversational speech			
Decision	**Guiding Information**		
Areas of Speech/Language Intrinsic to the Long-Term Goal	**Area of Speech/Language**	**Referent Taxonomy**	**Current Performance Level**
	Language Use	Language content/form/use Bloom & Lahey (1978); Lahey (1988)	Language functions restricted to request and demand
Subordinate Long-Term Goals	Amahl will: Use a range of language functions in conversational speech		

FIGURE 3.2b: MK-SLIP Subordinate Long-Term Goal Templates for Amahl

Deriving the Long-Term Goal			
Decision	**Guiding Information**		
Areas of Speech/Language to be Targeted, Referent Taxonomy, and Current Level of Performance	**Area of Speech/ Language**	**Referent Taxonomy**	**Current Performance**
	Language (Content/form/use)	C/F/U, complex sentences Lahey (1988); Bloom, Lahey, Lifter, Fliess (1980) Literate narratives story grammar Stein & Glenn (1979)	Mild, **moderate**, severe
Projecting a Prognosis	**Maintaining Factors**	**Severity**	**Current Performance**
	Cognitive	Mild Mod. Sev.	Mild delay
	Sensorimotor	Mild Mod. Sev.	Mild Hypotonia
	Psychosocial	Mild Mod. Sev.	
	Medical	Mild Mod. Sev.	
	Caretaker Attendance	Frequently	Intermittently	Rarely
Time Frame	Time Allotted	3 years	
Long-Term Goals	Darryl will: Produce personal, conjoined, and embedded goal-based causal chain narratives in a variety of contexts		

FIGURE 3.3a: MK-SLIP Long-term goal template for Darryl

Deriving Subordinate Long-Term Goal(s) Long Term Goal:			
Decision	**Guiding Information**		
Areas of Speech/Language Intrinsic to the Long-Term Goal	**Area of Speech/Language**	**Referent Taxonomy**	**Current Performance Level**
	Content/form interactions Microstructure of narrative discourse	Bloom & Lahey (1978), Lahey (1988)	Speaks primarily in single verb sentences
Subordinate Long-Term Goals	Darryl will: Produce a range of complex sentences with appropriate connectives Increase lexical variety across content categories within discourse Produce range of developmental morphemes in discourse contexts		

FIGURE 3.3b: MK-SLIP Subordinate long-term goals for Darryl

Deriving the Long-Term Goal			
Decision	**Guiding Information**		
Areas of Speech/Language to be Targeted, Referent Taxonomy, and Current Level of Performance	**Area of Speech/ Language**	**Referent Taxonomy**	**Current Performance**
	Content/form (Semantics/syntax)	Lahey (1988)	Uses one and two-word utterances to code existence and action, with much hesitation and phonetic groping Uses a mixture of English, Spanish, and Italian words, gestures, writing, and drawing Able to read single words
	Phonology		Displays characteristics of apraxia, resulting in irregular articulatory breakdowns, distorted consonants and vowels, literal and verbal Paraphasic errors, and neologisms
Projecting a Prognosis	**Maintaining Factors**	**Severity**	**Current Performance**	
	Cognitive	Mild Mod. Sev.		
	Sensorimotor	Mild Mod. Sev.	Right hemiparesis	
	Psychosocial	Mild Mod. Sev.	Mild depression; frustrated by not being understood	
	Medical	Mild Mod. Sev.	Coronary disease	
	Caretaker Attendance	Frequently	Intermittently	Rarely
Time Frame	Time Allotted			
Long-Term Goals	Produce 2-3 constituent utterances as contingent responses within conversations			

FIGURE 3.4a: MK-SLIP Long-term goals for Mr.B

Deriving Subordinate Long-Term Goal(s)			
Long Term Goal:			
Decision	**Guiding Information**		
Areas of Speech/Language Intrinsic to the Long-Term Goal	**Area of Speech/Language**	**Referent Taxonomy**	**Current Performance Level**
	Language use	Lahey (1988)	Speaks to direct listener's attention, comment, request
Subordinate Long-Term Goals	Produce language for a range of communicative functions		

FIGURE 3.4b: MK-SLIP Subordinate long-term goals for Mr.B

SUMMARY: DO'S AND DON'TS OF GOAL-WRITING

Having examined steps in the derivation of long-term goals, we have compiled a list of do's and don'ts of long-term goal-writing by way of summary. These include:

Do's

- ***Do*** write long-term goals in terms of functional communication regardless of the age of the client or the communication problem being addressed (e.g., language, voice, fluency, and phonology).

- ***Do*** describe long-term goals with reference to developmental or complexity hierarchies within linguistic or physiological taxonomies.

- ***Do*** specify linguistic categories of speech and language in the long-term goal.

Don'ts

- ***Don't*** write overly general long-term goals, such as "to improve client's receptive and expressive language" or to "improve functional language."

- ***Don't*** write long-term goals as isolated skills. Examples of isolated skills include recalling number sequences, identifying main ideas in reading passages, practicing fluency techniques while imitating the clinician, discriminating sound, and so on. These do's and don'ts are illustrated above.

EXERCISES

1. Identify the ***don'ts*** in each of the following long-term goal statements written for Amahl (with reference to the don'ts in the list).

   Amahl will increase attention span.

   Amahl will improve recall in the context of daily activities.

   Amahl will follow four-step commands.

2. Which of the following hypothetical long-term goals do not provide a clear taxonomy for the formulation of short-term goals?

   A. Adult client (aphasia) will respond appropriately to questions in all communicative contexts.

   B. Adult client (aphasia) will produce various two- and three-constituent utterances (agent–action–object relations) with words and gestures in all communicative contexts.

   C. Adult client (aphasia) will use compensatory strategies during moments of word-finding difficulty.

D. Child (6, 10; language and phonology) will demonstrate appropriate expressive language skills to support functional communication in all communicative contexts.

E. Child (6, 10) will produce complex causal chain narratives in a variety of contexts.

F. Adult client (aphasia) will produce higher-level cognitive skills across all communicative contexts.

G. Child (3, 7; phonology/language) will produce a range of complex sentences with appropriate connectives in conversational speech.

H. Adult client (aphasia) will decrease paraphasias.

ANSWER: C, D, F, H—there is no identifiable category of linguistic behavior, thus, no basis for subsequent goal planning.

3. *It may be useful to consider the following criteria in evaluating the appropriateness of the LTG.* It is helpful to ask what the goal represents.

A. A change in the individual's communication behavior within a linguistic, developmental, or physiological taxonomy of behavior?

B. A client data–based projection within a hierarchy of behaviors (i.e., a guide for STG planning)?

C. Highest projected level of communication change/performance in the individual in naturalistic contexts?

D. A change in observable communication behavior that may be recognized by a caregiver in a naturalistic context?

Do the following LTGs satisfy the above criteria? If not, which number(s) above is/are violated?

1. AC will coordinate the four subsystems of speech to produce an efficient voice pattern, appropriate to a range of pragmatic contexts.

2. CV will utilize relaxation exercises to decrease tension (e.g., in jaw, face, larynx, and torso) across communicative contexts.

3. TW will understand cognitive and psychosocial underpinnings of fluency disorders and use cognitive behavioral therapy to reduce secondary behaviors.

4. MC will initiate conversation and regulate the environment in all communicative contexts for functional communication.

5. The client will eliminate the use of phonological processes that are no longer age-appropriate in conversational contexts.

6. SB will produce age-appropriate developmental morphemes across all communicative contexts.

ANSWERS: 1. None; 2. A, B, C, D; 3. A, B, C, D; 4. C; 5. None; 6. None.

Appendix 3A

Bloom and Lahey (1978; Lahey, 1988) Content/Form Interactions

1. Bloom and Lahey's content categories (single words—three or more constituents)

Category	Example
Existence	Dog/It's a dog.
Disappearance	Doggie all-gone.
Recurrence	More doggie.
Action	The dog ate the bone.
Locative action	The dog jumped onto the chair.
Attribution	The doggie is brown.
Rejection	No dog!
State	The dog is sad.

2. Bloom and Lahey's complex interevent content categories (two or more verbs in one sentence).

Content Category/ Syntax	Semantic Relation between Clauses	Example
Additive/conjunction	Reversible clauses	I like cats and I like dogs.
Temporal/conjunction	Necessary sequence	The boy showered and then dried himself.
Causal/conjunction	Causally dependent	The boy dried himself cause he was wet.
Adversative/conjunction	Contrast	The boy was dirty, but towel is clean.
Epistemic/ complementation	Thought, belief	I think that this is important.
Notice/perception complementation	Sensing, perceiving	I saw that you hit the boy.
Communication/ complementation	A communicating act	I said that you are in trouble.
Object specification/ relativization	Complement of a noun phase (subject, or complement of VP prediction.	The boy ate a hamburger that was yummy.

Adult discourse analyzed with reference to Bloom and Lahey (1978) and Lahey (1988) Content/Form/Use Taxonomy

Sentence from Adult Discourse	Verb Relation Content Category	Coordinated Non–Verb Relation Categories*	Form
This is a shark's tooth	Existence	Possession	3+ constituents
I took my kids to the Museum of Natural History last week	Locative action	Possession Temporal	3+ constituents
They drove me crazy!	State	Temporal	3+ constituents
First, they wanted to eat	Internal state (desire)/mood		Complex 2-verb (infinitival complement)
Then, they had to go to the bathroom	Internal state (necessity)/mood		Complex 2-verb (infinitival complement)
Then, they wanted to go to the gift shop	Internal state (desire)/mood		Complex 2-verb (infinitival complement)
I told them that I wanted to see the dinosaur exhibit first, but Jordan complained that he had a belly ache!	Communication Internal state (desire)/mood Adversative Communication		Complex multiverb (conjunction, infinitival complement, sentential complement)
Then he started to cry so I took him to the gift shop	State (initiate)/mood Causal		Conjunction, infinitival complement

*Identified with three-constituent utterances.

chapter 4

Long-Term Planning: Formulating a Procedural Approach

READER WILL:

- Become familiar with the MK-SLIP template for procedure planning
- Become familiar with steps of decision-making and sources of information that guide procedure planning
- Identify premises of theories of learning and rehabilitation that guide procedure planning
- Identify maintaining factors that guide intervention planning

After planning long-term goals, it is natural to ask oneself, "How am I going to help my client achieve these competencies?" Thus, at the long-term planning phase the clinician turns to procedure planning. At this point in the planning process, we identify those sources of information that would be most useful in designing interactions and contexts that will help our client achieve his or her long-term goals. Those sources of information, in addition to the long-term goal statement itself, are (a) clinical research that bears upon treatment of the particular disorder being addressed, (b) theory-based premises of learning and rehabilitation, and (c) maintaining factors that require modification. The specification of learning and rehabilitation premises and maintaining factors to be addressed in the design of specific tasks constitutes the procedural approach.

58   **CHAPTER 4** Long-Term Planning: Formulating a Procedural Approach

Step 1: Survey the research evidence.

Procedure planning begins with a search for available research evidence about effective intervention approaches associated with the acquisition or rehabilitation of the specific aspect of communication specified in the long-term goal statement. For example, one long-term goal for Amahl involves the improvement of articulation/phonology related to apraxia. Research reveals that frequent, rapid productions of selected stimuli (drill) is most facilitative in cases of articulation intervention (Lass & Pannbaker, 2008; Shriberg & Kwiatkowski, 1982; Wanbaugh, 2002). In the case of Darryl, long-term goals involve producing causal-chain narratives and component complex sentences. Research indicates that narrative discourse and content/form interactions in young children are most readily achieved in the context of naturalistic routines, including storybook reading (Gillam & Ukrainetz, 2006; Hoggan & Strong, 1994) and play (Bloom & Lahey, 1978; Lahey, 1988; Lund & Duchan, 1988; Kim & Lombardino, 1991). Based on such evidence, tasks for Amahl would involve repetitive efforts to articulate specific phonemes; for Darryl, play and storytelling activities might be considered.

Turning to Mr. B, a growing body of research has documented the efficacy of communication-based intervention approaches in the rehabilitation of language in adults with aphasia. This can be contrasted with more traditional approaches targeting information processing skills (i.e., memory, retrieval) though rote drill (Salis, Hwang, Howard, & Lallini (2017). Meta-analyses of outcomes of such approaches have raised significant doubts about their effectiveness (e.g., Salis et al).

THE STATE OF THE EVIDENCE. It would be helpful if the research evidence relevant to each and every type of speech and language disorder was unequivocal; one identifiable intervention approach proved maximally efficacious. Reality reveals, however, multiple intervention approaches associated with many communication disorders. Two divergent approaches to intervention, for example, have been promoted for language delays associated with autistic spectrum disorders: operant (especially applied behavior analysis, Lovaas, 1987; verbal behavior, Carbone, 2013) and relationship-based pragmatic (most prominently, Greenspan's DIR program; Greenspan & Weider 2006). There is no experimental evidence to date, however, that unequivocally supports the efficacy of any of these approaches in the facilitation of speech/language or functional communication (Spreckley, 2009; Australian Government Department of Aging, 2006). This situation is common across many disorder areas. Interestingly, there *is* evidence in recent literature concerning what *NOT to do* (e.g., the use of nonspeech oral-motor exercises to treat articulation disorders; Lass & Pannbacker, 2008; Lof, 2003; Lof & Watson, 2008; Powell, 2008; the use of auditory processing exercises to improve expressive language; Fey, Richard, Geffner, Kamhi, Medwetsky, Ross-Swain, Wallach, Frymark, Schooling, 2011; Law, Garrett, & Nye, 2004). What do we do about this state of affairs?

First, we stay away from those procedures or techniques that have been shown to have no or questionable credibility (e.g., non-speech oral-motor exercises, Fast Forward, AIT, Facilitated Communication, auditory processing exercises). Second, as clinicians versed in clinical research, we can conduct our own research by writing goals in observable, measurable terms and assessing progress toward achievement of the long-term goal of functional communication.

Step 2. Identify theories of learning and rehabilitation intrinsic to clinical research and derive premises contained within the theories.

Theory-based premises of learning and rehabilitation represent the second information source that informs procedure planning. Theories serve multiple functions in procedural planning; perhaps the most important function served is as sources of premises about learning that can be used to derive concrete intervention procedures.

STEP 2A. IDENTIFY PREMISES INTRINSIC TO SELECTED THEORIES.

Theories of learning and rehabilitation may be understood through their representative premises; premises are assumptions about processes or cause-and-effect relations that explain how learning and rehabilitation take place. Premises are the basis for the derivation of procedures that will lead to the acquisition of a targeted category of behavior. For example, a premise of operant learning theory is that environmental consequences following a behavior strengthen or weaken the behavior. A procedure that may be derived from this premise is that clinicians should provide rewarding and extinguishing consequences to clients following the expression of behavior targeted for acquisition or extinction.

STEP 2B. DETERMINE WHETHER THE OUTCOME OF SUPPORTING RESEARCH IS FUNCTIONAL COMMUNICATION.

Theories are especially useful in helping to understand whether or not the outcome of a particular study may contribute to functional communication. Given situations in which multiple intervention approaches are associated with particular communication disorders, theoretical considerations may help the clinician choose among competing approaches. For example, the developers of Fast ForWord, the computer-based language processing program, have asserted that their training in the processing of acoustic input will improve language performance (e.g., Tallal, 2004). Other researchers, however, have demonstrated, that while children may improve in performance on program exercises, their general language performance did not manifest commensurate improvement (Gillam, Loeb, Hoffman, Bohman, Champlin, Thibodeau, Widen, Brandell, Friel-Patti, 2008).

FIVE THEORIES OF LEARNING AND REHABILITATION. In the discussion that follows we present an overview of five theories of learning and rehabilitation. In this overview, we summarize premises and procedures that emanate from each theory, specify the behaviors the theory addresses, and the implications for procedure planning.

Constructivism

Premises

Language expresses what individuals know about objects, attributes, states, procedures for solving problems, and causality. From a constructivist perspective, this knowledge is acquired as individuals attempt to achieve goals they set for themselves, create strategies to overcome problems, and reflect on the results of their attempts. The individual makes discoveries as a consequence of feedback that he or she receives from his or her own physical actions and from others as he or she acts to achieve personal goals. Goals evolve through the lifecycle. A young child's goal may be to reach a rattle, climb out of a crib, place a block to create a tower; an adult's goal may be to correct a defective speech sound or say his wife's name. Constructivist theories derive from the work of Jean Piaget (e.g., 1962, 1985).

Constructivism has been applied to explain the development of particular types of semantic relations or content categories such as knowledge of objects, attributes, states, temporal and causal relations, and so on (Bloom, 1995; Fosnot, 1996; Karmiloff-Smith, 1986; Piaget, 1985). Constructivism has also been applied to explain the acquisition of pragmatics of language: social knowledge (Muller, Carpendale, Budwig, Sokol, 2008), phonology (especially phonological development; e.g., Ertmer & Ertmer, 1998, Klein), and syntax as a product of word knowledge and case grammar (Miyagawa, 2010).

DERIVED PROCEDURES. The clinician planning intervention from a constructivist perspective would design procedural contexts in the following way:

1. Allow clients to set goals for themselves.

2. Engage the client in the manipulation of concrete objects and the identification of problems that interfere with goal achievement

3. Engage clients in conversations about their intent, objects being manipulated, and causal explanations for outcomes.

A constructivist approach to facilitate coding attribution with reference to size might be having a child try to park a large fire truck in a small garage. For an adult with aphasia the clinician might plan for the adult to adjust the ingredients for a zucchini soup to accommodate additional guests.

Social Cognitive Learning Theories

Social cognitive learning theories have been applied to almost every domain of speech and language (e.g., vocabulary, syntax, semantic relations, voice, fluency, articulation, etc.) These theories focus primarily on executive functions: strategies and knowledge that individuals use to communicate, resolve problems, and acquire additional knowledge.

Premises

Social cognitive theories identify scaffolding as the primary instructional interaction. The concept of scaffolding was articulated by Bruner in his studies of infant–caregiver interactions and game playing (e.g., Ratner & Bruner, 1978). Scaffolding refers to a mentoring-type of relationship between an expert and a novice. In scaffolding, experts initially take the lead in problem-solving by directing the novice's attention to important information, modeling procedures, offering verbal explanations, and so on (e.g., Grannott, 1993). The expert gradually turns the lead over to the student as the student internalizes the procedures modeled by the mentor and gains expertise. The student thus becomes increasingly self-directive.

The progenitor of social cognitive theories was Vygotsky (1934, 1987). Vygotsky coined the term "zone of proximal development." This term signifies that there is a window of opportunity in which it is possible to facilitate development. The requirement is that tasks presented to the individual be within his or her grasp given his or her present developmental level and that the teacher offer useful strategies for the learner to capitalize on information relevant to accomplishing the task (e.g., Feuerstein, Rand, & Hoffman, 1979; Torgesen, 2004; Wertch, 1984).

Social cognitive theories emphasize the role that executive functions play in learning and problem-solving. The novice learner internalizes verbal or text-based procedures for solving specific types of problems and suppressing interfering behaviors. The learner retrieves the appropriate procedures from long-term store, and applies the procedures when presented a relevant task, or when a relevant problem arises. Examples include finding the main idea in a story by asking oneself who, what, where, when, and why questions (Reid, 1988); employing articulatory and phonatory strategies to mitigate stuttering; utilizing reminders for maintaining a calendar or appropriate social behavior; and so on.

A popular line of thought in the domain of social cognitive theory involves the use of scripts and other stores of situational knowledge when approaching a task (e.g., Schank & Abelson, 1977). Scripts comprise knowledge structures about familiar events (e.g., going to a fast-food restaurant, going to school, etc.). Scripts provide the individual easy-to-enact approaches to familiar tasks. Scripts simplify information processing by allowing the learner to focus on novel information without being burdened by the additional familiar information contained within the script being applied to the task at hand.

DERIVED PROCEDURES. Clinicians following social cognitive premises may design intervention contexts in the following way:

1. Model target behaviors

2. Provide verbal (or text-based) rules and scripts for the client to use to compensate for language-learning or performance problems (Courtright & Courtright, 1976, 1979; Cole & Dale, 1986; Connell, 1987; Youmans & Youmans, 2010).

Relationship-Based Pragmatic Theories

Relationship-based pragmatic learning theories attempt to account for the development of conversational discourse and underlying content/form/use interactions.

Premises

Relationship-based pragmatic theories posit that language serves primarily relationship-based social and emotional functions. These relationship-based functions center on the process of *intersubjectivity*: the desire of the speaker to make content of mind and intent known by a significant other. *Content of mind* refers to what the individual is thinking about and feeling at any given moment. Relationship-based pragmatic theory suggests that language learning is a function of communicative engagement with another (Geller & Foley, 2008; Greenspan & Weider, 2006).

CHILDREN. According to Bloom (1995), intersubjectivity—the child's desire that her intent be acknowledged by others in the course of language use—drives language development. Along these lines, Greenspan (2005) delineated two conditions that promote language learning; these are (a) the establishment of *circles of communication* (contingent, cooperative, topic-sharing play, and linguistic exchanges between child and caregiver) and (b) social problem-solving (problem-solving requiring the assistance of another). In such communicative contexts, the adult's responsiveness to a child's affective state and intent promotes language acquisition.

Geller and Foley (2008) approach language intervention as necessarily interprofessional, with caregivers treated as partners and cotherapists. Clinicians are encouraged to identify multiple points of entry—ways to promote conversational exchanges between clinicians, children, and caregivers. Clinicians are encouraged to recognize dynamics of the *intersubjective field* established during communicative exchanges between the clinician, child, and caregiver. The intersubjective field comprises the feelings and intents of the participants, as well as the interpretation of feelings and intents of one participant by another. As such, the necessity of establishing relationships between clinician and caregivers, as well as clinician and child, is a second central principle of language intervention. Relatedly, reflection by participants about the personal interpretation of other's intents and perspective taking and shifting are important competencies relevant to intervention.

ADULTS. Relationship-based pragmatic intervention with adults was proposed, historically by A. Damien Martin (1981). Based on a "thought-centered" approach to intervention for aphasia developed by Wepman (1968), Martin (1981) proposed that the act of functional communication itself facilitates communication skills. Wepman's approach was a reaction to aphasia treatments that focused on information processing skills to the exclusion of communication for the purpose of transmitting ideas to a listener. Wepman wrote, "By changing therapy from the specifics of naming—the struggle for accuracy in word finding—to the realm of ideas, one hopes to increase the possibility of effecting change in what may be the basic discrepancy, the apparent limitation in the use of ideas" (1972, p. 205). Martin, like Wepman, emphasized the connection between thought and language, and the importance of supporting the individual in his or her expression of an intended message, even if that expression involves the use of impaired language. In proposing a communication-oriented approach to therapy, Martin declared that "As speech pathologists we are primarily interested in communication" (p. 150). Martin explained further that "The communication interaction does not depend on the successful transfer of a particular intended message, but rather on the assumption of the appropriate role to effect such transfer" (p. 150; see also Muma, 1975). In other words, a communication interaction depends on all parties assuming the role of listener and facilitator of message transference. Martin observed, however, that speech-language clinicians typically act as speakers and their clients as listeners. Martin proposed that clinicians adopt the role of facilitator and receiver of the client's intended message. As such, he redefined normal language functioning, disorder, and therapy as follows:

> Normal functioning can now be defined as the maintenance, with maximum efficiency, of appropriate receiver–sender roles in a conversational exchange. The disorder can then be viewed as the disruption of the interaction in which one of the participants is an aphasic through the failure of either or both participants as a receiver–sender in the exchange. Therapy would then become the attempt to maximize and improve performance as receiver-senders by both participants in the same situation. (p. 151)

DERIVED PROCEDURES. Relationship-based pragmatic theory guides the clinician as follows:

1. Establish conversational exchanges with clients and their families that allow free and trusting expression of intent.

2. Be responsive to the affective and intentional states of clients and families.

3. Bring caregivers and partners into therapy sessions as coclinicians.

With reference to this last principle, incorporating caregivers in therapy sessions empowers caregivers. Caregivers learn goals and procedures of intervention for follow-up and at the same time provide clinicians with personally and culturally relevant information, useful for procedure planning,

Motor Theory

Premises

Here is a category of learning theories concerned with the acquisition of patterns of behavior (i.e., sensorimotor representations as seen in the areas of phonology, voice, and fluency)—not conscious ideas or cognitive processes. Motor-learning theories apply to both the learning of new skills in the areas of articulation/phonology, voice, fluency and the rehabilitation of previously known behaviors. Processes identified in these *motor-learning* theories as central to the acquisition of behavior patterns include the exercise of motor patterns, self-correction in response to problematic feedback, and the differentiation, integration, and coordination of different and often conflicting behavioral patterns (Klein & Moses, 1999a, b).

Motor representations incorporate the use of various types of peripheral feedback (e.g., auditory, tactile, proprioceptive/kinesthetic from joints, tendons, muscles, and air- and bone-conducted pressure changes) and central feedback (from the brain) as part of the control mechanism for self-regulation of behavioral patterns. Two types of feedback loops have been implicated in the process of self-regulation: open and closed (Mass, Robin, Austerman-Hula, Wulf, Ballard, Schmidt, 2006; also see Leather & James, 1991; and Locke & Pearson, 1992). *Open-loop* control involves preplanning and the use of already-represented patterns exclusively during problem-solving. Open-loop control does not, however, allow the incorporation into procedural representations of new information from feedback received during efforts to compensate for problems. Open-loop control may be observed in the perseverative behavior of some children with autistic spectrum disorder and adults who suffer brain injury. In such cases, behaviors within the loop are not modifiable and not readily changed with treatment. *Closed-loop* feedback systems do use new information, thus amenable to modification, facilitating habilitation.

DERIVED PROCEDURES. The clinician addressing the acquisition or rehabilitation of motor representations would be guided by the preceding premises:

1. Create procedures that encourage the client to produce the target motor pattern.

2. Encourage the client to practice target patterns.

3. Modify behaviors in response to problematic efforts to produce the target pattern.

Operant Theory

Operant premises apply to learning across domains of language across the lifespan (e.g., see Lovaas, 1987; Sweeney-Kerwin et al., 2007, with reference to autistic spectrum and other child language disorders; McAffrey, 2008; Robey, 1998, with reference to aphasia; Onslow, Packman, & Harrison, 2003, with reference to stuttering; Butcher, Elias, & Raven, 1993, with reference to voice). The goal of behaviorism is the "prediction and control of [observable] behavior" (Watson, 1919/1994, p. 248). Behaviorism aims to explain the acquisition of observable behaviors that can be measured directly. Sets of observable behaviors that serve adaptive functions are termed *operants*. Operants are the means by which individuals operate on their environment (Skinner, 1957). For example, reaching, grasping, turning, and pushing represent components of a door-opening operant.

Premises

Operant theory presumes that operants—which include verbal behaviors—are shaped, strengthened, or weakened, and ultimately evoked by their consequences; behavioral consequences are environmental events that occur after the behavior has been expressed (Hayes & Hayes, 1992; Hedge, 1995; Goldfarb, 1981; Skinner, 1969). Thus, a door opening serves to reinforce the "door-opening" operant. Consequences that increase the probability that a behavior will be expressed again are termed *reinforcers* (i.e., S_R's); positive reinforcers involve the provision of something tangible, whereas negative reinforcers involve the removal of something noxious or uncomfortable following the expression of an operant. Consequences that decrease the subsequent rate of a behavior's expression are termed *extinguishers* or *punishments*. An extinguisher is the absence of a consequence following a behavior. A punishment involves the provision of a noxious stimulus following a behavior.

Stimuli that precede target behaviors are termed *discriminative stimuli* (S_D's). At the outset of an intervention, an S_D is typically a prompt by a clinician. Eventually, when the target behavior becomes spontaneous, the reinforcing consequence (S_R) becomes the S_D.

In an operant intervention, the long-term goal is dissected by the clinician (or curriculum author) into a series of simpler, learnable tasks; this process is termed *task analysis:* The series of tasks are then taught to the client applying operant techniques summarized earlier.

DERIVED PROCEDURES. According to the premises of operant theory the clinician should do the following:

1. Present a stimulus to prompt a target behavior.

2. If the client produces the target behavior, present a reinforcer (i.e., reward).

3. If the client does not produce the target behavior, present an extinguishing or punishing consequence.

Box 4-1 summarizes the premises derived from theories of learning reviewed earlier and their implications for intervention planning. Box 4-1 was designed to aid the clinician in identifying premises of learning and rehabilitation that could be useful in planning and justifying procedural approaches. Box 4-1 directs the clinician toward identifying (a) five learning theories and premises of learning derived from these theories, (b) speech/language domains (content/form/use) in which change is addressed, and (c) clinical research that bears upon the efficacy of these premises.

BOX 4-1: Five Theories of Learning and Rehabilitation with Corresponding Premises and Treatment Implications

Theories of Learning	Premises	Treatment Implications	Research Evidence
Constructivism	Language expresses what individuals know about objects, attributes, states, and procedures for solving problems in causal relations. This knowledge is acquired as individuals: attempt to achieve goals they set for themselves create strategies to overcome problems reflect on the consequences of their attempts (i.e., feedback)	Goal setting: Target functional communication (expressions of intent) and linguistic organization, developmentally appropriate content categories (syntax) Target language forms (vocabulary, narratives) that reflect client's content of mind (i.e., real-time focus of attention and interest) Procedure planning: Engage clients in play with concrete objects, promote problem-solving involving concrete objects Encourage clients to communicate about their intent, objects being manipulated, problem-solving procedures, and causal explanations for outcomes.	Theoretic: Bloom (1995) Forman and Hill (1990) Lahey (1988) Clinical: Moses, Klein, and Altman (1989)

| Relationship-based/ pragmatic | Language serves primarily social and emotional functions

Intersubjectivity, the desire of the speaker to make content of mind known to others, is the driving process in language acquisition and language use | Goal setting: Target language functions and contingent responses to others

Target *circles of communication* (conversation focusing on the client's intent)

Establish goals for caregivers as well as the child or adult who is the focus of intervention

Procedure planning: Establish conversational exchanges with clients and their families which allow free and trusting expression

Be responsive to the affective and intentional states of clients and families

Integrate caregivers and Partners into therapy sessions as coclinicians | Theoretic Geller and Foley (2008)

Clinical Greenspan and Weider (2006) Lahey (1988) |
|---|---|---|---|

Social cognitive	Language emerges from scaffolding (caregiver/ expert drawing attention to objects and relation-ships and modeling language and prob-lem-solving procedures) Scaffolding is most effective within the individual's "zone of proximal develop-ment" (appropriate for the client's stage of development) and within familiar routines Scaffolding leads to internalized verbal directives used to talk oneself through problem-solving (executive functions)	Goal setting: Target any linguistic structure or problem-solving procedure appropriate for the client's developmen-tal level of functioning Procedure planning: Model (verbal or text based) linguistic forms (vocabulary, sentences), rules, and scripts for the client to represent and apply to familiar and novel situations	Theoretic Bruner (1986) Nelson (2009) Wertch (1979) Clinical: Duchan (2004)
Motor learning	The expression of lan-guage is supported by the acquisition of motor representations; these emerge from practice with ges-tures required for speech production Representations may be modified in response to sensory feedback from failed efforts to produce the target pattern	Goal setting: Target articulation/ phonology, voice, fluency Procedure planning: Practice required gestures Modify gestures in response to problems in achieving target	Theoretic Adams (1971) Hikosaka et al. (2002) Maas et al. (2008) Clinical Grigos and Kolenda (2010) Knock et al. (2000)

Behaviorism/ operant	Language is viewed as *verbal behavior,* which is shaped, strengthened, or weakened, and ultimately evoked by consequences controlled by others	Goal setting: Target individual components of more complex skills; Establish observable, measurable goals Procedure planning: Schedule effective behavior-reinforcing and extinguishing consequences	Clinical: Lovaas (1987) Sweeney-Kerwin et al. (2007) McAffrey (2008) Robey (1998) Hegde and Davis (2010)

Several questions have been formulated to guide the clinician in selecting premises of learning theories when formulating procedural approaches. They direct the reader to the variety of premises that may provide rationales for procedural planning and suggest how premises from different learning theories together may help us devise an integrated procedural approach:

1. What is the area of communication targeted?

2. Is the client going to achieve change in the area targeted through (a) self-directed efforts at problem-solving; (b) engaging in reciprocal, interactive, circles of communication with the clinician and/or caregiver, or (c) through imitating and otherwise internalizing information presented by others?

3. What kinds of clinician–client interactions will encourage motivation, task orientation, and meaningful learning and development: clinician-directed or client-controlled?

4. What kinds of material will facilitate task engagement and language learning: manipulable concrete objects or symbolic items (words, pictures, text)?

5. What type of reward system should be employed to strengthen target responses?

Caution: Achieving Functional Communication

An important consideration in choosing among competing approaches is whether the specific tasks that participants perform contribute to functional communication. Regardless of the specific disorder type and related projected achievements, the ultimate long-term goal for all clients should be improved functional communication (see ASHA's mandate; Fratelli, Tompson, Holland, Wohl, & Ferketic, 1995). We need to emphasize, however, that functional communication is described with reference to the specific disorder type and achievement level expected of a client.

For example, there are many research studies that promote exercising executive functions (e.g., working memory, linguistic problem-solving procedures) as a basis for improving language and literacy in school-age children with language-learning disabilities (Marton & Schwarz, 2003; Rasmussen, Treit, Pei, 2010, Singer & Bashir, 1999). Results demonstrate improvement in planning and information recall within tasks specific to the studies (e.g., Rasmussen et al.). The question is, does the performance of those tasks contribute to functional communication? In the absence of empirical research, there is no absolute answer to this question, but there are tentative hypotheses that emerge from theory-based premises of learning.

From a social cognitive perspective, it is important to learn problem-solving procedures from experts; such procedures function as the basis for talking oneself through problem-solving tasks, and ultimately, transitioning from novice to expert. From this point of view, targeting executive functions to achieve functional language skills and literacy makes sense. Contrastively, constructive cognitive theories focus on developmental language achievements (Bloom, 1995; Moses, Klein, & Altman, 1990). Developmental achievements allow the individual to generate his or her own approaches to problem-solving and also achieve greater understanding of information presented by others. From this constructivist perspective, literacy tasks would need to include features that lead to developmental achievement, such as the learner's intentional, goal-directed, action-based problem-solving experiences, and not include merely verbal instructions provided by others.

Competing theories are not necessarily mutually exclusive. In Box 4-1, we presented a set of contrasting learning theories and their domains of applicability. The theories considered were behavioral, constructivist-cognitive, pragmatic, social learning, and motor. A clinician may favor one of these over another to explain learning. We suggested, however, that the clinician need not choose only one theory as a basis for developing an approach to speech/language intervention. Individual approaches are not universal in their explanatory power. Individual theories may account for the acquisition of some components of language but not others. Social learning theories, for example, may account for learning vocabulary, whereas constructivist theories may account for the achievement of content categories that the vocabulary represents. It is important, therefore, for the clinician to know an array of premises derived from theories and how specific premises can influence the design of clinical contexts.

Summary

At this point in the long-term planning phase, we have examined three sources of information that are used to establish a procedural approach: (a) the long-term goal statement, (b) findings from published research, and (c) premises derived from theories of language learning and rehabilitation (including the clinician's own beliefs about language and language learning). We will note the long-term goal for the particular client, clinical research that provides support for a particular approach to intervention, and premises that resonate with us.

We will also return to one other source of information that was introduced in the course of long-term goal-planning: nonlinguistic factors that may be maintaining the language disorder. The clinician will discover that recognition of nonlinguistic maintaining factors influences the other components of decision-making in the realm of procedure planning: the selection of premises of learning and rehabilitation, and the regulation of performance demands. Only after maintaining factors are considered can the procedural approach be finalized.

Maintaining Factors

In addition to research evidence and theoretic premises, a third body of information influences decisions about procedures: our knowledge about factors maintaining the specific disorder. Cognitive, sensorimotor, and psychosocial maintaining factors were discussed first in Chapter 2 in terms of their influence on goal-planning. We will now review these factors in terms of their influence on procedure planning. In the area of procedure planning, the identification of maintaining factors orients the clinician to speech- and language-related problems that the child needs to compensate for, modify, or eliminate in order to achieve the long-term goal.

Cognition

DEVELOPMENTAL COGNITION–LANGUAGE RELATIONS. The categories and types of object representations and relationships reflected in language content are very much a function of the developmental status of cognition, that is, an individual's awareness of their environment and use of that awareness in reasoning and problem-solving (Piaget, 1971). Consider Bloom and Lahey (1978; Lahey, 1988) who define language as "a code that represents *ideas about the world*….', not '…a code whereby the *real-world* is represented….'" Chomsky (2004, 2014) similarly has emphasized that semantics do *not* refer *to extramental objects*—objects outside of the mind; language employs only mentally represented linguistic objects. In the domain of semantics, these linguistic objects include representations of objects, actions, attributes, states, and so on, that is, types or categories of objects that humans attend to and the specific instances of each that individuals experience. Representations also refer to relations among objects and events (i.e., semantic relations, such as actor-action-object-instrument, additive, temporal, causal, epistemic, logically inclusive or exclusive, and so on; see Brown, 1972; Chomsky, 2013; Lahey, 1988).

Piaget's developmental taxonomies (e.g., Piaget, 1954, 1962, 1976, 1978) alert us to the relationship between stage of cognition and reasoning achieved by an individual.

Piaget's taxonomies also alert us to complexity of the topics and relationships within linguistic content categories referenced by individuals. There are different types of attributes, states, procedural and causal relations, and story grammars that individuals can produce and understand (e.g., Moses, Klein, & Altman, 1989).

Thus, long-term goals that target semantics at the lexical, sentential, and narrative levels also address cognition, that is, the representation of objects and relationships intrinsic to such goals. Cognition, furthermore, may be directly targeted within long-term goals for clients at prelinguistic developmental levels that address such cognitive competencies as pretend-play and prelinguistic functions of intentional communication.

The implication for procedure planning is that approaches to learning and rehabilitation need to be considered that promote the construction of mental representations, establishment of more complex relationship-making, and cognitive development.

EXECUTIVE FUNCTIONS AND METALINGUISTICS. Long-term goals (and subsequently short-term and session goals) may address metalinguistics and executive functions (i.e., the use of language to plan, direct oneself in the course of problem-solving, suppress or sequence behavior, etc.). Implicit in such objectives is that language itself, and constituent linguistic objects, become objects of awareness, to be intentionally reflected upon and manipulated.

The implication for procedure planning is that approaches to learning and rehabilitation need to be considered that make language and its components topics of awareness, to promote the use of language to regulate one's own behavior and the development of operational and verbal reasoning. Box 4-2 presents implications for intervention planning stemming from cognition as a maintaining factor.

BOX 4-2: Relationships between Cognitive Skills and Evidenced-Based Implications for Intervention Planning

Stage of Linguistic Performance	Associated Cognitive Skills	Implications for Intervention Planning	References
Prelinguistic: Reduplicative and variegated babbling Developing object and relational knowledge	Circular reactions (the child notices his or her own behavior and objects manipulated, repeats actions, experiments)	Establish goals related to: Pre-speech sound production Object manipulation Create procedures that: Encourage caregiver–child interactions Extend vocalizations and object manipulation	Piaget (1962) Greenspan and Weider (2006)

	Imitation of caregiver's production of sounds and gestures already generated by the child	Establish goals related to: The intentional expression of sounds and gestures; turn-taking, and other conversational devices Create procedures that: Facilitate caregiver–child communication	Bloom, Lightbown, and Hood (1974) Williams, Whiten, Sudendorf, and Perrett (2001)
	Intentional means–end behavior (intentionally setting a goal, such as getting daddy to repeat a favorite behavior, and using a familiar action, such as smiling to achieve a goal)	Establish goals that target: Intentional communicative functions: instrumental, regulatory, interactional, personal, heuristic Create procedures that encourage: Goal setting, Manipulating and combining objects	Halliday (1993) Greenspan and Weider (2006)
Single words through the beginning of syntax (two- to three-word combinations)	Object constancy (knowing that objects exist, even when displaced)	Establish goals for: Naming objects, commenting on their absence or recurrence	
	Creation of new means not already in the child's repertoire to achieve goals or solve problems (e.g., using a chair to retrieve a box of cereal from the top of the refrigerator)	Establish goals for: Commenting on objects, actions, and locations Create problem-solving opportunities involving means– end behavior (withswitch toys, mechanical toys, constructive objects)	Piaget (1954) Forman and Hill (1990)
	Single-scheme and combinatorial pretend-play (combining and separating objects and representing objects and their functions with toys)	Establish goals that target: Pretend-play (combinatorial scheme, scripts) Plan procedures that encourage: Play with toys, enactment of familiar routines	Piaget (1962, 1985) Nicolich (1981) Forman and Hill (1990)

Development of phonology of the language	Imitation of novel gestural and vocal movements not already in the child's repertoire	Target articulatory gestures and the production of specific word syllable, and root forms. Model and encourage imitation of word, syllables, and individual speech sounds	
Two- to three-word combinations through complex utterances	Multischeme pretend-play and script play (planning pretend activities involving a series of actions and pretending at familiar activities, such as going to a restaurant)	Goals target production of more complex semantic relations and narratives	Piaget (1962) Westby (1980, 2010)
	Early part–whole relations, classifications, and seriations requiring the manipulation of objects (involves distinguishing parts from the whole, grouping and regrouping objects according to attributes, and ordering objects according to a specific dimension (e.g., size)	Goals target semantic categories of: attribution, quantity, possession, and internal state comparatives and causal relations Plan procedures that involve: goal setting; problem-solving involving grouping, conceptualizing, and distinguishing attributes and internal states; means–end behavior; and more complex causality	Forman and Hill (1990) Piaget (1952)

| | Acts of conservation in which relations among multiple factors in the course of problem-solving are identified and evaluated and multiple possible approaches to problem-solving are envisioned | Target the use of language for planning and problem-solving
Target complex causal utterances
Create problem-solving procedures that address conservation | Karmiloff-Smith (1986)
Piaget (1976, 1978)
Moses, Klein, and Altman (1989)
Fischer and Rose (1998)
Fischer, Rotenberg, Bullock, and Raya (1993) |
| Literacy | Awareness of speech and language units that may be manipulated (i.e., sounds, syllables) | Set goals that address metalinguistic skills and knowledge, including phonologic awareness, word and sentence meaning, figurative language, and syntax | Karmiloff-Smith (1986) |

Sensorimotor

STABILITY, LOCOMOTION, AND SKILLED MOTOR ACTS. Beyond speech perception discussed in Chapter 2, the child's overall sensorimotor functioning has significance for speech-motor control and language performance. A child's ability to maintain stable, comfortable speech postures (e.g., sitting, standing), manipulate objects, execute motor acts, and ambulate (crawl, walk) is particularly relevant for speech and language. These sensorimotor abilities allow the child to learn about the world (i.e., acquire language content) through manipulating, exploring, and playing with objects and people (Iverson, 2010; Conner, Williamson, & Siepp, 1978). Sensorimotor achievements support phonologic and syntactic competence, as the child is able to generate speech movements and regulate respiratory function while engaged in ongoing activities (such as playing, eating, or sitting at a desk in school; see Green, Moore, Higashikawa, & Steeve, 2010).

IMPLICATIONS FOR INTERVENTION PLANNING. Generally, we work with the physical or occupational therapist to address stability and locomotion within intervention procedures (e.g., in positioning the client, using adaptive or augmentative devices, etc.).

SENSORY FEEDBACK. The processing of sensory information is an additional sensorimotor aspect that merits attention. Specifically, our focus is sensation and its relationship to motor control during goal-directed play and problem-solving. Every goal-directed motor act has a sensory feedback component (Mysak, 1980; Kent, 1999). This feedback component involves the sensing of movement and the gathering of information relevant to the individual's effort to achieve a goal or to communicate intent. The sense of movement involves proprioception and kinesthesis (feeling where the body is in space), vestibular activity (detecting and maintaining balance and uprightness), and tactile sensation (deep and light touch).

Children and adults need to be able to sense their movements (i.e., receive and process feedback information) in order to learn how to control their movements (Bobath & Bobath, 1986; Mysak, 1980). Individuals need to process feedback to ascertain progress in achieving a goal and to identify and compensate for problems. Individuals use feedback to represent objects that they interact with during sensorimotor activities and play (Piaget, 1971, 1985) and to control phonation and articulation. Obtaining comfort and pleasure from others through physical contact supports emotional responsiveness, positive feedback from others, and communication. Discomfort and displeasure from interactions with others interfere with communication and aspects of content, form, and use acquired through communication

Sensory processing problems are a feature of a number of syndromes and disorders; these include Down's syndrome, autistic spectrum disorder (Tomchek & Dunn, 2007), cerebral palsy (Bobath & Bobath, 1986; Mysak, 1980), and perhaps certain learning disabilities (Ayres, 1969; Cummins, 1991).

One of the most salient sensory processing problems—hearing loss—may become a consideration in the aging population. Approximately 30% of noninstitutionalized persons over 65 years of age have some degree of hearing loss and about 70%–80% of residents of nursing homes suffer from auditory dysfunction. Weinstein (1994) in a comprehensive chapter on presbycusis indicated that (a) age is a significant risk factor for hearing loss with mean hearing levels increasing as a function of age and (b) hearing levels in men are slightly poorer than those of women, especially in the high frequencies.

Difficulties in processing sensory feedback have also been implicated as a concomitant of apraxia. Martin (1974) suggested that oral apraxia may be related to a heightened threshold for processing sensory input from articulatory gestures.

IMPLICATIONS FOR PROCEDURE PLANNING. The ability to process sensory information, especially sensory feedback from goal-directed action, has important implications for procedural planning in the treatment of a broad range of speech and language problems, in the areas of content, form, and use.

The speech-language pathologist may collaborate with an appropriate allied professionals (e.g., an audiologist or occupational therapist) and caregivers or significant others to develop intervention procedures that intensify sensory input and facilitate sensory processing. Augmentative devices, hearing aids, and so on may be employed to help the client compensate for sensorimotor difficulties. Procedures that address sensory maintaining factors are discussed further in subsequent chapters addressing intervention planning for specific speech-language disabilities.

One caveat should be noted. There is no evidence that the treatment by occupational therapists of sensory integration problems, as advocated by Jean Ayres (1969; 2005), has any measurable effect on cognition or speech-language function (Schooling, Coleman, Cannon, 2012). (Box 4-3 describes essential sensorimotor functions and their implications for intervention planning.)

BOX 4-3: Relationships between Sensorimotor Functions and Evidence-based Implications for Intervention Planning

Sensorimotor Function	Implications for Intervention Planning	Evidence
Speech-related perception High-speed processing of phonologic features for phoneme identification and discrimination Ability to differentiate and attend to speech, given competing sound (speech and nonspeech)	Perceptual skills can be targeted as session goals relevant to articulation, language comprehension, and hearing	Tallal (1997, 2004)
Sensation and regulation of feedback from goal-directed activity contribute to the acquisition of language content/form/use	When planning procedures for goals addressing content/form/use interactions, provide sensorimotor experiences involving the manipulation of concrete objects (e.g., play, problem-solving)	Karmiloff-Smith (1986), Piaget (1985)
Tonicity, body stability, respiration, locomotion contribute to skilled motor acts relevant to articulation, voice, fluency, and language	When planning procedures for articulation, voice, fluency, language, work in collaboration with occupational and physical therapists to address tonicity, body stability (e.g., positioning) Target skilled motor acts as session goals when addressing speech acts	Connor, Williamson, and Siepp (1978); Mysack (1980) Shriberg and Kwiatkowski (1982)

Psychosocial

Geller and Foley (2008) have emphasized that speech-language intervention—and, ipso facto, intervention planning—needs to be relationship based. This point of view emerges from the recognition that language develops in a social context—within the caregiver–child relationship (Bloom, 1995; Greenspan & Weider, 2009). Language serves multiple social functions, including alerting others to one's intent (Bloom, 1995; Bloom & Tinker, 2001) and emotional state (Greenspan, 2005; Greenspan, Weider, & Simon, 1998), and establishing and maintaining interpersonal contact (Halliday, 1975; 1993). Furthermore, language is influenced by culture and is a medium for the transmission of culture (Champion, 2003; Seymour, 2006; Heath, 1983).

Given that language serves critical affective and social functions, difficulties in psychosocial functioning may contribute to a speech/language disorder. Psychosocial factors that affect speech/language functioning include (a) the individual's ability to engage in and benefit from social interactions; (b) the individual's typical affect and strategies for adapting to environmental demands, including reactions to communicative successes and failures; (c) the caregiver's or partner's efforts to facilitate communication development and their reactions to the individual's communicative attempts; and (d) the characteristic composition of the client's environment (caregivers, spouses, partners, friends, peers, siblings, culture, socioeconomic background, affect, languages spoken, etc.).

IMPLICATIONS FOR PROCEDURE PLANNING. In the course of procedure planning, we keep in mind that the long-term goal of all speech-language intervention is functional communication, that is, spontaneous communication in the social context of play and discourse with others. Thus, contexts are designed in which the client demonstrates mastery of intervention goals while communicating intentionally with others. Furthermore, the client's culture and the role of the caregiver or significant other in intervention is considered in the course of procedure planning. The influence of caregiver–child interactions and significant other–adult interactions and scaffolding on procedure planning was discussed earlier in the context of social cognitive and pragmatic learning theories. Inclusion of caregivers and significant others in intervention is highlighted as a premise of the relationship-based pragmatic paradigm of language learning and rehabilitation across the lifespan. Box 4-4 presents implications for intervention planning stemming from psychosocial variables as maintaining factors.

BOX 4-4: Psychosocial Achievements and Evidence-based Implications for Intervention Planning

Psychosocial Achievement	Age Expected	Implication for Intervention Planning	Reference
Calming eye gaze to caregiver during feeding	1 month	Potential goals: establishment of eye gaze and joint attention; goals may be established for caretaker as well as baby Procedures: Create naturalistic intervention context involving caretaker and child (e.g., cradling, feeding, and bathing)	Greenspan and Weider (2006) Geller and Foley (2008)
Baby attends to objects (rattle, keys, plush toy) given caregiver guidance	3–6 months	Potential goal: joint attention Procedures: Create naturalistic intervention context involving caretaker/clinician and infant, in which caregiver presents materials to and engages infant	Greenspan and Weider (2006) Uzgiris and Hunt (1965)

Child engages in scaffolded routines guided by caregiver, such as peek-a-boo, book reading	6 months on	Potential goals:
		  vocabulary comprehension
		  joint attention
		
		Procedures: Caregiver/clinician initiates routines, and actively engages child; caregiver/clinician works to allow child to initiate, extend, and modify routine
			Bruner and Ratner (1978), Greenspan and Weider (2006), and Westby (2010)

Child attends to caregivers comments on child's intentional activities, affect; caregiver's expansion of child's utterances	6–8 months on	Potential goals:
		  expansion of vocabulary,
		  content/form/use interactions
		
		Procedures: Allow child to engage in spontaneous play. Caregiver/clinician comments on child's object of interest and actions on objects. Caregiver may play alongside child. Caregiver avoids commands and questions. Caregiver's language is syntactically complete, but controlled for complexity with reference to the child's developmental level
			Bloom (1995); Greenspan and Weider (2006); Muller, Carpendale, Budwig, and Sokol (2008); Nelson (2009)

Child engages in routine experiences (school, shopping), role-play with peers	2 years on	Potential goals: acquisition of context-specific pragmatic skills pragmatic skills that reflect theory of mind culture-specific vocabulary figurative language pragmatic skills script play Procedures: Allow child to select and direct script. Caregiver/clinician may engage with child in the script-play routine. Caregiver converses with child naturally, in an effort to reflect child's intentionality and to extend script. Caregiver avoids commands and questions. Caregiver's language is syntactically complete, but controlled for complexity with reference to the child's developmental level	Lederer (2006) Westby (1980)
Child receives instruction and undergoes experiences relevant to cultural norms—acceptable behavior and prohibited behavior Development of intimate friendships Evolution of perspective, self-concept	4 years on	Potential goals: acquisition of cultural norms of communication (e.g., greetings, politeness, respect, attentiveness markers, request forms, etc.); context-specific pragmatic skills; identification of others' perspectives Procedures: Create conversational routines; allow client to engage in activities of interest (music, electronic games, etc.); create problem-solving experiences relevant to educational or social challenges; model target forms for client, as client models target forms for clinician	Geller and Foley (2008), Greenspan and Weider (2006)

Young adult prepares for and begins a career Chooses a significant other (to live with or marry) Begins to have children Becomes a member of a professional or vocational community Continued evolution of perspective, self-concept Older adults engaged with vocational, family, responsibilities Retirement Emotional responses to perceptions of progress, success, or failure pertaining to life's goals and experiences	Adulthood	Potential goals: continued development and refinement of context-specific pragmatic skills development of complex content/form/use interactions, narratives, and specialized vocabulary relevant to concepts and tasks associated with vocational training and experience Procedures: Create conversational routines incorporating client's interests and intents (social/vocational routines, etc.); clinician mediates routine; models target forms, incorporates significant others in the intervention Create problem-solving experiences relevant to social or vocational challenges	Moses, Klein, and Altman (1990)

Bilingualism and Bidialectism

As discussed in Chapter 2, within the broad area of cultural diversity, bilingualism and bidialectism are unique and important factors that need to be taken into account in intervention planning. Decisions need to be made about what language(s) to work on and what contexts to modify. Factors that contribute to decision-making relevant to goal and procedure planning include the following: The bilingual clients' language dominance, history as a simultaneous or sequential bilingual, baseline data concerning stage of language acquisition and/or language loss, and interlanguage, contextual information (additive or subtractive environments; family, peer, school attitudes toward bilingualism, bidialectism, mixing, etc.). Box 4-5 describes some cultural differences that have implications for intervention planning. It is important that the speech-language pathologist be aware of these differences when planning goals and procedures of intervention.

BOX 4-5: Stages in the Acquisition of a Second Language in Sequential Bilingualism

Stage of Acquisition	Behavioral Characteristics	Implications for Intervention Planning
Home language use/nonverbal	Avoidance of talking outside of the home within L2 context	Establish use of multipurpose utterances (vocabulary, phrases) as session and short-term goals
Formulaic language	Use of "default" or "stock" sentences or phrases in multiple contexts; for example, stating "That is good," whenever asked to comment on an activity	Sequence goals to proceed from use of multipurpose utterances to use of context-specific utterances
Interlanguage	Phonologic patterns (e.g., cluster reduction; general all-purpose verbs [GAP]) Errors of omission (e.g., omitting articles, irregular tense forms, markers for number agreement) Errors of commission (e.g., overgeneralizing regular tense patterns) Transfer of L1 features to L2 Phonological patterns Morphosyntax Transfer of morphological forms (accelerates learning if L1-L2 match, may delay learning if mismatch) May avoid L2 forms May use awkward forms Bilingual bootstrapping	Focus goals on language forms (e.g., sounds) that do not overlap between L1 and L2 Target use of function words following a developmental schedule

Early Stages of Second Language Acquisition in Sequential Second Language Learning (Tabor, 2008).

Summary

We have reviewed factors outside of the speech-language behavioral systems that appear to be interacting with speech and language to influence the communication problem under consideration. This information completes the procedural approach.

Illustrative Derivations of Procedural Approaches: Amahl, Darryl, and Mr. B

Long-term goal-planning was exemplified in Chapter 3 by following three clients: Amahl and Darryl, two children with speech/language disabilities, and Mr. B, an adult with aphasia. Figure 4.1 presents the template from the MK-SLIP APP for Planning the Procedural Approach. Figures 4.2 through 4.4 illustrate the derivation of procedural approaches for these three individuals—one addressing Amahl's phonological goals, one Darryl's language goals, and one Mr. B's goals. These exemplar procedural approaches will serve as a basis for illustrating the identification of specific acts of learning and task contexts that will constitute session goals and procedures.

Planning the Procedural Approach		
Decision	**Guiding Information**	
Ultimate Behaviors to Be Acquired	**Long-Term Goals and Corresponding Subordinate Long-Term Goal(s)**	
Approaches to Intervention	**Types of Evidence**	**Reference**
	Meta-Analysis	
	Experimental	
	Clinical Practice	
Premises about Language Learning or Rehabilitation from Clinical Research Relevant to Achieving Long-Term Goals	**Theory**	**Premises**
	Constructivism	
	Relationship-Based Pragmatic	
	Social Cognitive	
	Motor	
	Operant	
Maintaining Factors that Need to Be Addressed	**Maintaining Factors**	**Current Performance**
	Cognitive	
	Sensorimotor	
	Psychosocial	
	Medical	

FIGURE 4.1: MK-SLIP template for the long-term procedural approach

Planning the Procedural Approach		
Decision	**Guiding Information**	
Ultimate Behaviors to Be Acquired	**Long-Term Goal and Corresponding Subordinate Long-Term Goal(s)**	Produce three constituent utterances coding early content categories in conversational speech
		Use a range of language functions in conversational speech
		Produce a range of syllable and word structures and segmental features absent from and emerging in his repertoire
Approaches to Intervention	**Types of Evidence**	**Reference**
	Meta-Analysis	
	Experimental	
	Clinical Practice	Bloom (1995), Forman & Hill (1990) Lass & Pannbaker (2008) Shriberg & Kwiatkowski (1982) Wambaugh (2002)
Premises about Language Learning or Rehabilitation from Clinical Research Relevant to Achieving Long-Term Goals	**Theory**	**Premises**
	Constructivism	Reflection on feedback from the manipulation of concrete objects in context of goal directed behavior and problem solving facilitates language acquisition
		Feedback from articulatory gestures attempted in efforts to produce target sounds facilitates phonological development
	Relationship-Based Pragmatic	Communicative interactions between child and caretaker focused on child's content of mind and intent facilitates language acquisition
	Social Cognitive	Modeling promotes learning
	Motor	Practice producing articulatory patterns facilitates articulation
	Operant	Consequences following a behavior strengthens or weakens behavior
Maintaining Factors that Need to Be Addressed	**Maintaining Factors**	**Current Performance**
	Cognitive	Moderate developmental delay Provide Amahl perceptual support involving objects to manipulate
	Sensorimotor	Low tone, apraxic
	Psychosocial	Perseverates on routines. Aggressive when routines are broken Create and encourage familiar routines in collaboration with caregiver

FIGURE 4.2: MK-SLIP Long-term procedural approach for Amahl

Planning the Procedural Approach		
Decision	**Guiding Information**	
Ultimate Behaviors to Be Acquired	**Long-Term Goals and Corresponding Subordinate Long-Term Goal(s)**	Produce personal and causal chain narratives in a variety of contexts Produce a range of complex sentences with appropriate connectives Increase lexical variety across content categories within discourse contexts Produce the range of developmental morphemes in discourse contexts
Approaches to Intervention	**Types of Evidence**	**Reference**
	Meta-Analysis	
	Experimental	
	Clinical Practice	Geller & Foley (2008) Greenspan & Weider (2003) MacDonald (2004) Prizant & Wetherby (2003)
Premises about Language Learning or Rehabilitation from Clinical Research Relevant to Achieving Long-Term Goals	**Theory**	**Premises**
	Constructivism	Reflection upon feedback and from goal-directed play and problem solving facilitate the development of content of mind
	Relationship-Based Pragmatic	Circles of communication focusing on play and other topics of interest and feelings facilitate content/form/use interactions
	Social Cognitive	Modeling facilitates development
	Motor	
	Operant	Context, and consequences following behavior strengthen or weaken behavior
Maintaining Factors that Need to Be Addressed	**Maintaining Factors**	**Current Performance**
	Cognitive	
	Sensorimotor	Mild hypotonia
	Psychosocial	

FIGURE 4.3: MK-SLIP Long term procedural approach for Darryl

Planning the Procedural Approach		
Decision	**Guiding Information and Client Specific Details**	
Ultimate Behavior to be Acquired	**Long-Term Goals and Corresponding Subordinate Long Term Goals**	Produce 2-3 constituent utterances as contingent responses within conversations Produce context appropriate vocabulary to express a variety of content categories and communicative functions in conversation Demonstrate a variety of communicative functions
Approaches to Intervention	**Types of Evidence**	**Reference**
	Meta-Analysis	
	Experimental	
	Clinical Practice	Martin (1974); Chapey (1994); Lahey (1988)
Premises about Language Learning or Rehabilitation Derived from Clinical Research Relevant to Achieving Long-Term goals	**Theory**	**Premises**
	Constructivism	
	Relationship-Based Pragmatic	Participation in communicative exchanges aids rehabilitation
	Social Cognitive	Modeling facilitates rehabilitation
	Motor	
	Operant	Consequences following behavior strengthen or weaken behavior; acknowledgement of intent by conversational partner is reinforcing of the communication attempt
Maintaining Factors that Need to be addressed	**Maintaining Factors**	**Current Performance**
	Cognitive	
	Sensorimotor	Mild right hemiplegia, apraxia
	Psychosocial	Depressed; Frustrated when not understood
	Medical	History of cardiac issues; Taking Coumadin to prevent additional strokes

FIGURE 4.4: MK-SLIP Long-term procedural approach for Mr. B

The following are exercises designed to support an understanding of some of the necessary components of long-term procedure planning.

EXERCISES

1. Two contrastive interventions that address language delay in children with autistic spectrum disorder are applied behavior analysis (an operant intervention program) and Greenspan's floor-time (a relationship-based [social-pragmatic] program). Cite premises associated with each approach (see Box 4-1) that explain how content/form/use relationships would be acquired, and the implications for procedure planning that derive from the premises.

2. The following three syndrome categories are frequently associated with language disorders: autism, specific language impairment (SLI), and Down's syndrome. For each of these categories, identify the primary factors that may be maintaining the difficulty in learning language.

Our answers:

Question 1

Relationship-Based/Pragmatic Premise

The desire of the speaker to make content of mind known to others is the driving process in language acquisition.

Implication: Establish circles of communication in which children are permitted to express intentionality and in which caregivers speak to the child with reference to the child's intent.

Operant Premise

Language is shaped, strengthened or weakened, and ultimately evoked by consequences controlled by others

Implication: Evoke target utterances and follow the expression of target utterances with rewarding consequences.

Question 2

SLI:

*   Information processing deficit (e.g., Tallal, 1997; Bishop & Leonard, 2014)

*   Grammatical deficit (Bishop & Leonard, 2014; Lin, 2007)

*   Deficits in phonological memory (working memory; Bishop, 1994; Montgomery, 2000; Weismer & Evans, 2002)

Autism: Significant delays or impairment in

- forming and/or maintaining an emotional and/or social relationship with a primary caregiver.

- forming, maintaining, and/or developing communication.

- auditory processing skills (e.g., perception, comprehension, and articulation).

- processing of other sensations, including hyper/hypo-reactivity to visual-spatial, tactile, proprioceptive, and vestibular input processing of movement patterns (Greenspan, Weider, & Simon, 1998).

Down's syndrome (Trisomy 21, Global Down Syndrome Foundation, 2014)

- Moderate cognitive disability

- Hypotonicity (low tone)

- Difficulty in processing movement patterns

- Hearing problems, especially conductive hearing loss associated with otitis media.

chapter 5

Short-Term Planning: Short-Term Goals

READER WILL:

- Derive short-term goals with reference to baseline data from three clients: two children and one adult
- Become familiar with steps of decision-making and information that guide short-term goal planning
- Become familiar with the use of the MK-SLIP template as a tool for short-term goal planning

The focus of short-term planning is on identifying a set of behaviors (short-term goals) that can be acquired within several months or a semester, and that will advance the client toward the achievement of the long-term goal. The focus is also on making more specific procedural decisions.

Short-Term Goals Defined

A short-term goal is defined as an observable, measurable category of linguistic behavior, which is (a) targeted for acquisition within a three- to six-month period, (b) produced within a functional communication context, and (c) given priority within a hierarchy of achievements required for the realization of the long-term goal.

LINGUISTIC CATEGORY. Like long-term goals, a short-term goal incorporates a category of linguistic (communicative) behavior, such as phonological processes (targeted for elimination or reduction), content categories, or pragmatic contexts. These behaviors are categorical because they encompass a subset of similar behaviors. Thus, a phonological process affects a related set of phonemes (e.g., the process of stopping typically affects all fricatives); content categories refer to a potentially infinite number of utterances that code the same semantic relation, such as existence, action; locative, action (Lahey, 1988). Targeting a category of behavior is an effort to expand the individual's communicative system; the behavioral category is presumed to be the product of the mind's generative, organizational, relationship-making linguistic activity (i.e., language). The abstraction of such a category is believed to effect a general change throughout the system.

In some cases, as in the preceding examples, the behavioral categories are targeted directly. With disorders such as voice and fluency, however, the long- and short-term goals are targeted in the context of communicative performance. For example, a short-term goal for fluency may be formulated as "Client will coordinate the underlying systems of respiration, phonation, resonation, and articulation to produce three-constituent utterances, with controlled fluency as responses to questions." A similar goal may be formulated for voice disorders. Since we take the position that fluency and voice disorders require the coordination of the basic physiological processes to produce controlled fluency and efficient voice our sequence of goals are based on managing a taxonomy of contextual challenges: linguistic complexity, interlocutor expectations, and propositional demands.

OBSERVABLE AND MEASURABLE. The stipulation that short-term goals be observable and measurable addresses a requirement of idea legislation (PL-94-142ff) governing publicly funded speech-language services for children. A short-term goal (or any goal for that matter) must be formulated in terms of behaviors that can be measured (e.g., child will demonstrate the reduction of velar fronting to below 40%; an adult will demonstrate the functions, request and protest). A short-term goal cannot reference a mental function, for example, "to improve working memory"; memory occurs within one's mind and is therefore not observable or measurable.

EVALUATION CRITERIA. When we write short-term goals, we may include evaluation criteria to document achievement of target behavior. Criteria are usually written in terms of percentage or frequency of occurrence; for example, the child will reduce the process of stopping /s, z, f, v/ in phrases to 20%. In establishing this general procedure for writing short-term goals, we are adopting the format required by IDEA Legislation for writing short-term goals for children who are receiving speech-language intervention within a government-funded early intervention or educational program (e.g., New York State Education Department, 2005). Evaluation is typically by clinician observation.

FUNCTIONAL COMMUNICATION CONTEXTS. Short-term goals, like long-term goals, require the specification of a context in which the targeted behavior is expressed.

A consideration about nonlinguistic and linguistic characteristics of context is important because different contexts pose different challenges for the client.

At the short-term planning phase, the *nonlinguistic* context is described in terms of the type and amount of contextual support. Presence of manipulable objects, the clinician's verbal model of the behavioral target, and physical or verbal prompts offer the greatest degree of contextual support; spontaneous discourse about past or future events offers the least perceptual support.

The *linguistic* context is described in terms of the language surrounding the target utterance. The semantic, syntactic, pragmatic, and phonologic complexity and novelty of utterances surrounding the target behavior are the primary considerations in specifying the linguistic context for the expression of the target behavior. Taxonomies derived from the literature on typical development and linguistic universals provide a basis for evaluating linguistic complexity.

Formulating Short-Term Goals

Having identified taxonomies intrinsic to the long-term goal at the long-term planning phase, our task during the short-term planning phase is making prioritization decisions with reference to these taxonomies. How do we decide which behaviors should be learned before others on the road toward the designated long-term accomplishment? Systematic planning at the short-term phase involves the identification of a hierarchy of behaviors. This hierarchy represents the organization of behaviors within a taxonomy with reference to developmental or complexity levels that serves as a basis for sequencing goals.

Step 1: Identify a hierarchy of short-term achievements.

The term "hierarchy of achievements" has a number of implications. It suggests that the attainment of a long-term goal requires targeting a number of intermediate achievements or goals. It suggests, further, that intermediate goals can be arranged in such a way that each success serves as a foundation to the achievement of subsequent goals. Furthermore, the term "hierarchy" implies that there may be a natural configuration and order to a set of achievements. The naturalness and order is associated with achievement of the long-term goal. Bases for deriving hierarchies for the acquisition of certain speech/language behaviors may be different for children and adults.

STEP 1 FOR CHILDREN: REFER TO THE DEVELOPMENTAL TAXONOMY(IES) THAT GUIDED LONG-TERM GOAL PLANNING. As explained in the chapter addressing long-term goal planning, developmental taxonomies are the primary basis for establishing hierarchies of goal achievement for children. Examples of developmental taxonomies included Bloom and Lahey's content/form interactions (1978; Lahey, 1988), Halliday's (1975) functional communication; and Hodson and Paden's (1991) and Grunwell's (1985) phonological processes.

The two-dimensional nature of developmental taxonomies. Within developmental taxonomies, behavioral achievements may be viewed as proceeding in two directions. In the normal course of development, some achievements may be expected later than others. Still other achievements may be expected at the same time. This distinction between sequential and parallel achievements in child language development is illustrated in Bloom and Lahey's (1978) description of phases in the development of content/form interactions. There are a number of linguistic structures that children achieve during a single phase (parallel achievements), and there are other sets of structures that are attained later in development (higher-level achievements). For example, during the first phase of development, children use single words to code existence, recurrence, action, and negation (among others). In other words, a number of achievements occur at the same time. Single-word achievements occur at phase 1 before word combinations—a higher- level, phase 2, achievement. Figure 5.1 depicts the relationship between parallel and sequential achievements within a developmental hierarchy.

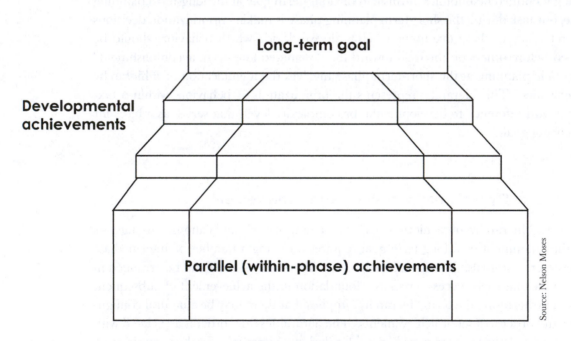

FIGURE 5.1: Relationship between Parallel and Hierarchical/Developmental Achievements

STEP 1 FOR ADULTS: REFER TO THE DEVELOPMENTAL OR COMPLEXITY TAXONOMY OR FRAMEWORK EMPLOYED TO ESTABLISH THE LONG-TERM GOAL. IF NECESSARY, CONDUCT COMPLEXITY AND DIFFICULTY ANALYSES WITH REFERENCE TO THE TAXONOMY TO ESTABLISH HIERARCHIES. With adults, two well-established considerations for ordering goals are task complexity and task difficulty (e.g., Chapey, 2008; Jenkins, Jimenez-Pabon, Shaw, Sefer, 1975; Klein & Moses, 1999b). The complexity of a task is determined based on an analysis of the information processing skills or linguistic organization demanded by that task (i.e., the number of syntactic transformations; the feature contrasts implicated in the processing of two discrete phonemes, the number of bits of information being held in working memory, etc.). For example, producing a phrase with a relative clause (e.g., "The man who painted the house fell on the lawn") reflects a greater degree of linguistic organization than the sentence, "The man is painting the house." The former is objectively more complex than the latter (e.g., van Riemsdijk & Williams, 1986). For a second example, consider two acts of productions of stress patterns, producing iambic and trochaic two-syllable words versus producing a variety of four-syllable stress contours. In the second goal, there are many more possible alternatives of stress/serial position interactions.

Degrees of ***complexity*** may be contrasted with perceptions of ***difficulty***. Ease or difficulty of a task depends, in part, on the experiences, skills, and attitudes of an individual. Keeping the degree of complexity consistent, a particular act may be more difficult for one person compared to another. For example, the production of a phrase with a relative clause in it referring to a location in Chile, South America, may be less difficult for a client with aphasia from Chile than a client from Canada.

HOW COMPLEXITY INHERENT IN CONTENT, FORM, AND USE MAY AFFECT SHORT-TERM GOAL DECISIONS FOR ADULTS. As noted earlier, prioritization decisions for children lean heavily upon developmental data. Developmental data, in addition to reflecting the order in which children acquire certain behaviors, suggest hierarchies of behavioral complexity. To reinforce a point first made in Chapter 3, when planning for adults, developmental taxonomies are useful indices of complexity for sequencing short-term goals. Developmental taxonomies may be used in making decisions about complexity of targeted achievements in short-term planning. To reiterate, developmental hierarchies of content/form interactions in children present, in a systematic manner, levels of complexity of the semantics and syntax of word combinations, sentences, and sequences of sentences (narratives).

The domain in which task complexity is ordered depends on the presenting disorder. For example, dysarthrias have been described as "a group of speech disorders resulting from disturbances in muscular control over the speech mechanism due to damage of the central or peripheral nervous system" (Enderby, 2012; ASHA, 2012). Because of the nature of this disorder we would sequence short-term goals with reference to the complexity of the motor act expected of the client. Task complexity would be approached somewhat differently in cases of linguistic disturbance (e.g., aphasia). Here short-term goals might be sequenced according to the complexity of linguistic structures, such as syntax, semantic relations, and so on.

Step 2: Establish a context within which the short-term target behaviors will be expressed.

As noted earlier, a description of the context in which the target behavior will be expressed is a component of the short-term goal statement. Decisions about the nonlinguistic context are made with reference to degree of contextual support that will be predictably necessary for the client's expression of the target behavior in light of the client's present level of functioning. Decisions about the linguistic context are made with reference to complexity of language surrounding the target behavior.

With reference to exemplar clients, Amahl and Mr. B, there are a number of context options. Amahl, who is apraxic and manifests an overall language delay, does not produce syllable-final consonants. Syllable-final consonants were targeted within one of his two long-term goals. With reference to this phonological target and Amahl's current level of functioning, a single-word and single-phrase context would be an appropriate level of linguistic complexity given Amahl's developmental characteristics. This decision leads to the potential short-term goal statement: "Amahl will demonstrate the reduction of final consonant (coda) deletion to below 40% in words and phrases." For the adult (Mr. B) working on language function, it was determined that familiar scenarios are more facilitative than novel experiences; this observation supports target language expressed in the context of familiar social scripts: A possible short-term goal incorporating the context is, "Client will demonstrate the functions, *request* and *protest*, in familiar social scripts (routines such as ordering food in a restaurant)."

An additional example comes from an articulation program for Sylvia, an adult who speaks English as a second language; research has shown that task formality influences accuracy of production (i.e., reading word lists are more facilitative of accurate productions than conversational speech; Leather & James, 1991). This finding guides the clinician in decision-making about the communication context in which an early short-term behavioral objective can be reliably expected: reading as opposed to open conversation.

Planning Short-Term Goals for Amahl, Darryl, and Mr. B

The following are short-term goals, corresponding long-term goals, and the taxonomies that guided their derivations for Amahl, Darryl, and Mr. B, the clients we are following as we explicate the intervention planning process.

Amahl (nine years old)

Long-Term Goals

Amahl will produce three-constituent utterances coding existence, action, locative action, and state to comment and request in a variety of contexts.

Amahl will produce a range of segmental features and prosodic components absent from and emerging in his repertoire.

Short-Term Goals and Derivation Sources

Amahl will code existence using three constituents in context of play (Lahey, 1988; taxonomy of content/form/use).

Amahl will code locative action using three constituents in context of play to comment, request, and direct (Lahey, 1988; taxonomy of content/form/use).

Amahl will produce two-syllable /CVCV/ words with anterior and dorsal stops in syllable initial position (Hodson & Paden, 1991; taxonomy of phonologic process dissolution).

Darryl (five years old)

Long-Term Goal

Darryl will produce a range of complex sentences with associated connectives.

Short-Term Goals and Derivation Sources

Darryl will produce complex sentences expressing temporal relationships in the context of problem-solving tasks (Moses, Klein, & Altman, 1989—taxonomy of causal semantic relations; Lahey, 1988—taxonomy of content/form/use interactions).

Darryl will produce complex sentences expressing causal relationships in context of problem-solving tasks (Moses, Klein, & Altman, 1989—taxonomy of causal semantic relations; Lahey, 1988—taxonomy of content/form/use interactions).

Mr. B (an adult with aphasia)

Long-Term Goal:

Mr. B will produce two- to three-constituent utterances as contingent responses within conversations.

Short-Term Goals and Derivation Sources

Mr. B will demonstrate the functions, *request* and *protest*, when engaged in familiar social routines (Lahey, 1988; content/form/use taxonomy).

Mr. B will produce 2+ word utterances coding existence plus attribution and rejection within familiar social routines.

Mr. B. will produce two-constituent utterances coding action, and locative action, in response to clinician's queries in a familiar social routine (Lahey, 1988; content/form/use taxonomy).

Summary

We have considered how short-term goals are formulated and prioritized. We planned short-term goals with reference to baseline data, information about maintaining factors, developmental hierarchies, and task complexity and difficulty. Task complexity and difficulty were evaluated with reference to developmental taxonomies and information about a particular client's social and cultural experiences.

Figure 5.2 presents the MK-SLIP template for establishing short-term goals. The derivations of short-term goals for Amahl, Darryl, and Mr. B on the corresponding MK-SLIP short-term goal templates are illustrated in Figures 5.3 to 5.5.

Deriving Short-Term Goals			
Decision	**Guiding Information and Client-Specific Details**		
Long-Term Goal and Corresponding Subordinate Long-Term Goals and Taxonomies Addressed	**Long-Term Goal and/or Subordinate Long-Term Goal(s)**	**Taxonomy**	**Current Performance Level**
Time Frame	**Time Allotted:**		
Short-Term Goal and Rationale	**Long-Term Goal Addressed:**		
	Short-Term Goal(s)		
	Rationale with reference to: development/complexity/difficulty		
	Subordinate Long-Term Goal Addressed:		
	Short-Term Goal		
	Rationale with reference to: development/complexity/difficulty		
	Short-Term Goal		
	Rationale with reference to: development/complexity/difficulty		
	Short-Term Goal(s)		
	Rationale with reference to: development/complexity/difficulty		

FIGURE 5.2: MK-SLIP Short-term goal template

Deriving Short-Term Goals			
Decision	**Guiding information and Client-Specific details**		
Long-Term Goal and Corresponding Subordinate Long-Term Goals and Taxonomies Addressed	**Long-Term Goal and/or Subordinate Long-Term Goal(s)**	**Taxonomy**	**Current Performance Level**
	Produce three constituent utterances coding early content categories in conversational speech	Bloom & Lahey (1978)	Produces single-word utterances that code existence, to request or demand
	Use a range of language functions in conversational speech	Lahey (1988)	Functions are limited to request, demand, and protest
	Produce segmental and prosodic features absent from and emerging in his repertoire	Bernhardt & Stemberger (2000)	Apraxic, produces only single syllable CV words and syllable structures, anterior stop consonants
Time Frame	**Time Allotted:** 4 mos.		
Short-Term Goal and Rationale	**Long-Term Goal Addressed:** Amahl will produce 3 constituent existence, action, and locative action utterances to comment, request, direct, respond to requests given clinician model		
	Short-Term Goal(s) Amahl will produce 3 constituent existence, action, and locative action utterances to comment, request, direct, respond to requests given clinician model **Rationale with reference to: development/complexity/difficulty** Produces single word utterances. 3 constituent and additional content categories represent next developmental steps		
	Subordinate Long-Term Goal Addressed: Produce segmental and prosodic features absent from and emerging in his repertoire		
	Short-Term Goal Amahl will produce two syllable /CVCV/ words with anterior and dorsal stops in syllable initial position **Rationale with reference to: development/complexity/difficulty** Produces single CV syllable word structures with anterior stops. Two syllables, with dorsal stops represent early developmental step		

FIGURE 5.3: Short-term template for Amahl

Deriving Short-Term Goals			
Decision	**Guiding information and Client-Specific details**		
Long-Term Goal and Corresponding Subordinate Long-Term Goals and Taxonomies Addressed	**Long-Term Goal and/or Subordinate Long-Term Goal(s)**	**Taxonomy**	**Current Performance Level**
	Produce conjoined/embedded causal chain narratives in a variety of contexts	Lahey (1988)	Content/form/use interactions are productive at Lahey's Phase 2 and 3 (e.g., existence, action, locative action, attribution, possession; comment, direct, respond to requests)
	Produce a range of complex sentences with appropriate connectives	Lahey (1988)	No complex sentences
	Increase lexical variety across content categories within discourse contexts	Lahey (1988)	Restricted range of vocabulary used to represent available content categories
	Produce the range of developmental morphemes in discourse contexts	Brown (1973)	Variable performance across Brown's morphemes
Time Frame	**Time Allotted: 6 mos.**		
Short-Term Goals and Rationale	**Long-Term Goal Addressed:** Produce conjoined/embedded causal chain narratives in a variety of contexts		
	Short-Term Goal(s) Darryl will produce complex sentences expressing temporal and causal relationships in context of problem-solving tasks in 80% of obligatory contexts **Rationale with reference to: development/complexity/difficulty** Complex sentences coding temporal and causal semantic relations are among the earlier complex sentences in children's repertoire. Darry is producing 3 constituent utterances presently. Such sentences will constitute the internal structure of causal narratives		
	Subordinate Long-Term Goal Addressed: Produce a range of complex sentences with appropriate connectives		
	Short-Term Goal Darryl will produce complex sentences expressing temporal and causal relationships in context of problem-solving tasks **Rationale with reference to: development/complexity/difficulty** Complex sentences coding temporal and causal semantic relations are among the earlier complex sentences in children's repertoire. Darryl is producing 3 constituent utterances presently. Such sentences will constitute the internal structure of causal narratives		

FIGURE 5.4: Short-term template for Darryl

Deriving Short-Term Goals			
Decision	**Guiding information and Client-Specific details**		
Long-Term Goal and Corresponding Subordinate Long-Term Goals and Taxonomies Addressed	**Long-Term Goal and/or Subordinate Long-Term Goal(s)**	**Taxonomy**	**Current Performance Level**
	Produce 2-3+ constituent utterances as contingent responses within conversations	Lahey (1988)	Uses one and two-word utterances to code existence and action, with much hesitation and phonetic groping, Uses a mixture of English, Spanish, and Italian words, gestures, writing, and drawing
	Produce language for a range of communicative functions in conversational speech	Lahey (1988)	He uses language to comment, respond and direct action. Responses are often on topic but not contingent
	Produce context appropriate vocabulary in conversation	Coca, word frequency list (www.English-corpora.org/COCA/)	
Time Frame	**Time Allotted: 6mos.**		
Short-Term Goal and Rationale	**Long-Term Goal Addressed:** Produce 2-3+ constituent utterances as contingent responses within conversations		
	Short-term goal #1. Mr. B will produce 2 word utterances coding attribution and rejection, within familiar social routines **Short-term goal #2:** Mr. B will produce 2- constituent utterances coding action and locative action in response to queries in social routines **Rationale with reference to: development/complexity/difficulty** Two-word and 2-constitutent utterances are next steps in complexity from single-word utterances Content, form, and function targeted are supported by routines		
	Subordinate long-term goal: Produce language for a range of communicative functions in conversational speech		
	Short-Term Goal #3 Mr. B will use language to request and protest **Rationale with reference to development/complexity/difficulty** These functions are readily motivated by contexts in his daily life		

FIGURE 5.5: Short-term template for Mr. B

Short-Term Planning: Operationalizing the Procedural Approach

READER WILL:

- Operationalize the procedural approaches established with reference to three clients: two children and one adult
- Become familiar with steps of decision-making and the derivation of implications for short-term procedure planning from premises of theories of learning and rehabilitation
- Become familiar with the use of the MK-SLIP template as a tool for short-term procedure planning

At the short-term planning phase, we *operationalize* the procedural approach established during long-term planning. The term *operationalize* signifies describing in concrete observable terms features of actual tasks derived from more abstract constructs and concepts—in this case, tasks derived from (a) premises of learning related to established theories and clinically relevant research, and (b) factors maintaining the speech-language problem.

We have adopted the term *operationalize* from the world of research. Researchers must create tasks in which they can actually manipulate causal factors being studied (independent variables) to produce observable, measurable outcomes (dependent variables).

Clinical interventions can be seen as *mini studies* in which clinicians gather evidence concerning the effectiveness of procedures in facilitating achievement of targeted goals.

In the course of operationalizing the procedural approach, the clinician describes the linguistic and nonlinguistic features of tasks that will be presented to the client. Designing an appropriate task context is an especially critical aspect of intervention planning. The acquisition and use of language is influenced by tasks in which the individual engages throughout the day (Fischer, 1980; Kovarsky, Duchan, & Maxwell, 1999; Moses, 1994; Klein, Moses, & Jean-Baptiste, 2010). Different task contexts can have different influences on linguistic performance. Vygotsky indicated that tasks within a child's *zone of proximal development* (i.e., that correspond to the child's developmental characteristics) are most accessible for learning by the child. Bloom (1995) indicated that contexts in which caregivers respond to a child's intent facilitate language acquisition. Language performance varies as individuals move from place to place, attempt to achieve different goals, and encounter different problems. Variability in linguistic performance is a consequence of variability in the nonlinguistic and linguistic qualities of tasks (Evans, 2008).

The *linguistic context* refers to speech directed to the client by another and the client's speech itself. A great deal of variation within the linguistic behavior of individuals has been attributed to linguistic context. For example, children appear to generate more complex utterances following a statement by an adult about something the child is doing. They generate less complex utterances in response to questions (Hubble, 1988; Shatz & Gelman, 1973). Similarly, phoneme production seems to be influenced by the phonetic, morphological, and prosodic environment surrounding the phoneme (Klein & Spector, 1985).

Nonlinguistic aspects of tasks involve the kinds of materials that will be used to achieve targeted goals during speech/language intervention. As is the case with language directed at the client, variability in material has been shown to influence language performance. For example, Klein, Moses, and Jean-Baptiste (2010) demonstrated that the proportion and category of complex sentences varies in relation to the spontaneity of tasks in which the children were engaged (free play with manipulables, story-retell, and barrier). Given the potential of context to influence linguistic behavior, the design of the linguistic and nonlinguistic context is an important procedural concern. The three categories of information identified in the procedural approach provide a basis for designing the linguistic and nonlinguistic characteristics of tasks that will be presented to the client.

Step 1: Review the research evidence cited in the procedural approach.

As noted earlier in deriving the procedural approach, clinical research provides insights into approaches to intervention for particular disorder categories and populations. Within this research are descriptions of contexts that clinicians create and tasks clients engage in during intervention. Two examples are found in the contrastive interventions, cited earlier, that address language delay in children with autistic spectrum disorder: applied behavior analysis (ABA) and Greenspan's floor-time. Many ABA programs are conducted in a school-like setting: The child is seated, an adult is seated across from or next to the child, and the adult is directing or making requests of the child verbally and sometimes physically modeling the desired response. The task for the child is to respond in a way dictated by the adult. Contrastively, floor-time typically involves a play setting: The child is positioned where he or she chooses (seated on the floor or at a table, inside a play house, on a swing, etc.). Materials given a young child are usually toys. The adult is positioned near the child, in a position appropriate for having a conversation. The adult comments on the activity that the child is engaged in and plays at the activity as well. Such clinical research provides clinicians with parameters for operationalizing the procedural approach.

Step 2a: Review theories of learning and rehabilitation and derivative premises identified in the procedural approach.

Step 2b: Infer types of nonlinguistic and linguistic contexts that flow from each premise.

The foundation of most clinical research is learning theory. As noted earlier, learning theories contain premises; premises are assumptions about processes that explain how learning and rehabilitation take place. Premises allow clinicians to derive procedures that will lead to the acquisition of a specified behavior.

At the short-term planning phase, we return to the premises cited in the long-term procedural approach. These premises should relate to procedures employed in the clinical research that may be guiding us. These theoretical premises will provide guidance for designing intervention contexts.

Let us consider again the interventions cited above for language delay in children with autistic spectrum disorder: ABA and Greenspan's floor-time. The first (ABA) is based on operant theory, the second (floor-time) on relationship-based social pragmatic theory. Operant theory incorporates the following premise:

Verbal behavior is shaped, strengthened or weakened, and ultimately evoked by consequences following the behaviors that are mediated by another person.

One can infer from this premise that to operationalize an operant procedural approach, the clinician must *identify and schedule effective behavior-reinforcing and extinguishing events.*

Contrastively, a premise underlying relationship-based pragmatic theory is that *Intersubjectivity, the desire of the speaker to make content of mind known to others, is the driving process in language acquisition.*

One can infer from this premise that establishing a clinical context reflective of a relationship-based procedural approach requires:

- *Providing materials of interest to the client*

- *Allowing the client freedom to interact with materials and people*

- *Establishing conversational exchanges with clients and their families that allow free and trusting expression of intent*

- *Being responsive to the affective and intentional states of clients and families*

- *Bringing caregivers and partners into therapy sessions as coclinicians.*

As we have just illustrated, clinical research is guided by premises that derive from learning theories. These premises provide justification for the design of intervention procedures.

Step 3a: Review the maintaining factors identified in the procedural approach.

Step 3b: Derive implications for context design.

Tasks presented to clients make demands on nonlinguistic behavioral systems (cognitive, sensorimotor, and social/emotional) that may be influencing speech or language performance. Any impairment in these systems may contribute to the speech or language disorder; thus, we refer to these system impairments as *maintaining factors*. Controlling demands on weakened behavioral systems is an important step in operationalizing a procedural approach.

In the area of *cognition*, we want to provide materials that make developmentally and functionally appropriate demands on the client's reasoning and problem-solving abilities (see Chapter 4, Box 4-1). In the *sensorimotor domain*, our choice of furniture, play materials, communication devices, and so on will be influenced by such factors as the individual's tonicity, stability, body segmentation and coordination, and sensory status (see Chapter 4, Box 4-2). We may need to collaborate with allied professionals with expertise in sensorimotor functioning to appropriately address such factors. We also want to establish relationships with our clients that take into consideration that individual's *social*, *cultural*, and *emotional history*. The context we design for intervention will reflect what a child has experienced in his or her interactions with caregivers, family, and friends (see Chapter 4, Box 4-3), what a child likes to play with and whether the child plays in a parallel fashion or cooperatively, what the adult expects of others, the nature of the individual's responses to male and female figures, the caregiver's perception of his or her child, the spouse's perception of his or her partner, and so on. We may also want to include families in the intervention. Greenspan, Weider, and Simon (1998) and Geller and Foley (2008) have emphasized (and IDEA legislation has mandated) that intervention planning should be conducted in collaboration with caregivers.

Operationalizing the Procedural Approach for Amahl, Darryl, and Mr. B

In order to exemplify the process of operationalizing a procedural approach, we will extend procedure planning for Amahl, Darryl, and Mr. B initiated at the long-term planning phase. As noted previously, operationalizing the procedural approach will require describing contexts (linguistic and nonlinguistic) that will be created to facilitate achievement of the specified short-term goals. The description of these contexts will include the types of materials, interactions, and elicitations that will be utilized. Figure 6.1 illustrates the template for operationalizing the procedural approach (from the MK-SLIP APP) at the short-term phase.

Operationalizing the Procedural Approach	
Decision	**Guiding Information and Client-Specific Details**
Short-Term Goals to be Addressed	

Derive Implications for Procedure Planning from Theory-Based Premises	**Constructivist Premise:**
	    Implication: Therefore the clinician will operationalize the procedural approach by
	
	Relationship-Based/Pragmatic Premise:
	    Implication: Therefore the clinician will operationalize the procedural approach by
	
	Operant Premise:
	    Implication: Therefore the clinician will operationalize the procedural approach by
	
	Social-Cognitive Premise:
	    Implication: Therefore the clinician will operationalize the procedural approach by
	
	Motor-Learning Premise:
	    Implication: Therefore the clinician will operationalize the procedural approach by

Derive Implications for Procedure Planning from Maintaining Factors	**Maintaining Factors**
	
	Cognitive:
	    Implication:
	Psychosocial:
	    Implication:
	Sensorimotor:
	    Implication:
	 Medical
	    Implication:

FIGURE 6.1: MK.SLIP template for operationalizing the procedural approach

Figures 6.2 through 6.4 summarize the process of operationalizing the procedural approaches that were established for Amahl, Darryl, and Mr. B.

Operationalizing the Procedural Approach	
Decision	**Guiding Information and Client-Specific Details**
Short-Term Goals to Be Addressed	Amahl will produce two syllable /CVCV/ words with anterior and dorsal stops in syllable initial position
	Amahl will produce 2-3 constituent existence, action, and locative action utterances to comment, request, direct, respond to requests given clinician model
Derive Implications for Procedure Planning from: **Theory-based Premises**	**Constructivist Premise:** Feedback from articulatory gestures attempted in efforts to produce target sounds facilitates phonological development **Implication:** Therefore the clinician will operationalize the procedural approach by encouraging Amahl to imitate model, accept attempts even if not perfectly articulated, and encourage to try again
	Relationship-Based/Pragmatic Premise: Comments reflecting the child's intent facilitate language learning **Implication:** Therefore the clinician will operationalize the procedural approach by presenting vocabulary and commenting with reference to Amahl's interests and focus
	Social-Cognitive Premise: Modeling promotes learning **Implication**: Therefore the clinician will operationalize the procedural approach by positioning Amahl and clinician so that Amahl can observe clinician modeling target utterance and articulation
	Operant Premise: Consequences following a behavior strengthen or weaken behavior **Implication:** Therefore the clinician will operationalize the procedural approach by following each successful client effort to produce target word, sound by a reinforcing event (toy to manipulate, high five, etc.); clinician will identify stimuli rewarding to Amahl prior to designing session
	Motor-Learning Premise: Practice producing articulatory patterns facilitates articulation **Implication:** Therefore the clinician will operationalize the procedural approach by structuring activities so that clinician models target word, sounds, sentences, to encourage Amahl to practice

FIGURE 6.2: Operationalizing the procedural approach for Amahl

Derive Implications for Procedure Planning from:	**Maintaining Factors**
	Cognitive: Moderate delay
	  Implication: Provide Amahl perceptual support involving objects to manipulate relevant to taget utterances
	
	Psychosocial: Demands familiar routines
	  Implication: Create and encourage familiar routines in collaboration with caregiver (routines should include target linguistic structures)

Maintaining Factors	**Sensorimotor**: Low tone **Implication:** Provide physical prompts to heighten feedback relevant to producing target articulatory patterns

FIGURE 6.2 CONTINUED: Operationalizing the procedural approach for Amahl.

Operationalizing the Procedural Approach	
Decision	**Guiding Information and Client-Specific Details**
Short-Term Goals to be Addressed	Darryl will produce complex sentences expressing temporal and causal relationships in context of problem-solving tasks

Derive Implications for Procedure Planning from Theory-Based Premises	**Constructivist Premise:** Feedback from goal-directed action in context of problem solving facilitates the development of language content
	    Implication: Therefore the clinician will operationalize the procedural approach by presenting with concrete problem solving tasks incorporating means-end sequences involving the manipulation of concrete objects
	
	Relationship-Based/Pragmatic Premise: Comments reflecting the child's intent facilitates the development of language form
	    Implication: Therefore the clinician will operationalize the procedural approach by commenting about the problem solving task and Darryl's actions while Darryl is engaged with the task
	
	Social-Cognitive Premise: Modeling facilitates language acquisition
	    Implication: Therefore the clinician will operationalize the procedural approach by modeling target behavior
	
	Operant Premise: Context and consequences following behavior strengthen or weaken behavior
	    Implication: Therefore the clinician will operationalize the procedural approach by being responsive to Darryl's intent and production of target behavior

Derive Implications for Procedure Planning from Maintaining Factors	**Maintaining Factors** **Sensorimotor:** Mild hypotonia **Implication:** Darryl will engage in problem solving tasks involving the manipulation of concrete objects to provide maximal sensorimotor feedback; Clinician will collaborate with the occupational therapist

FIGURE 6.3: Operationalizing the procedural approach for Darryl

Operationalizing the Procedural Approach	
Decision	**Guiding Information and Client-Specific Details**
Short-Term Goals to be Addressed	Mr. B will produce 2 word utterances coding attribution and rejection, within familiar social routines Mr. B will produce 2- constituent utterances coding action and locative action in response to queries in social routines Mr. B will use language to request and protest

Derive Implications for Procedure Planning from Theory-Based Premises	**Relationship-Based/Pragmatic Premise:** Participation in communicative exchanges reflecting the individual's intent (cognitive and emotional) aids rehabilitation
	    Implication: Therefore, clinician will create naturalistic contexts
	    involving routines with persons who are meaningful to Mr. B
	
	Social-Cognitive Premise:
	Modeling faciliates rehabilitation
	    Implication: Therefore, communication partners will
	    operationalize the procedural approach by providing contingent
	    content and form during conversations with Mr. B
	
	Vocabulary (written words) relevant to familiar routines will be
	available to Mr. B on assistive device
	
	Operant premise: Context and consequences following behavior strengthen or weaken behavior
	    Implication: Therefore the communication partners will
	    operationalize the procedural approach by acknowledging Mr. B's
	    intent, thus offering a rewarding consequence
	
	Motor-Learning Premise:
	    Implication: Therefore the clinician will operationalize the
	    procedural approach by

FIGURE 6.4: Operationalizing the procedural approach for Mr. B

| Derive Implications for Procedure Planning from Maintaining Factors | Maintaining Factors

Cognitive:
    Implication:

Psychosocial: Mild depression; Frustrated when not understood
    Implication: Mr. B will receive acknowledgement of his intent from communication partner

Sensorimotor: Mild right hemiparesis, apraxia
    Implication: Vocabulary relevent to routines will be programmed on assistive device (tablet, phone) according to routine. Mr. B's use of written words to support word retrieval and intelligibility will be encouraged

Medical: History of cardiac issues |

FIGURE 6.4 CONTINUED: Operationalizing the procedural approach for Mr. B

chapter 7

Session Planning Phase

READER WILL:

- Derive session goals with reference to baseline data from three clients: two children and one adult
- Become familiar with steps of decision-making and information that guide session goal and procedure planning
- Become familiar with the process of identifying and controlling performance demands
- Become familiar with the use of the MK-SLIP template as a tool for goal planning

We have finally arrived at the session planning phase—that phase of planning where the clinician actually creates specific activities that will be presented to the client to promote specific outcomes during an actual session! The formulation of session goals and procedures brings together information generated during procedure planning as well as goal planning.

Session Goal

The session goal is defined as *an observable behavior expressed in a specified task context that represents an act of learning that will lead to the acquisition of functional communication behavior targeted as a short-term goal* (Klein & Moses, 1999). This is a rather lengthy definition that includes a number of aspects that must be considered in the planning process.

An Act in the Process of Learning

We view session goals as means to an end; session goals are behaviors expressed in the process of learning or reacquiring communication competencies targeted as short-term and long-term goals. Therefore, we conceptualize session goals as acts of learning. As such, session goals are fundamentally different in comparison to long- and short-term goals. Long- and short-term goals are, by necessity, functional, communicative, and linguistic behaviors that are the products of acts of learning. Session goals may not represent functional communication; for example, signaling that /pat/ and /bat/ are different words as an articulation intervention exercise is a plausible session goal, not meant to be an act of functional communication.

AN OBSERVABLE BEHAVIOR. As discussed in context of long-term and short-term planning, accountability requires that we identify concrete evidence of goal achievement. Session goals, therefore, must be observable, measurable behaviors that constitute acts of learning. For example, we may decide that learning to discriminate between minimal word pairs and pictures is a necessary act of learning for an individual with aphasia to achieve the short-term goal of "using an augmentative communication device (iPad) to express actions." We cannot observe the process of "discrimination" directly. We need to identify an observable behavior that demonstrates the process we wish to exercise. We may decide that an eye gaze directed at one of two pictures in response to a clinician's directive is a sufficient response to indicate that the individual is learning to discriminate among named and pictured verbs. Thus, a session goal might read, "The client will gaze at one of two pictures depicting minimal-pair verbs (dump-jump, dip/sip) corresponding to the clinician's directive." In this example, eye gaze was targeted as a session goal because it is observable.

Located within a Series of Achievements Leading to the Acquisition of Short-Term Goal

The session goal is one step in a series of achievements *en route to the short-term goal*. In the example mentioned previously, "appropriate eye gaze" in a minimal-pairs exercise was believed to be a necessary step on route to operating an augmentative communication device to express action (the short-term goal).

Components of the Session Goal

The session goal has two components: (a) the behavioral objective/target and (b) the context in which the behavior is to be produced. The *behavioral objective* is the observable behavior the client is expected to produce in the course of achieving the established task. The task context refers to the nonlinguistic environment (objects, materials) surrounding the target behavior and the linguistic environment (language behavior of the clinician and the client).

Consider the first session goal introduced: "The client will gaze at one of two pictures depicting minimal-pair verbs (dump/jump, dip/sip) that correspond to the clinician's directive." The observable behavior of *gazing* at one of two pictures is the behavioral objective. The targeted behavior takes place in the nonlinguistic context of "two pictures depicting minimal-pair verbs" and the linguistic context of "the clinician's directive." Implicit in this description of the context is the client's task of discriminating the initial consonants of the words presented by the clinician (represented in the pictures).

Formulating Session Goals

Step 1: Identify guiding premises.

In order to formulate session goals, the clinician reviews premises of learning or rehabilitation identified in the procedural approach. These premises, derived from the theoretic foundations of clinical research, were operationalized during short-term planning. They serve as the basis for envisioning acts of learning and designing complementary task contexts.

Step 2. Identify maintaining factors.

The second step in formulating session goals involves addressing factors maintaining the particular communication problem. These factors were first identified during the long-term planning phase. Implications for designing contexts that address maintaining factors were then drawn at the short-term planning phase. As part of session goal and procedure planning, the clinician will design a specific intervention that incorporates treatment of the behavioral systems other than speech and language that are influencing the client's performance.

Maintaining factors also influence the next step of session goal and procedure planning: managing demands on performance made by behavior expected of clients, tasks presented to clients, and the environment in which tasks are situated.

Step 3: Regulate demands on performance.

A client's performance is challenged by the speech/language behavior (target) that he or she is expected to produce. The client is further challenged by the *linguistic and/or nonlinguistic context* in which the speech-language target is embedded. For example, in the area of phonology, relative challenges to the production of a sound may be imposed by the position of the sound in a word (syllable initial or final), the stress of the syllable in which the sound is embedded, or the phonetic environment of the target sound. Similarly, in the area of language, word comprehension may be promoted or reduced by the relative complexity of the semantics and/or syntax of the sentence in which the word is used. Other factors such as the availability or unavailability of environmental support in the form of the presence of objects being spoken about, models of target utterances, and/or printed materials may differentially challenge the client.

HOW PERFORMANCE DEMANDS RELATE TO VARIABILITY IN PERFORMANCE. Research in dynamic assessment as well as operant processes has demonstrated that aspects of the nonlinguistic and linguistic context influence speech and language performance. Typically developing children demonstrate variability in the complexity of productions that are generally acquired during a single developmental period (see Bloom, Miller, & Hood, 1975, with reference to sentence constituents, and Klein, 1981, with reference to phonology). Children with language and speech disorders have been shown to produce a newly acquired structure in some situations but not in others (e.g., Kent, 1982; Hedge & McCann, 1981; Rockman & Elbert, 1984). Kamhi (1988) has referred to contextual and production factors that influence such variability in performance as "performance factors." We shall refer to these factors as "performance demands" or "factors that contribute to the complexity of the learning task."

USING KNOWLEDGE OF PERFORMANCE DEMANDS TO FORMULATE SESSION GOALS AND PROCEDURES. Our knowledge about performance demands provides important information for the generation of a sequence of session goals and procedures. During a session, we will be asking our client either to produce a new communication form or to generalize one already being produced. In producing a communication form for the first time, we want to provide a context (linguistic and nonlinguistic) that makes as few demands as possible beyond the production of the new form. Optimally, the context will actually support production of the form (e.g., by being perceptually salient, facilitative of articulatory gestures, relevant to the content and function of the utterance, and facilitative of maintaining factors). In the case of linguistic forms already being produced, the clinician will want to manipulate the context so that the client is challenged, within reason, to generalize its use to novel linguistic or more complex contexts.

HOW PERFORMANCE DEMANDS RELATE TO GENERALIZATION. It is important to note that when we manipulate the complexity of tasks across sessions, we are promoting generalization. Issues of generalization have been part of the clinical process historically (e.g., Berry & Eisenson, 1956; Van Riper, 1939) and continue to be referenced within respected clinical paradigms (e.g., "phonological knowledge"; Elbert & Gierut, 1986). See also Fey's (1988) introduction to a clinical forum, in which generalization issues are addressed from a variety of theoretical viewpoints, and Thomson's (2007) introduction to a clinical forum on complexity in language learning and treatment with examples from phonology, semantics, and syntax.

With reference to the nature of the linguistic target (a new linguistic structure or generalization of a structure already being produced), the clinician will need to envision a sequence of learning tasks that will lead to the achievement of the short-term goal. Sequences derive from the clinician's estimates of the demands made on the learner in performing one particular task relative to another. These estimates of complexity help us to make decisions about which behavior to target and in which contexts—two integral components of the session goal statement.

A consideration of performance demands plays a critical role in decision-making for session goals and procedures. Consequently, we devote the next section of the chapter to a discussion of performance factors that need to be addressed in two disorder areas: language disorders and articulation/phonology. A similar analysis with reference to voice and fluency disorders may be found in Klein and Moses (1999, Volume I).

PERFORMANCE DEMANDS INTRINSIC TO TREATMENTS OF LANGUAGE DISORDERS. There is a set of variables that commonly influence the client's ability to produce content/form interactions and, therefore, need to be manipulated in the formulation of session plans. These variables are (a) perceptual support, (b) sensorimotor action, (c) lexical novelty, (d) syntactic complexity, (e) phonetic/phonological factors, and (f) cognitive demand of concepts underlying language content.

PERCEPTION AND ACTION. When children first learn language, they talk about objects that they are perceiving, usually in a play context. Only later do they use language to talk about objects and events that they are not presently observing or physically manipulating (e.g., Bloom & Lahey, 1978). Children learning language also often label and request in familiar game routines with caregivers, such as "peek-a-boo" or story time with a favorite book (Ninio & Bruner, 1978; Ratner & Bruner, 1978).

One implication of these findings is that the provision of *perceptual support* for children and adults learning or reacquiring a new content/form interaction may lessen the performance demand. The production of a specific content/form interaction to recollect or anticipate an event that is not observable could be targeted as a more advanced session goal.

A second implication is that *sensorimotor action* supports the production of language. Sensorimotor action involves the physical manipulation of objects related to achieving some goal and reflecting upon feedback from attempts. In Chapters 1 and 2, in discussing constructivist cognitive learning theory, children's reflection on feedback from their own actions was identified as foundational for the development of cognition and language content (Bloom, 1995; Bloom & Tinker, 2001; Moses, 1981; Piaget, 1985). This principle has been extended to adults as well (e.g., Fisher & Bidell, 2006; Moses, 1994; Piaget, 1970). From this point of view, it may be easier for children and adults to represent concepts underlying language while engaged in practical, constructive, problem-solving activities involving the manipulation of concrete objects. Practical, action-oriented, and goal-directed activities may also support problem-solving skills such as attending and information retrieval. It may be more difficult for clients to learn concepts and problem-solving skills from pictures, verbal explanations, metalinguistic "self-talk," or by being trained, behaviorally, to perform splinter skills, such as sitting or making eye contact.

Research suggests that listening to decontextualized explanations before engaging in concrete, contextualized experiences is like putting the cart before the horse (see also Forman & Hill, 1990; Fosnot, 1996). This is an especially critical principle to keep in mind for clients with language/learning disabilities. Learning concepts through language for an individual with a language/learning disability can be disabling. This is a likely consequence of the clinician insisting that the client learn by relying on a disabled behavioral system (language) rather than potentially enabled ones (e.g., sensorimotor action, vision, and reflection; Moses, Klein, & Altman, 1990; Gallagher & Reid, 2002).

Consider, for example, planning session goals for a six-year-old child with a cognitive impairment. The short-term goal targeted by both the speech/language pathologist and classroom teacher is "coding attribution with one or two words." In this case, baseline data revealed deficits in awareness and general knowledge of attributes.

Suppose that the clinician decides to focus on "size" as the first attribute for the child to code linguistically. A context should be created that would most facilitate the achievement of this goal. Box 4-2 is helpful in providing guidance (see the discussion on maintaining factors in Chapter 4). With reference to information contained in Box 4-2, coding attribution is related to "comparing and ordering objects according to a specific dimension" (e.g., size). As such, we might engage this child in an activity in which he or she manipulates objects of various sizes and is encouraged to make size comparisons (e.g., trying to get airplanes of various sizes into small garages or having to select from a jar of tiny cookies and a jar of large cookies while observing a playmate eating a large cookie). We would avoid using pictures of objects of different sizes, initially, to facilitate the coding of attribution. We might turn to pictures in familiar storybooks and later more abstract or unfamiliar pictures to "generalize" the use of this linguistic structure.

PRAGMATIC CONSIDERATIONS. There are a set of factors belonging to the area of pragmatics that may contribute to task complexity in language cases. The factors we identify are consistent with Bloom's (1995) principle of "relevance," Greenspan and Weider's (1998) "floor-time" approach to language intervention, and Lund and Duchan's (1988) conceptualization of "fine-tuning." Lund and Duchan define fine-tuning as "how adults alter what they say to children in response to what a child is presumed to be thinking or doing" (p. 64). They note that "the closer the match between the language input and the child's thinking, the better are the conditions for the child to understand and learn about language" (p. 64).

In a similar vein, Bloom and her colleagues (1975) compared the conditions under which children produced two- and three-constituent utterances. They found that children were more likely to produce three constituents when (a) the lexical items were familiar, (b) the utterance was supported by something in the adult's prior utterance, and (c) there were no new syntactic elements.

Knowledge of how certain pragmatic behaviors impact on linguistic performance in children can be derived from the literature on language intervention. For example:

1. Adult's comments that mirror a topic initiated by a child (in play or conversation) are easier to process than comments that shift topics. Lund and Duchan (1988) refer to this close relationship between the focus of a child's attention and understanding and the adult's subsequent utterance as "semantic contingency."

2. Adult's comments that reflect, reiterate, or expand upon a child's utterance are easier to process than comments that do not reflect the child's prior comment. Lund and Duchan (1988) view this relationship between the form of the child's utterance and the adult's subsequent statement as another component of semantic contingency.

3. Explicit reference (nominal-nominal) is probably easier to process than anaphoric reference (pronominal-nominal) for children just learning language.

4. Statements by adults to children that do not demand a particular response seem to be, paradoxically, easier to respond to than questions or imperatives. Similarly, *genuine questions*, to which the caretaker really does not know the answer and that are relevant to the child's ongoing actions are easier to respond to than imperatives, or questions that serve no real function for the child other than responding to the adult. Lund and Duchan (1988) term this relationship between the intent of the adult's statement and its demand on the child as "intentional contingency."

5. Lexical novelty and syntactic complexity increase performance demands.

The same principles apply to adults. For example, language processing in adults following traumatic brain injury and stroke is facilitated when utterances of a communication partner are contextualized, refer to familiar routines, and make demands consistent with the adult's linguistic and cognitive competency.

In sum, the clinician can "fine-tune" the linguistic context of the therapeutic session by (a) increasing the alignment between the clinician's utterances and the client's actions, (b) avoiding imperatives and questions meant only to provoke a response, and (c) minimizing lexical novelty and syntactic complexity. Introducing topic shifts and directives using novel linguistic forms would be a means of increasing performance demands.

PHONOLOGICAL FACTORS. There is a body of research that indicates that phonological factors may impact upon language learning, particularly at early stages of language development (Klein, 1982; Stoel-Gammon & Cooper, 1984). A number of researchers (e.g., Locke, 1983; Menn,1978; Stoel-Gammon & Cooper, 1984; Vihman, 1976, 1978) have found that the first words of normally achieving children are influenced by a child's idiosyncratic "favorite sounds," "most frequently produced categories of sounds" (stops, glides, nasals produced in anterior positions), and syllabic forms (CV) carried over from babbling. The implication is that careful consideration should be given to the phonetic characteristics of words that a child with a language delay is expected to learn. "First-word" vocabulary constituting stops, glides, and nasals produced in anterior positions, CV syllable forms, and the child's personally preferred sounds should be relatively easy to produce. Words containing fricatives, liquids, blends, and complex multisyllabic forms might pose a greater challenge.

DEVELOPMENTAL HIERARCHIES. Developmental hierarchies presented in the literature on typical child development often are useful resources for determining task complexity. Take, for example, the plan to work toward the coding of attribution with the child with cognitive impairment discussed earlier. The short-term goal did not specify the attribute to be coded by the child. The attribute targeted could impact upon the complexity of the learning task. Selecting an attribute to target would be facilitated if we could reference a published developmental hierarchy.

Such taxonomies, however, do not always exist. The taxonomy that we referenced to target attribution in the short-term goal (Bloom & Lahey, 1978) does not present a developmental sequence for specific attributes. We must look elsewhere to determine if such a sequence exists. If it does not, we will have to devise ourselves a basis for hypothesizing a sequence. In this case, a hierarchy was constructed based on information in the literature on young children's understanding of attributes (Smith, 1984) and observations of the child's behavior during play (i.e., the child appeared to make size comparisons rather than those based on shape or color).

Let us consider another example of a planning problem involving task complexity. A short-term goal statement indicates that the child will code a particular linguistic structure in the complex speech act, "narrative storytelling." Planning a session could be facilitated by additional developmental information. In this instance, there is a developmental schedule to reference—Lahey (1988). This schedule would serve as a guide for devising a sequence of session goals and procedures increasing in complexity.

PERFORMANCE DEMANDS INTRINSIC TO THE TREATMENT OF ARTICULATION DISORDERS. Disorders of articulation and phonology represent the second area that we will consider with reference to factors that contribute to performance demands. We identify traditional and phonological approaches to this issue. Traditionally, speech/language pathologists have organized the approach to speech/sound production on the basis of production demands with reference to length of unit (i.e., sound in isolation, syllable, monosyllabic word, multisyllabic word, phrase, sentence, and continuous speech) and position in word (initial, final, and medial). These sequences have become very popular because they represent an apparent hierarchy of production complexity. For detailed descriptions of such an approach, see seminal works by Van Riper (1978) and Winitz

(1969, 1975) and more recent updates (Creaghead, Newman, & Secord, 1989; Bernthal & Bankson, & Flipson, 2017).

More recently, with an emphasis on rule development, elimination of phonological processes, and "phonological knowledge," hierarchies have been formulated on the basis of children's own production patterns. It has been argued that children will demonstrate what they know (or don't know) about the sound system by how they pronounce words. This approach has directed the speech/language pathologist to examine the child's production pattern for information about which factors contribute to complexity (ability to produce a particular sound).

Some factors that have been isolated are stress and serial position of syllable containing the phoneme (Klein, 1981; Klein & Spector, 1985), phonetic context of sounds (e.g., Camarata & Gandour, 1984; Leonard, Devescove, & Ossela, 1987; Wolfe & Blocker, 1990), and underlying phonological representation or "phonological knowledge" (e.g., Gierut, 1989, 1990; Gireut, Elber, & Dinnsen, 1987; Elbert, Dinnsen, & Powell, 1984; Elbert, Dinnsen, Swartzlander, & Chin, 1990; Powell, 1992). These factors, as the more traditional, provide direction for the planning of a sequence of session goals. In the following section, we will discuss the way in which some of these factors may affect session planning.

WORD POSITION. Let us return again to the child who is fronting for an application of our knowledge of these factors related to performance demands. As is typical in intervention planning, a number of questions come to mind: (a) Which sound should we start with first, /k/, /g/, /n/, or all? (b) In which word position should the sound be introduced? (c) In which phonetic context should it be embedded? (d) How many syllables should the word contain? (e) How may exemplars would be sufficient for generalization to occur?

If we decide to start with /k/, research on phonological development informs us that the final position would be most facilitative, whereas for /g/ it would be the initial. This is because young children have been reported to more readily produce voiced plosives in the initial position and voiceless in the final (e.g., Ingram, 1989). Difficulties in the acquisition of voicing have been attributed to the complexity of mastering voice on set time adjustments (Bernthal, Bankson, & Flipson, 2017). It has also been suggested, however, that children only produce voiceless unaspirated stops in both positions (Macken, 1980), which are perceived by adults as voiced in the initial position and voiceless in the final position (Bernthal, Bankson, & Flipson, 2017). Word position variables, therefore, must be considered in planning a sequence of session goals. If we are targeting place (as with the fronting process) we would aim to facilitate the production by considering the most facilitating voicing environment. Edwards (1992) proposes similar hierarchical considerations involving place and voicing in her discussion of "process ordering."

PROSODY. Another factor that should be considered and is related to position is prosody. If we are interested in generalizing the production of a consonant to "within-word" position we must be careful about the stress and serial position of the syllable in which it is embedded. Klein (1981) demonstrated that children generally maintain consonants from stressed syllables occurring at the end of a sequence. These syllables, therefore, were hypothesized to be less demanding on the child's processing capacities than unstressed syllables beginning a sequence (i.e., giving rise to unstressed syllable deletion). More recent attention to nonlinear aspects of phonology underscores the importance of considering the relationship between segments and syllable structure and between segments and stress (see Schwartz, 1992, for a discussion of the relationship of nonlinear phonology to clinical phonology). Thus, stress and serial position of syllable are additional factors to consider in formulating a series of session goals.

PHONETIC ENVIRONMENT. Another factor that will help us to design a series of session objectives is the phonetic environment of the sound. It is well known that the phonetic environment of the sound will influence its production (e.g., Hodson & Paden, 1991; Kent, 1982). Some neighboring sounds may encourage target sound production, whereas other sounds may support the error production. For example, a child who is producing /t/ for /k/ will more likely produce a target /k/ in *cake* than in *kite*. The second /k/ in *cake* supports the initial /k/, whereas the final /t/ in *kite* encourages the production of the error segment in the initial position. Both are cases of assimilation, in which one sound becomes more like another; the first case is one of facilitating assimilation, and the second is nonfacilitating. It is important for the clinician to be aware of both types of assimilative contexts.

Examples of assimilative tendencies come from the literature on typically developing children and those with delayed speech development. Observation of typically developing children reveals that one sound (1) is more likely to come under the control of another (2) when (1) is not as firmly established in the child's repertoire as (2) (alveolars generally before velars; Maken, 1979; Stoel-Gammon, 1985) or when (2) is in a more favorite position than (1) (Smith, 1973). Although these assimilative tendencies are somewhat universal they need to be assessed for individual children. For example, Camarata and Gandour (1984); Leonard, Devescove, and Ossela (1987); and Wolfe and Blocker (1989) provide examples of unusual assimilative tendencies exhibited by speech-delayed children.

Assimilation tendencies have been described extensively with reference to clusters. It has been shown that certain clusters facilitate the production of singleton /s/ and /r/ targets (e.g., Swisher, 1973, cited in Kent, 1982). Also see a comprehensive articulatory classification of clusters by Grunwell (1985). This classification system suggests the articulatory mechanisms underlying the sequencing of consonants, resulting in possible assimilation tendencies. It also provides a very useful framework in which to organize children's cluster errors and plan a sequence of goals based on the complexity of the required articulatory gestures involved.

In summary, knowing about which sounds in words affect the target sound will help the clinician to develop a hierarchy of complexity within phonetic contexts (for a comprehensive discussion of the impact of aspects of the context on correct sound production—syllable stress and word or syllable position and adjacent sounds—see Bernhardt & Stemberger, 2000).

PHONOLOGICAL KNOWLEDGE. Another concern in determining what to do first with a speech-disordered client is the client's "phonological knowledge" (for an introduction to and clinical application of this model, see Elbert & Gierut, 1986). This model suggests that target sounds should be selected on the basis of the child's "phonological knowledge." This knowledge refers to the way in which "the idiosyncratic properties of morphemes are learned and stored in a speaker's lexicon or mental dictionary" (p. 49). Hierarchies of target achievement are developed with reference to most-to-least phonological knowledge or least-to-most phonological knowledge (i.e., Gierut, Elber, & Dinnsen, 1987). See also Powell's (1991) and Elbert's (1992) rationales for using the principle of "least phonological knowledge" in planning a sequence of goals.

Within the "phonological knowledge" approach, there has been increased systematic study of the phenomenon of generalization by Elbert and colleagues (e.g., Elbert, Dinnsen, & Powell, 1984; Elbert, Powell, & Swartzlander, 1991; Elbert, Dinnsen, Swartzlander, & Chin, 1990). These clinical phonologists have studied primarily the way in which a child's phonological knowledge and conditions of the environment influence the amount, extent, and type of generalization that occurs in intervention.

PERCEPTUAL SUPPORT. We can talk about perceptual support in the area of phonology in a number of ways. The first is stimulability. "Stimulability" signifies the ability to produce an utterance following a model. Here, the model serves as perceptual support (auditory and visual). Some sounds may be perceived both visually and aurally, for example, /f/ and /p/. For this reason, such sounds may be more stimulable, that is, more likely to be imitated. The stimulability of a sound is one of the factors that would be considered in determining which sound among a group of sounds (vulnerable to a particular process) would be targeted first.

A second issue related to perceptual support in the area of phonology concerns the linguistic/pragmatic context in which a child is expected to achieve a production. Should the production be imitative or spontaneous? Imitation of model utterances has traditionally been targeted as a goal before the child's spontaneous production, during the establishment phase (Bernthal, Bankson, & Flipson, 2017). Imitation may be seen as utilizing auditory and visual perceptual support for sound production.

Still another form of perceptual support is the printed orthographic symbol. There is no research or clinical data that directly focus on the use of printed material to facilitate sound production within a hierarchy of other tasks based on their complexity. It does, appear, however, that the printed symbol would serve as perceptual support for the reading child. Consequently, it may be reasonable to expect a child to have greater success in transferring the correct production of a sound to the reading of a word list before he or she will produce these sounds in words spontaneously (i.e., responses to questions or statements).

SUMMARY. In summary, we can see that there are a number of different ways to proceed in making decisions about which sounds (or sound groups) to target first and in which phonetic and prosodic contexts. According to leading clinical phonologists, it is best that one's guiding principles for the development of session goals (or "goal attack strategies"; Fey, 1992) be consistent with one's particular phonological theory. For a summary of various approaches to phonological intervention based on different phonological theories, see the contributions to a clinical forum (Edwards, 1992; Elbert, 1992; Fey, 1992; Hodson, 1992; Hoffman, 1992; Kamhi, 1992; Schwartz, 1992).

Boxes 7-1A and B list a number of contextual variables that can influence a client's performance and offer suggestions for addressing these performance demands when projecting a series of session goals. The clinician actively manipulates performance demands made on the client in the course of intervention (and in anticipation, in the course of intervention planning).

BOX 7-1A: Variables That Make Demands on Language Performance and Implications for Intervention Planning

Variables Influencing Intervention Planning	Basis of Variability	Implications for Planning	Selected Sources
Sensorimotor and perceptual support	Children learning language talk more readily when manipulating objects than when merely observing object and/or actions	Have individuals act on objects to support language before expecting language in the absence of the referent event	Lahey (1988) Forman and Hill (1984) Moses (1981) Piaget (1985) Bloom and Lahey (1978) Muma (1978)
	Language occurs more frequently with object/actions present than in the absence of objects/actions being referenced	Include objects when introducing a novel linguistic target; remove objects later	
Pragmatic context	Utterances have been found to be more complex when - lexical items are familiar, supported by aspects of adult's prior utterance - there are no new syntactic elements - they are closely aligned to child's actions - questions to child are genuine, not contrived	Provide the following supports when first introducing speech/language target: Provide model utterance that is contingent with topic of client's communication and actions Avoid using questions to stimulate speech	Bloom (1995) Lund and Duchan (1988)

Executive functions	The cognitive, semantic, syntactic, lexical, and morphological complexity of problem-solving procedures that individuals are presented verbally (by teachers) or in text	Design and sequence task contexts and problem-solving procedures presented to client with reference to: Piagetian stages/neo-Piagetian phases of cognition, Lahey (1988) content/ form/use taxonomy	C/F/U, Lahey (1988) morphology, semantic functions; Brown (1973) Nippold (2016) Piaget (1976, 1978) Karmiloff-Smith (1986)
	The number of individual linguistic items the individual is challenged to recall		
	The transparency of figurative language encountered	Nippold's taxonomy of figurative language	
		Client's cultural/ family history	
	Familiarity with lexical items and figurative expressions		

Note. The variables in this table are not exhaustive. Given a specific communication problem and an individual's unique speech/language profile, other contextual variables may be identified.

BOX 7-1B: Variables That Make Demands on Articulation/Phonology and Implications for Intervention Planning

Variables	Basis of Variability	Implications for Intervention	Sources
1. Word position	Certain syllable positions are more facilitative of particular sound groups than others, for example: • Fricatives often occur in final position before initial • Voiced stops occur before voiceless stops in initial and the converse is true for final	Begin with most facilitative position first Consider targeting a [-voice] stop first in final position	Klein (2005) Edwards (1992)
2. Prosody	Consonants in stressed syllables are more likely to be produced accurately than in unstressed syllables	Place new consonant target in stressed position (e.g., target within word /l/ in *balloon* rather than in *elephant*)	Klein (1981a, b) Klein and Spector (1985)
3. Markedness	Consonants with fewer marked features are acquired earlier than those with more marked features	Consider the number of marked features in selecting target sounds	Bernhard and Stemberger (2000)
4. Phonetic environment	Some neighboring sounds may support target production, and others may encourage error production. Knowing which sounds affect production of the target sound will aid in the development of an individualized hierarchy of complexity within phonetic contexts	To facilitate the production of an initial fricative, it would be more facilitative to include a final fricative rather than a stop (*fish* vs *fit*)	Kent (1982), Klein and Spector (1985), Hodson and Paden (1991)

5. Perceptual support	Perceptual support of a target sound in the form of a clinician's model or written symbol is generally viewed as facilitative during early stages of sound acquisition	Model sounds for the client's imitation. For children who recognize sound/symbol relationships, a printed symbol may be helpful	Bernthal, Bankson, and Flipsen (2017)
6. Linguistic context	The greater semantic/syntactic complexity of an utterance, the greater the challenge to articulatory performance. Conversely, children are more likely to produce final consonants if these consonants also code an additional morpheme	In the process of generalization, begin with simple phrases before sentences. The "z" may be more readily produced in the word *boys* than in the word *noise*	Bernthal, Bankson, and Flipsen (2017) Paul and Norbury (2012)
7. Response mode	Perception of target phoneme is often viewed as a less complex task than production and typically undertaken before production is initiated	Early sessions should include exercises in perception and then continued along with production exercises	Bernthal, Bankson, and Flipsen (2017); Klein, McAllister Byun, Davidson, and Grigos (2013)
8. Influence of first language or dialect pattern	It has been shown that it is more difficult for an individual to learn L2 sounds that are close to L1 than sounds that are very different from any sound in L1	Choose initial targets that are separated by more than one space on the L2 vowel chart	Leather and James (1991)

Note. The variables in this table are not exhaustive. Given a specific communication problem and an individual's unique speech/language profile, other contextual variables may be identified.

Deriving Session Goals and Procedures for Amahl, Darryl, and Mr. B

In this second half of Chapter 7, we illustrate and elaborate upon the decision-making process at the session phase of intervention planning. We derive session goals and procedures for the two children and one adult we have followed throughout this book—Amahl, Darryl, and Mr. B. In developing session goals and procedures for each client, we consider maintaining factors, principles from learning theories, and performance demands. It should be noted that the first two sections, premises and maintaining factors, remain the same for all session goals derived from the same long-term goals and corresponding short-term goals. If however, another long-term goal represents an additional disorder area (e.g., phonology in addition to language), different learning premises may be applicable. For example, there may be greater emphasis on motor theory for articulatory goals than constructive theory for language goals. In addition, performance demands are considered specifically for each session goal. See figure 7.1 for the session-goal template.

Deriving Session Goals and Procedures	
Decision	**Guiding Information and Client-Specific Details**
Long-Term Goal and Related Subordinate Goals	**Long-Term Goal:** **Subordinate Goals:**
For Each Short-Term Goal, Consider Implications of:	**Short-Term Goal:** **Taxonomy:**
Learning and Rehabilitation Premises	**Learning Theories** | **Implications Drawn (in the operationalized approach)** **Constructivism** | **Social Cognitive** | **Relationship-based pragmatic** | **Motor Learning** | **Operant** |
and **Maintaining Factors**	**Maintaining Factors** | **Implications Drawn (in the operationalized approach)** **Cognitive** | **Sensorimotor** | **Psychosocial** | **Medical** |

FIGURE 7.1: MK-SLIP, session goal template

Early Session Goal:

(#) Child will _____ given (non-linguistic context) _____ and (linguistic context) _____ in (achievement criteria) _____.

Performance Demands Controlled	Performance Variable Controlled	How the Variable is Controlled	Aspect of Session Goal Affected

Later Session Goal:

(#) Child will _____ given (non-linguistic context) _____ and (linguistic context) _____ in (achievement criteria) _____.

Performance Demands Controlled	Performance Variable Controlled	How the Variable is Controlled	Aspect of Session Goal Affected

FIGURE 7.1 CONTINUED: MK-SLIP, session goal template

As shown in this template, the performance demands responsible for the wording of the each session goal appears after each goal.

For each client, we present sample session goals and procedures leading to specified short-term goals. These comprise "early" session goals and procedures, which would be targeted during the first group of sessions in a given time period, and "later" session goals that would be targeted as the term progressed. We also summarize those sources of information that were referenced in the development of each goal (i.e., maintaining factors, learning principles, and sources of variability). In each goal statement, key words are underlined that refer to the particular aspects of the client's performance that were targeted as a result of consulting these sources of information.

Amahl

Step 1: Prioritizing short-term goals.

The first step in the derivation of session goals is to make a decision about whether to target all the short-term goals simultaneously (during the same session) or to prioritize these goals.

Short-Term Goals:

- Amahl will produce two syllable /CVCV /words with anterior and dorsal stops in syllable-initial position within three-constituent utterances.

- Amahl will code action and locative action using three constituents in the context of familiar routine.

In examining the goals listed, we can see that in both goals, three-constituent utterances are targeted, the first as a context in which to produce stop consonants, and the second is the content/form interaction itself.

We are attempting to stabilize sounds (stops) and word structures (CVCV already emerging in his repertoire (see Chapter 3, for baseline data). Working to stabilize sounds, the process of "generalization" to other phonetic and situational contexts is a gradual process that may take longer with older clients and clients with sensorimotor problems (Hodson & Paden, 1991; see also Bernthal, Bankson, & Flipson, 2017, for a summary of approaches to sound generalization).

Now that we have decided to target each of the short-term goals from the outset of therapy, we need to consider those factors that will help us formulate a sequence of session goals to reach each short-term target. We need to consider maintaining factors, principles from learning theories, and sources of variability (performance demands).

Step 2: Considering maintaining factors.

As we noted earlier, Amahl is viewed as having difficulties with cognitive, sensorimotor, and psychosocial maintaining factors. In designing a sequence of session goals, we must keep in mind the modification of or compensation for these factors in order to facilitate both the acquisition of segmental features and prosodic patterns absent from his repertoire and the development of content/form structures.

Regarding articulation, Amahl manifests apraxia related to sensory processing difficulties associated with his diagnosis of autistic spectrum disorder. Amahl will be challenged to avoid deletion of weak syllables in multisyllable words and, instead, to increase complexity of word and syllable structure. Reduplication and increasing syllable complexity from CV to CVC structure represents a developmental sequence seen in young children as children differentiate and reorganize sensorimotor behavior patterns. In addition to syllable and consonant deletion patterns, Amahl manifests stopping (difficulty maintaining oral air flow, given the pressure of a consonant) and fronting (difficulty differentiating tongue movements, and likely the use of intra-oral feedback from the articulators).

These specific articulatory difficulties relate to difficulties differentiating and executing contrasting tongue positions (i.e., front/back movements) and release patterns (continuing/stopping). According to the occupational therapist, difficulty with tongue movements is related to overall body low muscle tone, incoordination, and weakness, which are compounded by tactile defensiveness. With this knowledge in mind, our session goals will need to address some aspect of sensorimotor control. Our sequence of sensorimotor accomplishments will be directed by the occupational therapist.

With reference to content/form interactions, Amahl is producing single words to code existence, primarily. He is showing comprehension on a picture vocabulary test, suggestive of language competence beyond the single-word stage. It is likely that phonological limitations are interfering with expression of linguistic competence. Following Bloom and Lahey's taxonomy, expanding content and increasing complexity to form two- to three-constituent utterances is reasonable for the short-term framework. Since sensorimotor problems influencing phonology will be addressed in the course of treating the phonology delay, targeting three-constituent production over the term seems reasonable.

The learning premises that guide procedure planning for Amahl were derived primarily from social cognitive learning theory, operant theory, and motor learning theory (see Box 4-1). These principles now influence our session goal planning. We will provide models, reinforcing consequences, and abundant opportunities for practice.

Step 3: Controlling performance demands.

As is our practice in planning session goals and procedures, we consider conditions under which the child is expected to perform. The purpose is to systematically design contexts that facilitate learning and/or promote generalization. The following represents our reasoning about performance demands and identifies the variables we are controlling:

MARKEDNESS: Stop consonants are less marked than continuants.

SYLLABLE POSITION: Initial syllable positions for voiced stops are more natural than final syllable positions.

SYLLABLE STRUCTURE: CVCV word structure offers less demand on performance than does a CVC syllable structure.

SEMANTIC COMPLEXITY: Action relations are acquired before state relations, and object relations in single-verb sentences pose less linguistic complexity than interevent relations or relations in which additional content is coordinated.

Including objects to manipulate during session reduces performance demands as compared to talk about displaced objects. Figure 7.2 presents session goals for Amahl.

Deriving Session Goals and Procedures	
Decision	**Guiding Information and Client-Specific Details**
Long-Term Goal and Related Subordinate Goals	**Long-Term Goals:** Produce three constituent utterances coding early content categories in conversational speech Produce a range of syllable and word structures and segmental features absent from and emerging in his repertoire **Subordinate Goals:** Use a range of language functions in conversational speech
For Each Short-Term Goal, Consider Implications of:	**Short-Term Goal Amahl will:** Produce 2-3 constituent utterances coding existence, action, and locative action to comment, request, direct, respond to requests given model provided by communication partner Produce two syllable /CVCV/ words with anterior and dorsal stops in initial position **Taxonomy:** Content/form/use (Lahey, 1988) Non-linear phonology (Bernhardt & Stemerger, 2000)
Learning and Rehabilitation Premises	

Learning Theories	Implications Drawn (in the operationalized approach)
Constructivism	Objects such as small animals and vehicles that Amahl favors will be available for Amhl to manipulate and reference
Social Cognitive	Clinician will model SVC, VC targets, target vocabulary Amahl and clinician will be positioned so that Amahl can observe clinician modeling target utterance and articulation
Relationship-based pragmatic	Clinician will present objects, vocabulary and comments with reference to Amahl's interests and focus

FIGURE 7.2: Session goal template for Amahl

Motor Learning	Clinican will structure activities so that clinician models target word, sounds, sentences, to encourage Amahl to produce target word, sounds, sentences
Operant	Clincian will follow each successful client effort to produce target word, speech-sound by a reinforcing event (toy to manipulate, high five, etc.)

Maintaining Factors	Implications Drawn (in the operationalized approach)
Cognitive	Clincian will provide Amahl perceptual support involving objects to manipulate relevant to taget utterances
Sensorimotor	Clinican willl provide physical prompts to heighten feedback relevant to producing target articulatory patterns
Psychosocial	Clincian will encourage familiar routines in collaboration with caregiver (routines should include target linguistic structures)

The left column spans both tables and reads: **and Maintaining Factors**

Early Session Goal:

Amahl will *produce 2 -constituent action directives* containing *two-syllable /CVCV/ diminutive words* with *anterior and dorsal stops* in *syllable initial position* to command small toy animals (kitty, piggy, doggie to act—e.g., eat kitty, jump doggie) given toys and *clinician's verbal and physical model* 8/10 trials.

FIGURE 7.2 CONTINUED: Session goal template for Amahl

Performance Demands Controlled	Performance Variable Controlled	How the Variable is Controlled	Aspect of Session Goal Affected
	Syllable structure	CVCV structure is developmentally early	Target
	Word position	Stops in initial before final position.	Target
	Markedness	Stops less marked than fricatives	Target
	Tongue position	Dorsal and anterior stops after only anterior stops	Target
	Cogntive demand	Favorite objects available for manipulation and sensory feedback	Non-linguistic context
	Perceptual support	Verbal model before no model	Linguistic context

Later Session Goal

Amahl will produce /CVC/ words "woof", "huff", "puff" with /f/ in syllable final position, *modeled* by the clinician, within a routine in which animals "huff, "puff" and "woof" to make a boat float across a bowl 8/10 trials.

FIGURE 7.2 CONTINUED: Session goal template for Amahl

Performance Demands Controlled	Performance Variable Controlled	How the Variable is Controlled	Aspect of Session Goal Affected
	Word position	Fricative generally early in word final	Target
	Syllable structure	CVC early structure	Target
	Cognitive demand	Favorite objects available for perceptual support, and feedback	Non-lingustic context
	Perceptual support	Clinician's model before no model	Linguistic context
	Psychosocial demand	Routine before novel tasks	Non-linguistic contexts

FIGURE 7.2 CONTINUED: Session goal template for Amahl

Darryl

The next child considered for session planning is Darryl, the five-year-old boy with a developmental language disability.

Step 1: Prioritize short-term goals to target first.

Two short-term goals were prioritized at the short-term phase of intervention planning for Darryl, targeting complex temporal and causal content/form interactions. Two questions that provided direction for deciding which of these short-term goals to address first are (a) can the short-term goals be ordered according to a natural developmental hierarchy? and (b) is the client already producing the target structure in some contexts?

With reference to the first question, the two content/form interactions targeted as short-term goals emerge in typically achieving children at phase 5 of Lahey's C/F/U plan. With reference to the second, Darryl is not producing complex sentences in any context, only producing single-verb content/form interactions.

Step 2: Consider maintaining factors.

Having decided to work toward achieving two short-term goals, we turn to maintaining factors. We established at the long-term planning phase that cognitive, linguistic, and sensorimotor maintaining factors would be addressed in the design of the clinical context.

COGNITION. Darryl has demonstrated the ability to reference objects, locations, possession, and internal states, one at a time within single-verb sentences. At this point, we are helping Darryl refer to multiple content categories within single-verb utterances. Darryl also produces complex (two-verb) utterances while playing with concrete objects. We are hoping that in the future, Darryl will be able to produce complex utterances in other less perceptually supported contexts, such as narrative storytelling (the long-term objective).

We would also like to determine what aspects of cognitive functioning are supportive of our linguistic goals. Is there a developmental taxonomy that could guide us in addressing such aspects of cognition? Box 4-2 (Chapter 4) provides such information. A number of developmental cognitive competencies correspond with the acquisition and coordination of complex content/form interactions. These include the ability to engage in multischeme pretend and script play, make part–whole relations, and group objects according to specific attributes (Bloom, 1995; Piaget, 1977; Westby, 1980). We will need to create activities that exercise these cognitive skills. At the previous phase of intervention planning (short term), we began to think about such activities.

In addition to cognition, linguistic and sensorimotor factors were identified as possibly maintaining Darryl's language delay. Baseline data in the area of language indicate that Darryl may have problems perceiving morphemes of low phonetic substance. As such, the clinician will stress such structures when modeling. The clinician also will create pragmatic contexts that require Darryl to produce such morphemes with stress.

SENSORIMOTOR FACTORS. The influence of Darryl's sensorimotor functioning (mildly low tonicity) on linguistic performance also will be addressed in session. As noted at the short-term planning phase, play with concrete objects will provide Darryl the sensory feedback needed, as will our focus on language production. Darryl's overall problems with tonicity will be addressed by an occupational therapist (OT). The speech/language clinician will collaborate with the OT and may work with reference to goals set by the OT under the OT's supervision.

LEARNING THEORY. At the long- and short-term phases of procedural planning, we began to delimit a therapeutic context for Darryl based on selected principles derived from learning theory—particularly constructivist cognitive theory. The principles suggested how the clinician would interact with Darryl. At this session planning phase, each principle will suggest behavior that we will expect Darryl to demonstrate as a session goal and which we would expect the clinician to encourage in the session procedure. Correspondences between learning principles and behaviors expected of the child are illustrated in Box 4-1 (Chapter 4).

In sum, at this session phase of intervention planning, the behaviors corresponding to learning principles will be incorporated into session goal statements. Furthermore, these principles and behaviors will guide us in the creation of specific activities. An additional consideration in the design of activities concerns the complexity of the learning task. We want to make sure that clinician/child interactions and the activities we design are as supportive as possible for learning.

Step 3: Manage performance demands.

In designing activities and interactions, we know that subtle changes in linguistic and nonlinguistic context can influence performance. With this knowledge in mind, we wish to create a context that will stretch the child to either attempt a new or more complex behavior or generalize an already acquired behavior to a new context. We do not, however, want to overwhelm the child.

We have already made a number of decisions at the long- and short-term planning phase that bear upon the issue of task complexity. We envisioned materials and games that were commensurate with Darryl's interests and developmental level in the area of cognition and language. Furthermore, short-term goals were set commensurate with Darryl's current level of linguistic performance. The setting of goals and designing of therapeutic context with reference to the child's developmental level ("zone of proximal development," to quote Vygotsky, 1987) are an important control on task complexity. At this point, let us consider factors that may impact upon task complexity and generalization. The following factors and findings derived from the literature on typical language acquisition suggest a set of variables that may be manipulated to create a sequence of learning tasks.

PERCEPTUAL SUPPORT. It is easier for children to use a linguistic structure while manipulating concrete objects than it is to talk about a picture or to talk without referential objects present (Lahey, 1988; Tomasello & Farrar, 1984).

PRAGMATIC COMPLEXITY. Children use more complex language when talking spontaneously about personal action than when answering questions (Bloom & Lahey, 1978).

LINGUISTIC COMPLEXITY. Using a linguistic structure in a single utterance is less complex than using an utterance in a conversation or in a narrative (Lahey, 1988).

Based on these assumptions, it is possible to envision the following sequence of activities in which use of targeted linguistic structures changes over time:

- in familiar play contexts to describe personal action

- in play to respond to requests of the clinician

- in planning an activity without objects present or in reflecting on a just completed activity

- in a narrative about a past or imagined sequence of events, using pictures or objects for support

- in a narrative describing past or imagined sequences of events, without pictures or objects available.

Given Darryl's developmental level, we are holding off on targeting narrative production or comprehension until Darryl has achieved the prerequisite complex content/form interactions at the sentence level. However, looking to the future, the idea of Darryl producing targeted structures in narratives requires further consideration. Although the term "narrative storytelling" is relatively specific, it is possible to further delimit the type of narrative that Darryl will be expected to produce. Research on normal child development indicates that there is a hierarchy of story grammar complexity—the complex content–form interactions that account for the cohesiveness of a story (Lahey, 1988). For instance, Lahey (1988) indicates that stories comprising additive "story grammar" are less complex than stories comprising causal "story grammar."

A hierarchy of complexity linked to the child's familiarity with a story also can be identified. Telling stories about familiar real events or stories from books frequently read to the child would be less complex than creating novel stories about unfamiliar or entirely imagined events. Related to the interaction of perceptual support for utterances and task complexity, we expect that telling a story with props is a less complex task than retelling a story from memory alone.

SUMMARY. After considering maintaining factors and learning theories, we have envisioned sequences of activities for each short-term goal that we planned to address with Darryl. These activity sequences were based on inferences we made about factors that contribute to the complexity of tasks that we plan to present to Darryl. With this information in mind, we are now prepared to examine the template for session goals and procedures (Figure 7.3).

Deriving Session Goals and Procedures	
Decision	**Guiding Information and Client-Specific Details**
Long-Term Goal and Related Subordinate Goals	**Long-Term Goal:** Produce personal, conjoined, and embedded goal-based causal chain narratives in a variety of contexts **Subordinate Goals:** Produce a range of complex sentences with appropriate connectives Increase lexical variety across content categories within discourse Produce a range of developmental morphemes in discourse contexts
For Each Short-Term Goal, Consider Implications of:	**Short-Term Goal: Darryl will:** Produce complex sentences expressing temporal and causal relations in context of problem solving tasks **Taxonomy:** Complex sentences. C/F/U (Lahey, Lifter, Feiss, 1980); Cognition (Piaget, 1952; 1976; 1978)
Learning and Rehabilitation Premises **and**	<table><tr><td>**Learning Theories**</td><td>**Implications Drawn (in the operationalized approach)**</td></tr><tr><td>**Constructivism**</td><td>Means-end problem solving activities involving objects to manipulate will be available</td></tr><tr><td>**Social cognitive**</td><td>Clinician will model target sentences, vocabulary</td></tr><tr><td>**Relationship-based pragmatic**</td><td>Clinician will comment with reference to Darryl's focus during problem solving activity</td></tr><tr><td>**Motor Learning**</td><td>Clinican will encourage Darryl to produce target word, sounds, sentences</td></tr><tr><td>**Operant**</td><td>Clinician will be responsive to Darryl's intent and production of target behavior</td></tr></table>

FIGURE 7.3: Session goal template for Darryl

Maintaining Factors	Maintaining Factors	Implications Drawn (in the operationalized approach)
	Cognitive	Problem solving tasks will incorporate maniplables, and encourage goal direction, causal relations
		Clincian will provide Darryl perceptual support involving objects to manipulate relevant to problem solving tasks and target utterances
	Sensorimotor	Problem solving tasks will incorporate maniplables to maximize sensorimotor feedback
		Clinician will collaborate with the occupational therapist

Early Session Goal:

Darryl will produce *complex (two verb) sentences* expressing *temporal relations* (e.g., get on the elevator and go up) to *comment on the actions of a plush monkey riding on a manipulable* elevator given the toys and *clinician model* 5 X 30 minute session

Performance Demands Controlled	Performance Variable Controlled	How the Variable is Controlled	Aspect of Session Goal Affected
	Semantic Relation	Temporal before causal relations developmentally	Target behavior
	Language Use	Comments among earliest functions	Linguistic context
	Cognitive Demand	Problem solving using manipulable objects before problem solving using language, alone	Non-linguistic context
	Perceptual Support	Model target utterance before spontaneous	Linguistic context

FIGURE 7.3 CONTINUED: Session goal template for Darryl

Later Session Goal

Darryl will *produce complex sentences (2-verbs)* to express *cause-effect relation* (turn the key and open the door) to release a hamster from a cage given objects and *clinician's model* 5 X in 30 minute session.

Performance Demands Controlled	Performance Variable Controlled	How the Variable is Controlled	Aspect of Session Goal Affected
	Semantic relations	Causal relations After temporal	Target behavior
	Cognitive demand	Problem solving using manipulable objects before problem solving using language, alone	Non-linguistic context
	Perceptual support	Model target utterance before spontaneous	Linguistic context

FIGURE 7.3 CONTINUED: Session goal template for Darryl

Mr. B

Three short-term goals were established for Mr. B.

- Mr. B will demonstrate the functions, *request* and *protest*, when engaged in familiar social routines (Lahey, 1988; content/form/use taxonomy).

- Mr. B will produce 2 word utterances representing noun+attribution and noun+rejection within familiar social routines.

- Mr. B. will produce two-constituent utterances coding action, and locative action, in response to clinician's queries in a familiar social routine (Lahey, 1988; content/form/use taxonomy).

The first short-term goal is least complex—there are no syntactic demands incorporated. Comparing the second and third goals which do contain form elements, 2+ words is less complex requirement that two constituents (which infer syntax). Early session goals will address the first short-term goal. Later session goals will address the short-term goals targeting content/form interactions.

Step 1: Sequence short-term goals.

One short-term goal was established for Mr. B: Greet, request, and protest in social routines, using word relations and two-constituent utterances coding existence, rejection, action, locative action, state, and attribution. The need to prioritize a set of short-term goals is not an issue. A series of session goals will be devised to address this short-term goal.

Step 2. Apply premises from theory of learning and rehabilitation.

Premises of relationship-based pragmatic will guide procedure planning. Naturalistic routines involving persons meaningful to Mr. B will be re-created. Clinician and spouse will be sensitive and responsive to Mr. B's intent. Circles of communication in which topics are maintained through multiple turns will be facilitated by clinician and spouse.

Step 3: Consider maintaining factors and regulate performance demands.

Mr. B manifests medical issues that result in fatigue after relatively short periods of activity. Based on a consideration of this maintaining factor, Mr. B will attend treatment sessions three times a week for 30 minutes. The combination of these disorders leads to fatigue. Therefore, we must schedule rest periods, and vary complexity of tasks. We will begin sessions with a simple, familiar routine (greeting), introduce a novel or more complex routine, and conclude with a familiar routine (Goodbyes).

Mr. B has vacillations in his cognitive functions, including auditory agnosia. These maintaining factors can interfere with his ability to relearn communicative strategies. When his acoustic agnosia is more severe, we will use stimuli that are dissimilar, have the environment free of background distractions, and use visual cues to reinforce the verbal message. Then, when his acoustic agnosia is milder, we will reduce cues and challenge Mr. B to distinguish among stimuli having similar features (e.g., by manipulating wine or food selections during restaurant routine) .

Psychosocial issues must also be considered. We choose procedures that are familiar and culturally appropriate and of interest to Mr. B. Since Mr. B has intimate knowledge of the entertainment business and likes to talk about it, we will focus treatment tasks around restaurants, stars, movies, plays, food, wine, and politics. When he experiences oscillations in psychosocial status, we will help to reduce his general frustration by focusing his attention on the success of his communication rather than the specifics of his speech production. As he builds an acceptance of his communicative changes, his overall communicative success will improve. Mr. B is sensitive to rejection by others in response to his disability (a psychosocial maintaining factor). His communication partner will acknowledge his intent within conversational interactions.

The following summarizes considerations relevant to the regulation of performance demands:

SYNTACTIC COMPLEXITY: Two-constituent utterances are less complex than three-constituent utterances.

LANGUAGE USE: Earlier developing functions occur before later developing.

NOVELTY OF TASK: Familiar routines are more facilitative than novel or unanticipated situations.

Figure 7.4 summarizes the derivation of session goals and procedures discussed above.

Deriving Session Goals and Procedures	
Decision	**Guiding Information and Client-Specific Details**
Long-Term Goal and Related Subordinate Goals	**Long-Term Goal:** Produce 2-3 constituent utterances as contingent responses within conversations **Subordinate Goals:** Produce language for a range of communicative functions Produce context appropriate vocabulary to express a variety of content categories and communicative functions in conversation
For Each Short-Term Goal, Consider Implications of:	**Short-Term Goals:** Produce 2 to 3-word utterances coding existence, attribution, and rejection. (Lahey, 1988) Produce 2-3 constituent utterances coding action, and locative action within familiar social routines Demonstrate the functions comment, request and protest when engaged in familiar social routines. (Dore, 1972) **Taxonomy:**
Learning and Rehabilitation Premises **and**	<table><tr><td>**Learning Theories**</td><td>**Implications Drawn (in the operationalized approach)**</td></tr><tr><td>**Constructivism**</td><td></td></tr><tr><td>**Social Cognitive**</td><td>Communication partners will provide contingent content and form during conversations with Mr. B Vocabulary (written words) relevant to familiar routines will be available to Mr. B on assistive device</td></tr><tr><td>**Relationship-based pragmatic**</td><td>The clinician will create naturalistic contexts involving routines with persons who are meaningful to Mr. B</td></tr><tr><td>**Operant**</td><td>Communication partners will acknowledge Mr. B's intent, thus offering rewarding consequences</td></tr></table>

FIGURE 7.4: Session goal template for Mr. B.

Maintaining Factors	Maintaining Factors	Implications Drawn (in the operationalized approach)
	Sensorimotor	Vocabulary relevant to routines will be programmed on assistive device (tablet, phone) according to routine. Mr. B's use of written words to support word retrieval and intelligibility will be encouraged
	Psychosocial	Mr. B will receive acknowledgement of his intent from communication partner
	Medical	History of cardiac issues

Early Session Goal

Mr. B will *protest* his wife's suggestion to eat at "McDonald's" or "Popeye's" when *engaged in a conversation* about where to eat out five times in 30 minute session by *saying "no/no way."*

Performance Demands Controlled	Performance Variable Controlled	How the Variable is Controlled	Aspect of Session Goal Affected
	Syntactic complexity	Two word utterances less complex than two-constituent utterances	Target
	Pragmatic complexity	Familiar routine conversation before novel experiences	Linguistic context

Later Session Goal

Mr. B will *produce 2-3 constituent utterances* coding *action and state*, in *response to request* about desired order at a restaurant 3 times in 30 minute session (e.g., give me water; want a salad).

FIGURE 7.4 CONTINUED: Session goal template for Mr. B

Performance Demands Controlled	Performance Variable Controlled	How the Variable is Controlled	Aspect of Session Goal Affected
	Syntactic complexity	Two-constituent utterances more complex than two words, but less complex than three constituent utterances	Target
	Pragmatic complexity	Less complex functions (direct request vs. indirect request)	Target
	Cognitive demand	Familiar routines before novel experiences	Linguistic and non-linguistic context

FIGURE 7.4 CONTINUED: Session goal template for Mr. B

REFERENCES

Australian Gov't. (2006). ASD treatment efficacy.

Ayres, J. (1969/2005). Sensory integration and the child. LA: Western Psychological.

Battle, D. (2002). *Communication disorders in multicultural populations* (3rd ed.). Boston: Butterworth-Heinemann.

Bernhardt, B., & Stemberger, J. P. (2000). *Workbook in nonlinear phonology for clinical application*. Austin, TX: PRO-ED.

Bernthal, J. E., Bankson, N. W., & Flipsen, P. (2017). *Articulation and phonology disorders* (7th ed). Allyn & Bacon.

Berry, M. F., & Eisenson, J. (1956). Speech disorders: Principles and practices of therapy. NY: Appleton-Century-Crofts.

Bloom, L. (1995). *The transition from infancy to language: Acquiring the power of language*. Washington, D.C.: APA

Bloom, L., & Lahey, M. (1978). *Language development and language disorders*. New York: Wiley.

Bloom, L., Lahey, M., Hood, L., Lifter, K., & Feiss, K. (1980). Complex sentences: Acquisition of syntactic connectives and the semantic relations they encode. *Journal of Child Language, 7*, 235–261.

Bloom, L., Miller, P., Hood, L. (1974). Variation and reduction as aspects of competence in language development. *Papers and Reports on Child Language Development, 8*, 142–178.

Bloom, L., & Tinker, E. (2001). The intentionality model of language acquisition. *Monographs of the Society for Research in Child Development, 66*(4), 1–91.

Bobath, B., & Bobath, K. (1981). *Motor development in different types of cerebral palsy*. London: Heinemann.

Brown, R. (1973). *A first language: The early stages*. London: George Allen & Unwin.

Bruner, J. (1986). *Actual minds, possible worlds*. NY: Harvard University Press.

Bryant, G. A., & Barett, H. C. (2006). *Evidence of Universals in Infant-directed Speech. UCLA Department of Anthropology*. Retrieved from http://www.sscnet.ucla.edu/anthro/faculty/barrett

Camarata & Gandour. (1984)

Campbell, T. F., & Bain, B. A. (1991). How long to treat: A multiple outcome approach. *Language, Speech, and Hearing Services in Schools, 22*, 271–276.

Carbone, V. (2013). The establishing operation and teaching verbal behavior. *The Analysis of Verbal Behavior*, 29.

Champion, T. (2003). *Understanding storytelling among African-American children: A journey from Africa to America*. Mahwah, NJ: Erlbaum.

Chapey, R. (ed., 2008). *Language intervention strategies in Aphasia and related neurogenic communication disorders* (5th ed.). NY: Lippincott, Williams, & Wilkins.

Chomsky, N. (2004). Noam Chomsky on Linguistics - Poverty of Stimulus. Retrieved from https://www.youtube.com/watch?v=urrNTVxuCxs

Chomsky, N. (2013a). Problems of projection. *Lingua, 130*, 33–49

Chomsky, N. (2013b). What kind of creatures are we? Lecture 1: What is language? *The Journal of Philosophy, 90*, 645–662.

Chomsky, N (2014a). On human nature and language. Retrieved from https://www.youtube.com/watch?v=j1-jtAhcmoI

Chomsky. (2014b). Biology and language (Bio-linguistics). Retrieved from https://www.youtube.com/watch?v=Kek_YpJsSsg.

Chomsky, N. (1995). *The minimalist program*. Cambridge, MA: The MIT Press.

Conner, F., Williamson, G., and Siepp. (1978). *A transdisciplinary approach to intervention for children with neuromotor and other developmental; disabilities*. New York, NY: Teachers College Press.

Cole, K. N., Dale, P. S. (1986). Direct language instruction and interactive language instruction with language delayed preschool children: A comparison. *Journal of Speech and Hearing Research, 29*, 206–217.

Connell, P. H. (1987). An effect of modeling and imitation teaching procedures on children with and without specific language impairment. *Journal of Speech-Language- and Hearing Research, 30*, 105–113.

Courtright & Courtright. 1979. Imitative modeling as a language intervention strategy: the effects of two mediating variables. *Journal of Speech & Language Research, 22*, 389–402.

Dollaghan, C. (2007). *The handbook for evidence-based practice in communication disorders.* Baltimore: Paul H. Brookes.

Doody, R. S., Stevens, J. C., Beck C., Dubinsky, R.M., Kaye, J.A., Gwyther, L., Mohs, Dore, J. (1975). Holophrases, speech acts, and language universals. *Journal of Child Language, 2*, 20–40.

Eger, D. L. (1988). Accountability in action: Entry, measurement, exit. *Seminars in Speech and Language, 9*, 299–319.

Elbert, M., & Geirut, M. A. (1986). *Handbook of clinical phonology.* Martlets Way, UK: College-Hill Press.

Enderby, P. (2012). Disorders of communication: dysarthria. In (Handbook of Clinical Neurology). In M. J. Aminoff, F. Boller, & D. F. Swab (eds.). *Handbook of clinical neurology.* New York, NY: Elsevier.

Ertmer, D. J., & Ertmer, P. A. (1998). Constructivist strategies in phonological intervention facilitating self-regulation for carryover. *Language, Speech, and Hearing Services in Schools, 29*, 67–75.

Evans, J. (2008). Emergentism and language. In: M. Mody & E.R. Silliman (Eds.). *Brain, Behavior, and Learning in Language and Reading Disorders.* New York, NY: Guilford Press.

Feier, C. D., & Gerstman, L. J. (1980). *Sentence comprehension abilities throughout expression.* Cambridge UK: Cambridge University Press.

Feuerstein, R., Rand, Y., & Hoffman, M. B. (1979). *The dynamic assessment of retarded performers: The learning potential assessment device, theory, instruments, and techniques.* Baltimore, MD: University Park Press.

Fey, M. E. (1988). Generalization issues facing language Interventionists. *Language, Speech, and Hearing Services in Schools, 19*, 272–281.

Fey, M. E. & Justice, L. M. (2004). *Evidence-based practice in schools: integrating craft and theory with science and data.* The ASHA Leader.

Fey, M. E., Richard, G. J., Geffner, D., Kamhi, A. G., Medwetsky, L., Paul, D., Schooling, T. (2011). Auditory processing disorder and auditory/language interventions: An evidence- based systematic review. *Language, Speech and Hearing Services in Schools, 42*, 246–264.

Fischer, K. W. (1980). A theory of cognitive development: The control and construction of hierarchies of skills. *Psychological Review, 87, 477–531.*

Fischer, K. W., Rotenberg, E. J., Bullock, D. H., & Raya, P. (1993). The dynamics of competence: How context contributes directly to skill. In R.H. Wozniak & K.W. Fischer & Rose (1998, eds.). *Development in context: Acting and thinking in specific environments. The Jean Piaget Symposium Series* (pp. 93-117). Hillsdale, NJ: Erlbaum.

Forman, G., & Hill, P. (1990). *Piaget in the preschool.* Menlo Park, CA: Addison Wesley.

Fosnot, K. (1996). *Constructivism and teacher education.* New York, NY: Teacher's college press.

Frattali, C. M., Thompson, C. M., Holland, A. L. Wohl, C. B., & Ferketic, M. M. (1995). The FACS of life: ASHA FACS-a functional outcome measure for adults. *ASHA, 37*, 40-46.

Frost, L., & Bondy, L. (1994). The picture exchange system. *Focus on Autistic Behavior, 9*, 1–19.

Gallagher, J. K., & Reid, D. K. (2002). *The learning theory of Piaget and Inhelder.* Bloomington, IN: iUniverse.

Galloway, M., Blikman, A., Omaivboje, L. M., & O'Rourke, M. (2009). *Clinical application of evidence based practice: A guide for clinicians.* Atlanta, GA: Georgia State University Press.

Geirut, J.A. (1998). Treatment efficacy: Functional communication problems in children. *Journal of Speech, Language, Hearing Research in Children, 41*, S85–S100.

Geller, E., & Foley, G. M. (2008). Expanding the points of entry for speech-language pathologists. A relational and reflective model for clinical practice. *American Journal of Speech-Language Pathology, 18*(1), 4–21.

Geller, E., & Foley, G. M. (2008). Expanding the points of entry for speech-language pathologists. A relational and reflective model for clinical practice. *American Journal of Speech-Language Pathology*, Retrieved from http://ajslp.asha.org

Gillam, R. (2012). *Phonologic awareness: From research to practice.* New York, NY: Guilford Press.

Gillam, R., Loeb, D., Hoffman, L., Bohman, T., Champlin, C., Thibodeau, L., Widen, J., Brandel J., & Friel-Patti, S. (2008). The efficacy of fast forward language intervention in school-age children with language impairment: a randomized controlled trial. *Journal of Speech, Language, and Hearing Research*, 97–119.

Gillam, R. A., & Pearson, N. A. (2004). *Test of narrative language.* Austin, TX: Pro-Ed.

Gillam, R., & Ukrainetz, T. (2006). *Contextualized language intervention: Scaffolding* framework for management. *Journal of Speech and Hearing Disorders, 47,* 226–241.

Global Down Syndrome Foundation. (2014). Facts and FAQ's about Down Syndrome.

Greenspan, S., & Weider, S. (2006). *Engaging autism: Using the floortime approach to help children relate, communicate, and think.* Philadelphia: Merloyd- Lawrence/Perseus.

Greenspan, S., & Weider, S., & Simon, R. (1998). *The child with special needs.* Philadelphia: Perseus.

Greenspan, S. & Lewis, M. (2005). *The affect based language curriculum*, (2nd ed.). Interdisciplinary Council on Developmental and Learning Disorders.

Grunwell, P. (1985). *Phonological assessment of child speech (PACS).* San Diego, CA: College Hill Press.

Guttierez-Clellan, V.F., & Pena, E. (2001). Dynamic assessment of diverse children: A tutorial. *Language, Speech, and Hearing Services in Schools, 32,* 212–224.

Halliday, M. A. K. (1975). *Learning how to mean: Explorations in the development of language.* London: Edward Arnold.

Halliday, M. A. K. (1993). Toward and language based theory of learning. *Linguistics and Education, 5,* 93–116

Heath, S. (1983). *Ways with words: Language, life, and work in communities and classrooms.* Cambridge, UK: Cambridge University Press.

Hodson, B. W., & Paden, E. P. (1991). *Targeting intelligible speech: A phonological approach to remediation*, (2nd ed.). Austin, TX: Pro-Ed.

Hoggan, K. C., & Strong, C. J. (1994). The magic of once upon a time: narrative teaching strategies. *Language, Speech, and Hearing Services in Schools, 25,* 76-89.

Hubble, R. D. (1988). *A handbook of English grammar and language sampling.* Retrieved from http://www.global-downsyndrome.org/about-down-syndrome/facts-about-down-syndrome/#Whatis

Hubble, R. D. (1988). *A Handbook of English grammar and language sampling.* Berlin, Germany: Springer Science+Business Media

Ingram, D. (1981). Procedures for the phonological analysis of children's language. Baltimore, MD: University Park Press.

Jenkins, J. J., Jimenez-Pabon, Shaw, R. E., & Sefer, J. W. (1975). *Schuell's Aphasia in adults: Diagnosis, prognosis and treatment.* New York City, NY: Joanna Cotler Books.

Karmiloff-Smith, A. (1986). Stage/structure versus phase/process in modelling linguistic and cognitive development. In I. Levin (Ed.), *Stage and structure* (pp. 192-212). Norwood, NJ: Ablex.

Kamhii, A. (1988). A reconceptualization of generalization and generalization problems. *Language, Speech, and Hearing Services in Schools, 19,* 304–313.

Kent, R. D. (1999). Motor control: Neurophysiology and functional development. In Caruso, A., & Strand, E. (Eds.) *Clinical management of motor speech disorders of children.* New York, NY: Thieme.

Khamis-Dakwar, R. & Froud, K. (2007). Lexical processing in two language varieties: An event- related brain potential study of Arabic native speakers. In Mughazy, M. (ed.), *Perspectives on Arabic linguistics XX* (pp. 153–168). Amsterdam: John Benhamins.

Kim, T. Y., & Lombardino, L. J. (1991). The efficacy of script contexts in language comprehension intervention with children who have mental retardation. *Journal of Speech-Language-Hearing Research, 34,* 845–857.

Klein, H. B. (1981). Productive strategies for the pronunciation of early polysyllabic lexical `items. *Journal of Speech and Hearing Research, 24,* 389405.

Klein, H. B. (2005). Reduplication revisited: Functions, constraints, repairs, and clinical implications. *America Journal of Speech Language Pathology, 14,* 71–83.

Klein, H. B., Moses, & Jean-Baptiste, R.. (2010). Influence of context on the production of complex sentences by typically developing children. *Language, Speech, and Hearing Services in Schools, 41,* 289–302.

Klein, H. B., Grigos, M. I; McAllister Byun, T; Davidson, L. (2012). The relationship between inexperienced listeners' perceptions and acoustic correlates of children's /r/ productions. *Clinical Linguistics and Phonetics. 26*, 628–645

Klein, H. B., & Moses, N. (1999a). *Intervention planning for children with communication disorders.* (2nd ed.). Boston: Allyn & Bacon.

Klein, H. B., & Moses, N. (1999b). *Intervention planning for adults with communication disorders.* (2nd ed.). Boston: Allyn & Bacon.

Klein, H., Moses, N., & Baptiste, R. (2010). Influence of context on the production of complex sentences by typically developing children. *Language, Speech, and Hearing Services in Schools, 41,* 1–14.

Klein, H. B., & Spector, C. (1985). Effect of syllable stress and serial position on error variability in polysyllabic productions of speech-delayed children. *Journal of Speech and Hearing Disorders, 50,* 391-402.

Kovarsky, D., Maxwell, M., & Duchan, J. F. (1999). *Constructing incompetence: Disabling evaluations in clinical and social interactions.* New York, NY: Psychology Press.

Labov, W. & Waletzky, J. (1967). Narrative analysis. In J. Helm (Ed.), *Essays on the verbal and visual arts* (pp. 12–44). Seattle, WA: University of Washington Press

Lahey, M. (1988). *Language disorders and language development.* New York, NY: Macmillan.

Lass, N. J. & Pannbacker, M (2008). The application of evidence-based practice to nonspeech oral motor treatments. *Language, Speech, and Hearing Services in Schools, 39*(3), 408–421.

Law, J., Garrett, Z., & Nye, C. (2004). The efficacy of treatment for children with speech and language delay/disorder. *Journal of Speech, Language, Hearing Research, 41,*1114–1117.

Leather, J., & James, A. (1991). The acquisition of second language speech. *Studies in Second Language Acquisition, 13,* 305–341.

Lederer, S. (2006). *I can say that.* Children's Publishing.

Lee, L. (1974). *Developmental sentence analysis.* Evanstown, IL: Northwestern University Press.

Leonard, Devescove, & Ossela. (1987).

Levinson, D. J. (1978). *The seasons of a man's life.* New York, NY: Ballantine Books.

Loeb, D. F., Gillam, R. B., Hoffman, L., Brandel, J., & Marquis, J. (2009). The effects of Fast For Word language on phonemic awareness and reading skills of school-age children with language impairments and poor reading skills. *American Journal of Speech- Language Pathology, 18,* 376–387.

Lof, G. L., & Watson, M. M. (2008). A nationwide survey of nonspeech oral motor exercise use: Implications for evidence-based practice. *Language, Speech, and Hearing Services in Schools, 39*(3), 392–407.

Lonsbury-Martin, B. (2006). Advances in audiology research: An overview. *The ASHA Leader 11,* 1–22.

Lovaas, O. I. (1987). Behavioral treatment and normal educational and intellectual functioning in young autistic children. *Journal of Consulting and Clinical Psychology, 55,* 3–9.

Locke & Pearson

Lund, N. J., & Duchan, J. F. (1988). *Assessing children's language in naturalistic contexts,* (2nd ed.). Englewood Cliffs, NJ: Prentice-Hall.

Madell, J. R. (1994). *Professional standards in professional issues in speech-language pathology and audiology, Editors.* Singular Publishing Group, Inc., San Diego, CA.

Martin, A. D. (1981). The role of theory in therapy: a rational. *Topics in Language Disorders,* 63–72.

Marton, C, & Schwartz, R. (2003). Working memory capacity and language capacities in children with specific language impairments. *Journal of Speech, Language, and Hearing Research, 46,* 1138–1153.

Shatz, M., & Gelman, R. Modifications in the speech of young children as a function of listeners. *Monographs of the Society on Research in Child Development, 38*(5), 1–38.

Maas, R., Austermann Hula, S. N., Freedman, S., Wulf, G., Ballard, K. J., Schmidt, R. A. Principles of motor learning in treatment of motor speech disorder. *Speech Language and Hearing Sciences, 17,* 277–298.

McCabe, A., & Rollins, P. R. (1994). Assessment of preschool narrative skills. *American Journal of Speech Language Pathology, 3,* 45–56

Miyagawa, S. (2010). *Why agree? Why move? Unifying agreement-based and discourse-configurational languages*. Cambridge, MA: MIT.

Mody, M., & Silliman, E. R. (2008). *Brain, Behavior, and Learning in Language and Reading Disorders*. New York, NY: Guilford Press.

Moses, N. (1994). Procedural knowledge I adults engaged in a tractor-trailer task. *Cognitive Development, 9*, 103–130.

Moses, N., Klein, H., & Altman, E. (1990). An approach to assessing and facilitating causal language in learning disabled adults based on Piagetian theory. *Journal of Learning Disabilities, 23*, 220-229.

Muller, U., Carpendale, J. I. M., Budwig, N., Sokol, B. (2008). *Social life and social knowledge: Toward a process account of development*. New York, NY: Erlbaum.

Murray, E., McCab, F., Ballard, K. J. (2014). A systematic review of treatment outcomes for children with apraxia of speech. *American Journal of Speech Language Pathology, 23*, 1–19.

Mysak, E. D. (1980). Neurospeech therapy for the cerebral palsied: A neuroevolutional approach. New York, NY: Teachers College Press.

Nelson, K. (2009). Young minds in social world: Experience, meaning, and memory. Cambridge, MA: Harvard University Press.

Nicolich, L. (1977). Beyond sensorimotor intelligence: Assessment of symbolic maturity through analysis of pretend play. *Merrill-Palmer Quarterly* 23, 89–99.

Ninio, A., & Bruner, J. (1978). The achievement and antecedents of labeling. *Journal of Child Language, 5*, 1–15.

Nippold. (2016). *Later language learning*. Austin, Tx: Pro-Ed.

Olswang, L. B., & Bain, B. (1994). Data collection: Monitoring children's treatment progress. *American Journal of Speech-Language Pathology, 3*, 55–66.

Osgood, C. (1957). *A behavioristic analysis of perception and language as cognitive phenomena, contemporary approaches to cognition*. Cambridge, MA: Harvard University Press.

Paradis, J., Genesee, F., Crago, M. B. (2011). *Dual language development and disorders: A handbook on bilingualism and second language learning.* Baltimore, MD: Brookes.

Phillips, B., Ball, C., Sackett, D., Badenoch, D., Straus, S., Haynes, B., & Dawes, M. (1998/2009). *Levels of evidence*. Oxford Centre for Evidence-based Medicine. Retrieved from http://www.cebm.net/?o=1116

Piaget, J. (1962). *Play, dreams, and imitation in childhood*. New York, NY: Norton.

Piaget, J. (1971). *Biology and knowledge*. Chicago, IL: University of Chicago Press.

Piaget, J. (1976). *Grasp of consciousness*. Chicago, IL: University of Chicago Press.

Piaget. J. (1978). *Success & understanding*. Cambridge, MA: Harvard University Press.

Piaget, J. (1985). *The equilibrium of cognitive structures*. Chicago, IL: University of Chicago.

Piaget, J., & Garcia, A. (1991). *Toward a logic meaning*. Hillsdale, NJ: Erlbaum.

Syndrome Foundation. (2014). Facts and FAQ's about Down Syndrome. Retrieved from http://www.globaldown-syndrome.org/about-down-syndrome/facts-about-down-syndrome/#Whatis

Prizant, B. M., Wetherby, A. M., Rubin, E., Laurent, C. & Rydell, P. J. (2006). The SCERTS Model: A comprehensive educational approach for children with autism spectrum disorders. Baltimore, MD: Paul H. Brookes Publishing.

Rasmussen, T., & Pei. (2010). Memory interventions for children with language deficits. In: J. H. Stone, M. Blouin (Eds). *International Encyclopedia of Rehabilitation*. Retrieved from http://cirrie.buffalo.edu/encyclopedia/en/article/276

Ratner, N., & Bruner, J. (1978). Games, social exchange, & language. *Journal of Child Language*, 391–401.

Reese, E., & Cox, A. (1999). Quality of adult book reading affects children's emergent literacy. *Developmental Psychology, 35*, 20-28.

Rvachew, S. (1994). Speech perception training can facilitate sound production learning. *Journal of Speech and Hearing Research, 37*, 347–357.

Salis, C., Hwang, F., Howard, D., Lallini, N. (2017). Short-Term and working memory treatments for improving sentence comprehension in Aphasia: A review and a replication study. *Seminars in Speech and Language, 38*, 29–39.

Santrock, J. W. (1995). *Life span development*, Vol. 39. Madison, WI: WCB Brown & Benchmark Schools, 408–421.

Schank, R. C., & Abelson, R. P. (1977). *Scripts, Plans, Goals and Understanding: an Inquiry into Human Knowledge Structures*. Hillsdale, NJ: Erlbaum.

Shatz, M., & Gelman, R. (1973). The development of communication skills: Modifications in the speech of young children as a function of listener. Washington, D.C.: APA

Sheehy, G. (1995). *New passages*. New York, NY: Random House.

Shriberg, L., & Kwiatkowski, J. (1982). Phonological disorders II: A conceptual framework for management. *Journal of Speech and Hearing Disorders, 47*, 226–241.

Singer, B. D., & Bashir, A. S. (1999). What are executive functions and self-regulation and what do they have to do with language-learning disorders? *Language, Speech, and Hearing Services in Schools, 30*, 265–273.

Skinner, B. F. (1957). Verbal behavior. New York, NY: Appleton-Century Crofts.

Smith, T. T., Myers-Jennings, C., & Coleman, T. (2000). Assessment of language skills in rural preschool children. *Communication Disorders Quarterly, 21*(2), 99–113.

Spelke. (1991). In S. Carey and R. Gelman (Eds.). *Epigenesis of mind: Essays on biology and cognition.* Wiley online library.

Swain, D., Wallach, G. P., Frymark, T., & Schooling, T. (2011). Auditory processing disorder and auditory/ language interventions: an evidence-based systematic review. *Language Speech and Hearing Services in Schools, 42*(3), 246–264.

Spreckley, M., & Boyd R. (2009). Efficacy of applied behavioral intervention in preschool children with autism for improving cognitive, language, and adaptive behavior: a systematic review and meta-analysis. *Journal of Pediatrics, 154*, 338–344.

Stein, N. L., & Glenn, C. G. (1979). An analysis of story comprehension in elementary school children. In Freedle, R. (Ed.), *Discourse processing: Multidisciplinary perspectives*. Norwood, NJ: Ablex.

Tannen, D. (2005). Conversational style. London: Oxford University Press.

Tallal, P. (1997). *FastForWord*, Oakland, CA: Scientific Learning.

Tallal, P. (2004). Improving language and literacy is a matter of time. *National Review of Neuroscience, 9*, 721–728.

Thomson, C. K. (2007). Complexity in language learning and treatment. *American Journal of Speech Language Pathology, 16*, 3–5.

Torgesen, J. K. (2004). Lessons learned from research on interventions for students who have difficulty learning to read. In P. McCardle & V. Chhabra (Eds.), *The voice of evidence in reading research*. Baltimore, MD: Brookes.

Tyack, D., & Gottsleben, R. (1974). *Language sampling, analysis and training: A handbook for teachers and clinicians*. Palo Alto, CA: Consulting Psychological Press.

Van Riper, 1939ff

Wambaugh, J. L. (2002). A summary of treatments for apraxia of speech and review of replicated approached. *Seminars in Speech and Language: Apraxia of Speech: From Concept to Clinic, 23*, 293–308.

Weismer, S. E., & Evans, J. L. (2002). The role of processing limitations in early identification of specific language impairment. *Topics in Language Disorders, 22*(3), 15–29.

Wepman, J. (1968). The modality concept: Including a statement of the perceptual and conceptual levels of learning. In H. K. Smith (Ed.), *Perception and reading*. Newark, DE: International Reading Association.

Wertch, J., & Tulviste, P. (1992). L. S. Vygotsky and contemporary developmental psychology. *Developmental Psychology, 28*(4), 548–557.

Westby, C. (1980). Assessment of cognitive and language abilities through play. *Language, Speech, and Hearing Services in Schools, 11*, 154–168.

Westby, C. (2000). Revised Concise Symbolic Play Scale. Retrieved from *https://www.smartspeechtherapy.com/wp.../Revised-Concise-Symbolic-Play-Scale.pdf*

Wiig, E. H., Semel, E., & Secord, W. (2013). Clinical Evaluation of Language Fundamentals 5th ed. Psychological Corp.

Winitz, II. (1969). *Articulatory acquisition and behavior*. New York: NY: Appleton-Century-Crofts

Williams, J. H. G., Whiten, A., Suddendorf, T., & Perrett, D. I. (2001). Imitation, mirror neurons and autism. *Neuroscience and Behaviour Review, 25,* 287–295.

Wolfe & Blocker. (1990). Consonant-vowel interaction in an unusual phonological system. *Journal of Speech and Hearing Disorders, 55,* 561–566.

Youmans, G., Youmans, S. R., Hancock, A. B. (2011). Script training for adults with apraxia of speech. *American Journal of Speech-Language Pathology, 20,* 23–37.

PART 2

Selected Cases of Speech and Language Intervention in Children and Adults

chapter 8

Intervention Planning for Autism Spectrum Disorders

READER WILL:

- Define autism spectrum disorder
- Become familiar with evidence concerning applied behavioral analyses, relationship-based and constructivist approaches to intervention with autistic spectrum disorder
- Describe intervention planning (goal and procedure planning) for a child with an autistic spectrum disorder across the three phases of intervention planning

In this chapter, we apply our model of intervention planning to a child with autistic spectrum disorder (ASD). ASD is a diagnostic category for individuals who present with a heterogeneous group of developmental disabilities involving multiple behavioral systems. Greenspan and Weider (2003) described these characteristics as follows:

- Significant delay or impairment in forming, maintaining, and/or developing communication. This includes preverbal gestural communication as well as verbal and nonverbal communication (e.g., symbolic communication).

- Significant delay or dysfunction in auditory processing skills (e.g., perception, comprehension, and articulation).

- Significant delay or dysfunction in the processing of other sensations, including hyper-/hypo-reactivity to visual-spatial, tactile, proprioceptive, and vestibular inputs as well as the processing of movement patterns (e.g., sequencing).

The *Diagnostic and Statistical Manual of Mental Disorders* (*DSM-IV*; American Psychiatric Association, 2007) identified four subcategories of ASD: autism, Asperger syndrome, pervasive developmental disability–not otherwise specified (PDD-NOS), and Rett syndrome, each having its own behavioral characteristics. In 2013, the diagnostic criteria for ASD within the *DSM-V* were modified. Asperger syndrome and Rett syndrome were removed from designation of ASD. ASD was distinguished by two categories of symptomatology: (a) persistent deficits in social communication and social interaction across multiple contexts and (b) restricted, repetitive patterns of behavior, interests, or activities. Individuals diagnosed with ASD were classified with reference to a three-level severity scale within in each of the symptom categories: Level 1 = mild, requiring support; Level 2 = moderate, requiring substantial support; and Level 3 = severe, requiring very substantial support.

The following is an account of intervention planning for Jonathan, a five-year six-month-old boy with autism.

JONATHAN

Jonathan is a minimally verbal five-year and six-month-old boy who was diagnosed with an ASD at the age of three. Jonathan performs at the moderate range on the Child Autism Rating Scale (CARS), and at Level 2 (requiring substantial support) both in management of social communication and repetitive behavior (see Appendix for recent assessment data.) Jonathan had been enrolled in a preschool program for children with developmental disabilities. His parents described his progress as slow. Jonathan's parents are professionals, committed to extensive participation in intervention. Jonathan's family lives in Brooklyn, New York, and is monolingual—English-speaking.

Long-Term Planning

The first phase of intervention planning for Jonathan involves establishing one or more long-germ goals and a procedural approach. We begin with goal planning.

Establishing Long-Term Goals

The first step in establishing long-term goals is to examine baseline data concerning the child's speech-language functioning; these data will be drawn from the child's diagnostic evaluation and will be compared to norms for the child's age with reference to a research-based developmental taxonomy. The purpose is to understand where the child is presently functioning linguistically in comparison to expected language performance. This information will help us decide what goals to establish for Jonathan at the outset of treatment, and what outcome to expect in the long-term.

COMMUNICATION PERFORMANCE. As Jonathan's diagnostic report (see Appendix) indicates, Jonathan manifests a moderate delay in auditory comprehension and expressive language; Jonathan is producing single words and early word combinations to express the earliest developing semantic relations and communicative functions. In the area of phonology, Jonathan produces one- and two-syllable words, restricted stress patterns, and an incomplete phonological inventory manifested in a cluster of unsuppressed phonological processes.

Summary of Maintaining Factors

SENSORIMOTOR. Jonathan is mildly hypotonic. He is being seen by an occupational therapist who is working on sensory integration and fine motor skills.

COGNITION. Jonathan uses common objects functionally, sometimes producing brief gestures indicating recognition. He does not use objects symbolically. One would expect a child by five years of age to be engaging in symbolic script play, planning and combining play schemes, and reenacting familiar routines (see also Westby, 1980).

PSYCHOSOCIAL. Jonathan's parents are anxious to participate in treatment. Jonathan spends seven plus hours/day weekdays with his babysitter, who is bilingual (Spanish/English); her dominant language is Spanish. Jonathan has a typically developing seven-year-old sister.

Jonathan establishes brief, fleeting eye contact. He resists many forms of physical contact (e.g., being held and hugged). He enjoys tickling and roughhousing initiated by father. Communication is often by gesture or vocalization, to request food or continuation of the tickle or roughhousing routines, and protest. Jonathan is often unresponsive to speech directed to him. He is hypersensitive to high-pitch sounds and many forms of music.

TIME FRAME FOR LONG-TERM GOAL ACHIEVEMENT. Jonathan is early school age. Individuals with Disabilities Education Act (IDEA) legislation mandates formal reevaluation every three years, with ongoing evaluation of treatment outcomes. Given the three-year reevaluation schedule, long-term goals that can be achieved within the three-year period will be projected.

Considering baseline data, and a cautiously optimistic prognosis, the following are long-term goals and the taxonomies that served as a basis for goal-setting:

Taxonomies relevant to establishing long-term goals

Semantics, syntax, pragmatics (Lahey, 1988).

Phonology Grunwell, 1985, phonological processes; Klein, 1981a, b, multisyllabic words).

Long-Term Goals

1. Jonathan will produce complex sentences (two-verb content/form interactions) for a variety of discourse functions.

2. Jonathan will eliminate all phonological processes that are not age appropriate.

Subordinate goals

1. Jonathan will engage in the production of extended conversations with contingent utterances.

2. Jonathan will produce a variety of words to represent a range of content/form interactions.

Planning the Procedural Approach

Now that a set of long-term goals have been established for Jonathan, we prepare to plan procedures that will help Jonathan achieve those goals. We begin by exploring research on treating language delay in ASD.

RESEARCH EVIDENCE RELATIVE TO PROCEDURE PLANNING. Three approaches to the treatment of ASD stand out in the literature: operant programs, most notably applied behavior analysis; relationship-based pragmatic programs, most notably Greenspan's developmental, individual-difference, relationship-based (DIR) program; and social cognitive programs emphasizing executive functions. Each approach embodies a set of premises about language learning and related intervention procedures.

OPERANT PROGRAMS. Among published operant programs, Applied Behavior Analysis (ABA) is, arguably, the most touted (Lovaas, 1987; Carbone, 2013). ABA has been promoted as uniquely supported by experimental evidence demonstrating a significant effect on language performance. A second popular operant program, Picture Exchange Communication System (PECS; Frost & Bondy, 2005), is intended for preverbal children. The more recent "verbal behavior" approach by Carbone (2013) is also based on operant principles.

Operant interventions promote language acquisition by engineering antecedents to and consequences of target behavior (Hedge & Davis, 2010). Consequences are features of the environment that follow a behavior and serve to strengthen or weaken a behavior. Consequences that strengthen behavior are reinforcers (primary, secondary, positive, and negative S_R's). Consequences that weaken behavior are punishments or extinguishers. Antecedents, referred to as "discriminative stimuli (i.e., S_D's)," are stimuli that activate the behavior. ABA programs (e.g., Maurice, Green, & Luce, 1996) prescribe goal sequences that are intended to promote verbal behavior. .

Two meta-analyses of research bearing on language acquisition and ABA yielded somewhat conflicting results. Spreckley and Boyd (2009) evaluated four studies containing randomized comparison trials. They concluded that, compared with standard care, ABA programs did not significantly improve expressive or receptive language or adaptive behavior.

A second meta-analysis conducted by Lantz (2012) attempted to address variation in the methods, designs, treatment features, and quality standards of operant studies. Lantz applied sensitivity analyses, meta-regression, and dose–response measures to meta-analysis. Results suggested that long-term, comprehensive ABA intervention leads to significant long-term improvement of intellectual functioning, language development, daily living skills, and social functioning in children with autism. Language-related outcomes (IQ, receptive and expressive language, communication) were superior to nonverbal IQ, social functioning and daily living skills. The variable of total treatment hours had the greatest effect on language and adaptation composite scores.

The research reviewed in the preceding did not distinguish aspects of operant programs that might be effective (e.g., goal sequences, reinforcer type or frequency, intervention frequency or intensity). There are notable differences among programs, especially in terms of goals, goal sequences, and types of reinforcement employed.

OPERANT PREMISES AND RELATED PROCEDURES. The core premise of operant theory is that consequences of children's actions on their environment ultimately shape and exert control over their behavior. Implied procedures include the following:

1. Prompting desired behavior, and

2. Engineering consequences for the child to experience (i.e., rewards and punishments) following expression of desired or problematic behavior.

RELATIONSHIP-BASED, PLAY-ORIENTED, AND CONSTRUCTIVIST PROGRAMS. Relationship-based communication approaches for children with ASD include Macdonald's Echo program (1986), Greenspan and Weider's (2008) DIR Floortime, and Prizant et al.'s SCERTS program (Prizant Wetherby, Ruben, & Laurent, 2003). Relation-based programs attend to conversational interactions between child and caregiver as driving language acquisition (Bloom, 1995; Geller & Foley, 2010; Greenspan & Weider, 2008).

Especially important is the process of intersubjectivity, which refers to the child's drive to be social and to have a caretaker acknowledge his or her intent (Bloom, 1995).

In relationship-based programs, the caretaker/clinician engages in child-directed activities (usually play) and provides feedback (verbal and gestural) cueing the child that his or her expressions of intent have been recognized. For example, Greenspan's DIR program promotes *circles of communication*. Circles of communication may be initiated by the child or adult. Circles are extended as the adult responds to the child's intent and the child responds in turn to the adult's input, *closing one circle of communication*. A new circle begins when the child or adult extends the previous topic or starts a new one. McDonald's Echo program, which predates DIR, also promotes conversational interactions as the adult *echoes* the child's intention and communicative attempts.

 To date, there does not appear to be any experimental evidence regarding the efficacy of relationship-based programs. Greenspan and Wieder (2003) reviewed the charts of 200 children diagnosed with ASD and found that most children who received Floortime intervention for at least two years made significant improvement in all areas of development. All children in the study received 2 to 5 hours of Floortime interaction at home in addition to comprehensive services such as speech therapy. The researchers claimed that 58% of the participants made significant improvements in affect, social behavior, language, and symbolic play. In addition, the frequency of avoidant, self-stimulatory, perseverative behavior decreased in these children.

PREMISES INTRINSIC TO RELATIONSHIP-BASED PRAGMATIC PROGRAMS AND RELATED PROCEDURES. The core premise of relationship-based programs is that language content, form, and use develop as children engage with others in extended conversations that center on the child's intent. Procedures that can be derived from this premise are as follows:

1. Identify the child's intention

2. Promote extended circles of communication by engaging in activities initiated by the child and making comments acknowledging the child's intent.

SOCIAL COGNITIVE APPROACHES EMPHASIZING EXECUTIVE FUNCTIONS. Hill (2004) identified weaknesses in executive functions in children with ASD. These weaknesses are in the use of self-directed language (representing problem-solving procedures acquired from interactions with caregivers and teachers) and working memory during problem-solving. Weaknesses have also been identified in planning, flexibility, impulse control, and inhibition of off-topic behavior.

Research on the efficacy of direct teaching methods emphasizing executive functions suggests that modality of information presentation is a factor in the efficacy of such teaching methods with children with ASD. Visually based approaches have been found to be more effective than verbal-language-based methods in social and academic problem-solving strategy instruction (Kirk, Gallagher, & Coleman, 2011; Ganz, Earles-Vollrath, & Cook, 2011).

PREMISES INTRINSIC TO SOCIAL COGNITIVE PROGRAMS AND DERIVATIVE PROCEDURES. The central premises of programs based on social cognitive learning theory are that (a) ideation is promoted by associations that caretakers and teachers help individuals establish between words and referent objects, states, and attributes, and (b) problem-solving is promoted by teaching procedures that individuals can retrieve from memory and recite to themselves in the course of problem-solving. Two therapeutic procedures that clinicians may draw from these premises are as follows:

1. Direct the individual's attention to objects and events, while modeling related vocabulary, and

2. Describe and model relevant procedures for achieving tasks and solving problems that may arise.

Additional Theoretic Considerations

The following theoretical constructs have not been explicitly described as a driving force in the generation of procedures for the treatment of communication disorders related to autism. They have, nonetheless, contributed to the evolution of relationship-based and operant intervention programs.

CONSTRUCTIVIST. Constructivist premises are that semantic relations (the content or ideation underlying verbal expression) are established as a consequence of child's efforts to (a) achieve goals during play, (b) attend to feedback from their own behavior signaling success or failure, (c) compensate for errors, and (d) reflect upon experiences. Intervention procedures that we infer from these premises are as follows:

1. Create play contexts offering opportunities for goal-directed behavior

2. Encourage the child to elaborate on his or her play and to try to alter procedures if initial efforts to achieve a goal do not lead to success

3. Encourage the child to reflect upon his or her experiences.

MOTOR. As discussed in Chapter 4, motor theory represents a category of learning theories concerned with the acquisition of patterns of behavior and applies both the learning of new skills in the areas of articulation/phonology, voice, fluency, and the rehabilitation of previously known behaviors. An essential premise of motor theory is that the acquisition of behavior patterns include the exercise of motor patterns, self-correction in response to problematic feedback, and the differentiation, integration, and coordination of different behavioral patterns (Klein & Moses, 1999). Procedures that may be derived from this premise include encouraging the client to (a) produce the target motor pattern and (b) modify the behavior following problematic efforts to produce the target pattern.

CONCLUSION. We have reviewed the literature on three approaches to language intervention with children with ASD. Evidence concerning the efficacy of each of these approaches is inconclusive. The strongest evidence, however, supports operant techniques. There are, however, unanswered questions concerning operant approaches, namely, which components of operant interventions are effective (especially goal sequences that have been established, reinforcement procedures, and frequency of intervention) and precisely what aspects of language are influenced by operant processes. To date, the efficacy of the programs reviewed above is still uncertain. The clinician may continue to be guided, however, by a clear understanding of the theoretic premises and their associated procedures that underlie these programs (i.e., constructive, relationship based, operant).

Considering baseline data from Jonathan, the clinical evidence concerning effectiveness of treatments, and theoretic perspectives reviewed previously, the following procedural approach will guide intervention planning:

Procedural Approach

MAINTAINING FACTORS TO BE ADDRESSED: Cognition, sensorimotor, psychosocial

Guiding premises:

OPERANT THEORY: Consequences of a child's actions on the environment shape and exert control over the child's behavior.

RELATIONSHIP-BASED PRAGMATIC THEORIES: The expression of intent by the child to caretakers and the acknowledgment by caretakers of the child's intent facilitate language acquisition.

CONSTRUCTIVIST THEORY: Feedback from sensorimotor action received by the child during goal-directed play, goal-setting and problem-solving, and reflection upon experiences facilitates development of content of mind.

MOTOR THEORY: The practice of establishing target movement patterns and self-correction in response to problematic feedback is essential for the acquisition of motor patterns.

SOCIAL-COGNITIVE THEORY: Modeling and direct instruction facilitates the acquisition of language forms and development of executive functions

The maintaining factors and learning principles delineated in the procedural approach will be operationalized, during short-term and session procedure planning.

Short-Term Planning

As we progress to the short-term planning phase, we prepare to identify intermediate steps toward the achievement of the long-term goals that were established for Jonathan. Since we are operating with reference to a school calendar, we project objectives for a four-month period.

Establishing Short-Term Goals

Four long-term goals have been established addressing complex content/form/use interactions, phonology, contingent discourse, and vocabulary. Our job at this short-term planning phase is to prioritize from an array of possible achievements those that need to be accomplished first as a foundation for making continued progress. Baseline data in the area of speech and language will provide the starting point for goal planning. Short-term goals will be derived from the developmental taxonomies that guided the establishment of long-term goals.

LONG-TERM GOAL 1. The Bloom and Lahey (1978)/Lahey (1988) taxonomy of content/form interactions was referenced in planning the first long-term goal—*the production of complex (two-verb) content/form interactions for a variety of discourse functions.* This taxonomy outlines a developmental progression of content/form interactions that can serve as potential short-term achievements. Given Jonathan's optimistic prognosis, we expect him to produce more complex syntax as he attempts to express new and more complex semantic relations. Thus, we establish the following short-term goal: *Jonathan will produce two-to-three-constituent utterances to code existence, action, and locative action (coordinated with possession and attribution) in context of pretend play.*

LONG-TERM GOAL 2. Taxonomies by Grunwell (1985), Ingram (1981), and Hodson and Paden (1991) contributed to the derivation of the second long-term goal: Jonathan will *eliminate all phonologic processes which are no longer age appropriate.* We will look to these taxonomies of phonological processes to identify intermediate short-term behavioral targets. Jonathan is currently producing one- and two-syllable words (reducing syllable number when trying to produce three-syllable words. He uses a number of phonological processes. Most prominent are stopping of fricatives, final consonant deletion, and weak syllable deletion.

With reference to the taxonomy cited earlier, we project the following set of short-term goals in the area of phonology:

Jonathan will reduce the process of weak syllable deletion affecting three-syllable words with a variety of stress patterns, during conversational interchanges in play contexts.

Jonathan will reduce the process of stopping of fricatives (f,s)in syllable-initial and syllable-final positions in sentences.

Long-Term Goal (subordinate) 3. Developmental taxonomies in the area of language use from Greenspan (2005) and Lahey (1988) served as bases for the establishment of the third long-term goal: Jonathan will engage in the *production of extended conversations with contingent utterances.* The related short-term goals are as follows:

Jonathan will extend conversations with contingent utterances through five turns during play with a caretaker.

Long-Term Goal (subordinate) 4. *Jonathan will produce a variety of lexical items to represent a range of content/form interactions.*

The related short-term goal is:

Jonathan will increase the number of different lexical items coding action and attribution.

Operationalizing the Procedural Approach

Before we turn to session planning, we revisit the procedural approach established at the long-term planning phase. Our purpose is to further plan procedures for achieving goals that we have established for Jonathan. We will begin to operationalize the learning premises and develop procedures that address maintaining factors cited in the procedural approach.

Operationalizing Learning Premises

Four premises about learning were cited in the procedural approach. Three address primarily content/form/use interactions and one addresses phonology. With reference to content/form/use interactions, the first premise was derived from operant theory: *Consequences of a child's actions on the environment shape and strengthen or weaken the operant behavior.* Operationalizing this premise follows from its implications. One implication of this premise is that the successful achievement of goals children set for themselves will reinforce procedures children use to achieve their goals. Therefore, the clinician will encourage Jonathan to set goals for himself during play, help him to successfully achieve goals that he establishes, and comment on his efforts. Also, the clinician will tolerate error and encourage Jonathan to try again. Successful achievement of a goal should reinforce the successful procedure; failure should extinguish maladaptive behaviors and motivate Jonathan to try alternative solutions. In addition, the clinician's comments on Jonathan's play should provide social reinforcement for the expression of target behaviors.

The second learning premise was derived from relationship-based pragmatic theory: *Acknowledgment by caretakers of the child's intent facilitates language acquisition.* An implication of this premise is that the child should be permitted to express intent, and the clinician should respond to the child's expression of intent. To operationalize this premise during actual therapy sessions, a context will be designed that is "in tune" with the child's free expression of intentionality. Such a context, given a child of Jonathan's age and developmental level, would contain manipulable objects of interest to the child, and adults who allow the child to freely act upon these objects, and themselves. Within such a context we will observe the child and comment upon the child's activities. Our comments will reflect the language goals established for the session. We will also endeavor to interact with the child to expand his play.

The third learning premise was derived from constructivist theory: *Feedback from sensorimotor action during goal-directed play and problem-solving facilitates development of content of mind.* Operationalizing this principle will involve providing the child with concrete objects to manipulate during play (as already planned in line with social/pragmatic learning principles cited earlier). The clinician will interact with the child to extend play and expand relationships the child makes involving objects of play. Adults will, furthermore, mediate the child's play in ways that encourage goal-setting, problem-solving, and reflection.

With reference to phonology, efficacy research in the area of phonology has found that practicing articulatory gestures in an effort to match target vocabulary modeled by another is the most effective approach to establishing a phonological system (Shriberg & Kwiatkowski, 1981). The implication of the premise is straightforward: Encourage Jonathan to produce target phonemes multiple times during sessions. This approach is consistent with the premise of motor theory described in the procedural approach.

We project that target sounds will be practiced most frequently when the sounds are embedded in words that correspond with the child's own intentional state. Therefore, we will work on phonology in the context of play. We will provide Jonathan with toys that encourage the production of words that contain the target phoneme type (fricatives) and syllable structures. We will promote practice by modeling the target word(s). The choice of a specific phoneme (fricative) to target, and the linguistic context in which to promote its production, will be determined as we consider performance demands during session planning.

Maintaining Factors

The procedural approach is also operationalized with reference to factors related to speech and language that may be maintaining the presenting problems. As determined in establishing the procedural approach, Jonathan presents with three maintaining factors: Mild hypotonia in the area of sensorimotor functioning, a moderate cognitive delay, and psychosocial symptomatology typical of autism: avoidance of eye contact and physical interaction with others. The decision to employ play contexts and object manipulation addresses sensorimotor involvement; object manipulation should provide a stream of sensory feedback relevant to language content. In addition, the focus on production of target phonemes provide a type of articulatory exercise (i.e., oral-motor sensorimotor experiences) that should facilitate acquisition of phonologic features, which in turn should lead to the reduction of targeted phonologic processes. The idea of promoting the making of more complex object relations during play addresses Jonathan's cognitive delay. Finally, emphasis of circles of communication focusing on Jonathan's intent should encourage increased social interaction with caregivers.

Session Planning

Session planning involves creating a series of tasks for Jonathan. These tasks will be defined by action expected of the client, the materials he will encounter, and the clinician's actions. The planning process will be guided by decisions that have already been made at the long- and short-term planning phases.

RECAP. We planned long- and short-term goals targeting content/form/use interactions and phonology. At the long-term planning phase, we envisioned a procedural approach that entailed (a) addressing cognitive, sensorimotor, and affective maintaining factors, and (b) employing learning principles from intentionality theory, constructivism, and operant theory. We operationalized that approach by envisioning a play context containing manipulable objects, in which the clinician would encourage the child to establish goals for himself, and to attempt to achieve his own goals. Such an environment will address our core beliefs that feedback from sensorimotor action and communication with others relevant to the child's intentionality will promote language development. The clinician will provide toys and model vocabulary that incorporate target phonological features and word shapes. With these decisions as the foundation, we will now establish session goals with reference to each of Jonathan's short-term goals.

Planning Session Goals

PLANNING WITH REFERENCE TO SHORT-TERM GOAL 1: *Jonathan will produce two- to three-constituent utterances to code existence, action, and locative action (coordinated with possession and attribution) in context of pretend play.* This first short-term goal involves, specifically, identifying objects, representing possession, attributes of objects, actions, and locative action. Therefore, tasks involving changes of location, possession, and attributes of objects (e.g., colors, sizes) will be appropriate contexts for addressing session goals.

PERFORMANCE DEMANDS. A session goal is one of a series of manageable steps progressing toward achievement of a short-term goal. Engineering such a progression requires consideration of the demands each session task will make on the child, that is, performance demands. Across sessions, performance demands are typically intensified until the child has achieved the more demanding short-term goal.

Although Jonathan is presently coding existence using single words, he is coding action and locative actions with two constituents. Thus, we are working toward producing three-constituent utterances and utterances representing more than one content category. Producing novel syntax and semantic relations involves greater linguistic complexity—a significant performance demand. This complexity increases with the number of constituents. So we begin by targeting two-constituent utterances with the addition of another semantic category (a coordinated category).

A related performance demand is *semantic complexity*. This demand is intrinsic to the specific semantic relations that can be targeted. We refer to Lahey's taxonomy, which specifies which two-constituent semantic relations typically achieving children produce first. Lahey's taxonomy indicates "existence (two constituents) + possession (coordinated content)" and "existence (two constituents) + attribution (coordinated content)." Should these relations be targeted individually, in sequence, or simultaneously?

When *existence + attribution* is targeted as a session goal, particular attributes must be identified. In choosing attributes for Jonathan to talk about, developmental research indicates that size and color would be less advanced than shape, weight, and texture (deVilliers & deVilliers, 1978). Attributes that interest Jonathan would be less challenging than entirely foreign attributes (according to Bloom's [1995] relevancy principle).

DECISION. Taking everything into consideration, we decide to establish "existence + attribution" (size, for example, "that's a big truck") before "existence + possession" (e.g., "That's my truck") as the first session goal for Jonathan (we will accept two constituents, not press Jonathan to produce the contracted copula 's; that is, we will accept "that a big truck").

Planning Session Procedures

The content categories *existence + attribution* will be expressed as Jonathan is engaged in a specific task. We have already decided that the task should involve play with manipulable objects and that the clinician will encourage Jonathan to establish goals for himself and to work at achieving these goals. We now need to specify the materials that will be provided Jonathan and how the clinician will interact with him during the session.

To create a problem-solving scenario involving attributes of concrete objects, a decision is made to encourage play with a big fire truck, a small fire truck, and two fire houses: one with a garage door big enough for the large fire truck to fit into, and a second garage too small for the big fire truck. The choice of a fire truck was influenced by the second objective of the session discussed in the following (articulation of fricatives). The clinician will encourage Jonathan to try to drive the big truck into the small fire house; the clinician will state, "Oh my. That's a little fire house; That's a big truck." Thus, Session Goal 1 reads: ***Jonathan will code existence + attribution (size) with two constituents while engaged in play involving two fire trucks (big and little) and two firehouses (big and little) 3 times/30-minute session.***

Jonathan will not be expected to produce a correct /f/ in this context but be given the opportunity to hear the correct production, thus highlighting a sound that will also be a production goal.

Planning with Reference to Short-Term Goal 2

TARGET GOAL AND LEARNING PRINCIPLES. Phonology was established as a second target in consideration of Jonathan's general language delay. As such, the long-term goal is to expand Jonathan's phonological system (as opposed to correcting misarticulations). The derivative short-term goal involves the ***reduction of the process of stopping fricatives (f,s) in syllable initial and final position in sentences.***

We have already decided to provide Jonathan toys that encourage the production of the target segment—fricatives—and target word and syllable structures. The choice of a specific phoneme to target, and the linguistic context in which to promote its production, will be determined with reference to performance demands.

PERFORMANCE DEMANDS. There are several considerations that bear upon the choice of one or more fricatives that will be targeted and the context in which production will be expected. The first concerns the word position in which the + continuant feature is produced and in turn that the process of stopping will be suppressed: Developmental literature indicates that continuant + consonantal features (fricatives) are most naturally produced in word-final VC position (Bernhardt & Stemberger, 2000). Word-final position reduces performance demand. Another consideration, however, is *relevance*. Jonathan will be more likely to attempt production of a lexical item if the object it represents is of interest to him. We will select play objects that will potentially interest Jonathan and have a fricative in the word-initial or word-final (CV, VC) position (recognizing that word-initial position might pose a heightened performance demand).

The third performance demand concerns whether to target one phoneme or a few fricatives simultaneously. Hodson and Paden (1991) promote a cycles approach, in which more than one fricative would be targeted in an effort to reduce the process of stopping, in a recurring fashion with each sound in focus for no more than two or three sessions.

We established the following second goal, taking the performance demands discussed in the preceding as well as the first session goal discussed into consideration: ***Jonathan will produce /f/ in final position articulating "Huff" and "puff" modeled by the clinician in context of producing the wolf routine in the three little pigs story read by the clinician 8/10 trials.***

We have established two session goals corresponding to the first two short-term goals. We will wait to target *circles of communication* (the third short-term goal) within conversational discourse until Jonathan has advanced in the production of content/form/use interactions. Acquisition of complex content/form interactions will provide the developmental foundation for discourse.

CRITERIA FOR GOAL ACHIEVEMENT. The final consideration in session goal planning is related to the frequency or proportion of target responses to establish as criteria for goal achievement.

Regarding the language goal, Bloom and Lahey provide two statistics relevant to acquisition of linguistic structures. The first is *productivity*—five different examples of the structure. The second is achievement—proportion of utterances that match the adult form of a sentence. Since we have set as the objective two-constituent utterances (a non-adult form), productivity is an appropriate benchmark. We will establish *five* "two-constituent, existence + attribution utterances" as the production criteria for the language goal.

The phonology goal involves accomplishing an adult target. Hodson and Paden (1991) suggest frequency of production as an accomplishment criterion. Since the session we are planning will be Jonathan's first attempts to produce /f/ in a clinical setting, we settle on 8/10 trial across three sessions.

Figures 8.1 through 8.5 present a completed MK-SLIP intervention guide for Jonathan.

Deriving the Long-Term Goal			
Decision	**Guiding Information**		
Areas of Speech/Language to be Targeted, Referent Taxonomy, and Current Level of Performance	**Area of Speech/Language**	**Referent Taxonomy**	**Current Performance**
	Language	Bloom & Lahey (1978); Lahey (1988) (Content/form/use interactions, level 3 single-verb sentences)	Productive for content/form interactions at Lahey Phases 1,2,3 (Single words, early combinations, 2-3 constituents), modal+ infinitival complement
	Phonology	Grunwell (1985) Hodson & Paden (1991) Klein (1981a; 1981b) (Phonologic Processes)	Produces one- and two syllable words, restricted stress patterns, and incomplete phonologic inventory
Projecting a Prognosis	**Maintaining Factors**	**Severity**	**Current Performance**
	Cognitive	Mild Moderate Severe	Delayed symbolic play
	Sensorimotor	Mild Moderate Severe	Hypotonia
	Psychosocial	Mild Moderate Severe	Fleeting eye gaze
	Caretaker Attendance	Frequently	Intermittently	Rarely
Time Frame	Time Allotted	Three years (DOE reevaluation cycle)	
Long-Term Goals	1. Jonathan will produce complex sentences (two-verb content/form interactions) for a variety of discourse functions in context of pretend play and conversations 2. Jonathan will eliminate all phonological processes which are no longer age appropriate		

FIGURE 8.1a: Long term goals

Deriving Subordinate Long-Term Goal(s): Language			
Long Term Goal 1: Jonathan will produce complex sentences (two-verb content/form interactions) for a variety of discourse functions in context of pretend play and conversations			

Decision	Guiding Information		
Areas of Speech/Language Intrinsic to the Long-Term Goal	**Area of Speech/Language**	**Referent Taxonomy**	**Current Performance Level**
	Lexicon	Lahey (1988)	Uses narrow range of high frequency vocabulary; often references objects as "that"
	Pragmatics	Lahey (1988)	Narrow range of language functions Does not engage in extended interactions
Subordinate Long-Term Goals	1a. Jonathan will produce extended conversations reflecting self and other-directed topic cohesion 1b. Jonathan will produce a variety of lexical items to represent a range of content/form interactions		

FIGURE 8.1b: Subordinate goals for language and speech

Deriving Subordinate Long-Term Goal(s): Speech			
Long Term Goal 2: Jonathan will eliminate all phonological processes which are not age appropriate			
Decision	**Guiding Information**		
Areas of Speech/Language Intrinsic to the Long-Term Goal	**Area of Speech/Language**	**Referent Taxonomy**	**Current Performance Level**
	Substitution and deletion processes	Grunwell (1985) Hodson & Paden (1991) Klein (1981a; 1981b) (Phonologic Processes)	A wide range of processes are applied with great frequency
	Prosodic constraints		Produces only one- and two syllable words with restricted stress patterns
Subordinate Long-Term Goals	2a. Will reduce substitution and deletion patterns in conversational speech 2b. Will produce a range of syllable and stress patterns in conversational speech		

FIGURE 8.1b CONTINUED: Subordinate goals for language and speech

Planning the Procedural Approach		
Decision	**Guiding Information and Client Specific Details**	
Ultimate Behavior to be Acquired	**Long-Term Goals and Corresponding Subordinate Long-Term Goals**	Jonathan will: 1. Produce complex sentences (two-verb content/form interactions) for a variety of discourse function 2. Eliminate all phonological processes which are not age appropriate **Subordinate goals: Jonathan will:** 1a. Engage in the production of extended conversations with contingent utterances 1b. Produce lexicon to represent a range of content/form interactions 2a. Will reduce substitution and deletion patterns in conversational speech 2b. Will produce a range of syllable and stress patterns in conversational speech
Approaches to Intervention	**Types of Evidence**	**Reference**
	Meta-Analysis	Spreckley & Boyd (2009)
	Experimental	
	Clinical Practice	Geller & Foley (2008)
	Theory	
Premises about Language Learning or Rehabilitation Derived from Clinical Research Relevant to Achieving Long-Term goals	**Theory**	**Premises**
	Constructivism	Feedback from sensorimotor action received by the child during goal-directed play, goal setting and problem solving, and reflection upon experiences facilitates development of content of mind
	Relationship-Based Pragmatic	The expression of intent by the child to caretakers, and the acknowledgement by caretakers of the child's intent facilitates language acquisition
	Social Cognitive	Modeling and direct instruction facilitates learning
	Motor	The practice of establishing target movement patterns and self correction in response to problematic feedback is essential for the acquisition of motor patterns
	Operant	Consequences of a child's actions on the environment shape and exert control over the child's behavior
Maintaining Factors that Need to be addressed	**Maintaining Factors**	**Specific Aspect(s)**
	Cognitive	Moderate developmental delay
	Sensorimotor	Mildly Hypotonic
	Psychosocial	Avoids eye contact and physical interaction

FIGURE 8.2: Long-term procedural approach

Deriving Short-Term Goals			
Decision	**Guiding information and Client-Specific details**		
	Long-Term Goal and/or Subordinate Long-Term Goal(s)	**Taxonomy**	**Current Performance Level**
Long-Term Goal and Corresponding Subordinate Long-Term Goals and Taxonomies Addressed	1. Produce complex sentences (two-verb) content/form interactions)for a variety of discourse functions	Bloom & Lahey (1978); Lahey (1988)	Produces primarily single and two-word utterances and single verb sentences coding earliest developing semantic relations and communicative functions
	2. Eliminate all phonological processes which are not age appropriate	Grunwell (1985) Hodson & Paden (1991) Klein (1981a; 1981b) (Phonologic Processes)	Uses multiple substitution and deletion phonological processes Uses syllable structure processes and restricted stress patterns
Time Frame	**Time Allotted:** 4 months		

FIGURE 8.3: Deriving Short-term goals

Short-Term Goals And Rationale	**Long-Term Goal Addressed 1.** Will produce complex sentences (two-verb content/form interactions) for a variety of discourse functions
	Short-Term Goal Jonathan will produce two-to three-constituent utterances to code existence, action, and locative action (coordinated with possession and attribution) in the context of pretend play **Rationale with reference to: development/complexity/difficulty** Produces primarily single and two-word utterances and single verb sentences coding earliest developing semantic relations and communicative functions; 2-3 constituents are next, developmentally
	Long-Term Goal 2: Eliminate all phonological processes which are not age appropriate
	Subordinate Long-Term Goal 2a. Will reduce substitution and deletion patterns in conversational speech
	Short-term goal: Jonathan will reduce the process of stopping of fricatives (f, s) in syllable initial and final position in sentences **Rationale with reference to: development/complexity/difficulty** /f/ is among the early fricatives to be acquired; he is stimulable for /f/ production
	Subordinate Long-Term Goal 2b Will produce a range of syllable and stress patterns in conversational speech
	Short-Term Goal: Jonathan will reduce the process of weak syllable deletion affecting two-syllable words with trochaic and iambic stress patterns, during conversational interchanges in play contexts **Rationale with reference to: development/complexity/difficulty** Reduces two syllable words to one by deleting unstressed syllables Two syllable words are among the first to be acquired, especially with trochaic pattern

FIGURE 8.3 CONTINUED: Deriving Short-term goals

Operationalizing the Procedural Approach: Language	
Decision	**Guiding Information and Client-Specific Details**
Short-Term Goals to be Addressed	Produce 2-3 constituent utterances to code existence, action, locative action coordinated with possession and attribution
Derive Implications for Procedure Planning from Theory-Based Premises	**Constructivist Premise:** Feedback from sensorimotor action received by the child during goal-directed play, goal setting and problem solving, and reflection upon experiences facilitates development of content of mind 　**Implication:** Therefore, clinician will provide activities involving goals Jonathan can set for himself, object to manipulate **Relationship-Based/Pragmatic Premise:** The expression of intent by the child by the child to caretakers, and the acknowledgement by caretakers of the child's intent facilitates language acquisition 　**Implication:** Therefore, clinician will provide objects and activities of interest to Jonathan. Clinician will be responsive to Jonathan's intent **Social-Cognitive Premise:** Modeling and direct instruction facilitates acquisition of target behavior 　**Implication:** Therefore, clinician will mode target responses when appropriate **Operant premise:** Consequences of a child's actions on the environment shape and exert control over the child's behavior 　**Implication:** Therefore, clinician will identify rewarding consequences for client. Clinician will also monitor her responses to behavior that is maladaptive **Motor-learning Premise:** Establishing target movement patterns and self correction in response to problematic feedback facilitates the acquisition of motor patterns 　**Implication:** Therefore, clinician will encourage Jonathan to attempt alternate approaches to problems; encourage him when he runs into a problem

FIGURE 8.4: Operationalizing the procedural approach for language and speech

Derive Implications for Procedure Planning from Maintaining Factors	Maintaining Factors
	Cognitive: Moderate Delay **Implication:** clinician will encourage creation of object relations during play and reflection to support more complex ideation **Psychosocial: Avoids eye contact and physical contact** **Implication:** Clinician will encourage circles of communication focusing on Jonathan's intent to encourage increased social interaction with caregivers **Sensorimotor: Mild Hypotonicity** **Implication:** Clinician will create play contexts and encourage object manipulation to provide a stream of sensory feedback relevant to language content

FIGURE 8.4 CONTINUED: Operationalizing the procedural approach for language and speech

Operationalizing the Procedural Approach: Speech	
Decision	**Guiding Information and Client-Specific Details**
Short-Term Goals to be Addressed	Reduce the processes of stopping of fricatives (f, s) in syllable initial and final positions in sentences. Reduce the process of weak syllable deletion affecting two-syllable words with a variety of stress patterns, during conversational interchanges in play contexts

Derive Implications for Procedure Planning from Theory-Based Premises	**Constructivist Premise:**
	  Feedback from sensorimotor action received by the child during the production of articulatory gestures, including self-correction facilitates acquisition, representation, and organization, of phonologic features
	
	  Efforts to achieve goals facilitates learning
	
	  Implication: Encourage self correction, experimentation with novel articulatory gestures
	
	  Relate words articulated to acquiring, manipulating objects, activities of interest
	
	Relationship-Based/Pragmatic Premise:
	  The expression of intent by the child by the child to caretakers, and the acknowledgement by caretakers of the child's intent facilitates production of articulatory gestures required to make intent intelligible to others
	  Implication: Embed target sounds in words and sentences related to Jonathan's interests
	
	Social-Cognitive Premise:
	  Modeling and direct instruction facilitates acquisition of novel articulatory gestures, varied stress patterns, and phonologic features
	  Implication: Clinician will model and prompt articulatory gestures

FIGURE 8.4 CONTINUED: Operationalizing the procedural approach for language and speech

	Operant Premise:
	Consequences of a child's efforts to articulate language form shape the child's behavior
	    Implication: Clinician will identify rewarding consequences, and plan to present after target response
	
	    Relate words articulated to acquiring, manipulating objects, activities of interest to Jonathan (provided as rewards)
	
	Motor-Learning Premise:
	    Implication: The practice of establishing target movement patterns and self correction in response to problematic feedback is essential for the acquisition of motor patterns
	
	    Implication: Encourage production of articulatory gesture, and self correction

Derive Implications for Procedure Planning from Maintaining Factors	**Maintaining Factors**
	
	Cognitive: Moderate Delay
	    Implication: Clinician will draw Jonathan's attention and awareness to sounds in words
	
	Sensorimotor: Mild Hypotonicity
	    Implication: Clinician will stimulate areas in the oral-peripheral speech mechanism and intensify articulatory gestures to heighten feedback available to child
	
	Psychosocial: Avoids eye contact and physical contact
	    Implication: Clinician will encourage observation of articulatory gestures modelled by clinician and caregiver

FIGURE 8.4 CONTINUED: Operationalizing the procedural approach for language and speech

Deriving Session Goals and Procedures: Language	
Decision	**Guiding Information and Client-Specific Details**
Long-Term Goal and Related Subordinate Goals	**Long-Term Goal 1:** Jonathan will: Produce complex sentences (two-verb content/form interactions) for a variety of discourse functions **Subordinate Goals:** Jonathan will: 1a. Produce extended conversations reflecting self and other-directed topic cohesion 1b. Produce a variety of lexical items to represent a range of content/form interactions
For Each Short-Term Goal, Consider Implications of:	**Short-Term Goal:** Stg 1. Produce 2-3 constituents utterances to code existence, action, locative action coordinated with possession and attribution **Taxonomy:** Lahey (1988)
Learning and Rehabilitation Premises **and**	<table><tr><td><u>**Learning Theories**</u></td><td><u>**Implications Drawn (in the operationalized approach)**</u></td></tr><tr><td>**Constructivism**</td><td>Clinician will create a play context that encourages goal setting, problem-solving, and reflection upon an object and its attributes</td></tr><tr><td>**Social Cognitive**</td><td>Clinician will model target behavior</td></tr><tr><td>**Relationship-based pragmatic**</td><td>Clinician will comment in a way that reflects Jonathan's intent and provides a model reflecting the related language targets established for the session</td></tr><tr><td>**Operant**</td><td>Identify rewarding consequences for client. Clinician will also monitor her responses to behavior that is maladaptive</td></tr></table>

FIGURE 8.5: Session goals

Maintaining Factors	Maintaining Factors	Implications Drawn (in the operationalized approach)
	Cognitive	Play contexts and object manipulation will provide a stream of sensory feedback relevant to language content
	Sensorimotor	Clinician will create play contexts and encourage object manipulation to provide a stream of sensory feedback relevant to language content
	Psychosocial	Encourage circles of communication focusing on Jonathan's intent to encourage increased social interaction with caregivers

Early Session Goal Addressing STG1:

Jonathan will *code existence + attribution* (size) with *two constituent*s while engaged in play involving two fire trucks (big and little) and two firehouses (big and little), after clinician's model, 3x/30 minute session. Examples, "this big truck"; "that little house"

Performance Demands Controlled	Performance Variable Controlled	How the Variable is Controlled	Aspect of Session Goal Affected
	Conceptual complexity	Early content categories + embeddings before later categories	Target
	Syntactic complexity	2-before 3-constituents	Target
	Perceptual support	Use of concrete objects before no objects	Non-linguistic context
	Clinician's model	Model before no model	Linguistic context
	Cognitive complexity	Activity promoting comparison between attributes (big and little trucks, and corresponding garages)before static support	Non-linguistic context

FIGURE 8.5 CONTINUED: Session goals

CHAPTER 8 Intervention Planning for Autism Spectrum Disorders

Later Session Goal addressing STG 1:

Will code *action and locative action* with *two or three- constituents* while moving firetrucks in a *pretend play routine regarding a rescue.* Examples, Truck goes there; move truck there; you move truck; man drives truck, 3x in 30 minute session

Performance Demands Controlled	Performance Variable Controlled	How the Variable is Controlled	Aspect of Session Goal Affected
	Semantic complexity	Action and locative action after existence	Target
	Syntactic complexity	The expectation of 3-constitutents after 2-constituents	Target
	Cognitive complexity	Provision of familiar routine before novel routine	Non-linguistic context
	Perceptual support	Spontaneous after model	Linguistic context
	Perceptual support	Provision of manipulable toy fire set before no manipulables	Non-linguistic context

FIGURE 8.5 CONTINUED: Session goals

Deriving Session Goals and Procedures: Speech	
Decision	**Guiding Information and Client-Specific Details**
Long-Term Goal and Related Subordinate Goals	**Long-Term Goal 2:** Jonathan will eliminate all phonological processes which are not age appropriate 2a. Will reduce substitution and deletion patterns in conversational speech **Taxonomy:** Grunwell (1985); Hodson & Paden (1991); Klein (1981a; 1981b)
Learning and Rehabilitation Premises **and** **Maintaining Factors**	

Learning Theories	**Implications Drawn (in the operationalized approach)**
Constructivism	Encourage self correction, experimentation with novel articulatory gestures
Social Cognitive	Clinician will model target behavior
Relationship-based pragmatic	Embed target sounds in words and sentences related to Jonathan's interests
Motor Learning	Encourage production of articulatory gestures, and self-correction
Operant	Relate words articulated to manipulating objects, activities of interest to Jonathan (provided as rewards)

Maintaining Factors	**Implications Drawn (in the operationalized approach)**
Cognitive	Clinician will draw Jonathan's attention and awareness to sounds in words
Sensorimotor	Clinician will stimulate areas in the oral-peripheral speech mechanism and intensify articulatory gestures to heighten feedback available to child
Psychosocial	Clinician will encourage observation of articulatory gestures modelled by clinician and caregiver

FIGURE 8.5 CONTINUED: Session goals

Early Session Goal Addressing Short-Term Goal 2: Jonathan will reduce the process of stopping of fricatives (f, s) in syllable initial and final position in sentences 8/10 opportunities

Jonathan will *produce /f/* in articulating *"huff" and "puff" modeled by the cli*nician in context of producing the *wolf routine from the three little* pigs story read by the clinician 8/10 trials

Performance Demands Controlled	Performance Variable Controlled	How the Variable is Controlled	Aspect of Session Goal Affected
	Developmental consideration	'f' among earliest fricatives	Target
	Syllable/word position of target phoneme	Voiceless fricative /f/ is more frequently acquired in final than initial position	Target
	Perceptual support	Model before spontaneous	Linguistic context
	Familiarity of context	Target sound/word is embedded in context of familiar, motivating routine	Non-linguistic context

Later Session Goal Addressing Short-Term Goal 2

Jonathan will *produce /f/* in articulating *"fireman" and "firetruck, modeled by the clinician* in *context of play* with a fireman and fire truck, with 8/10 trials

FIGURE 8.5 CONTINUED: Session goals

Performance Demands Controlled	Performance Variable Controlled	How the Variable is Controlled	Aspect of Session Goal Affected
	Syllable position of target phoneme	Voiceless fricative /f/ embedded in word initial position of two syllable word after acquired in final position	Linguistic context
	Syllable number	/f/ embedded in two syllable word safer produced in single syllable words	Linguistic context
	Phonetic context	Labial /f/ in "fireman" followed by +labial /m/ and +anterior /n/	Linguistic context
	Perceptual support	Model before spontaneous	Linguistic context
	Context familiarity	Word in which target sound is embedded is presented in context of familiar, motivating routine	Non-linguistic context

FIGURE 8.5 CONTINUED: Session goals

REFERENCES

American Psychiatric Association (2007). Diagnostic and statistical manual of mental disorders (4th edition). NY: American Psychiatric Association.

American Psychiatric Association (2012). Diagnostic and statistical manual of mental disorders (5th edition). NY: American Psychiatric Association.

Bernhardt, B., & Stemberger, J.P. (2000). Workbook in nonlinear phonology for clinical application. Austin, TX: PRO-ED.

Carbone, V. (2013). The establishing of operation and teaching of verbal behavior. The Analysis of Verbal Behavior, 29, 2013.

Frost, L., & Bondy, L. (1994). The Picture Exchange System. Focus on Autistic Behavior, 9, 1- 19.

Ganz, J.B., Earles-Vollrath, T.L., & Cook, K.E. (2011). Visual modeling: A visually based intervention for children with Autistic Spectrum Disorder. Teaching Exceptional Children, 41, 8-19.

Ganz, J. B., Earles-Vollrath, T. L., Heath, A. K., Parker, R. I., Rispoli, M. J., & Duran, J. B. (2012). A meta-analysis of single case research studies on aided augmentative and alternative communication systems with individuals with autism spectrum disorders. *Journal of Autism and Developmental Disorders, 42,* 60–74.

Geller, E., & Foley, G.M. (2008). Expanding the points of entry for speech-language pathologists. A relational and reflective model for clinical practice. *American Journal of Speech-Language Pathology.*

Grunwell, P. (1985). Phonological assessment of child speech. San Diego, California: College-Hill Press.

Greenspan, S. & Weider, S. (2008). Engaging autism: Using the floortime approach to help children relate, communicate, and think. Philadelphia: Merloyd-Lawrence/Perseus.

Hegde, M.N., &Davis, M.A. (2010). Clinical methods and practicum in speech-language pathology. Clifton Park, NJ: Delmar

Hill, E. (2004). Executive dysfunction in Autism. Trends in Cognitive Science, 1, 26-32.

Hodson, B.W., & Paden, E. P. (1991). *Targeting intelligible speech: A phonological approach to remediation, 2nd Ed.* Austin, TX: Pro-Ed.

Kirk, S., Gallagher, J.J., & Coleman, M.R., Anastaslow, L. (2011). Educating exceptional children. NY: Council on Exceptional Children.

Klein, H. (1981a). Productive strategies for the pronunciation of early polysyllabic lexical items. *Journal of Speech and Hearing Research, 24,* 389405.

Klein, H. (1981b). Perceptual strategies for the replication of consonants from polysyllabic lexical models. *Journal of Speech and Hearing Research, 24,* 535551.

Klein, H. B., & Moses, N. (1999a). Intervention planning for children with communication disorders. (2nd Ed.). Boston: Allyn & Bacon.

Klein, H. B., & Moses, N. (1999b). Intervention planning for adults with communication problems.(2nd Ed.*).* Boston: Allyn & Bacon.

Lahey, M. (1988). Language disorders and language development. NY: Macmillan.

Lantz, J. (2001). Play time: An examination of play intervention strategies for children with autism spectrum disorders. *The Reporter, 6,* 1-7.

Lovaas, O. I. (1977). *The autistic child: Language development through behavior modification.* New York: Irvington Press.

Maurice, C., Green, G., & Luce, S.C. (1996). Behavioral intervention for young children with Autism: A manual for parents and professionals.

Prizant, B.M., Wetherby, A.M., Rubin, E., & Laurent, A. C. (2003). The SCERTS Model: A Transactional, Family-Centered Approach to Enhancing Communication and Socioemotional Abilities of Children With Autism Spectrum Disorder**.** *Infants and Young Children. 16,* 296–316.

Spreckley, M., & Boyd, R. (2009). Efficacy of Applied Behavioral Intervention in Preschool Children with Autism for Improving Cognitive, Language, and Adaptive Behavior: A Systematic Review and Meta-analysis, *Journal of Pediatrics, 154*, 338–344

Westby, C. (1980). Assessment of cognitive and language abilities through play. *Language, Speech, and Hearing Services in Schools, 11*, 154-168.

Long Island University

Speech-Language-Hearing Disorders Clinic

SPEECH AND LANGUAGE EVALUATION

Client Name: _____Jonathan_____ Primary Disorder: Autistic Spectrum

Chronological Age: __Five years, one month_____

Statement of the Problem:

Jonathan is a five-year and one-month-old boy, who was seen at LIU's Speech and Hearing Clinic, for a speech and language evaluation. Mr. K, Jonathan's father, was present during the course of the evaluation and provided pertinent background history. According to his father, Jonathan was referred to Committee on Special Education (CSE) for a full evaluation, due to continued concern with his "overall language and pronunciation of words." He also reported that "Jonathan continues to use simple sentences to express himself at five years."

Jonathan was diagnosed with Autism Spectrum Disorder at the age of three, and more recently, with an auditory processing delay. Jonathan attends X Early Learning Center; Jonathan's father described his progress as slow. English is the only language spoken by the family. Jonathan's sitter, however, is Spanish-speaking with limited English proficiency. Family history is positive for Asperger's, psychological disorders, and learning disabilities. Jonathan lives in Brooklyn, New York, with his parents. Jonathan receives special education services, as well as a range of private services, including occupational therapy and social skills training.

Medical History:

Mr. K reported that his wife's pregnancy was unremarkable. Jonathan was the product of a full-term pregnancy. He was delivered via a C-Section and weighed 7 lbs, 6 ozs at birth. Jonathan was breast-fed for 2.5 years. Jonathan produced his first words by 10 months of age and word combinations by 18 months of age. He walked by 13 months of age. He stopped speaking at 24 months, however, and began exhibiting unusual behaviors, such as staring at objects and avoiding eye contact, according to his father. He was toilet-trained by four years of age and learned to dress himself by 4.5-years.

Assessment Information

Behavioral Observations:

Jonathan presented as a handsome boy. Upon meeting the evaluator, he turned and walked away. He avoided eye contact throughout the evaluation, except when a desired object was withheld. He then jumped up and down, clapped his hands, and gazed at the evaluator. He tended to produce noncontingent speech when asked social questions (e.g., "Is your name Jonathan?"). He referred to himself as "Mabel." when asked his name (Mabel is the sitter). Jonathan labeled when asked to "point only." Jonathan presented with excessive movement. He moved around and touched the testing manual repeatedly. When a desired toy was shown to him, even with significant cues, he was unable to inhibit these behaviors. His sentences were of single-verb structures. He engaged primarily with Thomas trains and balloons. Multiword utterances were significantly unintelligible .

Results of Communication Assessment

Language

CONTENT/FORM/USE ANALYSIS OF SPONTANEOUS LANGUAGE. A spontaneous language sample of 100 utterances was collected during play and analyzed for content/form/use interactions (Lahey). Results were as follows:

Content/Form Interactions

Developmental Phase	Strong Evidence (Four or More Exemplars)	Emerging Evidence (Three or Less Exemplars)	Syntax
Phase 1	Existence Action	Nonexistence	Single word
Phase 2		Action Locative action	Two constituents Prep + noun
Phase 3	Quantity (-s) (numbers)	Action + specification Existence + quantity Locative action Locative state mood	Three constituents Three constituents Two constituents Modal + infinitival complementation

Jonathan's language was productive for two- to three-constituent utterances coding content/form interactions through phase 3. Jonathan produced complex sentences to code mood (modal + infinitival complement).

LANGUAGE USE. Jonathan's use of language was evaluated, and frequencies of utterances serving identified language functions were calculated. Results were as follows.

Functions	Proportions of Utterances Serving Each Function
Comment—others	0.08
Comment—self	0.02
Comment on object functions and actions	0.43
Total comment	**0.53**
Regulate—direct action	0.08
Regulate—focus attention	0.03
Regulate—obtain response	0.08
Total regulate	**0.18**
Discourse—respond	0.16
Discourse—acknowledge	0.06
Total discourse	**0.22**

Jonathan used language primarily to comment (on object functions and actions), obtain a desired object in the possession of another, and respond to questions given perceptual support (presence of objects referenced).

Preschool Language Scale—fifth edition (PLS-5):

The PLS-5 was administered to assess receptive and expressive language skills in a primarily symbolic context. Results were as follows:

PLS-5 Subtests	Raw Score	Standard Score	SS Range 90% Confidence	Percentile Rank	Percentile Range 90% Confidence
Auditory comprehension	38	66	62–75	1	1–5
Expressive communication	41	74	70–81	4	2–10
Total LS— language score	140	68	64–75	2	1–5

AUDITORY COMPREHENSION. Auditory comprehension scores obtained placed him 1.5 standard deviations below the age-equivalent mean. This is indicative of a moderate delay. Jonathan completed simple analogies ("You sleep in a bed." "You sit on a _____[chair].”). He identified letters, colors, and shapes. He identified objects in pictures given pre-noun elaboration ("Show me the white kitten") and spatial terms ("under"). He identified body parts. He did not identify quantitative concepts. He identified figures according to gender given gender-specific pronouns. He did not identify quantitative, temporal, and state concepts. He did not recall story detail or sequences. He did not identify rhymes or initial sounds of words. He did not respond to *Why* questions.

EXPRESSIVE COMMUNICATION. Jonathan's expressive language skills were 2.0 standard deviations below the age reference mean. This is indicative of a moderate expressive language delay. Jonathan uses present progressive tense. He answers *What* and *Where* questions given perceptual support (reference objects or pictures). He names described common objects (ball). He tells how an object is used (Question: "What do you do with a towel?" Answer: "*dry*" [dwaɪ]. He did not use possessives. He did not answer questions logically (Question: "What do you do when you are tired?" Answer: "um, um, um."). He did not use qualitative concepts (short, long). He did not use modifying noun phrases. He did not respond to "Why" questions" with specific information (Question: Why do you brush your teeth? Answer: "um, um, um."). He did not use synonyms. He did not use rhymes or repeat sentences. He did not attempt to retell a story.

CRITICAL DIFFERENCE. There was a critical difference between auditory comprehension and expressive communication. The critical difference value is .15.

Phonology:

PRESCHOOL LANGUAGE SCALE AND PHONOLOGIC PROCESS ANALYSIS. An assessment of Jonathan's articulation skills using the Preschool Language Scale—fifth edition—Articulation Screener, yielded an articulation raw score of 8. Performance typical for age-level peers is 16 or more. With a score of 11 or less, according to the PLS-5, a phonological involvement may be present. This score corroborated the findings obtained via the language sample analysis. Jonathan's most frequently used processes: fronting, stopping, weak syllable deletion, gliding, vocalization, derhoticization, and cluster reduction. When Jonathan produced single-word utterances, he was mainly intelligible, with a shared context. Intelligibility decreased when he produced discourse-level comments. When the evaluator modeled desired forms, he tended to imitate standard production, indicating that he is stimulable for standard production given a model.

Phonological Process	Target Word	Word Produced
Gliding	ring; light	[wɪn]; [waɪt]
Vocalization	people	[pipo]
Stopping	five	[paɪb]/[paɪ]
Deaffrication	chicken; jump	[tɪkɪn]; [dʌp]
Derhoticization	zipper	[dipo]
Cluster reduction	blue; friend	buʊ]/[bwʊ];[fen]
Weak syllable deletion	elephant; potato	[efɪn]; [teto]

GOLDMAN FRISTOE. The *Goldman Fristoe-2* was administered to evaluate articulation, in a single-word context. Results were as follows:

Raw Score	Standard Score	90% Confidence Interval	Percentile Rank
42	58	52 to 64	5

Results indicate that Jonathan scored 2.5 standard deviations below the age reference mean. This is indicative of a severe phonological impairment. He substitutes, omits, and distorts consonants. He tended to produce sounds, which should be produced at the velar region of his mouth, to the alveolar. The scores derived from the *PLS-5 Articulation Screener*, and *Goldman Fristoe-2*, corroborated the findings obtained from the language sample analysis.

Associated Behavioral Systems

Sensorimotor

ORAL PERIPHERAL/VOCAL QUALITY/RESONANCE. Observation and evaluation of oral-peripheral structures and their functions are as follows. Facial, lingual (tongue), and labial (lip) symmetry were observed. Jonathan displayed a closed-mouth posture at rest. His tongue appeared typical with regard to symmetry and color. Jonathan was uncooperative in following instructions or imitating oral-motor gestures (tongue lateralization and elevation). Speech volume was judged to be extremely variable. Vocal quality was nasalized. Impaired intelligibility and, relatedly, multiple unsuppressed phonology processes suggest oral apraxia,

HEARING HISTORY. Jonathan responded to speech and environmental sounds at typical conversational levels. A recent audiologic examination revealed hearing within normal limits.

Psychosocial

Upon meeting the evaluator, Jonathan turned and walked away. He avoided eye contact throughout the evaluation, except when a desired object was withheld. He then jumped up and down, clapped his hands, and gazed at the evaluator. Jonathan labeled when asked to "point only."

Jonathan avoids eye contact, except to obtain an observable, desired object in the possession of another. He avoids joint action routines (such as "peek-a-boo") initiated by others. He does not seek physical contact. Jonathan used language primarily to comment as he manipulated objects (label objects), to obtain a desired object in the possession of another, and to respond to questions given perceptual support (presence of objects referenced). He referred to himself as "Mabel." when asked his name (Mabel is the sitter).

Cognition

BAILEY SCALES OF INFANT DEVELOPMENT (BSID). BSID was administered at 32 months of age. Jonathan manifested a mild delay in cognitive functioning and a moderate delay in receptive and expressive language (cognitive composite score, 72.2; language composite score, 63.4). During assessment at five years of age, Jonathan manifested object permanence, circular reactions (repeated actions on objects), and ability to identify part–whole relations (as manifested in expression of attribution coordinated with action and existence).

Summary

Jonathan is a five-year and one-month-old boy who was diagnosed with autism spectrum disorder at the age of three, and more recently, with an "auditory processing delay." Results of a speech-language evaluation revealed a moderate delay in production and comprehension of content/form interactions; language was used primarily to comment as he manipulated objects (comment on his actions and the functions of objects manipulated), to obtain a desired object in the possession of another and to respond to questions given perceptual support (presence of objects referenced). He was also found to have a severe delay in phonological development, secondary to apraxia. He was observed to use a wide range of phonological processes affecting individual segments, syllable shape, and syllable number.

A prognosis regarding Jonathan's degree and rate of progress in language and speech, with intervention, is guarded due to the possible effect of related behavioral systems. Jonathan manifests a mild cognitive delay and mild sensorimotor involvement. He avoids eye contact, except to obtain observable, desired objects in the possession of others. He avoids joint action routines (such as "peek-a-boo") initiated by others. He does not seek physical contact. Despite these deterrents to achievement, Jonathan does spontaneously engage in goal-directed play with objects and is stimulable for standard forms of misarticulated phonemes given a model. These strengths suggest that Jonathan will make noticeable progress given speech/language intervention.

chapter 9

Intervention Planning for Speech-Sound Disorders in Children

READER WILL:

- Define speech-sound disorders: articulation, phonological
- Differentiate disorders ranging in severity
- Differentiate between two major models guiding the evaluation and treatment of phonological disorders
- Describe intervention planning (goal and procedure planning) for a child with a severe phonological disorder.

Persistent speech-sound disorders (SSD) have been viewed as "clinically significant," maintained beyond the age of eight and going beyond typical substitutions and distortions (Wren, Miller, Peters, Emond, & Rulestone, 2016); children with such disorders have been found to contribute to a substantive portion of clinicians' caseloads (e.g., Broomfield & Dodd, 2004; Gierut, 1998). Whether a child's presenting difficulties are mild or severe, the underlying source of the problem is not always obvious. Motivated by the interest in discovering the etiology of the problem, two primary underlying causes have been explored: phonetic and phonological (motoric and linguistic).

Through the decades SSDs have been referred to in a variety of ways; this change over time is vividly represented in the evolving title of one of the most frequently used texts in the area: Bernthal and Bankson (and more recently the addition of Flipson, Jr.). In the initial publication (1981) the book was entitled *Articulation Disorders*; beginning with the second edition (1987), the title changed to *Articulation and Phonological Disorders*. By the sixth edition (2008), this title was appended with the subtitle, *Speech Sound Disorders in Children*, which is currently maintained in the eighth edition (2017).

The 1981 title likely represents the view that problems in the production of speech sounds were primarily motor based involving a challenge to the articulatory mechanism. The change in title to *Articulation and Phonological Disorders* reflects the rapidly changing view of articulation, recognizing that speech-sound development and disorders also involve higher-level linguistic processes: the organization of a phonological system, one level of the grammatical system's structure. The position of articulation as a component of the phonological system has met with controversy in the literature. Some prefer the term *phonological disorder* as a superordinate diagnostic label for SSDs (e.g., Shriberg & Kwiatkowski, 1980; Gierut, 1998). They suggest that the phonological system comprises cognitive/linguistic (phonemic) and motor processes (phonetic) that may be challenging to differentiate as the underlying cause of a speech-sound disorder. Adhering to this view, all SSD may be accurately termed *phonological disorders*. This view contrasts most saliently with a position taken by Bauman-Waengler in the first four editions of her book (1999-2008), *Articulatory and Phonological Impairments: A Clinical Focus*, which emphasizes the differentiation of phonemic and phonetic disorders for the planning of goals and procedures.

The added subtitle in the Bernthal, Bankson, and Flipson (6th edition, 2008), *Speech Sound Disorders in Children* and the most recent Bauman-Waengler edition's new title, "Articulation and Phonology" in *Speech Sound Disorders* (2016) may reflect an updated view. These modifications may be an attempt to sidestep the controversy and consider phonological and articulation disorders, disorders of speech-sound production, regardless of etiology. In the present book, we follow suit in focusing on the SSD profile presented, severity of the disorder, and the status of the related behavioral systems related to speech-sound production. These areas of assessment are most crucial in planning goals and procedure.

SAM

Sam, a 11.11-year-old male child, presented with a severe phonological disorder. A summary of Sam's baseline data appears in the diagnostic report in the Appendix.

Long-Term Planning

The first phase of intervention planning for Sam involves establishing one or more long-term goals and a procedural approach. We begin with goal planning.

Establishing Long-Term Goals

To begin the formulation of long-term goals it is necessary to identify where Sam's communication behavior is with reference to a research-based developmental taxonomy. Since Sam presents with both language and speech-sound problems, we need to locate developmental hierarchies within both areas. The process of identifying a research-based developmental hierarchy is essential in providing *evidence-based* support for our goal choices.

With phonology, Sam's most serious problem area, we have two options in selecting a meaningful hierarchy of development. We could identify hierarchies in either phonological processes or nonlinear phonology, two major models guiding articulatory development and disorders. The phonological process model introduced by Stampe (1973) for typical development and modified by others for speech disorders (e.g., Hodson & Paden, 1991; Ingram, 1974; Shriberg & Kwiatkowski, 1980; Grunwell, 1985) represents a model of elimination of developmental processes on the road to learning the ambient sound system. The contrasting model of nonlinear phonology introduced to the field of speech-language pathology by Bernhardt and Stoel-Gammon (1994), and more recently Bernhardt and Stemberger (2000), represents a phonological learning process within which children acquire the sound system by the systematic addition of features, syllables, and stress patterns with development.

Sam is almost 12 years old and well past the typical age of acquisition. At this age, we view Sam as modifying his sound system by eliminating or reducing the inefficient articulatory gestures he has acquired (early processes) and heightening his ability to distinguish among these gestures. Most of the ambient sounds are within his phonetic repertoire but require stabilization. A few others must be established. Given Sam's phonological profile, the most fitting model appears to be phonological processes (Grunwell, 1985; Ingram, 1981). This model directs us to the elimination or reduction of inefficient behaviors (processes) that interfere with the production of expected sounds. We will also refer to the Bloom and Lahey model (Lahey, 1988) for decisions regarding changes in language content, form, and use.

Data regarding Sam's levels of achievement within speech and language hierarchies will be drawn from the child's diagnostic evaluation (Appendix). The information reported here provides the basis for supporting the goals formulated at each phase of intervention planning.

PHONOLOGY. Sam demonstrates the ability to produce the articulatory gestures for almost all sounds in the language (with the exception of /ʧ/, /ʤ//, and /r/). He does, however, maintain a large number of processes that operate frequently and affect a wide range of speech sounds. By age 11 years and 11 months, all processes should have been eliminated. Sam, however, continues to use these processes between 15% and 100% in single-word contexts and between 24% and 100% in continuous speech contexts. Our long-term goals therefore reflect a consideration of the range and frequency of process application.

Dissolution needs to be initiated for those processes applied in 100% of obligatory contexts. Others that have begun dissolution need to be targeted for reduction. Other factors must also be considered in formulating realistic goals: those factors maintaining his disorder. Sam has demonstrated deficits in sensorimotor, cognitive, and psychosocial arenas. He exhibits low motor tone and lack of awareness of body-part location and movement; he is also easily frustrated with and unwilling to perform challenging tasks. Given this knowledge, it is possible to predict that Sam will not achieve consistent production of all sounds of his language. Given his motor difficulty and his low frustration tolerance, a decision was made to target the increase in correct production for those variable sound and syllable productions, structures *within* his repertoire, affected by a range of *substitution* and *deletion* processes. Those structures not yet established must also be targeted for dissolution. The first long-term goal reads:

1. Sam will decrease the application of all phonological processes in conversational contexts.

It would not be realistic to expect the elimination of this wide range of processes but instead improvement that would be guided by how well he is understood in conversational contexts. Sam's processes affect the production of individual segments (substitution processes) as well as a range of syllable structures in continuous speech, with variable rates of application. Syllables are affected by a range of processes from one of the earliest, final-consonant deletion to a later developing process, cluster reduction. Since the segmental and syllable-structure processes may be viewed within separate developmental (elimination) hierarchies, we will consider targeting these two different sets of processes as subordinate long-term goals: 1a and 1b.

   1a. Sam will decrease the application of substitution processes across all categories to the point of intelligibility.

   1b. Sam will decrease the application of syllable-structure processes across all categories to the point of intelligibility.

LANGUAGE CONTENT AND FORM. Sam's language structures are consistent with development in the later phases of the Bloom and Lahey model of content, form, and use (Bloom & Lahey, 1978; Lahey, 1988). In conversational contexts, he presents evidence of a moderate range of complex sentence content: volition-intention, additive, temporal, causal, specification, notice, communication, with a narrow range of connectives: *and*, *when*, and *how*.

Attempts at narratives consist of two- to three-utterance samples. His content knowledge appears to be ahead of its execution with form. In other words, it appears that Sam's attempts at longer narratives are thwarted by difficulties in being understood. Until his speech-sound production improves, it is difficult to determine how much of his problem with narrative is the organization of ideas or the difficulty in phonological production. Nevertheless, narrative production of causal chains has been selected as a goal because Sam is producing short narratives that demonstrate primarily additive and temporal sequences, and he appears to be aware of cause–effect relations (present in complex sentences). Given his language profile, a second long-term goal for Sam reads:

2. Sam will produce causal chain narratives in discourse contexts.

Related to and supportive of narratives are morpheme endings and complex sentences, two linguistic taxonomies also requiring attention; goals for these areas are viewed as subordinate long-term goals. These, as other long-term goals, may be guided by evidence-based developmental hierarchies specific to each area of language. The baseline data on Sam's production of grammatical morphemes suggest that early developmental morphemes are generally absent from his productions in conversational speech. These are copula, third-person singular, possessive, past irregular, and past regular. All of these morphemes are vulnerable to phonological processes of weak syllable deletion, final-consonant deletion, and cluster reduction—prominent in Sam's production pattern. Morpheme endings, therefore, will be targeted as a context for the reduction of final-consonant deletion, cluster reduction, and weak syllable deletion. Sam's diagnostic report also indicates that Sam is missing some complex sentence categories (e.g., epistemic and adversative) and presents with a very narrow range of connectives within each category. In consideration of these two deficient linguistic taxonomies, two long-term goals, related to and subordinate to Goal 2 were formulated.

Subordinate long-term goals read:

   2a. Sam will increase frequency and variety of multiverb content/form interactions (complex sentences) and their associated connectives.

   2b. Sam will produce context-appropriate morpheme endings.

Determining a Time Duration for Goal Achievement

In reviewing background information relevant to Sam's clinical history, we learn that Sam has received speech/language therapy since the age of three. Therapy has focused primarily on eliminating the processes of backing, stopping, and final-consonant deletion. For these and other processes, progress in prior therapy suggests that achievements are slow and regression is frequent. Until now, treatment of his phonological impairment has been provided by a speech/language pathologist working independently. She has not collaborated with his school speech/language pathologist or his occupational therapist. The school speech/language pathologist has focused primarily on syntactic errors and comprehension. Although a prognosis is still uncertain, collaboration of the occupational therapist and speech/language pathologist is expected to improve stability of performance. Based, however, on Sam's achievement history, it is not likely that we can expect the processes he now uses to be eliminated entirely. This projection is also made with reference to the factors believed to be maintaining Sam's speech-language problems.

Baseline data from assessment reports provide information about factors that may be maintaining Sam's speech/language disorder. Based on results achieved on WISC-R, Sam presents with much inter-intra subtest variability. Lowest scores were obtained on tasks involving the visualization of part–whole relationships and analyzing and synthesizing designs and matching symbols to numbers. These tasks involve attention to detail and differentiating similarities and differences between items. These difficulties also may be represented in attention to speech sounds, syllables, and syntactic elements. Therefore, cognitive factors may be depressing speech/language performance and impacting on estimated long-term goal duration.

The sensorimotor domain is perhaps the most problematic for Sam and probably the primary maintaining factor of his severe phonological impairment. From the time of his first interview at three years of age, Sam was described by his mother as having coordination difficulty. Now at the age of 11 years and 11 months, he is described by the occupational therapist as having a number of sensorimotor difficulties, including low muscle tone and incoordination and weakness in overall body movements (see Appendix). These sensorimotor symptoms are likely to affect movement, coordination, and sensation associated with the production of speech sounds. This maintaining factor is perhaps the most influential in determining the level of goal achievement and expected time frame for the achievement of targeted goals.

Psychosocial factors also may be maintaining Sam's speech/language problem. Based on standardized tests administered by the psychologist, Sam is described as "anxious," "sad," "vulnerable," and having "low self-esteem." A frequent response to a perceived challenge is, "I can't do it." This behavior also has been observed by the speech/language pathologist and occupational therapist. While Sam can occasionally be encouraged to complete a task, the clinician will often need to end testing or task production because of Sam's refusal to continue. Sam's psychosocial picture is further complicated by his tactile defensiveness (particularly around the mouth). This attitude poses a constraint on the clinician who needs to touch him in order to demonstrate a motor action or phonetic placement. As we can see, psychosocial factors are additional maintaining factors that need to be considered in projecting long-term goals and time frames.

It is difficult to make a projection of the time duration for the completion of the goals formulated. The difficulty in making a specific projection about time has to do with Sam's inconsistent and slow progress in prior treatment, his age, the extent of involvement of those factors maintaining his speech/language problem, and the potential effect of speech-sound improvement on other areas of language targeted (inflectional morphemes, complex sentences and narratives). These factors suggest that improvement will continue to be slow and variable; the current plan, however, includes treatment designed through collaboration of a speech/language pathologist and occupational therapist. We also know that Sam will be receiving speech/language intervention with a more consistent approach by one speech/language pathologist three times weekly. (He had been receiving therapy from two different clinicians.) Given this information, we project that Sam will achieve the long-term goals we have set within three years.

Given the results of baseline data in speech and language, potential maintaining factors for a child Sam's age, and the outcome of prior interventions, we are prepared to complete the long-term and subordinate long-term goal templates (Figures 9.1a; 9.1b).

Deriving the Long-Term Goal			
Decision	**Guiding Information**		
Areas of Speech/Language to be Targeted, Referent Taxonomy, and Current Level of Performance	**Area of Speech/Language**	**Referent Taxonomy**	**Current Performance**
	Phonology	**Phonological processes:** Stoel-Gammon & Dunn (1985), Grunwell (1985)	1. Wide range of phonological processes applied with high frequency: substitution and syllable structure
	Language	**Morphemes,** Brown (1972)	2. Numerous morpho-phonemic errors
			3. Complex sentences have narrow range of connectives
		Narrative: Bloom and Lahey (1988); Stein and Glen (1979)	4. Narratives typically 2 or 3 utterances; phonological impairment interfered with intelligibility
Projecting a Prognosis	**Maintaining Factors**	**Severity**	**Current Performance**
	Cognitive	Mild Mod. Sev.	On WISC-R, full scale IQ is 75, verbal 86, performance, 68
	Sensorimotor	Mild Mod. Sev.	Results on tasks of speech functions were below age expectancy; report of occupational therapist revealed low muscle tone, tactile defensiveness, rapid fatigue, incoordination and weakness, immature hand function
	Psychosocial	Mild Mod. Sev.	Psychological testing revealed perseverative responses, anxiety, sadness, vulnerability, and low self-esteem
	Caretaker Attendance	Frequently	Intermittently	Rarely
Time Frame	Time Allotted	Within 3 years	
Long-Term Goals	Sam will: 1. Decrease the application of all phonological processes in conversational speech 2. Produce causal chain narratives in conversational contexts		

FIGURE 9.1a: Sam's long-term goals

Deriving Subordinate Long-Term Goals: Speech			
Long Term Goal: 1. Sam will decrease the application of all phonological processes in conversational speech			
Decision	**Guiding Information**		
Areas of Speech/Language Intrinsic to the Long-Term Goal	Area of Speech/Language	Referent Taxonomy	Current Performance Level
	Phonology Substitution and syllable structure processes	Grunwell (1985) Stoel-Gammon and Dunn (1985)	Frequent use of a wide range of phonological processes
Subordinate Long-Term Goals	Sam will: 1a. decrease the application of substitution processes across all categories to the point of intelligibility 1b. decrease the application of syllable structure processes across all categories to the point of intelligibility		

Deriving Subordinate Long-Term Goals: Language			
Long Term Goal: 2. Sam will produce causal chain narratives in conversational contexts			
Decision	**Guiding Information**		
Areas of Speech/Language Intrinsic to the Long-Term Goals	Area of Speech/Language	Referent Taxonomy	Current Performance Level
	Language Complex sentences Developmental morphemes	Lahey (1988) Complex sentences Brown (1972) Developmental morphemes	Narrow range of content and connectives Variable production of morphemes, likely phonologically based
Subordinate Long-Term Goals	Sam will: 2a. increase frequency and variety of complex sentences and their associated connectives 2b. produce context-appropriate morpheme endings		

FIGURE 9.1b: Subordinate long-term goals for Sam

The Derivation of a Long-Term Procedural Approach

EVIDENCE-BASED APPROACHES TO TREATMENT. Goal planning reflects the model one uses to guide approaches to selecting phonological targets; thus, the clinician may be targeting either the elimination of a process or the acquisition of segments or syllable structures. Approaches to procedure planning may be less differentiating. Clinicians using contrasting models to guide goal planning may derive similar procedures for the facilitation of targets. Over the past seven plus decades, numerous procedures have been advanced to facilitate target achievement. Although these procedures have differed with reference to sounds addressed and materials or devices utilized, they may all be encompassed within two primary categories: motor and linguistic.

Motor-based treatment approaches focus primarily on perception and production of targets; these approaches are often viewed as traditional approaches (Bernthal, Bankson, & Flipson, 2017). Here the emphasis is on the perception/discrimination and placement and movement of articulators. Exercises generally follow a series of prescribed steps beginning with perceptual training, leading to the initial production of the sound, and to the eventual use of the sound in conversational contexts. Although motor practice is an essential integral part of this approach, it must be noted that this refers to practice of speech sounds, not nonspeech oral motor exercises (e.g., Lass & Panbacker, 2008; Lof, 2003).

Recent research reports studying the relevance of perceptual training along with target production have found an advantage for subjects given perceptual training as a precursor (e.g., Lousada, Jesus, Cepalas, Margaca, Simoes, Valente, Hall, & Joffe, 2013; Schiller, Rvachew, & Brosseau-Lapré, 2010). From one of the earliest text books in our field (i.e., Van Riper, 1939) until today, clinicians employ the traditional approach alone or in conjunction with the linguistic approach. See Bernthal, Bankson, and Flipson (2017) for a comprehensive description of the motor approach.

Linguistically based treatment approaches stress the importance of phoneme contrasts, application of phonological rules regarding where to use the targeted structure, and understanding that using this structure will make a difference in being understood. Within a linguistic focus, an additional consideration is for the initiation and spreading of the phonological change throughout the system. Two approaches frequently reported in the literature appear to define this area of treatment: minimal pairs and cycles. The minimal-pair approach teaches clients to differentiate two words (or word-like pairs) based on a minimal difference of one phoneme, for example, /ti/ki/ (difference between consonants) or /bɪg/bæg/ (difference between vowels). The minimal-pair approach is designed to highlight two contrasting sounds, differing by one or more features, as responsible for differences in word meanings. Initially introduced by Weiner (1981), it has been modified to include multiple oppositions, more than two contrasting sounds (e.g., Williams, 2000) and maximal feature differences between sounds (e.g., Gierut, 1991).

The cycles approach, introduced by Hodson and Paden (1991), focuses on the change in the phonological system by beginning dissolution of processes operating between 60% and 100% in obligatory contexts. Operating on the premise that phonological change is gradual, a number of processes are targeted during a short-term period with each targeted for a few sessions and then recycled/revisited if necessary. Complete dissolution is not the goal of treatment. The beginning of dissolution is expected to result in continued improvement by the client. This approach, which includes perception and production practice, is directed toward overall changes in the phonological system that should result in improved intelligibility.

IDENTIFYING MAINTAINING FACTORS THAT NEED TO BE ADDRESSED. In our earlier consideration of Sam's maintaining factors, we concluded that Sam's production patterns were primarily maintained by his sensorimotor difficulty. Severely impaired articulation appears to be depressing the production of morphemes, complex sentences, and narratives. It is expected that procedures designed to facilitate the acquisition of speech sounds also will facilitate improvement in the other language areas. His baseline data further suggest that cognitive and psychosocial factors may play a role in the maintenance of impaired speech/language performance in all areas.

At this point, it is possible to begin to formulate the first part of the procedural approach in which we specify the maintaining factors that will need to be addressed in the course of intervention and the related communication areas targeted in the long-term goal statement: All long-term goals will be facilitated by modifying sensorimotor, cognitive, and psychosocial maintaining factors.

IDENTIFYING LEARNING PREMISES THAT WILL GUIDE OUR PROCEDURAL APPROACH. In identifying the premises that apply to the elimination of phonological processes and acquisition of new linguistic structures, we find that the most appropriate derive from motor learning theory, social cognitive theory, and Piagetian cognitive theory. With reference to social cognitive theory, learning is facilitated by

- efforts to match models presented by the clinician

- noticing similarities and distinctions between actions and events mediated by adults.

From a constructivist theory perspective, learning is facilitated by

- efforts to successfully convey meaning and overcome miscommunication

- reflection upon personal behavior.

From a motor theory perspective, learning is facilitated by

- sensory stimulation (i.e., sensory feedback) from movement involved in the performance of articulatory gestures.

Sam, as an almost-12-year-old, enjoys engaging in social interactions. The impact of improved intelligibility, which was targeted in the long-term goal statements, will be social in nature. Our focus on producing narratives as a long-term goal is also social in nature. It is for these reasons that we will employ a social reward system to facilitate the achievement of all goals. The impact of maintaining factors and learning theories is shown in Figure 9.2, the template for long-term procedures.

Planning the Procedural Approach		
Decision	**Guiding Information**	
Ultimate Behaviors to Be Acquired	**Long-Term Goal and Corresponding Subordinate Long-Term Goal(s)**	**Long-Term Goals** 1. Decrease the application of all phonological processes in conversational speech 2. Produce causal chain narratives in conversational speech **Subordinate Long-Term Goal(s):** 1a. decrease the application of substitution processes across all categories to the point of intelligibility 1b. decrease the application of syllable structure processes across all categories to the point of intelligibility 2a. increase frequency and variety of complex sentences and their associated connectives 2b. produce context-appropriate morpheme endings
Approaches to Intervention	**Types of Evidence**	**Reference**
	Meta-Analysis	Lass & Panbacker (2008)
	Experimental	Klein et al (2013) case study Schiller, Rvachew, & Brosseau-Lapré (2010); Lousada, Jesus, Cepales, Margaca, Simoes, Valente Hall & Joffe (2013)
	Clinical Practice	Hammer (2014) Webinar: 'r' intervention
	Theory	
Premises about Language Learning or Rehabilitation from Clinical Research Relevant to Achieving Long-Term Goals	**Theory**	**Premises: Language is facilitated by:**
	Constructivism	Efforts to successfully convey meaning and overcome miscommunication; reflection upon personal behavior
	Social Cognitive	Efforts to match models presented by the clinician; noticing similarities and distinctions among actions and events mediated by adults
	Motor	Sensory stimulation (i.e., sensory feedback) from movement involved in the performance of articulatory gestures
Maintaining Factors that Need to Be Addressed	**Maintaining Factors**	**Current Performance**
	Cognitive	Provide perceptual support when possible
	Sensorimotor	Modify motor and perceptual processes
	Psychosocial	Avoid excessive challenge

FIGURE 9.2: Long-term procedural approach

The Derivation of Short-Term Goals

The first step in the derivation of short-term goals involves making a decision about which long-term goals to address during the first contracted time period (in this case a semester). We can choose to work only on phonological goals, only language goals, or both. Since Sam is at the later phases of childhood and has deficiencies in both areas, it would be more expedient to consider both areas and how they may interact in treatment. We also need to reference developmental hierarchies in each area to guide our decisions. We formulated two long-term goals and four long-term subordinate goals.

1. Sam will decrease the application of all processes in conversational contexts.

    1a. Sam will decrease the application of substitution processes across all categories to the point of intelligibility by people unaware of his speech pattern.

    1b. Sam will decrease the application of syllable-structure processes across all categories to the point of intelligibility.

2. Sam will produce causal chain narratives.

    2a. Sam will increase frequency and variety of multiverb content/form interactions and their associated connectives.

    2b Sam will produce context-appropriate morpheme endings.

Short-term goals will be derived from the developmental taxonomies that guided the establishment of long-term goals.

Short-Term Goals 1 to 3 derive from LTGs 1a and 1b. Taxonomies by Grunwell (1985), Hodson and Paden (1991), Ingram (1981), and Stoel-Gammon and Dunn (1985) contributed to the derivation of the first long-term goal and the two subordinate goals.

We will look to the expected dissolution of substitution and syllable-structure phonological processes to identify intermediate short-term behavioral targets. Sam is currently using a wide range of phonological processes with variable rates in both single-word productions and conversational contexts. These processes affect early developing as well as later developing sounds. He is also reducing three-syllable words in single-word productions 25% of the time and 100% of attempts in conversational contexts. With reference to the taxonomies cited previously, we propose the following set of short-term goals in the area of phonology:

SHORT-TERM GOAL 1. *Sam will reduce the processes of fronting and backing.*

These substitution processes affect some of the earliest emerging sounds, alveolar and velar stops. Although these processes are applied moderately in single-word and continuous speech, their maintenance suggests that Sam is not consistently aware of his tongue position. Continued attention to differentiating these early developing sounds is essential for bringing attention to tongue position as well as increasing intelligibility.

Short-Term Goal 2. *Sam will reduce the process of weak syllable deletion affecting three-syllable words with a variety of stress patterns in conversational contexts.*

This is an early syllable process, and Sam's deletion of syllables in words of three or more syllables severely impacts his intelligibility, which ultimately compromises his expression of complex sentences and narratives.

Short-Term Goal 3. *Sam will produce /ɝ/ in single words.*

This short-term goal begins to address sounds out of the repertoire. From a developmental perspective /r/ would be the first sound to target. Although /r/, according to most developmental schedules, is designated to be achieved by six years of age, this acquisition references only the consonantal /r/; vocalic /r/: /ɝ/, which is the basis of consonantal /r/ generally occurs earlier (Hammer, 2014; Hodson & Paden, 1991; Klein et al., 2013).

Short-Term Goal 4. *Sam will produce final /s/, /z/ and derivative clusters coding plural, copula, possessive, and third-person singular.* This last goal selected for the first short-term period addresses Long-term Goal 2b. *Sam will produce context-appropriate morpheme endings.* This language goal was selected for the first short-term period because it intersects both phonology and language deficits. Sam produces fricatives with variable rates of accuracy and deletes or distorts most morphemes that are marked by fricative singletons or clusters (see process application in the diagnostic report). Brown's (1973) taxonomy of developmental morphemes was referenced in planning the fourth long-term goal: This taxonomy outlines a developmental progression of morpheme achievements, which indicates that plural, copula, and possessive are early occurring morphemes, with third-person-singular somewhat later. These were considered together, however, because variable production of each may be due to the same underlying challenge: fricative production.

Short-term Procedural Approach

Operationalizing Learning Premises

Four premises about learning were cited in the long-term procedural approach: three address content/form/use interactions and phonology, and one addresses phonology. With reference to language and phonology, the first two premises were derived from social cognitive theory: *Learning is facilitated by efforts to match models presented by the clinician and noticing similarities and distinctions among actions and events mediated by adults.* These premises suggest that elicitation of linguistic structures or sounds involve (a) modeling targeted segments in words or sentences and (b) presenting comparisons between target and error sounds.

The third learning premise was derived from constructivist theory: *Learning is facilitated by efforts to successfully convey meaning and overcome miscommunication.* Operationalizing this premise involves creating situations in which Sam is faced with communicative breakdown due to mispronunciation or insufficient information.

The fourth premise is derived from motor theory: *Learning is facilitated by sensory stimulation (i.e., sensory feedback) from movement involved in the performance of articulatory gestures.* This premise is primarily directed to phonological learning. It may, however, also apply to the intersection of phonology and morphology when phoneme targets are produced in the context of morpheme endings. Following this premise, the clinician will help Sam reflect on how phonetic gestures, sound, feel, and look. It has been shown that practicing articulatory gestures in an effort to match target vocabulary modeled by another is the most effective approach to establishing a phonological system (Shriberg & Kwiatkowski, 1982).

THE INFLUENCE OF MAINTAINING FACTORS. The procedural approach is also operationalized with reference to factors related to speech and language that may be maintaining the presenting problems. As determined in establishing the procedural approach, Sam presents with three maintaining factors: sensorimotor, cognitive, and sensorimotor. He exhibits low motor tone and lack of awareness of body-part location and movement; he is also easily frustrated with and unwilling to perform challenging tasks. One measure to address the sensorimotor deficits will be engagement of an occupational therapist to participate in planning. This is essential for addressing Sam's general body orientation in addition to oral awareness.

Cognitive and psychosocial deficits will be considered in weighing the task demands accompanying the production of specific sounds or linguistic structures. Sam is reluctant to perform any task he views as too challenging. Although he must be encouraged to attempt tasks outside his comfort zone, this must be done with caution in order to ensure necessary persistence. Session goals will be planned to consider linguistic and nonlinguistic demands on his performance and provide sufficient experiences of success. See Figures 9.3 and 9.4 for completed templates for short-term goals and short-term procedures, respectively.

Deriving Short-Term Goals			
Decision	**Guiding information and Client-Specific details**		
Long-Term Goal and Corresponding Subordinate Long-Term Goals and Taxonomies Addressed	**Long-Term Goal and/or Subordinate Long-Term Goal(s)**	**Taxonomy**	**Current Performance Level**
	1. Sam will decrease the application of all phonological processes in conversational speech. 1a. decrease substitution processes across all categories to the point of intelligibility. 1b. decrease the application of syllable structure processes across all categories to the point of intelligibility.	Phonological processes (Grunwell, 1985; Hodson & Paden, 1991; Stoel-Gammon & Dunn, 1985)	A wide range of substitution and syllable structure processes applied with high frequency
	2. Sam will produce causal chain narratives in discourse contexts.	Narrative Development (Lahey, 1988)	Narratives reduced in length and scope with missing connectives and absence of grammatical morphemes
	2a. increase frequency and variety of multiverb sentences and their associated connectives.	Complex sentences (Lahey, 1988)	Missing content categories and connectives in complex sentences
	2b. produce context-appropriate morpheme endings.	Developmental morphemes (Brown, 1973)	Reduced range of final-word marked morphemes, likely related to articulatory difficulty

FIGURE 9.3: Sam's short-term goals

Time Frame	Time Allotted: 6mos.
Short-Term Goals and Rationales	**Long-Term Goal Addressed:** Sam will decrease the application of all processes in conversational speech
	Short-Term Goal(s): See subordinate long-term goals: **Rationale with reference to: development/complexity/difficulty**
	Subordinate long-term goal addressed: Decrease substitution processes across all categories to the point of intelligibility
	Short-Term Goal 1: Reduce the processes of fronting and backing **Rationale with reference to: development/complexity/difficulty** Although these processes are applied moderately in single-word and continuous speech, their maintenance suggests that Sam is not consistently aware of his tongue position. Continued attention to differentiating these early developing sounds is essential for bringing attention to tongue position.
	Subordinate Long-term goal addressed: Decrease the application of syllable structure processes across all categories to the point of intelligibility
	Short-term goal 2: Reduce the process of weak syllable deletion affecting three-syllable words with a variety of stress patterns in conversational contexts **Rationale with reference to: development/complexity/difficulty** This is an early syllable process, and Sam's deletion of syllables in words of three or more syllables severely impacts his intelligibility, which ultimately compromises his expression of complex sentences and narratives.
	Subordinate long-term goal addressed: Decrease substitution processes across all categories to the point of intelligibility.
	Short-term goal 3: Produce /ɝ/ in single words **Rationale with reference to: development/complexity/difficulty** Vocalic /r/: /ɝ/, is the basis of consonantal /r/, therefore, occurs earlier
	Long-term goal addressed: Sam will produce causal chain narratives in discourse contexts
	Subordinate long-term goals addressed: produce context-appropriate morpheme endings
	Short-term goal 4: Produce final /s/, /z/ and derivative clusters coding plural, copula, third person singular and possessive **Rationale with reference to: development/complexity/difficulty Long-term** This goal intersects both phonology and language deficits. Sam produces fricatives with variable rates of accuracy and deletes or distorts most morphemes that are marked by fricative singletons or clusters

FIGURE 9.3 CONTINUED: Sam's short-term goals

Operationalizing the Procedural Approach	
Decision	**Guiding Information and Client-Specific Details**
Short-Term Goals to Be Addressed	Sam will: 1. Reduce the processes of fronting and backing 2. Reduce the process of weak syllable deletion affecting three-syllable words with a variety of stress patterns in conversational contexts 3. Produce /ɝ/ in single words 4. Produce final /s/, /z/ and derivative clusters coding copula, third person singular and possessive
Derive Implications for Procedure Planning from: **Theory-based Premises**	1. **Premise**: Learning is facilitated by efforts to successfully convey meaning and overcome miscommunication; reflection upon personal behavior. **Implications**: Clinician will ask Sam to reflect on tongue position of targeted sounds. 2. **Premise**: Learning is facilitated by sensory stimulation (i.e., sensory feedback) from movement involved in the performance of articulatory gestures. **Implications**: Clinician will ask Sam to produce speech sounds and morpheme endings. 3. **Premise**: Learning is facilitated by efforts to match models presented by the clinician. **Implications**: Clinician will ask Sam to produce structures after a model 4. **Premise:** Learning is facilitated by noticing similarities and distinctions among actions and events mediated by adults. **Implications**: Clinician will ask Sam to differentiate speech-sounds produced by self or another.

Derive Implications for Procedure Planning from:
 	
Maintaining Factors
	Maintaining Factors
	Cognitive:
	    Implication: Tasks will consider familiarity of perceptual support
	    of materials
	Psychosocial:
	    Implication: Level of task challenge will be considered
	Sensorimotor:
	    Implication: Tasks will address perceptual and motor limitations

FIGURE 9.4: Operationalized procedural approach for Sam

Session Planning

Session planning involves creating a series of achievements for Sam on route to a short-term goal. These steps are described by (a) what Sam is expected to do, (b) the materials he will encounter, and (c) the clinician's actions. The planning process will be guided by decisions that have already been made at the long- and short-term planning phases, with one exception: *performance demands*. As described in Chapter 7, it is necessary to identify the possible demands on the client's performance imposed by the choice of target and or the context (linguistic and/or nonlinguistic) in which the target is embedded.

Planning Session Goals

Planning with reference to Short-Term Goal 1: *Sam will reduce the processes of fronting and backing.* At this time, Sam's intelligibility interferes with his production of a sequence of ideas (i.e., narratives). His unintelligibility may be attributed to the use of a large number of processes, the frequent use of processes, the maintenance of unusual processes (i.e., backing), and very early processes (e.g., assimilation). What also adds to his unintelligibility is the use of process combinations (i.e., deaffrication and backing, /jar/ = [ga]). The frequency of process application increases in conversational speech. Because Sam's unintelligibility may be a deterrent to the production of more complex linguistic structures, we decide to target phonological goals among the first.

Fronting and backing, which are applied less frequently than the others, continue to be evident after many years of treatment. Fronting should be eliminated by age three, and backing is an unusual process, infrequently used by typically developing children. Due to the reversibility of the processes (backing or fronting, with no identifiable contextual determiners) and the long duration of operation, sensorimotor involvement is postulated. This maintaining factor must be considered in our goal expectations. Thus, the expectation is to reduce the operation of the process still further without necessarily being able to eliminate it.

Given that Sam produces alveolar and velar stops with great variability, it is assumed that Sam may require further attention to auditory and tactile discrimination of the sounds. For a child his age, it would be appropriate to begin treatment with a focus on differentiating these sounds based on interpersonal discrimination tasks and tasks of tactile awareness. Recent research has demonstrated a production advantage in children exposed to tasks of perceptual awareness (e.g., Lousada, Jesus, Cepalas, Margaca, Simoes, Valente, Hall, & Joffe, 2013; Rvachew, 1994; Rvachew, Nowak, & Cloutier, 2004; Schiller, Rvachew, & Brosseau-Lapré, 2010). Based on Sam's documented maintaining factors and research results, the first two session goals formulated for Sam focus on perceptual changes: *1. Sam will match the clinician's production of the first consonant in monosyllable words to a printed representation of the sounds /t, d, k, g/ with 80% accuracy. 2. Sam will indicate the part of the tongue involved with the production of monosyllabic words with the sounds /t,d,k,g/ by saying "front" or "back" with 80% accuracy.*

PERFORMANCE DEMANDS. Considering Sam's reluctance to perform tasks he perceives to be too challenging, a decision was made to keep performance demands low. The first session goal considers response mode; it makes minimal demand on vocal (oral) production. It only requires a perceptual judgment. Goal 2 does not only require a percentage of production accuracy but also a perceptual judgment of position. Goal 1 is viewed as precursory to Goal 2 with reference to the cognitive demand imposed. The identification and discrimination (existence) of an entity (the "t" or the "k") must be accomplished before appreciating any specific feature of the entity (attribution) and the determination of tongue position (see Piaget, 1954, regarding the development of object knowledge). Finally, number of syllables must be a consideration in the choice of stimuli, since a monosyllabic word would present less of a processing challenge than a greater number of syllables.

Planning with reference to Short-Term Goal 2: *Sam will reduce the process of weak syllable deletion affecting three-syllable words with a variety of stress patterns in conversational contexts.* In reviewing Sam's diagnostic report (Appendix), we observe that he is reducing three-syllable words in single-word productions 25% of the time and 100% of attempts in conversational contexts. Syllable reduction of three-syllable words should be eliminated by three+ years of age (e.g., Stoel-Gammon & Dunn, 1985). Given that this is an early process and one that seriously impacts intelligibility, a third session goal was formulated to address syllable production. *Sam will produce three-syllable familiar words with a 132 (primary, low, secondary stress) contour (elephant, telephone, microphone, telescope, calendar, dinosaur, etc.) after the clinician's model in 8/10 attempts.* Performance demands considered are the following:

1. Number of syllables: three syllables after two syllables. Two-syllable words are reduced less frequently (see diagnostic report).

2. Stress placement: First and final syllable stress are less vulnerable to deletion than unstressed syllables in those positions (e.g., Bernhardt & Stemberger, 2000; Klein, 1981a, b).

3. Familiarity of material: Common words he uses frequently or has demonstrated familiarity with will be chosen to avoid the perception of a challenge.

4. Perceptual support: after a model before spontaneous production (e.g., Lahey, 1988).

PLANNING WITH REFERENCE TO SHORT-TERM GOAL 3. *Sam will produce /ɝ/ in single words.* /ɝ/ is one of the most challenging sounds to the child developing phonology and certainly a challenge to an individual with a phonological disorder (e.g., Klein et al., 2013). The challenge may even be exacerbated in an individual like Sam who is already beyond the expected age for the development of this sound and one who is reluctant to perform under a perception of difficulty. Given this situation, we must proceed slowly and with minimal expectation. An approach to /ɝ/ will begin with auditory discrimination; the fourth session goal reads, *Sam will rate the production accuracy of the clinician's /ɝ/ in monosyllabic words on a three-point scale, with 80% accuracy*. Performance demands considered are the following:

1. Number of syllables: one before two syllables

2. Response mode: reception less demanding than expression

3. Cognitive support: use of a scale to a support judgment on a continuum (Klein, Grigos, Davidson, & McAlister-Byun, 2012).

Planning with reference to Short-Term Goal 4: *Sam will produce final /s/, /z/, and derivative clusters coding plural, copula, possessive, and third-person singular.* Children have begun to produce all of Brown's developmental morphemes by three years of age and complete the hierarchy by approximately by five years of age (Miller, 1981). In children with deficiencies in syntax and phonology, the phonological problem will impact the production of sounds that signal morphological endings. Sam's baseline data reveal that two of the most frequent processes operating during the production of conversational speech are final-consonant deletion and cluster reduction. These two processes clearly impact the production of morphological endings, which are often missing in Sam's expressive language. In order to produce morpheme endings (i.e., s, z, and consonant +s), Sam must be able to produce final-consonant singletons and clusters. Because of the interaction of these two levels of grammar it appears most natural to target them together. Our fifth and last session goal reads: *Sam will produce /z/ and C+S or C+Z to mark plural in words, representing pictures of single or multiple objects, after clinician's model in 80% of instances.*

According to Brown (1973), plural is one of the earliest morphemes signaled by a change in word ending. This morpheme is a useful context for focusing on final fricatives and early developing clusters. Plural may be coded by either singleton final /z/ (bees, shoes) or consonant clusters (hats, books, dads, eggs). With variable production of /s/, /z/ and a high percentage of cluster reduction, a goal targeting the interface of syntax and phonology is expected to be appropriate for Sam, whose chronological age is beyond expected limits in both domains. It has also been shown that children tend to produce final consonants more readily in morphological endings than in noninflected contexts (Paul & Shriberg, 1982). Recognizing the importance of reducing the initial challenge, this early goal will be achieved with the presentation of models.

Performance demands considered for facilitating Short-Term Goal 4 are as follows:

1. Developmental level: Plural is among the earliest of Brown's morphemes (Brown, 1973).

2. Number of syllables: monosyllable before bisyllabic words (Aichert & Zeigler, 2013).

3. Number of cluster segments: Two segments before three segments follow developmental expectations (e.g., Grunwell, 1985).

4. Perceptual support: following a model before spontaneous (e.g., Bernthal et al., 2017).

Session Procedures

As noted earlier, the procedural aspect at the session phase is guided by our selection of applicable theoretical premises and knowledge of maintaining factors. The five session goals formulated all have a phonological focus. For that reason, we can identify the components of the procedural approach that will be suitable across all five goals, the number of goals believed to be appropriate for Sam.

MAINTAINING FACTORS. Knowledge of maintaining factors has influenced a decision regarding the number of goals targeted at the session phase. In making decisions about how many goals to target, we considered language-related systems such as cognitive, psychosocial, and sensorimotor. Although Sam's cognitive level is still questionable (on the basis of psychologist's report), he did receive "average" scores in information, similarities, and comprehension, which are language-based areas. Average cognitive performance is a positive prognosticator for the ability to handle more than one goal at a time. In addition, the psychologist's report indicated that it is often possible to encourage Sam to persevere when he feels he cannot do something. Although the baseline data indicate that Sam has many sensorimotor problems, the recent initiation of occupational therapy is a positive indicator for the management of the goals set for Sam. In addition to the work of the occupational therapist, Sam must be directed to areas of oral articulation. Each of the five session goals makes demand on Sam to either recognize sounds produced by another or by himself. In Goals 3 and 5 he is encouraged to produce variable structures or sounds outside his repertoire.

Sam's cognitive and psychosocial deficiencies are considered by the level of demand of the tasks. For each goal, targets are chosen with reference to degree of cognitive complexity and perceived challenge (see performance demands). Sensorimotor factors are also considered with reference to the motor demands of the tasks. As demonstrated here, all early goals make little motor demands; they initially involve perception tasks. When a motor target is addressed it is accompanied by perceptual support. The presence of a model is often recommended as a crucial support in initial learning (Bloom & Lahey, 1978; Lahey, 1988).

THEORETICAL PREMISES. Operational premises were delineated in the preceding explication of the short-term-phase procedural approach. Now these premises apply to the procedural aspect of the session goals.

Learning is facilitated by

1. *efforts to match models presented by the clinician.* This premise will be incorporated in procedures for each goal. Models will be provided for each response that Sam is required to make even if the response is one of matching or recognition. The clearest application of the premise appears for Session Goals 3 and 5, for which a motor response is required and a model provided before each response.

2. *noticing similarities and distinctions among actions and events mediated by adults.* This premise is foundational for Goals 1, 2, and 4. For each of these tasks, Sam must make perceptual distinctions: among speech sounds, between tongue positions, and among ratings of accuracy.

3. *efforts to successfully convey meaning and overcome miscommunication.* This premise underlies the task in Session Goal 5, which is designed to elicit responses representing single or multiple objects. Sam will receive feedback on his accuracy by being shown the comparisons between visual representations of the singular and plural objects.

4. *sensory stimulation (i.e., sensory feedback) from movement involved in the performance of articulatory gestures.* Session Goals 3 and 5 are the only goals requiring oral articulation. Here the feedback from movement is believed to enhance both articulatory feedback for the development of a motor representation and semantic feedback required for the maintenance of word meaning and morphophonemic word endings. Being asked to produce the phonemes and phoneme combinations will provide practice for the development of motor and auditory representations.

See Figure 9.5 for examples of session goal development. Samples include early and later session goals for short-terms goals 1 and 2.

Deriving Session Goals and Procedures	
Decision	**Guiding Information and Client-Specific Details**
Long-Term Goal and Related Subordinate Goals	**Long-Term Goals:** **1. Sam will decrease the application of all phonological processes in conversational speech** **2. Sam will produce causal chain narratives in discourse contexts** **Subordinate Goals:** 1a. decrease the substitution processes across all categories to the point of intelligibility 1b. decrease the application of syllable structure processes across all categories to the point of intelligibility 2a. increase frequency and variety of multiverb sentences and their associated connectives 2b. produce context-appropriate morpheme endings.
For Each Short-Term Goal, Consider Implications of:	**Short-Term Goals:** Sam will: 1. Reduce the processes of fronting and backing 2. Reduce the process of weak syllable deletion affecting three-syllable words with a variety of stress patterns in conversational contexts. 3. Produce / ɝ/ in single words. 4. Produce final /s/, /z/ and derivative clusters coding copula, third person singular and possessive. **Taxonomy:** 1. Substitution processes 2. Syllable structure processes 3. Development of /r/ 4. Brown's morphemes
Learning and Rehabilitation Premises	<table><tr><td>**Learning Theories**</td><td>**Implications Drawn (in the operationalized approach)**</td></tr><tr><td>**Constructivism**</td><td>Clinician will ask Sam to reflect on tongue position of targeted sounds</td></tr><tr><td>**Social Cognitive**</td><td>Clinician will ask Sam to produce speech sounds, morpheme endings</td></tr><tr><td>**Relationship-based pragmatic**</td><td>Clinician will ask Sam to produce structures after a model</td></tr><tr><td>**Motor Learning**</td><td>Clinicians will ask Sam to differentiate speech-sounds produced by self or another</td></tr></table>

FIGURE 9.5: Session goals for Sam

Maintaining Factors	Maintaining Factors	Implications Drawn (in the operationalized approach)
	Cognitive	Clinician will consider familiarity and conceptual complexity of materials
	Sensorimotor	Tasks will address perceptual and motor limitations
	Psychosocial	Level of task challenge will be considered

Short-term goal 1: Early Session Goal:

Sam will *match* the clinician's production of the first consonant (non-linguistic context) to a *printed representation* of the sounds */t,d,k,g/* and (linguistic context) in *monosyllable words* (achievement criteria) with 80% accuracy.

Performance Demands Controlled	Performance Variable Controlled	How the Variable is Controlled	Aspect of Session Goal Affected
	Developmental level	Early sounds and variably produced	target
	Response mode	Perceptual judgment; discrimination before production of target	target
	Perceptual support	Presentation of an auditory or visual model before no model	non-linguistic context
	Cognitive demand	Identification before discrimination	non-linguistic context
	Syllable number	Monosyllabic before bisyllabic	linguistic context

Later Session Goal: Sam will *indicate* the part of the tongue ("front" or "back") involved with the clinician's production given (non-linguistic context) <u>none</u> and (linguistic context) of *monosyllabic words with the sounds /t,d,k,g/* (achievement criteria) with 80% accuracy.

FIGURE 9.5 CONTINUED: Session goals for Sam

Performance Demands Controlled	Performance Variable Controlled	How the Variable is Controlled	Aspect of Session Goal Affected
	Response mode	Articulation judgment before production	target
	Perceptual support	Presentation of an auditory model before no model	linguistic context
	Syllable number	Monosyllabic before bisyllabic	linguistic context
	Cognitive demand	Discrimination after Identification	non-linguistic context

Short-term goal 2: Early session goal

Sam will *produce three-syllable familiar words* given (non-linguistic context) none and (linguistic context) with a *132 (primary, low, secondary) stress contour* (elephant, telephone, microphone, telescope, calendar, dinosaur, etc.) after the *clinician's model* (achievement criterion) in 8/10 attempts.

Performance Demands Controlled	Performance Variable Controlled	How the Variable is Controlled	Aspect of Session Goal Affected
	Response mode	Production after discrimination	target
	Perceptual support	Presentation of an auditory model before no models	linguistic context
	Syllable number	3-syllables after 2-syllable stress contours	target
	Stress contour	132 stress contour less vulnerable than one with unstressed first syllable	target
	Familiarity of materials	Familiar and picturable before unfamiliar words	target

FIGURE 9.5 CONTINUED: Session goals for Sam

Later Session Goal

Sam will *produce three-syllable familiar words* given (non-linguistic context) none and (linguistic context) with a *313 (low, primary, low) stress contour* (banana; familiar, amazing, annoying, discover, etc.) after the *clinician's model* (achievement criterion) in 8/10 attempts.

Performance Demands Controlled	Performance Variable Controlled	How the Variable is Controlled	Aspect of Session Goal Affected
	Response mode	Production after discrimination	target
	Perceptual support	Presentation of an auditory model before no models	Linguistic context
	Stress contour	313-more challenging than 132 due to initial and final unstressed syllables	target
	Familiarity of materials	Some unpicturable words after familiar picturable words	target

FIGURE 9.5 CONTINUED: Session goals for Sam

SUMMARY

This chapter has presented an approach to phonological intervention with a child who has a severe speech-sound disorder accompanied by a moderate language impairment. The treatment approach followed the basic tenets of intervention planning outlined in the first section of this book. As with any disorder of speech or language the clinician must consider a number of interrelated factors in formulating goals and procedures at three phases of intervention planning. These factors include (a) the nature of the problem, (b) circumstances maintaining the problem, (c) theories of learning, and (d) variables affecting an increased/decreased demand on performance. How these factors contribute in designing an intervention plan for Sam demonstrates how clinicians may perform systematic and accountable treatment.

REFERENCES

Aichert, I. & Zeigler, W. (2013). Segments and syllables in treatment of apraxia of speech: An investigation of learning and transfer effects. *Aphasiology, 27*, 1180–1199.

Bauman-Waengler, J. (2016). *Articulation and phonology in speech sound disorders* (5th Ed.). New York: Pearson

Bernhardt, B., & Stoel-Gammon, C. (1994). Non-linear phonology: Introduction & clinical application. *Journal of Speech and Hearing Research, 37,* 123–143.

Bernhardt, B. & Stemberger, J. (2000). *Nonlinear phonology for clinical application.* Austin, Tx: Pro-ed.

Bernthal, J., & Bankson, N. (1981). *Articulation disorders.* Englewood Cliffs, N.J. : Prentice-Hall

Bernthal, J. & Bankson, N. (1987). *Articulation and phonological disorders* (2nd Ed.). Englewood Cliffs, NJ: Prentice-Hall.

Bernthal, N., Bankson., & Flipson, Jr. P. (2008). *Articulation and phonological disorders. Speech sound disorders in children.* (6th Ed.). New York: Pearson

Bernthal, N., Bankson, N., & Flipson, Jr. P. (2017). *Articulation and phonological disorders: speech-sound disorders in children* (8th Ed.). New York: Pearson

Bloom, L. & Lahey, M. (1978). *Language development and language disorders.* New York: Wiley

Broomfield, J. & Dodd, B. (2004). Children with speech and language disability: caseload characteristics. *International Journal of Communication Disorders, 3,* 303-324.

Brown. R. (1973). *A first language, the early stages.* Cambridge, MA: Harvard University Press.

Gierut, J. (1998). Treatment efficacy: functional phonological disorders in children. *Journal of Speech and Hearing Research, 41,* s85–s100.

Grunwell, P. (1985). Phonological assessment of child speech (PACS). San Diego, CA: College Hill Press.

Hammer, D. (2014, February 5). Those Darn R's! Strategies for Remediation for Persistent R Distortions in Childhood Apraxia of Speech. *Casana live webinar.* Retrieved from http://www.apraxia-kids.org/upcoming-webinar-those-darn-rs-strategies-for-remediation-

Hodson, B., & Paden, E. (1991). *Targeting intelligible speech.* San Diego, CA.: CollegeHillPress.

Ingram, D. (1974). Phonological rules in young children. *Journal of Child Language, 1,* 49–64.

Ingram, D. (1981). *Procedures for the phonological analysis of children's language.* Baltimore, Md.: University Park Press

Klein, H. (1981). Productive strategies for the pronunciation of early polysyllabic lexical items. *Journal of Speech and Hearing Research, 24,* 389405.

Klein, H. Moses, & Jean-Baptiste, R.. (2010). Influence of context on the production of complex sentences by typically developing children. *Language, Speech, and Hearing Services in Schools, 41,* 289–302.

Klein, H.B., Grigos, M.I; McAllister Byun, T; Davidson, L. (2012). The relationship between inexperienced listeners' perceptions and acoustic correlates of children's /r/ productions. *Clinical Linguistics and Phonetics. Vol. 26,* No. 7: 628–645.

Klein, H.B., McAllister Byun, T., Davidson, L., & Grigos, M. I. (2013). A multidimensional investigation of children's /r/ productions: perceptual, ultrasound, and acoustic measures. American Journal of speech Language Pathology, 22, 540–553.

Lahey, M. (1988). *Language disorders and language development.* Needham Heights, MA: Allyn & Bacon.

Lass, N. J., & Pannbacker, M. (2008). The application of evidence-based practice to non-speech oral motor treatments. *Language, Speech, and Hearing Services in Schools, 39,* 408–421.

Lof, G.L. (2003). Oral motor exercises and treatment outcomes. *Perspectives on language Learning and education, 10,* 7–11.

Lousada, M., Jesus, L.M., Capelas, S., Margaça, C., Simões, D., Valente, A., Hall, A., & Joffe, V.L. (2013). Phonological and articulation treatment approaches in Portuguese children with speech and language impairments: a randomized controlled intervention study. *International Journal of Language Communication disorders48,* 172–187.

Miller, J. (Ed.) (1981). *Assessing language production in children: Experimental procedures*. Baltimore: University Park Press.

Paul, R & Shriberg, L.D. (1982). Associations between Phonology and Syntax in Speech-Delayed Children. *Journal of* Speech, Language, and Hearing Research, *25*, 536–547.

Piaget, J. (1954). *The construction of reality in the child*. New York: Basic Books

Rvachew, S. (1994). Speech perception training can facilitate sound production learning. *Journal of Speech and Hearing Research, 37*, 347–352.

Rvachew, S., Nowak, M., Cloutier, G. (2004). Effect of phonemic perception training on the speech production and phonological awareness skills of children with expressive phonological delay. *American Journal of Speech-Language Pathology, 13*, 250–263.

Schiller, D., Rvachew, S., & Brosseau-Lapré, F. (2010). Importance of the Auditory Perceptual Target to the Achievement of Speech Production Accuracy. Canadian Journal of Speech-Language Pathology and Audiology, 34(3), 181–192.

Shriberg, L. & Kwiatkowski, J. (1980). *Natural Process Analysis (NPA). A procedure for phonological analysis of continuous speech samples*. New York, Wiley.

Shriberg, L., & Kwiatkowski, J. (1982). Phonological disorders II: A conceptual framework for management. Journal of Speech and Hearing Disorders, *47*, 242–256.

Stampe, D. (1973). *A dissertation on natural phonology*. New York: Garland Publishing.

Stein, N., & Glenn, C. (1979). An analysis of story comprehension in elementary school children. In R. Freedle (Ed.). *New directions in discourse processing* (Vol. 2, pp. 53–120). Norwood, NJ: Ablex.

Van Riper, C. (1939). *Speech correction: Principles and methods*. New York: Prentice Hall.

Weiner, F. (1981). Treatment of phonological disability using the method of meaningful minimal contrast. *The Journal of speech and hearing disorders 46*, 97–103.

Williams, A.L. (2000). Multiple oppositions: Theoretical foundations for an alternative contrast intervention approach. *American Journal of Speech-Language Pathology, 9*, 282–288.

Wren, Y., Miller, L. Peters, T. J., Emond, A. & Rulestone, S. (2016). Prevalence and predictors of persistent speech sound disorder at eight-years-old: Findings from a population cohort study. *Journal of Speech, Language and Hearing Research, 59*, 647.

Appendix

University Speech-Language-Hearing Disorders Clinic

Street Address

City, State

SPEECH AND LANGUAGE EVALUATION

Client Name: <u>Sam F.</u>   Date of Birth: _____ Date of Testing:_____

Chronological Age: <u> 11/11 </u>   Primary Disorder/ICD-9: <u>speech/language</u>

Parent/Caregiver Name: _____   Language of Testing <u>English</u>

Clinician: _____

Supervisor:_____

Statement of Problem and Background Information.

Sam, an 11-year and 11-month-old boy, was brought to the clinic for a reevaluation and possible treatment. He was seen here initially when he was 3.4 years old. At that time, he was essentially unintelligible due to a severe articulation problem marked by an unusually high degree of homonymy. Language content/form/use interactions were also below age expectancy. Speech/language delay was associated primarily with impaired sensorimotor functioning. A psychological report highlighted considerable difficulty in the "spatial motor" area (i.e., judging where his body is in space and interpreting feedback from his actions). He was described as frequently bumping into things, occasionally falling, and demonstrating imprecision in manipulating blocks and pegs. Reports from the occupational therapist and psychologist revealed deficits in sensorimotor and cognitive functioning.

Speech and language intervention at that time that commenced at our center focused on the elimination of backing (he produced no velar consonants), stopping of /f/, and final-consonant deletion. Phonological goals were embedded in Bloom and Lahey (1978) phase 3 content/form interaction goals. Three-constituent utterances were targeted. After approximately two years of treatment, therapy was terminated at the parents' request. At this point, Sam was at Bloom and Lahey's phase 5, producing a range of three-constituent utterances with embeddings of other content categories, and had begun to suppress the phonological processes targeted as goals. Least success was achieved with the elimination of backing.

For the past six years, he has been receiving speech/language therapy from a speech/language pathologist in private practice. In addition, he sees a speech/language pathologist at his school. The primary focus of private therapy has been the phonological problem, and in school the focus has been "language reception and expression."

He is currently in a special school program for children with communication and behavior problems, receives speech/language intervention at the school, and has private treatment once weekly by an occupational therapist.

Assessment Information

Behavioral Observations during Assessment

Sam was cooperative throughout the examination, although he questioned the need for certain procedures and was reluctant to perform them (e.g., Peripheral Speech Mechanism Exam).

Results of Communication Assessment

Language

Nonstandard Assessment: Language sample analysis (conversational sample and narrative sample)

A. Form-Content

Complex Sentence Analysis:

Evidence of volition-intention, additive, temporal, causality, specification, notice, communication, and internal-state connectives produced: *and*, *when*, and *how*

Narratives:

Attempts consisted of two- to three-utterance samples. Unintelligibility of utterances and necessity for continuous probing for the continuation of a sequence of ideas interfered with the completion of an adequate narrative sample.

Additional Syntactic Data:

Errors with the following syntactic structures may have been phonologically based (marked by word endings):

1. Plural—I tell jokes [aɪ tɛ dot]

2. Copula—"What's this?" [wa di]; "Who's there?" [hu geg]

3. Third-person singular—"My mother knows" [ma mʌno:]

4. Possessive—"Brother's room" [bʌgwum]

5. Past irregular—"made" [me]

6. Past regular—"wanted" [wʌd]

B. Use

Linguistic Context: Questions and responses generally contingent on prior statements or questions. Topics are typically extended by not more than two statements.

Function: Uses language to comment, direct action, obtain responses, routine, inform protest, negate, and amuse.

Discourse skills include acknowledgment of speaker's utterances, repair when not understood (primarily due to phonological impairment).

Initiates and responds to speech appropriately.

Standardized testing

Test of Language Development (TOLD): Was not testable. Did not appear to understand requirements of the first two subtests and refused to continue Peabody Picture. *Vocabulary Test (PPVT-R):* raw score, 78; language age, 8 to 6; percentile rank, 2.

One Word Picture Vocabulary Test (EOWPVT). Raw score, 91; standard score equivalent , 69; percentile rank, 2; Stanine, 1.

Phonology/Articulation:

Standardized testing: *The Photo Articulation Test (PAT)* was administered for the purpose of identifying sound production in single words, not as a normative measure.

Single-word productions elicited by pictures from the PAT revealed the following:

1. Consonants never produced as targets: ʧ, ʤ, θ, ʃ, ʒ, r, ŋ

2. Consonants produced only as substitutions : ʧ, θ,,ŋ

3. Phonological processes and percentage of occurrence.

Substitution Processes

Fronting of velars: k, g (43%)

Backing: t, d (15%)

Deaffrication: ʧ, ʤ (60%)

Stopping: f, v (43%); θ, ð (33%); s, z (18%); ʃ, ʒ (60%)

Gliding: l, r (44%)

Vocalizing: −1 (100%).

Syllable-Structure Processes

Final-consonant deletion: d, t, d, g, z, s, 1 (27%)

Weak syllable deletion: two-syllable (12%); three-syllable (25%)

Cluster reduction (90%)

Other processes and process combinations

Assimilation "balloon" [bum]

Stopping and backing "jar" [ga]

Fronting of velars and stopping "shoe" [tu]

Continuous speech sample:

Phonological processes and percentage of occurrence:

Fronting of velars (24%)

Backing (38%)

Stopping (77%)

Gliding (100%)

Vocalization (100%)

Final-consonant deletion (74%)

Weak syllable deletion (two syllable, 33%; three syllable, 100%)

Cluster reduction (100%)

Stopping + Backing (five instances)

Deaffrication + Backing (50%)

Deaffrication + Fronting of Palatals (50%)

Contextual patterns:

Words omitted (generally monosyllable, weakly stressed function words)

Neutralization of medial consonants: "writer" [waɪjʌ], "Steven" [tijɪ]

Coalescence: "brother"—"he" [bi]; "wanted" [wʌd]

Assimilation "to school" [sɔsu]; "ready" [wɛwi]; /k/ becomes [t] after a front vowel "week" [wit]; "make" [met]

Fluency: within normal limits

Voice: within normal limits

Associated Behavioral Systems (Factors maintaining or supporting Communication Behavior).

Sensorimotor

Results on the OSMSE-R

1. Appearance of lip, tongue, and palate was normal.

2. Nonspeech functions not accomplished were puffing cheeks, directing tongue to alveolar ridge, and directing tongue tip left of lips (tongue deviated toward right during these tasks).

3. Refused to imitate drawing tongue tip along hard palate.

4. Results on tasks of diadochokinesis were below age expectancy.

5. Repetitions were executed with spurts in speed and rhythmic changes. He refused to complete all tasks.

Reports of occupational therapist:

- Low muscle tone: This affects posture, stability, and balance-related activity. This is believed to be associated with motor-planning problems. Low muscle tone is observed about his face. It is still difficult to determine whether tonal problems of the oral cavity are all low or mixed due to his tactile defensiveness (particularly about the head and shoulders).

- Tactile defensiveness: He is reactive to being touched or handled, which interferes with oral and medical examinations. This behavior is being targeted indirectly with pushing and pulling exercises that require strong proprioceptive input.

- Fatigue: He fatigues rapidly when standing, sitting, and moving. He appears exhausted after hammering nails into a board for 5 minutes. The appearance of fatigue may be confounded by his labored breathing. The appearance of breathing difficulty is believed to be result of allergies, anxiety and resistance, overweight, and low muscle tone. Breathing appears more labored when he is pushed to complete a task.

- Incoordination and weakness: Sam has difficulty using the top part of his body against the lower part, and using the right side against the left side. Thus, he has problems using two arms in a coordinated manner, together or alternately. Part of the difficulty stems from the low muscle tone, which results in the general inability to pull into flexion against gravity. He compensates for postural instability by using a wide base of support when walking, standing, and sitting.

- Immature hand function: Sam presents with a set of immature or primitive grasp–release patterns, which are related to muscle tone, motor planning, and incoordination. He demonstrates poor joint stability and an inability to use thumb in opposition to fingers. There is a lack of stability that affects finger movements, demonstrated when Sam grasps a pencil and tries to write. It also appears that Sam lacks motor memory for how to hold the pencil and succeed.

- The occupational therapist's report was based on informal clinical observation rather than standardized testing. Sam is generally not cooperative in formal testing situations (Lefkofsky, personal communication, June 1992).

Cognition: Report from psychologist

Results on WISC-R: verbal IQ, 8; performance IQ, 68; full-scale IQ, 75

During the testing Sam occasionally stated, "I can't do it," but it was possible to make him persevere. On the basis of much inter-intra subtest variability, the psychologist concluded that results are a "minimal estimate" of his ability. Subtests' results ranged from *far below average* (areas assessed as "deficient" were block design and object assembly) to *average* (information, similarities, comprehension, and picture arrangement). Low scores were obtained on tasks involving visualizing part–whole relationships, analyzing and synthesizing abstract designs, and matching symbols to numbers.

Psychococial

Rorschach result: Psychologist indicated that Sam's responses were perseverative, reporting the perception of "bat" on many of the cards. He named the color of the blots rather than integrating color and form; this was interpreted as evidence of a neurological problem.

Thematic Apperception Test: Responses to pictures revealed anxiety, sadness.

SUMMARY: Sam, an 11-year and 11-month-old male presents with a severe phonological/articulation and language disorder. His phonological/articulation disorder is more prominent, evident since early childhood and involving a wide range of substitution and syllable-structure processes with variable rates of occurrence. His language disorder is characterized by deficits in content, form, and use. Form is largely compromised by the severity of the phonological disorder. Prognosis is guarded due to the long-term existence of the problem with negligible results of prior treatment programs. Sam's sensorimotor, cognitive, and psychosocial deficits appear to be major factors impacting his treatment progress.

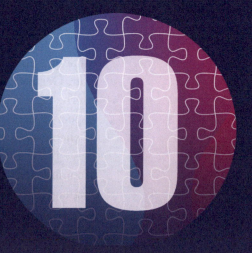
Intervention Planning for Second Language Phonology

THE READER WILL:

- Define the concept of "interlanguage" and its relationship to the acquisition of second language phonology (L2)
- Identify the content/form/use interactions that affect the learning of L2 phonology
- Identify the factors that maintain inauthentic L2 productions
- Demonstrate the application of principles of learning to the acquisition of L2 phonology
- Describe the derivation of a management plan for an adult designed to eliminate or reduce L1-induced dialectal patterns

Although clinicians have long been involved with the remediation of "foreign accents," assessment and remediation procedures have generally not been driven by L2 acquisition theory or based on research findings with L2 populations (see "speech correction" texts as far back as Raubicheck, 1952). Even current texts in articulation/phonology, although beginning to recognize the need to address pronunciation differences associated with particular dialectal or cultural backgrounds, omit any theoretical foundation for planning remediation for this population (e.g., see Bernthal, Bankson, & Flipson, Jr., 2017).

An acquaintance recently told us that of the five languages he speaks fluently (Romanian, German, French, Hebrew, and English), none are produced without an accent (Stern, personal communication, September, 2016). Dr. Stern may be unusual with respect to the many languages he speaks fluently but not with respect to the difficulty he encounters with their phonologies. Learning the phonology of more than one language is a complex, challenging process, involving many interacting variables. We are becoming more aware of these variables and their interactions as studies in second language (L2) phonology emerge with greater abundance. Described as "a relatively neglected area in the study of second language learning" (Leather & James, 1991, p. 305), the area of L2 speech continues to receive attention. Over the past few decades, research studies from a number of related disciplines (phonetics, phonology, psychology, speech-language pathology, second language acquisition, etc.) have converged, yielding new insights into the acquisition of L2 speech. Much of this research focuses on the nature of the "interlanguage" (derived from the interaction between L1 and L2; e.g., Dickerson, 1987; Selinker, 1992); constraints on the acquisition of L2, which may also be viewed as variable factors maintaining a foreign accent (e.g., Flege, 1992, 1995b; Leather & James, 1991; Long, 1990; Major, 1994); predictions about hierarchies of difficulty for the L2 learner (e.g., Carlisle, 1994; Eckman, 1981, 1985, 1987, 1991; Eckman & Iverson, 1994; Edge, 1991; Major, 1986; Yavas, 1994), and, more recently, "theoretical and methodological choices and problems of interpretation that enhance and undermine the usefulness of L2 pronunciation research findings" (Munro & Derwing, 2015, p. 1; Thomson & Derwing, 2015). These results of these studies, accordingly, begin to provide an important theoretical foundation for intervention planning with L2 adults.

Nature of the Problem

The major focus of this chapter is intervention planning for individuals learning to pronounce a nonnative language. An ancillary focus is to present some of the findings from L2 research, especially from those related disciplines outside of speech-language pathology, and to demonstrate how this material may be foundational for formulating goals and procedures at three phases of intervention planning.

The content of this chapter is obviously different from that of Chapters 8, 9, 11, and 12; it doesn't deal with disorders. But it deals with adults who may desire assistance with learning the pronunciation of a nonnative language. According to the American Speech-Language Association, "accent reduction" is within our scope of practice (ASHA, 1996). "The speech-language pathologist may also be available to provide elective clinical services to nonstandard English speakers who do not present a disorder" (ASHA, 1983, p. 24). Given that there are many L2 speakers from a great diversity of language backgrounds who visit speech-language pathologists (SLPs) yearly, this chapter will follow the other chapters in our SLP approach to intervention planning.

Sources of Information for Intervention Planning

Content/Form/Use Interactions

As with typically developing and impaired L1 systems, the acquisition of a second language involves the interaction of three linguistic components, form/content and use. Although this chapter focuses on L2 speech (the form of language), it is clear that other aspects of form (i.e., lexical items, syntax), content (meaning to be communicated), and use (conditions under which the speaker pronounces) will interact with the accuracy of speech-sound productions. First let us examine the object of our discussion, L2 phonology.

What Is L2 Phonology?

Most current researchers of L2 phonology ascribe the phonetic/phonemic patterns of the L2 speaker to a rule system that is distinct from that of the L1 and the L2. These patterns comprise some sounds resulting directly from L1 interference (substitutions by L1 sounds), and others from hybrid changes resulting from attempts to target phonetic units of L2 (modifications found in neither language). These new pronunciation patterns that derive from the interaction between any two languages along with other related interacting factors are referred to as "interlanguage (IL)" (Selinker, 1969, 1992). During the past few decades, a number of publications have been directed toward the elucidation of the interlanguage phenomenon—its characteristics and derivational bases.

In his seminal writings on interlanguage, Selinker (1969) states,

An interlanguage may be linguistically described using as data the observable output resulting from a speaker's attempt to produce a foreign norm, i.e., both his errors and nonerrors. It is assumed that such behaviour is highly structured. It must be dealt with as a system not an isolated collection of errors (fn 5).

More than 20 years later, Selinker (1992) concludes that "the IL Hypothesis is [still] a reasonable theoretical story" (p. 246). The IL Hypothesis has been stated as follows:

. . . in attempting to express meanings in an L2 and in attempting to interact verbally with native, as well as other non-native speakers of that L2, at least the following occur.

1. People create a (partly) separate linguistic system.

2. In that system, interlingual identifications and language transfer are central.

3. One selectively uses the NL [native language] by context.

4. One fossilizes [keeps from changing] at least parts of the IL.

5. One selectively fossilizes differentially according to linguistic level and discourse domain.

6. The IL one is creating is susceptible to the force of several types of language universals, as well as interlanguage universals.

7. The IL one is creating is susceptible to the training and learning strategies that are adopted.

8. The IL one is creating is susceptible to simplification and complexification strategies (p. 247). [brackets are ours]

This description suggests that interlanguage is viewed as an independent rule system derived from the interrelationship of at least two languages. These rules may be considered variable, given the range of fluctuation in pronunciation observed with a variety of alternating factors. These include the nonlinguistic and linguistic contexts (e.g., function of utterance, formality level, interlocutors, phonotactic constraints); linguistic universals (e.g., developmental schedules, markedness phenomena, phonological processes); individual strategies (e.g., production and perception processes, monitoring ability), training approaches and learning styles. Researchers (e.g., Leather & James, 1991; Major, 1994) support the viability of these variables and others in comprehensive reviews. Some of the variables affecting the acquisition of L2 speech (i.e., maintenance of an interlanguage) will be examined in the sections on maintaining factors and performance demands appearing later in this chapter.

Interactions with Content and Use

FORM/CONTENT. Lexical factors may affect L2 learning and pronunciation accuracy. Mack, Tierney, and Boyle (1990), as cited by Flege (1992), found that L2 speakers recognized frequently occurring words better than infrequent ones; this was especially true when words were computer generated. The converse, however, was found with reference to production. Less familiar words were produced with greater accuracy than more familiar. Fledge suggests that this comprehension/production learning discrepancy pattern would be expected if L2 speakers tended to mispronounce some of the earlier words they learn, before the establishment of stable phonetic categories; they then have difficulty in modifying these productions once categories have been established for the L2 sounds.

Pronunciation of L2 words may also be negatively affected if a given L2 word has a cognate (related L1 word). Flege and Munro (1994) found that voice onset time (VOT) values in English /t/ were less accurate in an English word with a Spanish cognate (i.e., *taco*) than in words without cognates. Similarly, we found, in our clinical practice that a Haitian French speaker produced English words with /r/ (e.g., republic) less authentically when these words had Haitian cognates.

FORM/USE. The discourse context and function of the speech event has been reported to affect the type and degree of sound transfer from L1 (i.e., the frequency with which L1 for L2 substitutions are made). Leather and James (1991) reviewed a number of research studies, generally concluding that more formal contexts (e.g., word list reading, reading of minimal pairs) are more facilitative of target attainment than intermediate formal (e.g., dialogue reading), which in turn is more facilitating than least formal (i.e., free speaking). Dickerson (1987) reports similar findings and attributes this variability within the interlanguage to the amount of attention paid to speech (i.e., the monitoring of one's speech). He suggests that L2 learners be taught formal pronunciation rules in addition to oral work so as to help them monitor their own utterances. By contrast, it has also been shown that the "vernacular" style of the developing interlanguage when compared with the "formal" style is more robust in withstanding the influence of L1 (Leather & James, 1991). This suggests that the stylistic variants of language in use may also affect the type and degree of influence of L1 on L2 in any acquisition context.

Related to the formality of the context is the background of the interlocutor. It has been reported that speakers will often accommodate their pronunciation (use language-specific variants of L2) when aware of the listener's native language (Beebe, 1977). Beebe showed that Chinese Thai bilingual speakers more readily used a Thai accent when speaking to Thai listeners and a Chinese accent when speaking to Chinese listeners even when the Chinese listeners spoke authentic Thai.

FORM/CONTENT/USE. The form of an utterance may also be affected by the requirement to communicate *meaning*—to avoid *communication breakdown*. In this instance, an interaction among all three components becomes obvious.

Weinberger (1994) emphasizes the difference between functional and phonetic constraints on L2 phonology. He argues that the L2 learner has two goals: (a) a phonetic goal—to learn speech sounds that approximate the target language—and (b) a functional goal—to keep words and sentences intelligible. It is this second goal that relates to language content and use, particularly the awareness of listener knowledge and communication breakdown. Weinberger explains that this functional goal influences the types of processes an L2 learner may adopt. For example, it has been shown that in an effort to simplify an L2 syllable structure (e.g., facilitate the production of the second C of a Consonant Vowel Consonant), an adult second language speaker will use the process of epenthesis rather than final consonant deletion (typical of a child). An example taken from Weinberger to illustrate the result of application of alternative processes is as follows: If the word *seed* is pronounced with epenthesis (insertion of a vowel) as [sidə], it may be confused with a limited number of English words—*seed* and *cedar*. If, however, the process of final consonant deletion is used, the number of words that would be possible candidates would be significantly greater (e.g., seed, seat, seep, seek, seize, siege, etc). Thus, the motivation to maximize lexical contrasts in order to maintain meaning in communication (content/use) interacts with the form component of language.

IMPLICATION FOR INTERVENTION PLANNING. From the foregoing discussion, it is clear that knowledge about the nature of the interlanguage and the way in which it interacts with the other language components guides the clinician in decision-making about goals and procedures across three phases of intervention planning. For example, the interlanguage affects long-term and short-term goal planning: Clinicians can differentiate between L1/L2 substitutions and new sounds (present in neither language). With knowledge of the client's phonological system, a complexity hierarchy may be generated to guide goal development. Knowledge of conversational interactions (form/use) may guide procedural planning in determining choices of linguistic and nonlinguistic contexts.

Maintaining Factors

As noted earlier, efforts to explain variability within the interlanguage have invoked a wide range of nonlinguistic and linguistic factors affecting pronunciation. To be consistent with the model presented in this book, a number of these factors will be organized within the categories of maintaining factors introduced in Chapter 1 and elucidated in Chapter 4: psychosocial, cognitive, and sensorimotor. An additional factor will be added—the phonological system itself. In our book on intervention planning for children (Klein & Moses, 1999) we explain that "syntax and phonology display unique organizational properties apparent in no other behavioral system" (p. 30). Moreover, the segments themselves and their interactions (i.e., markedness values) contain inherent relative difficulty (e.g., Eckman, 1977, 1985, 1991; Greenberg, 1965), which contributes to the maintenance of a nonnative dialect.

Psychosocial

Psychosocial factors may influence communication because they involve the individual's ability to engage in and benefit from social interactions and to adapt to the social and vocational demands of adulthood.

Current research in interlanguage phonology has highlighted several factors affecting the developing L2, which may be categorized as psychosocial. Those having the potential to affect intervention planning for the acquisition of a second phonological system are (a) age (Long, 1990; Major, 1994; Patkowski, 1994); (b) amount of native language use (Flege, Frieda, & Nozawa, 1997); (c) motivation (Leather & James, 1991); and (d) gender (Leather & James, 1991).

AGE. After a careful study of three comprehensive texts, a review article and three studies, Patkowski (1994) makes the following claim about age-related differences in the ability to learn the phonology of a second language:

There is a period ending around the time of puberty (operationally defined to mean somewhere between the ages of 12 and 15 years), during which it is possible, but not inevitable, for learners to acquire, as an end-product of a naturalistic L2 acquisition process, full native-like fluency in the phonological system of a second language, and after which such a possibility does not exist anymore. Thus a comparison between older and younger learners of their long-term achievement (operationally defined to mean that naturalistic exposure has occurred for at least 5 years or so under "advantaged" sociological, cultural, psychological, and affective circumstances) should reveal (a) that only younger learners can sometimes be shown to attain full native-like phonological L2 competence, and (b) that overall, there is a strong statistical difference in the long-term achievement of younger and older learners (p. 206).

Long (1990), who reports a growing preference for the term "sensitive" period, supports an age-related constraint on the acquisition of authentic L2 phonology, but suggests that this constraint may set in as early as age 6. Long's position is stated as follows:

There are sensitive periods governing the ultimate level of first or second language attainment possible in different linguistic domains, not just phonology, with cumulative declines in learning capacity, not a catastrophic one-time loss, and beginning as early as age 6 in many individuals, not at puberty as is often claimed (p. 255).

Although there appears to be little dispute regarding the "critical period" (or sensitive period) view, there continue to be conflicting explanations of this phenomenon. Those in the tradition of Lenneberg (1967) support a biological view of the sensitive period. For example, Long (1990) asserts that with maturation there is loss of the brain's plasticity due to the myelinization of neural pathways; in contrast, Flege (1992) opposes the notion of a biological or neurological basis to the sensitive period. According to the latter researcher, the maintenance of a foreign accent is more likely owing to differences in perceptual processing and representational mechanisms between older L2 learners (sequential bilinguals) and L1 learners. Flege suggests, in addition, that adults may not receive phonetic input as rich as the input directed to children learning a first language. It may also be that adults do not maintain attention to words as long as children because adults learn to recognize words more rapidly.

AMOUNT OF NATIVE LANGUAGE USE. It is likely that many of us know someone who began to learn a second language as a child (below age 10) and still maintains an accented L2, as an adult. Empirical research by Flege, Frieda, and Nozawe (1997) addressed this issue. As part of another study, Flege and his associates (Flege, Munro, &

MacKay, 1995) observed that some Italian adults who emigrated to Canada before the age of 10 (some at three years of age) continued to exhibit a foreign accent despite many years of experience with English. This appeared to contradict the critical period hypothesis or at least to indicate that other factors may also be constraining authentic L2. This finding prompted further investigation. One factor considered by Flege et al. (1997) was the continued influence of L1 on L2. To test this consideration, Flege et al. studied the relationship between the amount of L1 use and degree of accent in L2 of Italian L1 subjects; the subjects were matched for age of introduction to L2 and experiences in learning English as an L2. The researchers found that in their "HiUse" subjects (self-reported using L1 36% of the time on a daily basis), accents were significantly stronger than in "LoUse" subjects (L1 used 3% of the time on the average). The authors asserted that these results challenge the critical period hypothesis as a sufficient explanation of nonnativeness in second language speech.

MOTIVATION. Another psychosocial factor affecting the acquisition of L2 phonology is the individual's motivation for accurate L2 pronunciation. Leather and James (1991) suggest that various factors may be responsible for motivating an individual to attempt "native-like" authenticity in his/her speech. Factors for aspiring to authentic L2 speech include (a) the degree of concern felt by the learner about sounding like a native speaker (based on prevailing attitude of L1 culture); (b) the need to produce native-like speech for employment reasons (e.g., using telephone, holding interviews, lecturing; (c) the attitude toward the culture and society of the L2 (e.g., how much cultural identification is desired). As an example of (c) a multilingual acquaintance of ours has often noted that Americans do not pronounce their words clearly enough. Motivated by this notion, her attempts at English are heavily based on orthographic representations (aspiring to pronounce every consonant in the printed word, especially final stops). This approach results in an overarticulated, inaccurate version of American English devoid of appropriate allophonic variations (including the absence of flaps within and between words).

GENDER. Leather and James (1991) propose that the gender of the speaker may also affect the variety of L2 pronunciation used. They cite the work of Gussenhoven (1979), who found that female speakers were more favorably oriented toward the use of "prestige" forms than males. A gender difference in the use of prestige forms was also illustrated by the work of Adamson and Regan (1991), who examined the pronunciation of the "-ing" morpheme by Cambodian immigrants. They found that the [ɪŋ] variant (generally considered more prestigious than the [ɪn]) was used more frequently by the females than the males. In addition, the females produced the [ɪŋ] more frequently as the context became more formal. An interesting finding was that among males, the use of [ɪn] decreased as style became more formal. The authors were uncertain about why this should be the case. They suggested that the use of [ɪn] may reflect the desire of the males to accommodate to a male speaker, which they probably perceived to be [ɪn]) rather than an overall norm.

To summarize, psychosocial factors such as age of acquisition, frequency of L1 use, motivation, and gender should be considered in planning intervention. These factors are likely to affect planning of goals and procedures, especially in the long-term phase, when expectations for outcome and predictions about time duration must be made.

Sensorimotor

For the second language learner, we are most concerned with sensorimotor functioning as it affects the perception and production of speech sounds. Related to peripheral perception and production processes are those processes involved with discrimination, evaluation of similarities and differences, and the construction of an underlying representation based on perceptual cues and mnemonic factors—a representation that forms the basis for production attempts. Although the higher-level processes may be more cognitive in nature, they emanate from sensorimotor processes and therefore will also be addressed here.

PRODUCTION AND PERCEPTION. It is probably safe to assume that every speech-language pathologist has been well oriented toward a consideration of both perceptual and production factors in treating L1 clients with articulatory/phonological difficulties. Most texts on articulatory/phonological disorders focusing on L1 phonology describe procedures for assessing and remediating deficient perceptual and production skills. (See, for example, Bauman-Waengler, 2016; Bernthal, Bankson, & Flipson, Jr., 2017.) This consideration of perceptual and production mechanisms underlying the phonetic change implies an assumption that speech errors result from deficiencies in either or both of these variables (e.g., Bernthal, Bankson, & Flipson, Jr., 2017; Fey, 1992).

How production and perception factors affect the acquisition and maintenance of speech sounds has also received some attention in second language research. Although it is still difficult to precisely determine the contribution of each factor to the speaker's interlanguage (e.g., Leather & James, 1991; Flege, 1992, 1995a; Major, 1994), some points of view regarding the roles of perception, production, and their relationship have been expressed.

1. PRODUCTION. With reference to *production* capacities, Leather and James (1991) write,

Learners receiving explicit training in L2 articulation must adjust the configurations and movements of their articulators according to verbally formulated instructions, and the accuracy with which they are able to do this will ultimately be limited by tactile and proprioceptive feedback. Even naturalistic learners who receive no formal instruction must effect some match between target sounds and articulatory configurations during the production of an L2 (p. 311).

Flege (1992) expresses a similar point of view on the basis of his research on Japanese /r/ and /l/, Spanish learners' word-final fricative production, and Chinese speakers' difficulty in producing a contrast between plosive cognates (+ or − voicing) in word-final position. According to Flege, "difficulties in L2 production could arise from an inability to *modify* previously established patterns of segmental production or to develop *new ones*" (p. 567). He points out that although Japanese speakers have more difficulty in producing /r/ and /l/ in word-final singletons than word-initial singletons and word-initial clusters, the opposite pattern obtains for perception; this would suggest that the errors cannot be due only to faulty perception. Flege also points out that Spanish learners have more difficulty with the production of /s/ in final than initial position and that this may be attributable to the paucity of word-final consonants in Spanish; the presence of final consonants, therefore, create a more complex syllable structure, possibly posing a greater motoric challenge. In the case of Chinese speakers attempting English plosives, Flege suggests that the inability to produce an effective contrast in final position (though it is possible in initial position) may be due to the difficulty in sustaining closure voicing in word-final consonants to the same extent as speakers of English. This type of articulatory/voicing synchrony has been reported to be difficult for young L1 learners and results generally in consonant devoicing, vowel epenthesis (Klein, 1978), or nasal epenthesis (Fey & Gandour, 1982). When such processes are employed in L1, they are generally attributed to motoric difficulty because it is assumed that they are attempts to preserve surface contrast (apparently perceived, e.g., Fey & Gandour).

Motoric difficulty may also exist for the production of vowels. Flege (1989) found that Spanish speakers use a narrower vertical range of tongue positions to produce Spanish /i, a, u/ than English speakers in producing English /i, ɑ, u/. It is reasonable to hypothesize that given only 5 vowels in Spanish as compared with 14 in English, there would be some difficulty in making the subtle articulatory changes even when perception of these distinctions is possible.

2. PERCEPTION. Many researchers have viewed the role of perception as more influential than that of motor ability in the pronunciation patterns of L2 (of the interlanguage). It has been argued that differences in pronunciation between native and nonnative speakers are probably due to underlying perceptual differences. These differences are generally described with reference to the nature of the sound categories established for the L2. (For reviews of this area, see Flege, 1992, 1995b; Leather & James, 1991.) Flege asserts that correct production of an L2 sound depends to a great extent on how similar the speaker perceives this sound to be to an L1 phoneme. If the L2 sound is "identical" to an L1 sound or "so similar" to an L1 sound that differences are unnoticeable, the sound is said to be "equated with" or "equivalent" to the L1 sound, and likely to be produced authentically. In such a case, there is no reason for the L2 learner to establish a new L2 sound category. If the L2 sound differs substantially from the L1 sound, the L2 sound is again expected to be produced authentically; in this case, however, the significant *difference* is anticipated to generate the formation of a new sound category. The situation that is seen as most challenging is when an L2 sound is different enough from any L1 (perhaps only in minor details such as timing, amplitude, or placement) so that the substitution of L1 for L2 would be noticed but not different enough to motivate the formation of a new category. It should be noted that Flege (1992) uses the word "sound" to refer "to a class of phones that can be used to contrast meaning" (p. 566). He postulates the concept of class even at a "position-sensitive allophonic level, rather than at a more abstract phonemic level" (1995, p. 239).

Let us illustrate some of Flege's (1992, 1995b) conceptualizations regarding sound categorization with reference to a native Spanish learner of English. The /i/'s of Spanish and English are close enough for the individual to produce English /i/ authentically. The /æ/ of English has no close counterpart in Spanish so that it is likely that the formulation of a new category be triggered. Because Spanish /i/ has been described as lower than English /i/, somewhat closer to /ɪ/ (Flege, 1989), it is likely that both English /i/ and /ɪ/ will be attempted with the Spanish /i/ and no new category will be formed for /ɪ/. This will result in an i/ɪ substitution, contributing to a listener's perception of an accent. These alternate possibilities are encapsulated by Flege (1992) in the following statement, "Perhaps an L2 vowel will be treated as 'new' [forming a separate phone category] only if it is found in a portion of the acoustic phonetic vowel space that is unoccupied by an allophone of an L1 vowel category. Such may be the case of English /æ/ but not English /ɪ/, which is located in a portion of the space occupied by Spanish /i/ (especially the realizations of Spanish /i/ in closed syllables)" (p. 583).

Second language research has also addressed equivalence and nonequivalence in consonants. (See the work of Flege and his colleagues, reported in Flege, 1992 and 1995b.) Those consonants receiving most research interest have been /r/ and /l/ produced by Japanese learners and /p,t,k/ by native French and Spanish learners of English. In general, the research has shown that although a sound may be identified as "new" for a learner, distinct from the consonants in his or her language, it may not be produced correctly by the adult learner. For example, /l/ and /r/ could be viewed as new for Japanese (there is no /l/ in Japanese, and the /r/ is produced as a voiced tip-alveolar flap (Price, 1981). This situation would predict the formation of new sound categories for the production of /r/ and /l/ and authentic production expected. Research evidence, to date, has not consistently supported this prediction (Flege, 1992, 1995b). The situation is different for the production of English /p,t,k/ by French and Spanish speakers. In this case, the difference in L1 and L2 consonants is more subtle; the French and Spanish voiceless stops differ from English only in voice onset time (VOT, with longer VOT for English). Owing to this subtle difference, it would be expected that the L1 versions would be perceived as equivalent to the L2 and not produced authentically. Research evidence supported these predictions for adult learners (Flege, 1992).

Because it is often difficult to evaluate the extent to which perception and production separately, or interactively, contribute to phonological performance, both are often considered to be maintaining factors of error productions in L1 (Fey, 1992; Hodson &

Paden, 1991); a similar case may be made for the influence of these variables on learning the phonology of L2. When L2 sounds are found in the L1 repertoire or are similar, the intended target is usually an authentic L2 sound, and the articulatory plan to achieve the target is known. If, however, a "new" sound must be learned, "the speaker presumably refers to some less well formed perceptual target and enacts a motor program based on less well known production rules. . . Success in the production of L2 sounds would thus be limited . . . by inadequate knowledge of (a) the phonetic target and/or (b) the means of attaining it" (Leather & James, 1991, p. 314).

Cognition

Cognition is viewed as another possible maintaining factor for the maintenance of inauthentic L2 productions. There are a number of cognitive processes implicated in the acquisition of second language phonology that must be engaged in order to achieve authentic speech patterns.

LEARNING INVOLVES MENTAL ORGANIZATION OR REORGANIZATION. Based on a number of studies by Flege, and Flege with his associates (reported in comprehensive reviews, Flege, 1992, 1995b), a compelling argument is made for the process of phonetic system reorganization as a basis for authentic L2 pronunciation. This concept was broached in the foregoing section on perception and production processes, and will be reexamined here because of its cognitive implications.

A powerful theme emerging from Flege's (1992) review is that the primary task of the L2 learner is to perceptually differentiate L1 and L2 sounds (i.e., to distinguish between "new" and "similar" sounds) and *formulate new phonetic categories*. It is well known that older children (beyond the age of 6 or 7) and adults have greater difficulty in learning L2 sounds than younger children (see earlier section on critical period). This difficulty has been described as a diminished ability to establish additional phonetic categories for new L2 sounds (Flege, 1992). Flege attributes this reduced ability to a "phonetic system shift," which occurs between the ages of five and seven and is characterized by the development and stabilization of the phonetic system. The "5 to 7" shift is seen as reflecting general cognitive changes related to an increase in metalinguistic awareness. As a result, there is greater focus on specific aspects of stimuli, such as segment-sized rather than syllable-sized units in speech processing. This is shown in reading readiness research (Nesdale, Herriman, & Tunmer, 1984) and studies of metaphonological abilities (e.g., Klein, Lederer, & Cortese, 1991).

Flege (1992) characterizes the phonetic system shift as affecting the existing phonetic categories in two major ways: (a) the primary acoustic features of prototypes of each phonetic category and the relative saliency of these features will become better defined, (b) the range of exemplars representing each category will increase. The first change is believed to stabilize the category center, although the second defines the boundaries between categories. For the L2 learner, the "shift" increases the number of possible variants permitted within a category, thereby, reducing "uncommitted" vowel space not occupied by any L1 category. For example, an L1 has an [o] sound with [ɔ] and [ɑ] as acceptable variants; this L1 [o] phoneme will be used in the place of an L2 [ɔ] or [ɑ] and, thus, not perceived as different enough to trigger a "new" reaction. An example from an L1 Spanish speaker may further clarify this issue. For a native Spanish learner of English, the /æ/ (which is not a separate phone category in L1 or a variant of any other phone) would be likely to find a location in uncommitted space (not overlapping with any other L1 phonetic category, perhaps, requiring a somewhat different tongue posture).

The cognitive process of recognizing equivalence between or among phonemes is considered to be an adaptive process for L1 learners but nonadaptive for older children and adults (Flege, 1992). Young children must learn to regard variations on a phoneme as belonging to the same phoneme in order to find perceptual constancy and acquire necessary phoneme contrasts. The same process appears to hinder L2 learning because the overextension of perceptual boundaries may cause a "new" sound to be included within an existing boundary (perceived as equivalent) and produced as the L1 sound (contributing to an accent).

Within the framework of phonetic reorganization, it has also been hypothesized that as new phonetic categories are established in L2, other already established categories may demonstrate some regression (i.e., become more L1-like, Nathan, 1990). The establishment of new L2 categories may even lead to the loss of L2 sounds that are similar to L1. Major (1994) points out that the reciprocity between languages L1 and L2 may also contribute to the attrition in L1 (from the modification of sounds to complete loss). This phenomenon may help to explain the difficulty in maintaining authentic pronunciation in any one of the five languages spoken by Dr. Stern (referenced at the beginning of this chapter).

INDIVIDUALS MAY PASS THROUGH THE SAME PHASES OF COGNITION IN A CYCLICAL FASHION, EACH TIME THEY FIND THEMSELVES IN A COMPLEX, NOVEL, PROBLEM-SOLVING SITUATION. This cyclical concept from cognitive theory applies to second language phonology because it has been observed that L2 learners often approach difficult pronunciation targets as would L1 learners (e.g., Major, 1987, 1994). Guided by principles from natural phonology (reflecting the innate capacity of the human organism, Stampe, 1969), Major indicates that the acquisition process for L2 learners is similar in many ways to children's learning of a first language. First, acquisition in both cases proceeds via the elimination of processes that do not conform with the language standard production. The process of elimination is somewhat different, however, between the L1 and L2 learner. At the earliest stage, the child's pronunciation is constrained by a full set of universal processes (found in all the world's languages); as these processes are modified or suppressed, sounds of the ambient language are permitted to emerge (Stampe, 1969). For the adult, the initial array of universal processes has been reduced by those already mastered with L1. The adult learner, however, must eliminate two sets of processes: developmental and interference ("due to *interference* or transfer of processes, patterns, and structures of one's first language to the second language [e.g., a French speaker's substitution of [R] for English [r]", Major, 1987, p. 208]).

Second, in both L1 and L2 similar sounds are substituted for similar targets. For example, L2 learners modify final voiced stops very much as would children, by devoicing, deleting, or adding schwa to the final stop (even if the L1 had no final voiced stops). This pattern will be discussed later in the section on performance demands. Other processes occurring in L2 English, reminiscent of L1, are consonant cluster reduction and preference for open rather than closed syllables. In contrast, some L1 processes never appear in L2—those that have already been suppressed in L1 (e.g., fronting of velars or stopping of fricatives in English) and those that do not appear in any adult language (e.g., assimilation, reduplication, or diminutive).

With reference to his *Ontogeny* model, Major (1986) makes predictions about the relationship between interference processes and developmental processes during the L2 acquisition period. This model claims that "chronologically, errors due to transfer processes decrease, but errors due to developmental processes increase and then decrease" (p. 455). On the basis of his own research with L2 Spanish and L2 English learners, he argues against the common notion that all error types will decrease as one gains more experience with the target language. His research has demonstrated that transfer processes that predominate at the early stages of learning a language prevent developmental processes from surfacing. As transfer processes are suppressed, developmental processes become more obvious, before they too are eventually eliminated and authentic pronunciation may be accomplished. An illustrative example from Major (1987) comes from a speaker of Brazilian Portuguese learning English prevocalic /r/. The acquisition of /r/ is described to occur in five stages. In stage 1, the speaker attempts to substitute the /r/ with a sound from L1 [x] in Portuguese. In stage 2, [ø] (a form of /r/, which is considered a developmental substitution) alternates with [x]. Stage 3 exhibits three variant forms for the target ([x], [ø], an [r]). In stage 4, these variants are reduced to two, ([ø] and [r]). [r] is produced authentically in stage V. It is interesting to note that the variation (during stage 3) was observed to emerge after a more stable first two attempts.

Increased variability on the way to learning a target sound has also been documented in L1 development (e.g., Klein, 1981). This variability between the two process types and within the developmental processes supports a constructivist-cognitive orientation—incorporating behavioral variation and self-monitoring as facilitative learning mechanisms. It is the learner's task to unconsciously or consciously (metalinguistically) overcome both process types. As with children, the application of phonological processes acts to maintain productions that are different from the adult standard.

In summary, when working with an adult client one must consider the systemic nature of L2 acquisition and the cognitive (organizational) difficulties inherent in acquiring a language late.

The Phonological System as a Source of a Nonnative Accent

To speak of the phonological system itself, in the case of learning a second language, is really to speak of at least three phonetic/phonemic systems (L1 and L2) and their interactions (their developing interlanguage). Some of the challenges confronting the L2 learner in differentiating L1 and L2 have been discussed earlier within the categories of psychosocial, sensorimotor, and cognitive maintaining factors. Additional challenges inherent in the characteristics of phonological systems will now be addressed.

DIFFERENT LANGUAGES HAVE DIFFERENT PHONOLOGICAL FEATURES. Because the phoneme categories and allophone distributions differ with different languages, it is to be expected that learning one language will affect the learning of another. One of most important influences, therefore, on second language acquisition is L1 transfer to L2 pronunciation (Major, 1994). A knowledge of this potential transfer motivated the formulation of the Contrastive Analysis Hypothesis (CAH). In its strongest form, this hypothesis states that "one can predict the errors a language learner will make on the basis of a comparison of the descriptions of the native and target language" (Eckman, 1977, p. 316). This statement suggests that the L2 learner will experience greater difficulty with some sounds than with others owing to feature similarities and differences between both languages. Guided by this hypothesis, linguists attempted to explain all nonnative substitutions as motivated by the transfer process. Some substitutions could actually be explained in this manner; for example, the L1 Spanish speaker's use of /d/ for English initial [ð], the German speaker's production of English final voiced stops as voiceless, and the Chinese speaker's substitution of /r/ for English /r/ and /l/—the English targets (L2) comprising features absent from the L1. Linguists, however, soon became aware that some substitutions could not be explained through transfer processes (e.g., sound productions not found in either language). In addition, some predicted errors occurred where others did not. Where the CAH was found to be most lacking, however, was in its inability to predict why certain phonemes were acquired before others. Thus, the CAH hypothesis was useful to a point. It helped to identify areas of contrast between languages (similar and different features) in order to begin to speculate about relative difficulty and predicted order of acquisition.[1]

---

[1] Note: The concept of contrastive analysis in the form of model replica charts has been adapted for studies of phonological acquisition in typically developing children (see Ferguson, 1968, Klein, 1978) and for the assessment of phonological disorders (e.g., Ingram, 1981; Klein, 1984). These charts provide a graphic comparison or "contrast" between the adult phonological system and the emerging child system. These forms will be applied with the L2 learner later in this chapter in order to contrast L1 and L2 sounds.

SEGMENTS ARE UNIVERSALLY MARKED. As a reaction to the inadequacies of the CAH, Eckman (1977) introduced the Markedness Differential Hypothesis (MDH). This hypothesis was intended to extend the CAH by introducing a measure of "universal" (independent of any given language) relative difficulty among segments identified as having the potential for difficulty (not present in L1).

Markedness has been defined in a number of different ways. The term "marked" or "more marked" is used to express the idea that some segments are "less natural" or "less basic" to the capacities of the human speech and hearing mechanism. Least marked structures are acquired first by children and are more likely to occur in all language inventories (e.g., Schane, 1973). For Eckman "'degree of difficulty' corresponds to the notion 'typologically marked'" (p. 520). Let us first look at Eckman's definition of "markedness." Eckman states,

A phenomenon A in some language is more marked than B if the presence of A in a language implies the presence of B; but the presence of B does not imply the presence of A (p. 320.).

With this definition of markedness, Eckman proposes the following hypothesis:

> The areas of difficulty that a language learner will have can be predicted on the basis of systematic comparison of the grammars of the native language, the target language and the markedness relations stated in universal grammar, such that, (a) Those areas of the target language which differ from the native language and are more marked than the native language will be difficult. (b) The relative degree of difficulty of the areas of the target language which are more marked than the native language will correspond to the relative degree of markedness. (c) Those areas of the target language which are different from the native language, but are not more marked than the native language will not be difficult.

Eckman (1977) argued that if typological markedness is incorporated into the CAH, the degree of difficulty, not only the areas of difficulty, may be predicted. The following example, from Eckman, illustrates his position. The phoneme /ʒ/ occurs in initial, medial, and final positions in French; in English it occurs only in medial and final position. According to the CAH, one would predict that English speakers would have difficulty learning initial /ʒ/. This, however, is not the case. If, on the other hand, universal markedness relations are referenced (these markedness relations come from studies on language universals, e.g., Dinnsen & Eckman, 1978; Greenberg, 1965), the reason that /ʒ/ is, in fact, not difficult becomes clearer.

Based on the work of Dinnsen and Eckman (1978), Eckman (1977) proposes that languages may be typed (or typologized) according to whether or not a voice contrast is maintained. Those with a contrast medially do not necessarily have one finally, and those with an initial contrast do not necessarily have this contrast medially. Thus, an "implicational relationship" exists among these positional sound contrasts—a contrast in final position implies a contrast in medial and initial, and a contrast in medial implies one in initial. The hierarchy is based on the distribution of features across the world's languages. Moreover, those features that occur in most languages are considered to be learned with less difficulty than those that are rarer. With reference to this hierarchy, an English L1 speaker learning French should find the initial /ʒ/ unchallenging. Given that English does maintain a voicing contrast in medial and final positions, the L2 initial position is implied. Other markedness relationships that have also been derived from descriptive studies on language universals deal with clusters (Greenberg, 1965) and segments permitted in final position (Eckman, 1985). A final stop + stop is more marked than a final fricative + stop, C1C2C3# is more marked than C1C2#; C2C3# (Greenberg, 1965). In final position, the most marked segment is a voiced obstruent (e.g., /d/), followed by voiceless obstruent (e.g., /t/), sonorant consonants, and vowels least marked (Eckman, 1985).

In another publication, Eckman (1991) further delineated his views on markedness. He introduced the interlanguage Structural Conformity Hypothesis (SCH), which states, "The universal generalizations that hold for the primary languages hold also for interlanguages" (p. 24). Eckman argues that this is a stronger hypothesis than the MDH because it makes predictions based only on implicational universals in the absence of a difference between L1 and L2 (as required for the MDH). Because of this difference, it would be possible to explain an L2 learner's difficulties with certain features, evidenced in the interlanguage, on the basis of implicational universals within the L2 itself. Eckman (1991) illustrates this point with findings from Altenberg and Vago (1983) regarding adult native Hungarian speakers learning English. These L2 learners devoiced word-final obstruents of English targets. This situation cannot be explained by the MDH because it cannot apply (make any predictions) unless there is a difference between the L1 and L2 with reference to this feature. As it happens, both languages contain a voice contrast in final position. According to the SCH, however, systematic difficulty with voicing in final position would be predicted on the basis of implicational universals (within the L2 itself)—voicing in this position is most marked universally.

Other studies in L2 acquisition have further specified universal hierarchies of difficulty for the production of final stops and consonant clusters. These studies have focused on the interactions between structures known to be most marked universally (voicing contrasts in final stops and clusters of increasing numbers of segments) and the phonetic environments in which they are produced. These interactions will be discussed in the section on performance demands that follows.

One may ask how this information on markedness informs us about maintaining factors. It is our point of view that any deterrent to learning helps maintain a problem. The fact that two languages differ in their phoneme categories and allophonic variants makes learning the second language difficult. Utilizing the CAH (identifying differences between and among languages) gives us a starting point to make predictions about potentially difficult areas. Certain sounds, sound combinations, and production contexts are intrinsically more difficult than others regardless of the language spoken. Increased difficulty (or markedness), in addition, deters authentic productions. A consideration of any available hierarchy addressing relative complexity of linguistic features may be utilized (as suggested by the MDH and SCH hypotheses). This knowledge would be informative for planning short-term and session goals, in which cases it is necessary to determine treatment priorities.

PROSODY INFLUENCES SEGMENT PRODUCTION. Another phonological deterrent to authentic pronunciation may be the difference in prosodic characteristics of the contrasting languages. Major (1987) states, "Prosodic processes also affect the acquisition of a second language because to a large extent the prosody of a language governs the segmental processes" (p. 218). He explains that there is a difference in syllable reduction in stress-timed languages when compared with syllable-timed languages. This is because degree of stress governs certain processes, as exemplified in the production of the flap (e.g., `atom [ærəm] vs a`tomic [ətamIk]).

In stress-timed languages "syllables recur at regular intervals of time, regardless of the number of intervening unstressed syllables, as in English" (Crystal, 1991, p. 329); in syllable-timed languages "the syllables are said to occur at regular intervals of time as in French" (pp. 339–340). Because prosodic processes represent differences between L1 and L2, Major (1987) considers these *interference* processes (see section on cognition), which take precedence at early learning phases. These processes are believed to interfere with the production of segments. English speakers, accustomed to stress-timed productions, reduce unstressed syllables in Spanish to /ə/; Spanish speakers (who use syllable-timed speech) fail to reduce unstressed syllables to /ə/ and instead produce a full vowel (e.g., America [amerika]). As the rhythm of the new language is mastered, these segmental differences are expected to decrease.

SUMMARY. A number of conditions affect the successful acquisition of authentic L2 (or the maintenance of accented speech). These may be categorized as (a) psychosocial (age of acquisition, motivation level, and gender of the learner), (b) sensorimotor (the perception—differentiating new and equivalent sounds—and production of speech sounds, (c) cognitive (the organization of new phoneme categories and the elimination of interference and developmental processes and (d) phonological (the segmental and prosodic differences inherent in two different languages and the universal relative difficulty of features—markedness of segments, segment combinations, and contexts). Clinicians working with adults learning L2 phonology need to be aware of those conditions contributing to the maintenance of a foreign accent. It is only with this knowledge that the clinician will be able to plan procedures to facilitate target pronunciation. It should be noted that the information appearing in this section revealed a number of diverse points of view as to the primary source of a foreign accent. Not all of these views will be applicable to each client or appeal to every clinician. Knowledge of these potential maintaining factors, nevertheless, should aid the clinician in the decision-making necessary in intervention planning.

Theories of Learning

If we consider the maintaining factors of foreign accent presented in the last section, we can see that there are two major tasks for the L2 speaker: the phonetic task of differentiating and producing accurate L2 replicas, and the phonological (organizational), recognizing new sound categories and boundaries. If these are the learner's tasks, how may these best be facilitated? To answer this question, we turn to theories of learning presented in Chapter 4. Principles from the following theories (operant, constructivist, social-cognitive, relationship-based pragmatic theory, and motor theory) appear appropriate in providing guiding principles for procedure planning with individuals learning second language phonology. Although the focus of this chapter is on L2 phonology, principles from these theories may also be applicable to changes in expressive language.

Operant Theory

As was noted in Chapter 4, principles from operant theory apply to observable behaviors and may be applied to learning across the life span. In addition, behavioral principles apply to the strengthening of behaviors already in the individual's repertoire, or the establishment of new behaviors that reflect *already established* developmental/organizational parameters. This description makes operant principles applicable to the modification of "similar" sounds and the establishment of new sounds (in conjunction with constructivist-cognitive principles). Treatment tasks guided by operant principles such as the rapid production of stimulus words have been found to be highly successful in learning accurate sound productions in L1 (Shriberg & Kwiatkowski, 1982).

A behavioristic orientation to treatment of foreign accent is reviewed by Leather and James (1991). The authors explain that this theoretical position was most prevalent in the 1960s, consonant with the CAH framework in vogue. At that time the focus was on teaching the L2 learner "a new set of 'habit structures' namely, S-R pairings" (p. 325). This approach was weakened as a cognitive interpretation to learning new sound patterns became more popular. The cognitive orientation was influenced by the mentalism of generative grammar and Selinker's (1969) conception of interlanguage as language transfer, implying the learning of new structures rather than habit patterns (Leather & James). More will be said about the cognitive orientation in the next section.

APPLICATION TO GOAL PLANNING. As described in Chapter 4, in this text, goal planning from a behavioristic perspective includes a systematic task selection and analysis. This type of procedural orientation may be illustrated with planning for the acquisition of speech sounds by an L2 learner of English. The derivation of session goals may be facilitated through a task analysis such as the following: (a) identification of a target phoneme and phonetic/syllabic context, (b) production of nonsense monosyllabic syllables with the target sound in desired context following a model, (c) production of the sound in monosyllabic lexical items following a model, (d) production of the target in bisyllabic words following a model, (e) production of target in CVC or bisyllabic words when identifying pictures, etc. This type of task analysis will be discussed again in the section on performance demands later in the chapter when the determination of a hierarchy of context difficulty is discussed.

APPLICATION TO PROCEDURE PLANNING. If a clinician follows a behavioristic model, procedure planning will center on the identification of an effective reward system. For an adult L2 client, awards may be either external to the client (e.g., social praise) or intrinsic to the client (the achievement of a personally set goal—achieving the accurate sound).

Constructivist

Although constructivist principles may be most directly applicable to cases of adult language disorders, higher levels of cognitive organization may be present in other problem-solving situations such as *defining new speech-sound categories* (e.g., Karmiloff-Smith, 1986). Linguists have begun to explain L1 transfers to L2 in cognitive terms. For example, Hammerberg (1990) showed that the transfer of L1 Swedish to L2 German may be viewed as an "inferencing" type strategy in which "the learner makes use of prior linguistic knowledge to interpret L2 intake" (p. 199). He describes three levels of analysis involved with transfer.

(a) at the level of *strategy*, with regard to the learner's plan of action to solve a particular problem in acquiring some phonological regularity in L2; (b) at the level of *execution*, with regard to the event, or process of carrying out the strategy; and (c) at the level of *solution*, with regard to the product of the applied strategy (pp. 198–199).

Actual treatment data based on these notions are not available, yet a knowledge of constructivist principles may be useful in designing treatment contexts for the facilitation of phonemic representations.

APPLICATION TO GOAL SETTING. Constructivist theories allow for the development of organizational parameters of behavior throughout life. These theories, therefore, are applicable to the promotion of phonological reorganization in the adult L2 learner. Long- and short-term goals, therefore, are formulated to target changes in organizational patterns (e.g., phonetic/phonemic categories). Leather and James (1991) describe the "best fit" model of L2, the speech-learning process, as one that makes primary the "construction of phonetic prototypes to which processes of both perception and production may be geared" (p. 320). These prototypes (i.e., target phonemes) are believed to be the basis for guiding perception and monitoring articulation attempts (tokens) of the target.

APPLICATION TO PROCEDURE PLANNING. Based on cognitive principles, procedure planning may include the following:

1. the creation of tasks that are appropriate to the adult learner and challenging enough to provoke developmental changes (category boundaries and allophonic variations);

2. the creation of tasks that involve concrete execution of sensorimotor procedures to achieve the task or solve the problem (production and perception tasks); and

3. provoking the act of reflecting—specifically on perception/production relationships and causal mechanisms related to nonauthentic productions or successes.

Social-Cognitive Theory

According to social-cognitive principles, learning target language sounds would be facilitated by (a) noticing similarities and distinctions among actions and events mediated by those who set the standards, (b) imitation, and (c) practice. A number of cognitive theories of second language learning have been summarized by Ellis (1994). These theories and models of L2 acquisition (e.g., "The Monitor Theory" [Krashen, 1981], Bialystok's Theory of L2 Learning [1978]) view "L2 acquisition as a mental process involving gradual mastery of items and structures through the application of general strategies of perception and production" (p. 392). Although models such as these focus primarily on syntax, they too have the potential for application to the acquisition of phonology.

These principles will affect both the planning of goals and procedures of intervention.

APPLICATION TO GOAL PLANNING. As you can see, much of what we have said about the tasks of the adult L2 learner involves the enhancement of both perceptual and productive skills. These principles support the selection of the session objective, as either perceptual identification or production of a model. The client will be expected to either identify similarities and distinctions among target sounds (based on clinician-directed strategies), talk about these distinctions (using metacognitive strategies), and/or produce these targets.

APPLICATION TO PROCEDURES. Following social-cognitive principles, the clinician will design the clinical context to provide effective "scaffolding" devices (i.e., demonstrations, directions, models of procedures and strategies—see Chapter 7 for suggestions about interpersonal interactions and linguistic and nonlinguistic contexts in which these devices may be applied). A number of Teaching English as a Second Language (TESOL) publications focus on the development of social, metacognitive, and cognitive strategies in establishing control over selected pronunciation features (see Bailey & Savage, 1994; Celce-Muria, 1987; Morley, 1987, 1994).

Relationship-Based Pragmatic Theory

In Chapter 4 of this book, relationship-based pragmatic theories suggest that

> language serves primarily relationship-based social and emotional functions. These relationship-based functions center on the process of intersubjectivity:

the desire of the speaker to make content of mind and intent known by a significant other. Content of mind refers to what the individual is thinking about and feeling at any given moment. Relationship-based pragmatic theory suggests that language learning is a function of communicative engagement with another (p. 59).

Although this theory is most often used to explain the learning of language in children, it may also apply to communicative engagement of adults, especially adults who may be learning a new language or dialect.

APPLICATION TO GOAL PLANNING. Pragmatic theories affect goal planning at each goal planning phase because it is expected that an outcome of learning new sounds involves interacting with another individual. At the session phase, the individual is likely the clinician, but at the short-and long-term phases it may be a variety of interlocutors.

APPLICATION TO PROCEDURE PLANNING. For individuals who are learning a new language and dialect pattern, and feeling unsure of their communicative abilities, it may be wise to

1. be responsive to the affective and intentional states of clients and families

2. integrate caregivers and partners into therapy sessions as coclinicians.

Motor Theory

Klein and Moses (1999) describe motor-learning theories as follows:

> Motor learning theories are concerned with the learning of sensorimotor schemes, which are patterns of behavior—not conscious ideas or cognitive processes. Learning mechanisms cited in these theories include the exercise of motor patterns, self correction in response to problematic feedback, and the differentiation, integration, and coordination of different and often conflicting behavioral patterns. . . . Motor learning theories are most often applied to explain the acquisition of speech skills in the areas of phonology, voice, and fluency (p. 37).

It has been suggested at various points in this chapter that one of the major tasks of the second language learner is the mastery of articulatory gestures (the phonetic aspect); the performance of articulatory gestures serves to develop a motor representation based on various types and levels of feedback: first, peripheral feedback from air and bone-conducted pressure changes and from the joints, tendons and muscles (auditory, tactile, proprioceptive /kinesthetic)—"closed loop"; second, central feedback from within the brain, which is responsible for monitoring of muscular activity—"open loop" (Leather & James, 1991). Because "open-loop" feedback relies on matching a current production with a known motor plan or perceptual signal, it would not be appropriate for learning new sounds and, thus, is predicted to be used less by the new L2 speaker.

APPLICATION TO GOAL PLANNING. Motor theories most directly affect goal planning at the session phase. Operating from a motor theory approach, a clinician would be reminded to include a sensorimotor activity as a session goal (i.e., the execution of an utterance). Examples of such activities can be found in some TESOL approaches to pronunciation practice (e.g., Catford's 1987; Temperley, 1987).

APPLICATION TO PROCEDURE PLANNING: The clinician's role would be to

1. engage the client in activities that require the production of utterances (i.e., producing sounds, syllables, words, sentences, etc., imitatively or spontaneously).

2. model or physically shape the sensorimotor act

SUMMARY. This section has examined the way in which theories of learning may be a useful source in making decisions about intervention planning. See Box 4-1, pp. 68–70 for the principles derived from each theory and the way in which they may be used to guide the clinician in the formulation of goals and procedures. It is expected that not every theoretical model will appeal to the belief system of every clinician; similarly, not every model will be applicable to each client. Part of the challenge of intervention planning is to choose those learning principles that appear most useful to goal and procedure planning with each client, with each session, and even within sessions. As stated in Klein and Moses (1999), "Thus, it is our position that procedural planning does not involve committing to any single theory to the exclusion of others. Procedure planning requires selecting principles from theories relevant to a particular client's . . . problem and differentially applying these principles to design comprehensive therapeutic contexts. . . " (p. 40). Box 10-1 summarizes the way in which learning theories affect the planning of session goals.

Performance Demands

Until this point, three bodies of knowledge believed to be useful in intervention planning have been presented—knowledge about (a) content/form/use interactions, (b) maintaining factors, and (c) theories of learning. The fourth and last source of information for intervention planning is knowledge about those factors that increase or decrease the complexity of a task involved with learning to produce the sounds of a second language. The demands made on a client's performance at any time during the

BOX 10-1: Application of Learning Theories to Intervention Planning for Accented Second Language Speech

	Derived Principles	Application to Goal Planning	Application to Procedure Planning
Operant	Target-sound production is facilitated by: 1. the ability to discriminate stimuli associated with the target sound. 2. events following a behavior that can reinforce or extinguish a behavior.	Guides in the formulation and sequencing of session goals.	Supports a consideration of: • motivational events • behavioral reinforcers
Constructivist Cognitive	Target-sound production is facilitated by: 1. tasks that are complex enough to pose developmental challenges; 2. the execution of sensorimotor procedures to achieve tasks or solve problems; 3. the act of reflecting—specifically on task demands.	Influences the conceptualization of long-term and short-term goals as the acquisition of L2 phonetic categories (involving awareness of allophonic variation and category boundaries).	Supports the encouragement of: • variations in production attempts • self-reflection on performance
Social Cognitive	Target-sound production is facilitated by: 1. noticing similarities and distinctions among speech sounds produced by a standard model; 2. imitation of target sounds; 3. practice of target sounds.	Guides in the formulation of session goals that include discrimination and production activities.	Supports the clinician's role as one who: • models target sounds • suggests metalinguistic strategies for differentiating "new" from "similar" sounds

(continued)

Motor	Target sound is facilitated by peripheral (sensory) and central feedback from movement involved in the act of articulation.	Influences the performance of a production activity within a session goal.	Supports the clinician's role in: • engaging the client in activities that require the production of sounds, syllables, words, sentences, etc., (imitatively or spontaneously). • modeling or physically shaping the sensorimotor act.
Relationship-Based/ Pragmatic	Language serves primarily social and emotional functions Intersubjectivity, the desire of the speaker to make content of mind known to others, is the driving process in language acquisition and language use.	Suggests variation in context of L2 productions, to include, especially, native L1 speakers.	Suggests the encouragement of: • more frequent episodes of L2 conversations and • fewer episodes of L1 speech. • family members or caregivers

intervention process have been referred to as "performance demands" (see Klein & Moses, 1999, and Chapter 7 of this book). Information about performance demands most directly affects the planning of session goals. It is at this point in intervention planning that three important questions need to be answered: (a) What sound, sound groups, or features should be targeted first? (b) In what linguistic context should this target be embedded? (c) What constitutes a sequence of hierarchically organized steps through which the client will generalize this sound (i.e., reach the short-term goal)? The answers to these questions may be found in a review of those variables contributing to performance demands in learning to pronounce a second language.

Klein and Moses (1999) presented a comprehensive review of a number of variables believed to contribute to the demands made on a client's performance of session goals in the area of L1 articulation/phonology. It was shown that the production of a target segment may be affected by (a) the position of the target sound in a given syllable (e.g., initial/onset or final/coda), (b) the phonetic environment (vowels and consonants surrounding target sound), (c) the prosodic contour of word (specifically the stress of the syllable in which the sound occurs), (d) the response mode (described by Klein & Moses,

1999, as a way of differentiating between responses that require production of target with those that do not require production of target [i.e., the targeting of discrimination rather than production of sounds]), and (e) the presence or absence of perceptual support (is the response expected after a model [i.e., imitative] or without a model [spontaneous]). Also, see Box 7-1B.

Research in second language acquisition suggests that these performance demands may be equally valid for planning session goals for the adult L2 client. This section, therefore, will be organized with reference to the variables previously listed ; two additional factors often discussed in L2 phonology, "intrinsic complexity" of segment and "formality of task," will also be examined.

Intrinsic Complexity of Segment

Whether a clinician is targeting the elimination of a phonological process or acquisition of a class of sounds, one of the first considerations, generally, is which sound to target first (e.g., Gierut, Morrisette, Huges, & Rowland, 1996; Powell, 1991). How does one identify this representative sound or *target* sound. Some of the most common criteria for selecting a target sound in cases of L1 phonological disorders are the following: presence in the child's repertoire, stimulability, generalizability, and developmental schedule (see Edwards, 1992; Elbert & Gierut, 1986; and Hodson & Paden, 1991, who suggest distinct criteria for choosing an initial target). Although not stated explicitly, all these criteria reflect a consideration of relative complexity (difficulty in production) as compared with other segments. For example, sounds already present in a child's repertoire are probably earlier on the developmental hierarchy (see commonly referenced schedules such as Prather, Hedrick, & Kern, 1975; Sander, 1972; Smit, Hand, Freilinger, Bernthal, & Bird 1990; Templin, 1957) and, thus, presumably less complex than those not produced. These sounds would likely be more stimulable. These earlier developing, more stimulable sounds are currently thought to develop even without intervention, whereas less stimulable sounds (those more complex) should be targeted first for wider generalizability (e.g., Elbert & Gierut, 1986; Gierut et al., 1996).

More explicit specifications about target complexity as a clinical measure have been made with reference to (a) markedness criteria (Cairns, Cairns, & Williams, 1974; McReynolds, Engmann, & Dimmitt, 1974), (b) implicational laws (e.g., Dinnsen, Chin, Elbert, & Powell, 1990), and (c) consonant specifications (Bernhardt & Stoel-Gammon, 1994).

MARKEDNESS OF SEGMENTS. The concept of markedness (defined above) that developed within the Prague School of Linguistics was subsequently elaborated and applied to generative phonology by Chomsky and Halle (1968). The markedness framework provides for the differentiation of phonemes on the basis of being "marked" or "unmarked" for a particular feature; the unmarked state represents the less complex or natural. Thus, for example, linguistic theory views an optimal consonant as one made in the extreme forward part of the mouth. Consonants that are [+ anterior] (labials and dentals) will be unmarked for this feature [U for anterior]; consonants such as palatals and velars (which are [-anterior]) will be marked [M] for the feature anterior. The total complexity of the phoneme is indicated by the number of marked features or M's. In an effort to verify this theory, Cairns, Cairns, and Williams (1974) developed an inventory of markedness values that they used as a basis for a research study. Within this framework (receiving a complexity score of 0) would be a /t/ unmarked for vocalic, anterior, coronal, continuant, strident, voiced, lateral, and nasal. The most complex segment (with a score of 4) is the /ð/, marked for coronal, continuant, strident, and voiced. Cairns et al. used these values to analyze articulation errors of three dialect groups of elementary schoolchildren (Standard American English, Black American English, and Mexican American English). The results of this study demonstrated that "markedness theory can predict a substantial portion of the substitutions not due to dialectal or second language influences" (p. 166). Some attempts to use Cairns et al. markedness values to predict substitution patterns in children with articulation disorders (McReynolds et al., 1974), or for children learning to pronounce polysyllabic words (Klein, 1978) did not support Cairns et al's findings. Intrinsic segment complexity, measured by "markedness," has not yet been sufficiently supported as an independent predictor of difficulty in L1 or L2 learners. Word position and phonetic environment must be considered in conjunction.

IMPLICATIONAL LAWS. Related to markedness are implicational laws that also predict which sounds or sound classes are more complex than others. Sloat, Taylor, and Hoard (1978) identify the existence of an implicational law between two sounds when the presence of one sound generally implies the presence of the other. To illustrate this phenomenon, they compare /t/ and /d/. Because there are languages that have a /t/ and not a /d/ but not the reverse, the presence of /d/ implies the presence of /t/ but not the reverse. The segment that implies the presence of another, in this case the /d/, is considered to be the more marked (i.e., more complex and less natural). Other markedness relationships cited by Sloat et al. are as follows:

1. Voiced obstruents are more marked than voiceless

2. Liquids are more marked than obstruents

3. Fricatives are more marked than stops

4. Affricates are more marked than fricatives

5. [n] is the least marked nasal

6. [s] and [h] are the least marked fricatives

7. Low vowels are the least marked vowels

8. High vowels are more marked than midvowels

9. High back vowels are more marked than high front vowels

10. The CV syllable is the least marked followed by CVC.

Implicational hierarchies have been used to describe error patterns and suggest remediation hierarchies for children with phonological disorders (Dinnsen et al., 1990). These hierarchies have also been used to explain relative difficulty in the production of clusters in second language phonology (e.g., Carlisle, 1994; Eckman & Iverson, 1994).

Phonetic Environment

After decisions about a target segment or group of segments are made, the next important consideration is the context in which the target will be embedded. L1 treatment approaches to target facilitation have long recognized the effect of the phonetic environment (e.g., Hodson & Paden, 1991; Kent, 1982). Researchers of L2 acquisition have also shown that the phonetic environment will affect the production of certain segments, especially those found to be most problematic for second language learners of English: final consonants and clusters.

Greenberg's (1965) classic study, based on approximately 104 languages, established implicational universals for the length of codas (final consonants) and onsets (initial consonants) and for the segments coexisting within codas and onsets. In general, the longer the onset and coda, the greater the likelihood that cluster reductions will occur. This reduction results in fewer marked clusters (Carlisle, 1994). Greenberg also proposed that certain cluster combinations were more marked than others (if length of cluster was kept constant); therefore, the presence of certain combinations implies the presence of others. For example, if a language has a two-consonant coda with a stop-stop ("backed" [bækt]), it will also have one with a fricative-stop ("laughed" [læft]). If a language has a word-final coda of fricative-fricative ("laughs" [læfs]), it will also have stop-fricative ("looks" [lʊks]), or fricative stop. Stop-stop and fricative-fricative, therefore, are viewed as the more marked sequences. Greenberg also proposed universals for syllable onsets. One of these universals is that if a language has an obstruent-nasal ("snow") onset, then it will have an obstruent-liquid onset ("sleep"). The presence of the former implies the presence of the latter, indicating that the first is more marked than the second. Based on Greenberg's (1965) summary of findings (p. 29), the following markedness (complexity) relationships (appropriate to English) are proposed:

1. Shorter clusters are less complex than longer clusters.

2. Clusters that are analyzable into subclusters are less complex than unanalyzable clusters. For example, [skw] may be reduced to a subcluster /sk/. Some languages were found to present with unanalyzable clusters.

3. Homorganic nasals + obstruents (nd, mb) are less complex than heterorganic nasals + obstruents (ng).

4. Clusters in which sonorants are closer to the peak of the syllable (vowel) are favored over clusters in which obstruents are closer to the peak (e.g., in English initial clusters with two or three consonants must begin with an obstruent and end with a liquid, nasal, or glide—"slow," "splash," "swim," "squeeze,"). Codas, similarly, are guided by the requirement to maintain sonority close to the syllable peak. This is illustrated by the reverse order of consonant sonority relationships in "else," "elf," and "dance." Studies by Carlisle (1988), addressing onsets, and Eckman (1991), addressing codas, support these proposed universals.

Carlisle (1994) summarizes a number of his studies (1988, 1991), involving variability in the use of vowel epenthesis by native Spanish speakers learning English. Vowel epenthesis (the insertion of a vowel between two consonants within a cluster [e.g., class → kəlæs] or at the end of a syllable [e.g., seed →sidə]) has been described as a strategy used more frequently by L2 than L1 learners in an effort to simplify complex syllable structures (Weinberger, 1994). Carlisle also examined the occurrence of vowel epenthesis before specific cluster combinations in order to specify markedness relationships of the interactions between the proceeding segment and the cluster composition (e.g., /sl/ the less marked vs /st/ the more marked; /sl/ the less marked and /sN [collapsed category of /sn/ and /sm/]) the more marked. A consistent finding from all Carlisle's studies (reported in Carlisle, 1994) has been that nonepenthesis (the target variant) occurs significantly more frequently after vowels (the less marked) than after consonants and before the less marked of the cluster combinations. Carlisle concluded that cluster environments can be in a markedness relationship just as the clusters themselves can, and the less marked environment will induce a higher frequency of target variants than will more marked environments. On the basis of his findings, Carlisle proposed a hierarchy of difficulty that may be useful in planning goals for second language learners. The following hierarchy, organized in increasing order of difficulty, is consonant with Carlisle's (1994) suggestions for an instructional approach.

1. two-member onsets before three-member onsets (sp before spl)

2. two-member onsets with initial onsets should be

   approached in the following order: /sl/, /s+nasal/, /s+stop/

3. two-member onset interactions (with different preceding sounds)

   vocalic environment with /sl/

   vocalic environment with /sm/ and /sn/

   vocalic environment with /st/, /sp/, and /sk/

   consonantal environment with /sl/

consonantal environment with /sm/ and /sn/

consonantal environment with /st/, /sp/, and /sk/" (p. 245).

4. three-member onsets.

In contrast to Carlisle (1994), who studied syllable onsets, Eckman and Iverson's (1994) research focused on syllable codas (final consonants). These researchers were interested in describing production patterns affecting syllable final single consonants from different feature classes. Coda consonant errors (affecting obstruents, nasals, liquids, and glides) made by Cantonese, Korean, and Japanese were analyzed. Findings, in general, indicated that relatively marked coda obstruents of English are generally more difficult for speakers of each of the L1 backgrounds studied than are English sonorants. This was even true of the subjects whose L1 had rich coda structures (including both nasals and stops). Eckman and Inverson discuss pedagogical implications based on their findings. Unlike Carlisle (who proceeds from less to more complex), Eckman and Inverson argue for structuring treatment hierarchies that follow implicational principles. These principles would suggest that final consonants that are found to be more problematic should be targeted first. Mastery of a consonant in a final position implies mastery in an initial position, whereas the converse is not true. The authors also note that pronunciation problems with coda consonants may not always be predicted by the presence of these consonant types in the L1.

Position in Syllable

Final syllable position, especially for the production of stops, has been the focus of a number of studies in second language phonology (e.g., Eckman, 1981; Edge, 1991; Weinberger, 1994; Yavas, 1994). Although stops occur in all the languages of the world, many languages do not include stops in final position, and some languages permit only voiceless stops. A restriction on voiced stops appears to be the most common condition (Yavas, 1994). Second language learners whose L1 systems do not permit voiced stops have been observed to have difficulties when learning English. When encountering a voiced stop in final position, an L2 learner of English will most likely use any of the following processes: terminal devoicing (Eckman, 1981), final consonant deletion, and vowel epenthesis (Weinberger, 1994). According to Weinberger, vowel epenthesis is used more frequently than final consonant deletion because it is more likely to preserve lexical contrasts (see discussion on final consonant production earlier in this chapter).

Other studies attempted to further specify difficulties with the production of final voiceless stops by examining the environment of the final segment. For example, Edge (1991) examined the segments following word-final voiced obstruents. Various environments included those before a pause, before a vowel, before a voiced consonant, and before a voiceless consonant. Edge found that there were differential effects for the different environments. Most cases of devoicing occurred before a pause; the next most frequent context was before a voiceless consonant; then, before a voiced consonant and the last the context before a vowel. Yavas (1993, cited in Yavas 1994) extended Edge's consideration of the environment by the place of articulation of the stop and the height of the vowel preceding the stop. Yavas found that subjects devoiced more frequently as the point of articulation went from bilabial to alveolar and then to velar. Although changing the vowel from low to high did not affect the bilabial stop, it made a significant difference with the alveolar and velar stops.

These later two studies have important implications for planning of session goals. Based on Edge's study, a clinician targeting final stops would be wise to consider the environment following the stop. Edge's findings suggest the following hierarchy (of increasing difficulty) of environmental conditions:

1. before a vowel

2. before a voiced consonant

3. before a voiceless consonant

4. before a pause

Yavas (1994) discusses the implications for targeting voiced stops in final position based on his findings. His suggestions may also be organized within a complexity hierarchy of increasing difficulty.

1. bilabial stops preceded by low vowels (nonhigh, e.g., tub, rob, cab).

2. bilabial stops preceded by high vowels (e.g., bib).

3. alveolar stops preceded by a low vowel (e.g., bed, bad, red).

4. alveolar stops preceded by a high vowel (e.g., bead, food, kid).

5. velar stops preceded by a low vowel (e.g., bag, dog, egg).

6. velar stops preceded by a high vowel (e.g., big, pig).

7. bisyllablic words and words with initial clusters may become appropriate contexts for final voiced contexts next.

The Prosodic Contour of Word (specifically, the stress of the syllable in which the sound occurs).

As noted earlier, prosodic processes also affect the acquisition of L2 consonants and vowels (Major, 1987). Vowel reduction and the production of certain consonant allophones (e.g., the intervocalic /t/ produced as a flap), appear problematic to L2 learners of English. On the basis of these tendencies, one would conclude that target sounds should first be introduced in most salient contexts (stressed) before contexts reduced in stress. In addition, when targeting word stress patterns it would be wise to consider sounds already in the learner's repertoire. These principles conform with those currently expressed in nonlinear phonology. Within the nonlinear framework, it is suggested that segmental and prosodic aspects not be targeted simultaneously (i.e., follow the principle of using old forms to express new functions and new forms for expressing old functions, Bernhardt & Stoel-Gammon, 1994).

Response Mode

In the section on maintaining factors, it was demonstrated that both perception and production factors are involved with the learning of L2 sounds. The clinician must decide which modality to target first when formulating session goals. These decisions are often based on points of view expressed in published procedural approaches on the correction of foreign accents (e.g., Catford, 1987; Morley, 1994; Wong, 1987). Clinicians can also be guided by results of research in the area of L1 articulation treatment when making decisions about which modality to target first.

PERCEPTION. Leather and James (1991) review a number of studies designed to improve the phonetic ability of L2 speakers. These studies were designed to determine which modality should be trained first, perception or production, to affect the most efficient carryover to the other. Of the nine studies noted, training perception first revealed a slight advantage. The authors, however, concluded that the inconsistent and inconclusive findings were probably due to the differences in methodology and conceptualizations of perceptual and production knowledge.

The "perception first" explanation, nevertheless, continues to gain support. Leather and James (1991) point out that one of the reasons that the adult L2 learner rarely attains native-like pronunciation is that attempts to communicate occur before much prior perceptual exposure to the target language sound pattern (unlike L1 learners). In a similar vein, Neufeld (1980) hypothesizes (based on research data) that if L2 learners begin to pronounce before being sufficiently exposed to standard productions, they will misshape their developing phonetic "templates," which will then continue to guide inauthentic productions.

PERCEPTION AND PRODUCTION. Offering another point of view regarding the relationship between perception and production, Leather and James (1991) suggest that the speech-learning mechanism has the capacity to interrelate perceptual and productive knowledge which is conditioned by particular contexts and circumstances. In support of this position, they submit research findings from one of the authors (i.e., Leather, 1990) on the learning of Chinese tones by Dutch and English speakers. Using computerized techniques, some subjects were trained first in perception, whereas others were trained in production. These findings indicated that neither perception nor production training appeared to be prerequisite. Rather, training in either modality facilitated performance in the other.

Perceptual Support

Klein and Moses (1999) describe perceptual support in two major forms: the clinician's model and orthographic symbols. Each of these support devices is used by clinicians to decrease the performance demand on individual's learning to pronounce. A recent model of a target sound or word facilitates articulatory attempts and thus often becomes an early step in treatment (e.g., Bernthal, Bankson, & Flipson, Jr., 2017; Schmidt, 1997). Adult second language speakers may also be guided by the support of the printed word. This form of support would also lessen the demand made on production.

Box 10-2 summarizes the way in which performance demands affect the planning of session goals.

SUMMARY. The first part of this chapter explored four bodies of information believed to be basic to the intervention planning process. Each may be referenced at various phases of intervention planning and for specific aspects of the process (i.e., goals and/or procedures). The first, knowledge of content/form/use interactions in L2 learning, helps the clinician to understand the nature of the L2 sound system (and the concept of an interlanguage); this knowledge is essential in formulating realistic long- and short-term phonology goals. The second, a knowledge of maintaining factors, orients the

BOX 10-2. Performance Demands That Influence the Formulation of Session Goals

Areas of Performance Demand	Aspect of Goal Affected
Intrinsic complexity of segments or sound classes	Target: Selection of target sound or sound group: more or less marked/natural/complex or developmental expectation
Syllable position	Linguistic context: Syllable context in which target is embedded: onset or coda
Phonetic environment	Linguistic context: Phonetic environment of target sound, surrounding segments and/or cluster compositions
Prosodic contour of word	Linguistic context: Stress of syllable in which target is embedded: stressed or unstressed
Response mode	Target: The response expected of client: verbal or nonverbal
Perceptual support	Linguistic context: Clinician's model vs. spontaneous Nonlinguistic context: The presence or absence of visual support as a basis of the client's performance
Task formality	Nonlinguistic context: Degree of propositionality of task: read minimal word pairs versus conversation

clinician to the linguistic and nonlinguistic sources of variability in learning the L2; this should be useful knowledge for (a) identifying those areas requiring modification as a basis for the achievement of L2 targets, and (b) predicting the time necessary for goal accomplishment. The third, a knowledge of learning theories, is expected to guide the clinician in determining the most appropriate procedural approach for a given client (i.e., how best to facilitate the production of L2 targets). The fourth body of knowledge, performance demands, directs the clinician to those linguistic and nonlinguistic factors that affect the ability of a client to carry out a given task; information about factors influencing performance is most important for envisioning a series of session goals.

The next section introduces an L1 Spanish adult (Manuel) learning English. His case history, including results from testing, appears in Appendix A. A plan for treatment management follows.

The Management Plan—Manuel

The Long-Term Phase

LONG-TERM GOALS

As an L2 learner, Manuel's functional communication will be enhanced by improvement in content/form interactions (i.e., vocabulary, written and oral syntax, figurative language) and phonological knowledge and performance. Baseline data (Appendix A) indicate that Manuel presents with numerous L1-influenced syntactic patterns (in written and oral language), inappropriate morpheme use, and difficulty in the comprehension and interpretation of figurative expressions. The phonological analysis reveals a number of interlanguage patterns affecting consonants, clusters, vowels, and prosody, all typical of an L1 Spanish speaker (see Diagnostic report in Appendix A and Contrastive Analysis Charts in Appendix B).

Deriving the Long-Term Goal

In light of baseline data, the following two long-term *superordinate* (primary) goals are planned for Manuel (see Figure 10.1). For the purpose of delineating specific taxonomies, each primary long-term goal has been expressed as subordinate goals, which address separate taxonomies although possibly undertaken simultaneously (see Chapter 3 for the explication of subordinate goals, and Figures 10.2a and 10.2b for subordinate long-term goals in each area).

Deriving the Long-Term Goal			
Decision	**Guiding Information**		
Areas of Speech/Language to be Targeted, Referent Taxonomy, and Current Level of Performance	**Area of Speech/Language**	**Referent Taxonomy**	**Current Performance**
	Speech	Acquisition of segmental and suprasegmental features: Bernhardt and Stemberger (2000)	L1 influence on L2 consonants, vowels, clusters, prosody
	Language	Form/content, use interactions: Klein and Moses (1999)	Evidence of morphological difference Some difficulties in comprehending and using figurative language
Projecting a Prognosis	**Maintaining Factors**	**Severity**	**Current Performance**
	Cognitive	Mild Mod. Sev.	Lacks awareness of L1/L2 phonological distinctions
	Sensorimotor	Mild Mod. Sev.	Restricted vowels space and articulatory proficiency for new sounds
	Psychosocial	Mild Mod. Sev.	Anxious about speaking to new people and in novel situations
	Caretaker Attendance	Frequently	Intermittently	Rarely
Time Frame	Time Allotted	2 years	
Long-Term Goal	1. Reduce dialectal phonological patterns in a variety of social and vocational contexts. 2. Eliminate dialectal patterns affecting language production in conversational speech.		

FIGURE 10.1: Manuel's long-term goals

Deriving Subordinate Long-Term Goal(s)			
Long-Term Goal: Reduce dialectal phonological patterns in a variety of social and vocational contexts			
Decision	**Guiding Information**		
Areas of Speech/Language Intrinsic to the Long-Term Goal	**Area of Speech/Language**	**Referent Taxonomy**	**Current Performance Level**
	Segmental phonemes (consonants, vowels) and clusters	Consonant and vowel feature complexity: Bernhardt and Stemberger (2000); Cluster complexity, Grunwell (1985)	Frequent and variable substitutions affecting vowels, consonants, and clusters
	Prosodic structures	Stress and syllable interactions: Bernhardt and Stemberger (2000), Klein and Spector (1985)	Unstressed L2 syllables are given full vowel value
Subordinate Long-Term Goals	1. Reduce the use of dialectal patterns affecting consonants, consonant clusters, and vowels in all pragmatic contexts. 2. Reduce the use of dialectal prosodic patterns in conversational speech.		

FIGURE 10.2a: Subordinate long-term goals for speech intervention

Deriving Subordinate Long-Term Goal(s)			
Long-Term Goal: Eliminate dialectal patterns affecting language in conversational contexts			
Decision	**Guiding Information**		
Areas of Speech/Language Intrinsic to the Long-Term Goal	**Area of Speech/Language**	**Referent Taxonomy**	**Current Performance Level**
	Morphemes	Morpheme complexity: Brown (1973)	Frequent and variable morpheme differences in oral and written language
	Figurative Language	Figurative language (transparency): Nippold and Rudzinski (1993)	Difficulty in comprehending and expressing figurative language
Subordinate Long-Term Goals	1. Use contextually appropriate morphemes in written and oral expression. 2. Use a variety of figurative expressions appropriately in conversational contexts.		

FIGURE 10.2b: Subordinate long-term goals for language intervention

As you can see, speech and language long-term goals for Manuel have been written with differentiated expectations. For example, the goals addressing phonological aspects target *reduction* of given patterns, not *elimination*. Decisions regarding the final outcomes of treatment for these goals are based on a number of factors operating against the prospect of long-term unaccented speech.

Primary among these delimiting factors is the age at which Manuel started to learn English—21 years. Research indicates that phonological learning after the age of 6 is generally marked by some accent (Flege, 1992; Long, 1990; Patkowski, 1994). Another deterrent of unaccented speech is the amount of time Manuel spends speaking his L1. It has been shown that speakers who use their L2 the greater proportion of the time make more progress than those who use the L2 less (Flege et al., 1997). Manuel also has a history of depression, inability to concentrate, and anxiety, which may also impede his achievement of authentic pronunciation. Personality factors have also been shown to play a part in the acquisition of authentic L2 speech (Major, 1994).

The achievement of content/form interactions expressed in accurate morphology as well as figurative language may be achieved more completely than phonology (*super*ordinate goal 2 and related *sub*ordinate goals). Manuel reports already making strides in vocabulary acquisition and the ability to express himself. In addition, the literature is less consistent with reference to as early a critical period as with phonology (e.g., Major, 1994).

It is anticipated that Manuel will be a good candidate for treatment and will achieve our Long-term goals in approximately three years. The client presents with a number of characteristics operating for L2 improvement. He is highly motivated (e.g., Leather & James, 1991); he voices serious concern about his inability to express himself in groups and when addressing a class. He is eager to improve his use of English as a means toward academic and professional achievement. In addition, he appears to be a committed, conscientious, and intelligent student.

The Procedural Approach

As outlined in Chapter 4, the procedural approach addresses the modification of maintaining factors and the utilization of premises from relevant theories of learning. As suggested in the baseline data presented in Appendix A, Manuel's accented speech may be maintained by both psychosocial and sensorimotor factors. Although we cannot modify his late onset of L2, we may encourage him to increase the percentage of time in which L2 is currently used. As an adult L2 learner, Manuel must learn to expand his categories of L2 sounds, especially vowels (e.g., Flege, 1995a), and learn new articulatory gestures (e.g., Leather & James, 1991). A focus on modifying these maintaining factors is expected to facilitate the modification of inauthentic productions. For clients like Manuel, who are unlikely to achieve authentic L2 speech sounds, it might also be wise to consider the position of Behrman (2017), who has demonstrated that a focus on *clear speech*, "increased intelligibility and ease of understanding" may be preferable to striving for production accuracy.

A procedural approach for Manuel will be guided primarily by principles from each of four theories presented in Box 4-1: constructivist-cognitive, social-cognitive, relational based-pragmatic, and motor. The premises from these four theories appear in Figure 10.3, the procedural approach. The way in which these premises guide decision-making about procedures of treatment will be discussed in the next section, on short-term goal planning.

Planning the Procedural Approach		
Decision	**Guiding Information**	
Ultimate Behaviors to Be Acquired	**Long-Term Goals and Corresponding Subordinate Long-Term Goal(s)**	1. <u>Reduce dialectal phonological patterns in a variety of social and vocational contexts.</u> 1a. reduce the use of dialectal patterns affecting consonants, consonant clusters, vowels in all pragmatic contexts. 1b. reduce the use of dialectal prosodic patterns in conversational speech. 2. <u>Eliminate dialectal patterns affecting language production in conversational speech.</u> 2a. Use contextually appropriate morphemes in written and oral expression. 2b. Use a variety of figurative expressions appropriately in conversational contexts.
Approaches to Intervention	**Types of Evidence**	**Reference**
	Meta-analysis	Munro and Derwing (2015)
	Experimental	Behrman (2017); Carlisle's (1994); Flege (1995); Leather and James (1991); Major (1987); Schmidt (1997); Sloat, Taylor, and Hoard (1978); Weinberger (1994); Yavas (1994); Yavas and Goldstein (1998)
Premises about Language Learning or Rehabilitation from Clinical Research Relevant to Achieving Long-Term Goals	Theory	
	Theory	**Premises**
	Constructivism	**Premises** Target-sound production is facilitated by tasks that are complex enough to pose developmental challenges; the execution of sensorimotor procedures to achieve tasks or solve problems; the act of reflecting on task demands.
	Relationship-Based Pragmatic	Language serves primarily social and emotional functions.
	Social Cognitive	Target sounds are facilitated by noticing similarities and distinctions among speech-sounds produced by a standard model; imitation of target sounds; practice of target sounds.
	Motor	Learning speech-sounds is facilitated by peripheral (sensory) and central feedback from movement involved in the act of sound production.
	Operant	Target-sound production is facilitated by the ability to correctly identify stimuli associated with the target; events following behavior that can reinforce or extinguish behavior.
Maintaining Factors that Need to Be Addressed	**Maintaining Factors**	**Current Performance**
	Cognitive	Lack of awareness of articulatory positions and sounds differences
	Sensorimotor	Lack of differentiation of L1 and L2 consonants, vowels, and stress patterns
	Psychosocial	Infrequent use of L2 in social and vocational contexts

FIGURE 10.3: Long-Term Procedural approach

The Short-Term Phase

THE SHORT-TERM GOAL As suggested in Chapter 1, the short-term phase of intervention planning is one of making decisions about priorities. We must decide which of the long-term goals to address and how to address each (i.e., what sequence of steps do we take to reach the long-term goal?). A set of short-term goals for our *first* long-term goal has been added to the Management Plan in Figure 10.4. As you can see, both subordinate long-term phonology goals have been addressed. This is because segmental and prosodic features interact in the pronunciation of words, (e.g., Major, 1987). If this chapter covered all aspects of learning a second language, we would have also listed our second primary goal. It is often efficient and useful to target both phonology and syntactic goals during the same period of treatment (see Klein & Moses, 1999) for a number of examples of such multicomponent targets). Now let us examine the derivation of the given short-term goals.

The first decision made was to work on subordinate long-term goals addressing phonology simultaneously—prosodic and segmental aspects. Because Spanish is a syllable-timed language, Manuel gives substantial stress to each syllable. This results in full-vowel nuclei rather than L2 expected schwa in certain syllable positions. The listener, therefore, perceives the schwa as being replaced by any number of other identifiable vowels (e.g., æ, e, u). It appears necessary to work on word prosody early (goal 1) in the treatment process because it does influence segment production (Major, 1987). Next, we needed to consider which vowels, consonants, and clusters to target during this first period.

Making priority decisions within sound categories required a number of considerations. First, we wanted to address a pattern that affects a substantial number of phonemes rather than an individual substitution or phonetic difference (e.g., trilled /r/) affecting a single sound. Second, we wanted to recognize contrasts between L1 and L2. As we discussed earlier, in the section on perception and production, L2 sounds that are most problematic for adult learners are those that are absent from the L1 repertoire, but close enough to L1 sounds, not to trigger the spontaneous creation of a new category. Our third consideration was that we would be guided by available universal patterns affecting vowels, consonants, and clusters. Short-term goals 2 to 4 were derived with reference to these considerations.

Goal 2 targets the reduction of the pattern of tensing of lax vowels. This pattern affects a number of vowels, most consistently the production of /ɪ/, /ʊ/, which are differentiated primarily on the basis of tense versus lax. It also affects /ɛ/,/ʌ/ and /ɔ/ and other lax vowels which engage in more variable substitutions. Although Spanish does not contain any of these vowels, each is close enough to a Spanish vowel to deter the development of a new category (i/ɪ; ʊ/u; e/ɛ, o/ʌ, ɔ); thus, targeting the tense–lax distinction is supported by the number of sounds affected and also by the improbability of spontaneous improvement (Flege, 1992, 1995b).

Goal 3 targets the reduction of final devoicing and of epenthesis. This goal is supported with reference to a variety of sources. First, a glance at the contrastive analysis chart, Figure B.1 in Appendix B, shows that Spanish has very few final consonant sounds and no opportunity for voicing contrasts. Voicing contrasts, especially among final stops, are among the most marked, universally (e.g., Eckman, 1977) and therefore predicted to be problematic for L2 learners. Adding to the difficulty is the subtle quality of the voicing feature as the only difference, a feature, as with subtle vowel differences, is not striking enough to signal the development of a new category. Final devoicing and epenthesis are generally alternative strategies to maintain a word-final consonant (Weinberger, 1994) and therefore appropriate to target together. Other consonant mismatches affect fewer sounds and have received less attention in terms of universal patterns.

Goal 4 addresses the reduction of cluster reduction in word-final position in words. As noted in baseline data, Manuel presents with a number of mismatches in producing L2 final and within word clusters. A decision was made to target final clusters because we are also working with final consonants. Those clusters involving final voiced consonants are expected to interact well with final singleton voicing. Final clusters also have a more predictable pattern than within word clusters: most prominent were those ending in /t/ (lt, st, kst, nst) or /z/ (gz, dz).

Deriving Short-Term Goals			
Decision	Guiding Information and Client-Specific Details		
Long-Term Goal and Corresponding Subordinate Long-Term Goals and Taxonomies Addressed	Long-Term Goal and/or Subordinate Long-Term Goal(s)	Taxonomy	Current Performance Level
	1. Reduce dialectal phonological patterns in a variety of social and vocational contexts.	Consonant, vowel, cluster and prosodic complexity: Bernhardt and Stemberger (2000); Sloat, Taylor, and Hoard (1978)	Variable dialectal patterns affecting vowels, consonants, clusters, and prosody
	1a. Reduce the use of dialectal patterns affecting consonants, consonant clusters, vowels in conversational speech.	Consonant, vowel and cluster complexity: Grunwell, 1985; Carlisle's (1994); Yavas (1994); Edge (1991)	Frequent and variable substitutions affecting vowels, consonants, and clusters
	1b. Reduce the use of dialectal prosodic patterns in conversational speech.	Stress pattern complexity in multisyllabic words: Klein and Spector (1985)	Unstressed L2 syllables are given full vowel value
Time Frame	Time Allotted: 6 months		

FIGURE 10.4: Deriving Manuel's Short-term Goals

Short-Term Goals and Rationale	Long-Term Goal Addressed:
	Short-Term Goal(s) **Rationale with reference to: development/complexity/difficulty**
	Subordinate Long-Term Goal Addressed: Reduce prosodic dialectal patterns in conversational speech.
	Short-Term Goal 1 Produce unstressed syllables in polysyllabic words. **Rationale with reference to: development/complexity/difficulty** Because Spanish is a syllable-timed language, Manuel gives substantial stress to each syllable. This results in full vowel nuclei rather than L2 expected schwa in certain syllable positions. The listener, therefore, perceives the schwa as being replaced by any number of other identifiable vowels (e.g. æ, e , u). It appears necessary to work on word prosody early in the treatment process since it does influence segment production (Major, 1987).
	Subordinate Long-Term Goal Addressed: Reduce the use of dialectal patterns affecting consonants, consonant clusters, vowels in all pragmatic contexts.
	Short-Term Goal 2: Reduce the pattern of tensing lax vowels in words and phrases **Rationale with reference to: development/complexity/difficulty** While Spanish does not contain any of these lax vowels, each is close enough to a Spanish vowel to deter the development of a new category (i/ɪ; ʊ/ʌ; e/ɛ, o/ʌ, ɔ); thus, targeting the tense lax distinction is supported by the number of sounds affected and also by the improbability of spontaneous improvement (Flege, 1992; 1995).
	Short-Term Goal 3: Reduce the pattern of final consonant devoicing and epenthesis in words and phrases. **Rationale with reference to: development/complexity/difficulty** Final devoicing and epenthesis are generally alternative strategies to maintain a word-final consonant (Weinberger, 1994) and therefore appropriate to target together. Other consonant mismatches affect fewer sounds and have received less attention in terms of universal patterns.
	Short-Term Goal 4: Reduce the pattern of cluster reduction in final position of words. **Rationale with reference to: development/complexity/difficulty** Those clusters involving final voiced consonants are expected to interact well with final singleton voicing. Final clusters also have a more predictable pattern than within word clusters: most prominent were those ending in /t/ (lt, st, kst, nst) or /z/ (gz, dz).

FIGURE 10.4 CONTINUED: Deriving Manuel's Short-term Goals

Operationalized Procedural Approach (Premises and Implications)

At this point in management planning for Manuel, we must make decisions about the nonlinguistic and linguistic contexts that will best facilitate the goals we have targeted.

In planning the *nonlinguistic context*, we need to consider the nature of goals targeted and the age, abilities, and interests of the client. Treatment procedures for L2 phonology learners closely resemble procedures of intervention for disordered L1 phonology (Schmidt, 1997). The client will need materials that are appropriate to and facilitative of the targets he is expected to produce, those that will maintain his interest, and those that he perceives as academically and professionally useful.

Next, we turn to the *linguistic* context. Here, decisions are made about the role of the clinician in the treatment context and are guided by the premises from learning theories stated in the long-term goal section. The selected premises of learning direct the clinician to enhance Manuel's phonological productions by presenting contrasting sounds for discrimination, modeling specific targets for imitation, and helping Manuel reflect on his articulatory movements (see Figure 10.5). These actions on the part of the clinician are also expected to reduce the sensorimotor maintaining factors identified at the long-term phase. In addition to, and perhaps compounding his phonological difficulties, are a number of psychosocial factors. Linguistic and nonlinguistic considerations guiding procedure planning appear in Figure 10.5.

Operationalizing the Procedural Approach	
Decision	**Guiding Information**
Short-Term Goals to be Addressed	1. Produce unstressed syllables in polysyllabic words. 2. Reduce the pattern of tensing lax vowels in words and phrases. 3. Reduce the pattern of final consonant devoicing and epenthesis in words and phrases. 4. Reduce the pattern of cluster reduction in final position of words.

Derive Implications for Procedure Planning from Theory-Based Premises	**Constructivist Premise:** Production is facilitated by reflection on production attempts.
	  Implication: Therefore the clinician will operationalize the procedural approach by presenting contrasting sounds for identification or judgment of same/difference; helping client to reflect on kinesthetic and auditory cues.
	
	Relationship-Based/Pragmatic Premise: Language serves primarily social and emotional functions.
	  Implication: Therefore the clinician will operationalize the procedural approach by encouraging Manuel to engage in greater use of L2 with family and friends and at work.

FIGURE 10.5: Operationalized procedural approach for Manuel

	Social-Cognitive Premise: Sound learning is facilitated by imitating models.
	
	  Implication: Therefore the clinician will operationalize the procedural approach by modelling target sounds in words or phrases for imitation.
	
	Motor-Learning Premise: The acquisition of motor representations emerges from practice with gestures required for production.
	
	  Implication: Therefore the clinician will operationalize the procedural approach by encouraging frequent practice.
	
	Operant Premise: Target-sound production is facilitated by the ability to correctly identify stimuli associated with the target sound; events following behavior that can reinforce behavior.
	
	  Implication: Therefore the clinician will operationalize the procedural approach by facilitating feedback for goal achievement.

Derive Implications for Procedure Planning from Maintaining Factors	**Maintaining Factors**
	
	Cognitive: Reduced awareness of L2 sound differences
	  Implication: Reflect on productions
	
	Psychosocial: Anxious about speaking to new people and in novel situations
	  Implication: Use L2 patterns with friends, family, at work and in social situations.
	
	Sensorimotor: Restricted vowels space and articulatory proficiency for new sounds
	  Implication: Perception and production exercises

FIGURE 10.5 CONTINUED: Operationalized procedural approach for Manuel

The Session Phase

Session Goals and Procedures

We are now at the phase of intervention planning that is most tangible. It is during the session with the client that we have the opportunity to apply what we planned during phases 1 and 2 and observe the accomplishment of "an act of learning." As discussed in Chapter 1, this act of learning is both *observable and measurable* and is expected to be one step in a *series of steps* leading to the short-term goal.

DECIDING ON A GOAL APPROACH STRATEGY. As the final stage in intervention planning, we bring to bear all our prior sources of information on the formulation of session goals and procedures. In planning goals at this point, therefore, we reference the client's baseline data, implications from maintaining factors and from learning theory premises, and information about performance demands relative to phonological change. Referencing these sources of information helps us to decide on a goal approach strategy. This involves answering at least the following three questions: (1) Do we wish to target all short-term goals within the first few sessions? (2) Would it be more efficient to target certain goals before others? (3) How do we approach the achievement of each short-term goal we target.

With reference to questions 1 and 2, let us review the short-term goals we have selected for Manuel (Figure 10.4). These goals target prosody, vowels, final singleton consonants, and clusters. Of these four areas, the two that are most directly related are final consonants and clusters. Recall that Manuel has difficulty with the production of final voiced stops and clusters containing these stops. Some of this difficulty may be explained by the inability to terminate the articulatory gesture simultaneously with the cessation of voicing (because he does not have L1 experience with this feature). When voicing ceases before the articulatory gesture is completed, a voiceless final consonant is produced; if voicing continues beyond the completion of the articulatory gestures, epenthesis of a schwa occurs. There is, however, another strategy for maintaining voice in a final stop consonant—the addition of a voiced continuant (as demonstrated for child language by Fey & Gandour, 1982). For Manuel, this would mean the production of final voiced stop followed by voiced fricatives (bz. dz, gz). It is reasonable to predict that the production of voiced final singletons would be facilitated by the introduction of final voiced clusters; thus goal 4 should precede goal 3 by a number of sessions. Of the other goals, there are no obvious priority needs, and they will be addressed in cycle fashion during the first short-term goal period (Hodson & Paden, 1991). The introduction of a number of separate deviation patterns within a contracted period (e.g., a semester) has been found to be efficient for the remediation of developmental phonological disorders—it is this interference with habitual patterns that generates greater reorganization of the individual's phonological system (Hodson & Paden). It is likely that the same rationale is appropriate for an adult who exhibits an interlanguage system, constituting a number of patterns, which requires reorganization.

Now let us turn to question 3. On the basis of our decision-making at earlier phases of intervention planning, we have already established some guidelines for approaching session planning across the various goals. First, we know that we must begin to modify those factors hypothesized to maintain Manuel's accented speech. For Manuel, we have determined that these are sensorimotor and psychosocial. As an adult second language learner, we can expect that Manuel will have difficulties with both the discrimination and the production of L2 speech sounds and prosody. In addition, the frequent use of his L1 and his anxiety about certain speaking situations adds a psychosocial deterrent to his progress with L2. These maintaining factors will be targeted now, at the session phase, by incorporating a discrimination or production task at each session. Attempts will also be made, when appropriate, to modify the frequency of his use of L2 and his sensitivity to new speaking situations.

Session goals are also shaped by our knowledge of learning theory. At the second phase of intervention planning, we selected premises from learning theories most suitable for this client (see Figure 10.5). We will now use these premises to guide us in the development of session procedures. For example, the premise from cognitive theory suggests that the clinician present items for discrimination that range in complexity; the premise from social cognitive theory suggests that the clinician model desired utterances; the motor-learning premise implies that the client must engage in frequent practice.

Finally, the approach to goal formulation is greatly influenced by our knowledge of the variables that contribute to increasing or decreasing demands on a client's performance. Earlier in this chapter, we outlined a number of variables known to influence the performance of a phonological task; these include intrinsic complexity of segments or sound classes, syllable position, phonetic environment, prosodic contour of word, response mode, perceptual support, and task formality. These variables will be addressed as a systematic means of modifying complexity and difficulty as a series of session goals is projected.

At this point, we are prepared to plan the session goals that should lead to each short-term goal. It is generally not possible to plan ahead the full number of session goals for each short-term goal. We can never be sure how any client will react to our plans and how much progress he or she will make. Moreover, it is not necessary to plan for more than one goal at a time. With the information previously outlined to guide us, we continue to modify our targets, and procedures for reaching them, as we monitor the clients performance. To illustrate the way in which the above sources of information contribute to (a) the formulation of session goals and (b) the modification of goals via an increase or decrease in task complexity and/or difficulty, two session goals will be formulated for each of the short-term goals: an early session goal and a late session goal. Session goal derivations across all short-term goals will be described in the text; in addition, session goals for two of these short-term goals will be illustrated in the session goal template (Figure 10.6, Phase 3 of the Management Plan). Words italicized in each goal statement serve to highlight the specific aspects of the goal that have been derived through a consideration of maintaining factors, learning principles, and performance demands.

Derivations for each session goal are discussed below.

SHORT-TERM GOAL 1: Manuel will reduce unstressed syllables in polysyllabic words. Manuel demonstrates the lack of stress reduction in most polysyllabic words, especially with three or more syllables. Because Manuel's L1 was a syllable-timed language, he has little experience with the various stress contours possible in English. It has been shown that English has eight primary stress (or intonation) patterns affecting words of two to four syllables (Sikorski, 1991). Thus, Manuel must learn to differentiate and produce a range of stress contours in polysyllabic words. How to proceed within a series of sessions leading to the achievement of this goal requires, first, hypotheses about those variables contributing to gradations of difficulty and/or complexity with reference to learning L2 stress contours. One factor often associated with increased demands on performance is increased syllable number (Bernthal, Bankson, & Flipsson, Jr., 2017; Bleile, 1995; Lowe, 1994). As syllable number increases from two to three and four, the number of alternative intonation patterns increases. Thus, greater complexity is present in the patterns possible for three- and four-syllable words. Because Manuel will also be introduced to new vowel and consonant targets during this phase of treatment, it is probably wise to start with only two-syllable words, including the two basic patterns trochaic (strong-weak) and iambic (weak-strong). Performance demands, therefore, may be increased by targeting an increase in syllable number and introducing other stress patterns. Other factors that are likely to promote gradations in performance demands are the linguistic and nonlinguistic contexts in which these words will be produced.

A nonlinear approach to phonological change suggests that new segmental and prosodic targets be targeted separately during the early stages of treatment (e.g., Bernhardt & Stoel-Gammon, 1994). It is suggested that when a new prosodic structure is introduced, the segmental content should be selected among established sounds. This approach suggests that performance demands would also be controlled by modifying the segmental content of two-syllable words by increasing the intrinsic complexity of segments or sound classes (with reference to Manuel's L2 phoneme repertoire; see Appendix B.). Perceptual support and task formality are two nonlinguistic areas that may be modified in increasing performance demand in the development of session goals leading to short-term goal 1. Articulatory treatment for adults as well as for children prescribes the use of a clinician's model to facilitate the attainment of a target response. Imitation of a model is generally an expected step before spontaneous production (e.g., Bernthal, Bankson, & Flipsson, Jr., 2017). Moving in the direction of reduced perceptual support, therefore, is a move in the direction of increased demand on performance. Task formality has also been shown to be related to accuracy of target achievement (e.g., Dickerson, 1987; Leather & James, 1991). The more formal tasks (i.e., word lists, minimal pairs) have been found to produce a greater proportion of L2 targets than the less formal tasks (dialogue, conversation). These research findings suggest that short-term goals may be made more challenging by altering the formality of the task.

The two session goals directed to the achievement of short-term goal 1 appear in Figure 10.6. You will note that a number of items are italicized in the statement of the goal. These italicized items represent decisions that have been made on the basis of a consideration of the sources of information discussed previously. We will examine each of these items in order to understand the basis for their selection.

The word *produce* is italicized because the hypothesized maintaining factors suggest that Manuel should have the opportunity to practice an act of discrimination or production at each session. Manuel has already demonstrated that he can identify the difference between two contrastive two-syllable word stress patterns. Both *trochaic* and *iambic* word patterns have been differentiated receptively, and production of this contrast, as with segments in minimal pairs, may serve to support the distinction. *After the clinician's model* is stipulated because this is an early goal and Manuel has not yet produced structures of this type accurately. *18/20* items appear a reasonable basis for any advance to more difficult prosodic contours. *List* is highlighted because it has been shown that L2 speakers are more likely to achieve the L2 target in words in more formal tasks.

The clinician utilizes premises from social-cognitive theory by modeling, and comparing his productions with the model; motor theory, by requesting imitation; and constructivist cognitive by helping him reflect on his productions. A later session goal is derived by modifying syllable number, the nature of perceptual support (written material rather than a clinician's model), the additional cognitive task of categorization. Premises from learning theories and maintaining factors remain essentially the same.

SHORT-TERM GOAL 2. Manuel will eliminate the pattern of tensing lax vowels in words and phrases. The substitution pattern for these vowel pairs is very consistent and related primarily to the absence of lax vowels in Spanish (see Appendix B, Figure B.2). Thus, it is necessary for Manuel to learn to receptively differentiate these vowels before he can produce them accurately. Consequently, *identification*, rather than production becomes the target of the early goal. *Identification* was also the choice over an alternative approach, "same-different." This is because the literature has shown that some clients make greater progress with this approach (Lively, Pisoni, Yamada, Tohikura, & Yamada, 1994; Logan, Lively, & Pisoni, 1991) and actually prefer it (Flege, 1995b). *Pointing* is italicized to make the act of learning to differentiate observable and measureable to the clinician. *After hearing the clinician's productions* incorporates the use of a familiar model before an unfamiliar model. It has been shown that listening to a variety of models in the process of phoneme identification facilitates learning distinctions (Lively et al., 1994). As pointed out in the derivation of the first session goal, syllable number is viewed as an important variable contributing to performance demands. To minimize task difficulty *monosyllabic words* are selected. Again *80%* accuracy gives us minimal assurance that we can proceed with increasing goal complexity. The sensorimotor maintaining factor is addressed in the act of discrimination, which requires modification. Finally, referencing the premises from social-cognitive theory by providing Manuel with the opportunity to compare speech sounds, and constructivist-cognitive theory, requiring the client to reflect on auditory and kinesthetic differences.

The later session goal listed in Figure 10.6 illustrates a goal occurring later in the sequence with the expected additional complexity. At this time, Manuel is asked to *formulate phrases*. This task has the added complexity of an expressive response, the inclusion of both vowels in the same phrase, and the spontaneous nature of the expression. As this goal is closer to the end of the first short-term period a *90%* accuracy criterion is reasonable. With this session goal we attempt to modify the motor aspect of the sensorimotor maintaining factor by practicing the production of the /ɪ, i/; /ʊ,u/ phonemes in a phrase context. In addition to the learning premises applied for the early goal we add a premise from motor-learning theory, encouraging production practice.

SHORT-TERM GOAL 3. Manuel will eliminate the pattern of final consonant devoicing and epenthesis in words and phrases. To choose an early target for this short-term goal we referenced a hierarchy based on Yavas' (1994) research. This research indicated that consonant placement and prior vowel contributed to an L2 speaker's ability to produce final stop consonants. Among these combinations, bilabial position with low vowel appeared to be most facilitative of final voiced consonant. For this reason the production of bilabial stops preceded by low vowels (e.g., tʌb, rob, cab) were selected to be an early session goal. Later goals will follow the remainder of this hierarchy (described earlier in this chapter). As was noted before, when a new sound is introduced it is generally *modeled* by the clinician for the client to imitate. Maintaining factors addressed are sensorimotor by focusing on production of words. The clinician's actions are guided by principles from social-cognitive theory, prescribing modeling, and constructivist-cognitive, requiring reflection on behavior.

A later session goal directed to the achievement of short-term goal # 3 increases performance demands in a number of ways. Now, Manuel will be asked to read short phrases containing final voiced stops. Manuel will be using the printed material as perceptual support rather than the clinician's model. The linguistic context will also be more of a challenge in progressing from single words to phrases. All voiced stops /b/, /d/, and /g/ will now be included. The construction of the phrases will be controlled with reference to the words following the stop. In this session, the point at which phrases are introduced, the words following the stop will be words beginning with a vowel or a voiced consonant. This selection is based on Edge's (1991) hierarchy of phonetic contexts for facilitating the production of final voiced stops. Performance demands will be increased in future sessions by introducing contexts that are more challenging for the production of a final voiced stop: a voiceless consonant and a pause. There is no change in the maintaining factors or premises from learning addressed.

SHORT-TERM GOAL 4. Manuel will eliminate the pattern of cluster reduction in final position of words. An early goal will be for Manuel to *read* rather than spontaneously produce words. *Single words* are typically first in the hierarchy of linguistic contexts for generalization. The reading of words is also found to be among the most formal contexts, associated with greater accuracy. Final clusters *constituting two consonant, stop + fricative* (e.g., eggs; words) are described as universally less marked than three-consonant cluster combinations, and thus the basis of one approach to the achievement of clusters. (It should also be noted that some researchers advocate starting with more marked targets early in treatment, e.g., Eckman, 1977). Lastly, stop + fricative are considered to be less marked than two stop clusters (Greenberg, 1965) and follow the approach of less marked first in treatment. (Even less marked are fricative-stop cluster (/st/) or sonorant + stop clusters (lt), but stop + fricative combinations were also chosen to facilitate the production of final voiced stops, as explained earlier). Sensorimotor factors are targeted in the *production* of words. Premises from motor theory and cognitive-constructivist are followed.

In a later goal directed toward the achievement of goal 4, Manuel is expected to *produce 2 and 3 element clusters* in *phrases* while answering questions posed by *his wife*, with *70%* accuracy. This goal illustrates the way in which performance demands have increased. We have progressed from two- to three-element clusters, from words to phrases, from perceptual support in the form of reading material to spontaneous productions. In addition, the interlocutor has changed. The construction of this goal makes attempts to address the psychosocial maintaining factor in addition to the sensorimotor by incorporating the client's wife. She represents a novel English conversational partner, because they usually speak Spanish at home. Premises from learning theories include constructive and relationship-based pragmatic, which guide the clinician to have the client produce phrases and to help the client reflect on his productions.

It should be noted that for this later session goal as well as for the other examples of later goals all the modifications in complexity do not necessarily occur at once. That is, the modifications illustrated between the first and second goal examples may in reality occur over a number of intervening sessions.

Deriving Session Goals and Procedures	
Decision	**Guiding Information and Client-Specific Details**
For Each Short-Term Goal, Consider Implications of:	**Long-Term Goal:** Manuel will <u>reduce the use of dialectal patterns affecting the phonology of American English in all pragmatic contexts</u> **Subordinate LTG:** <u>Reduce Prosodic Dialectal Patterns</u> <u>**Short-Term Goal #1**: Produce unstressed syllables in polysyllabic words</u>
Learning and Rehabilitation Premises	<table><tr><td><u>Learning Theories</u></td><td><u>Implications Drawn (in the operationalized approach)</u></td></tr><tr><td>Constructivism</td><td>Present contrasting sounds for discrimination and reflection on his articulatory movements</td></tr><tr><td>Social cognitive</td><td>Model specific targets for imitation</td></tr><tr><td>Relationship-based pragmatic</td><td>Encourage use of new sounds in a variety of situations</td></tr><tr><td>Motor learning</td><td>Encourage practice as much as possible</td></tr><tr><td>Operant</td><td>Facilitate feedback for goal achievement</td></tr></table>

FIGURE 10.6: Manuel's sessions goals

and Maintaining Factors	

Maintaining Factors	Implications Drawn (in the operationalized approach)
Cognitive	Encourage reflection on auditory and kinesthetic changes
Sensorimotor	Encourage practice
Psychosocial	Encourage use of new sounds in a variety of situations

Early Session Goal:

Manuel will *produce trochaic* (strong-weak) and *iambic* (weak-strong) word patterns **given (non-linguistic context)** *a list of selected words* ***and (linguistic context)*** after the *clinician's model* **(achievement criterion) for** 18/20 items. **Sample words:** SW (attic, bacon, candy, father, funny); WS (today, because, attack, reply, delay)

Performance Demands Controlled

Performance Variable Controlled	How the Variable Is Controlled	Aspect of Session Goal Affected
Syllable number	Two-syllable before 3+	Target
Task formality	Lists before spontaneous speech	Nonlinguistic context
Perceptual support	After model before spontaneous	Linguistic context

Later Session Goal

Manuel will *read* words **given (nonlinguistic context)** a prepared list of stress-patterns from four categories of randomly presented *3-syllable word-stress contours* **(achievement criterion)** with 80% accuracy. **Sample words:** banana (313); telephone (132); kangaroo (231); skeleton (133)

FIGURE 10.6 CONTINUED: Manuel's sessions goals

Performance Demands Controlled	Performance Variable Controlled	How the Variable Is Controlled	Aspect of Session Goal Affected
	Syllable number	3+ syllable contours after 2-syllable words	Target
	Perceptual support	Orthographic support before spontaneous Nonmodeled after modeled	Nonlinguistic context Linguistic context
	Task formality	Lists before self-formulation	Nonlinguistic context

Subordinate LTG: Manuel will reduce dialectal patterns affecting consonants, consonant clusters, and vowels of American English.

Short-Term Goal #2: Manuel will reduce the pattern of tensing lax vowels in words and phrases.

Early Session Goal:

Manuel *will* identify lax/tense vowels, comprising the following pairs: /ɪ, i /; /ʊ, u/ **given (nonlinguistic context)** by *pointing* to the phonetic symbol representing each sound **and (linguistic context)** after the clinician's model **(achievement criterion)** with 80% accuracy.

Performance Demands Controlled	Performance Variable Controlled	How the Variable Is Controlled	Aspect of Session Goal Affected
	Perceptual support	Phonetic symbol before no visual support	Nonlinguistic context
	Response mode	Discrimination before production	Target
	Linguistic unit	Phonemes before words	Target

FIGURE 10.6 CONTINUED: Manuel's sessions goals

Later Session Goal:
Manuel will produce *minimal pairs of contrasting lax/tense vowels (e.g., bit of beet)* **given (linguistic context)** *self-formulated phrases* **(achievement criterion)** with 90% accuracy.

Performance Demands Controlled	Performance Variable Controlled	How the Variable Is Controlled	Aspect of Session Goal Affected
	Perceptual support	Spontaneous after imitation	Linguistic context
	Linguistic unit	Phrases after words	Linguistic context
	Number of contrastive sounds	One sound difference before multiple	Target

FIGURE 10.6 CONTINUED: Manuel's sessions goals

Summary

This chapter has presented an approach to intervention with individuals learning the phonology of a second language. The approach has followed the basic tenets of intervention planning for speech-language disorders. This is because in planning goals and procedures to facilitate the acquisition of L2 phonology, consideration must be given to the same categories of information as with disorder types. In preparing for treatment with an L2 client, one must consider (a) the nature of the problem, (b) factors maintaining the problem, (c) theories of learning new sounds, and (d) those factors that contribute to increased demand on performance. It is knowledge of these categories of information relative to each client that makes goal and procedure planning a systematic and accountable endeavor.

REFERENCES

Adamson, H. D., & Regan, V. (1991). The acquisition of community speech norms by Asian immigrants. *Studies in Second Language Acquisition, 13*, 1–22.

Altenberg, E. P., & Vago, R. M. (1983). Theoretical implications of an error analysis of second language phonology production. *Language Learning, 33*, 427–447.

American Speech-Language Hearing Association. (1983). Position paper: Social dialects and implications of the position of social dialects. *ASHA, 25*, 23–27.

American Speech-Language Hearing Association. (1996, Spring). Scope of practice in speech-language pathology. *ASHA, 38*(Suppl. 16) 16–20.

Bailey, K. M., & Savage, L. (1994). *New ways in teaching speaking.* Alexandria, VA: TESOL.

Bauman-Waengler, J. (2016). *Articulation and phonology in speech sound disorders* (5th ed.). New York: Pearson.

Beebe, L. M. (1977). The influence of the listener on code-switching. *Language Learning, 27*, 332–339.

Behrman, A. (2017). A clear speech approach to accent management. *American Journal of Speech-Language Pathology, 26*, 1178–1192.

Bernhardt, B., & Stoel-Gammon, C. (1994). Nonlinear phonology: Introduction and clinical application. *Journal of Speech and Hearing Research, 37*, 123–143.

Bernthal, J. E., Bankson, N. W., & Flipson, P., Jr. (2017). *Articulation and phonological disorders: Speech-sound disorders in children* (8th ed.). New York: Pearson.

Bialystok, E. (1978). A theoretical model of second language learning. *Language Learning, 28*, 69–84.

Bleile, K. M. (1995). *Manual of articulation and phonological disorders.* San Diego, CA: Singular Publishing Group, Inc.

Cairns, H. S., Cairns, C. E., & Williams, F. (1974). Some theoretical considerations of articulation substitution phenomena. *Language and Speech, 17*, 160–173.

Carlisle, R. S. (1988). The effect of markedness on epenthesis in Spanish/English interlanguage phonology and syntax. *Issues and Developments in English and Applied Linguistics, 3*, 15–23.

Carlisle, R. S. (1994). Markedness and environment as internal constraints on the variability of interlanguage phonology. In M. Yavas (Ed.), *First and second language acquisition* (pp. 233–249). San Diego, CA: Singular Publishing Group, Inc.

Catford, J. C. (1987). Phonetics and the teaching of pronunciation: A systemic description of English phonology. In J. Morley (Ed.), *Current perspectives on pronunciation* (pp. 83–100). Washington, DC: TESOL.

Celce-Muria, M. (1987). Teaching pronunciation as communication. In J. Morley (Ed.), *Current perspectives on pronunciation* (pp. 1–12). Washington, DC: TESOL.

Chomsky, N., & Halle, M. (1968). *The sound pattern of English.* New York: Harper & Row.

Compton, A. J. (1983). *Phonological assessment of foreign accent (1963).* San Francisco, CA: Carousel House.

Crystal, D. (1991). *A dictionary of linguistics and phonetics* (3rd ed.). Cambridge, MA.: Blackwell Publishers.

Dickerson, W. (1987). Explicit rules & the developing interlanguage phonology. In A. James & J. Leather (Eds.), *Sound patterns in second language acquisition* (Chapter 7, pp. 121–140). Dordrecht, Netherlands: Foris.

Dinnsen, D. A., Chin, S., Elbert, M., & Powell, T. (1990). Some constraints on functionally disordered phonologies: Phonetic inventories and phonatactics. *JSHR, 33*, 28–37.

Dinnsen, D. A., & Eckman, F. R. (1978). Some substantive universals in atomic phonology. *Lingua, 45*, 1–14.

Eckman, F. R. (1977). Markedness and the contrastive analyses hypotheses. *Language Learning, 27*, 315–330.

Eckman, F. R. (1981). On predicting difficulty in second language acquisition. *Studies in Second Language Acquisition, 4*, 18–30.

Eckman, F. R. (1985). Some theoretical and pedagogical implications of the markedness differential hypothesis. *Studies in Second Language Acquisition, 7*, 289–307.

Eckman, F. R. (1987). The reduction of word-final consonants in interlanguage. In A. James & J. Leather (Eds.), *Sound patterns in second language acquisition* (Chapter 8, pp. 143–162). Dordrecht, Netherlands: Foris.

Eckman, F. R. (1991). The structural conformity hypothesis and the acquisition of consonant clusters in the interlanguage of ESL learners. *Studies in Second Language Acquisition, 13*, 23–41.

Eckman, F. R., & Iverson, G. K. (1994). Pronunciation difficulties in ESL: Coda consonants in English interlanguge. In M. Yavas (Ed.), *First and second language acquisition* (Chapter 11, pp. 251–265). San Diego, CA: Singular Publishing Group, Inc.

Edge, B. A. (1991). The production of word-final obstruents in English by L1 speakers of Japanese and Cantonese. *Studies in Second Language Acquisition, 13*, 377–393.

Edwards, M. L. (1992). In support of phonological process. *LSHSS, 23*, 233–240.

Elbert, M., & Gierut, J. (1986). *Handbook of clinical phonology: Approaches to assessment and treatment.* San Diego, CA: College Hill Press.

Ellis, R. (1994). The study of second language acquisition. New York: Oxford University Press.

Ferguson, C. A. (1968). Contrastive analysis and language development. In C. A. Ferguson (Ed.), *Language structure and language use.* Stanford, CA: Stanford University Press.

Fey, M. E. (1992). Clinical forum: Phonological assessment and treatment: Articulation and phonology: Inextricable constructs in speech pathology. *Language Speech and Hearing Services in Schools, 23*, 225–232.

Fey, M. E., & Grandour, J. (1982). Rule discovery in phonological acquisition. *Journal of Child Language, 9*, 70–82.

Flege, J. E. (1989). Differences in inventory size affect the location but not the precision of tongue positioning in vowel production. *Language & Speech, 32*, 123–147.

Flege, J. E. (1992). Speech learning in a second language. In C. H. Ferguson, L. Menn, & C. Stoel-Gammon (Eds.), *Phonological development, models, research, implications* (Chapter 21, pp. 565–604). Timonium, MD: York Press.

Flege, J. E. (1995a). Two procedures for training a second language phonetic context. *Applied Psycholinguistics, 16*, 425–442.

Flege, J. E. (1995b). Second language speech learning theory, findings, and problems. In W. Strange (Ed.), *Speech perception and linguistic experience* (Chapter 8, pp. 233–277). Timonium, MD: York Press.

Flege, J. E., Frieda, E. M., & Nozawe, T. (1997). Amount of native language (L1) use affects the pronunciations of an L2. *Journal of Phonetics, 25*, 169–186.

Flege, J. E., & Munro, M. J. (1994). The word unit in L2 speech production and perception. *Studies in Second Language Acquisition, 16*, 381–411.

Fledge, J. E., Munro, M. J., & Mackay, I. (1995). Factors affecting degree of perceived foreign accent in a second language. *Journal of the Acoustical Society of America, 97*, 3623–3641.

Gierut, J. A., Morrisette, M. L., Hughes, M. T., & Rowland, S. (1996). Phonological treatment efficacy and developmental norms. *Language, Speech, and Hearing Services in Schools, 27*, 215–230.

Greenberg, J. H. (1965). Some generalizations concerning initial and final consonant clusters. *Linguistics, 18*, 5–34.

Grunwell, P. (1985). *Phonological assessment of child speech (PACS).* San Diego, CA: College-Hill Press.

Hammerberg, B. (1990). Conditions on transfer in phonology. In J. Leather & A. James (Eds.), *New Sounds 90* (pp. 198–215). Amsterdam, Netherlands: University of Amsterdam.

Hodson, B. W., & Paden, E. P. (1991). *Targeting intelligible speech* (2nd ed.). Austin, TX: Pro-Ed.

Ingram, D. (1981). *Procedures for the phonological analysis of children's language.* Baltimore, MD: University Park Press.

Karmiloff-Smith, A. (1986). From meta-processes to conscious access: Evidence from children's metalinguistic and repair data. *Cognition, 23*, 95–147.

Kent, R. D. (1982). Contextual facilitation of correct sound production. *Language Speech and Hearing Services in Schools, 13*, 66–76.

Klein, H. B. (1978). *The relationship between perceptual strategies and productive strategies in learning the phonology of early lexical items* (Unpublished doctoral dissertation). Columbia University.

Klein, H. B. (1981). Productive strategies for pronunciation of early polysyllabic lexical items. *Journal of Speech and Hearing Research, 24,* 389–405.

Klein, H. B. (1984). A procedure for maximizing phonological information from single-word responses. *Language, Speech and Hearing Services in Schools, 15,* 267–274.

Klein, H. B., Lederer, S. H., & Cortese, E. E. (1991). Children's knowledge of auditory/articulatory correspondences: Phonologic and metaphonologic. *Journal of Speech and Hearing Research, 34,* 559–564.

Klein, H. B., & Moses, N. (1999). *Intervention planning for children with communication disorders.* Boston, MA: Allyn & Bacon.

Klein, H. B., & Spector, C. C. (1985). Effect of syllable stress and serial position on error variability in polysyllabic productions of speech-delayed children. *Journal of Speech and Hearing Disorders, 50,* 391–402.

Krashen, S. (1981). *Second language acquisition and second language learning.* Oxford: Pergamon.

Leather, J. (1990). Perceptual and productive learning of Chinese lexical tone by Dutch and English speakers. In J. Leather & A. James (Eds.), *New Sounds 90* (pp. 72–97). Amsterdam, The Netherlands: University of Amsterdam Press.

Leather, J., & James, A. (1991). The acquisition of second language speech. *Studies in Second Language Acquisition, 13,* 305–341. Amsterdam, The Netherlands: University of Amsterdam Press.

Lenneberg, E. H. (1967). *Biological foundations of language.* New York: Wiley.

Lively, S. E., Pisone, D. B., Yamada, R. A., Tohikura, Y., & Yamada, T. (1994). Training Japanese listeners to identify English /r/ and /l/: Long-term retention of new phonetic categories. *Journal of the Acoustical Society of America, 89,* 2076–2087.

Logan, J. S., Lively, S. E., & Pisoni, D. B. (1991). Training Japanese listeners to identify English /r/ and /l/: A first report. *Journal of the Acoustical Society of America, 89,* 874–883.

Long, M. H. (1990). Maturational constraints and language development. *Studies in Second Language Acquisition, 16,* 251–285.

Major, R. C. (1986). The ontogeny model: Evidence from L2 acquisition of Spanish. *Language Learning, 36,* 453–504.

Major, R. C. (1987). The natural phonology of second language acquisition. In A. James & J. Leather (Eds.), *Sound patterns in second language acquisitio*n. Providence: Foris Publications.

Major, R. C. (1994). Current trends in interlanguage phonology. In M. Yavas (Ed.), *First and second language acquisition* (pp. 181–204). San Diego, CA: Singular Publishing Group, Inc.

McReynolds, L. V., Engmann, D., & Dimmitt, K. (1974). Markedness theory and articulation errors. *Journal of Speech and Hearing Disorders, 39,* 93–103.

Morley, J. (1987). *Current perspectives on pronunciation.* Washington, DC: TESOL.

Morley, J. (Ed.) (1994). *Pronunciation pedagogy and theory.* Alexandria, VA: TESOL.

Munro, M. J., & Derwing, T. M (2015). A prospectus for pronunciation research in the 21st century: A point of view. *Journal of Second Language Pronunciation, 1,* 11–42.

Nathan, G. (1990). On the non-acquisition of an English sound system. In J. Leather & A. James (Eds.), *New sounds 90* (pp. 294–299). Amsterdam: University of Amsterdam.

Nesdale, A. R., Herriman, M. L., & Tunmer, W. E. (1984). Phonological awareness in children. In W. E., Tunmer, C. Pratt, & M. L., Herriman (Eds.), *Metalinguistic awareness in children* (pp. 56–72). Heidelberg, Berlin, Germany: Springer.

Neufeld, G. G. (1980). On the adult's ability to acquire phonology. *TESOL Quarterly, 14,* 285–298.

Nippold, M. A., & Rudzinski, M. (1993). Familiarity and transparency in idiom explanation: A developmental study of children and adolescents. *Journal of Speech and Hearing Research, 36,* 728–737.

Patkowski, M. S. (1994). The critical age hypothesis and interlanguage phonology. In M. Yavas (Ed.), *First and second language acquisition* (pp. 204–221). San Diego, CA: Singular Publishing Group, Inc.

Powell, T. W. (1991). Planning for phonological generalization. An approach to treatment target selection. *American Journal of Speech, Language Pathology, 1,* 21–27.

Prather, E., Hedrick, D., & Kern, C. (1975). Articulation development in children ages two to four years. *Journal of Speech and Hearing Research, 40,* 179–191.

Price, P. J. (1981). *A cross linguistic study of flaps in Japanese and American English* (Ph.D. Dissertation). University of Pennsylvania, Philadelphia, PA.

Raubicheck, L. (1952). *Speech improvement* (pp. 103–131). Englewood Cliffs, NJ: Prentice-Hill, Inc.

Sander, E. (1972). When are speech sounds learned? *Journal of Speech and Hearing Disorders, 37,* 55–63.

Schane, H. (1973). *Generative phonology.* Englewood Cliffs, NJ: Prentice-Hall, Inc.

Schmidt, A. M. (1997). Working with adult foreign accent: Strategies for intervention. *Contemporary Issues in Communication Science and Disorders, 24,* 53–62.

Selinker, L. (1969). Language transfer. *General Linguistics, 9,* 67–92.

Selinker, L. (1992). *Interlanguage.* New York/London, England: Longman.

Shriberg, L., & Kwiatkowski, J. (1982). Phonological disorders II: A conceptual framework for management. *Journal of Speech and Hearing Disorders, 47,* 256–270.

Sikorski, L. D. (1991). *Mastering effective English communication* (2nd ed.). Santa Ana, CA: LDS.

Sloat, C., Taylor, S. H., & Hoard, J. (1978). *Introduction to phonology.* Englewood Cliffs, NJ: Prentice-Hall Inc.

Smit, A. B., Hand, L., Freilinger, J. J., Bernthal, J. E., & Bird, A. (1990). The Iowa articulation norms project and its Nebraska replication. *Journal of Speech and Hearing Disorders, 55,* 779–798.

St. Louis, K. O., & Ruscello, D. M. (1987). *Oral speech mechanism screening examination revised.* Austin, TX: Pro-Ed.

Stampe, D. 1969. The acquisition of phonetic representation. In R. T. Binnick, et al. (Eds.), Papers from the Fifth Regional Meeting of the Chicago Linguistic Society, 443–454.

Temperley, M. S. (1987). Linking and deletion of final consonant clusters. In J. Morley (Ed.), *Current perspectives on pronunciation* (pp. 59–82). Washington, DC: TESOL.

Templin, M. (1957). *Certain language skills in children: Their development and interrelationships.* Institute of Child Welfare Monograph 26. Minneapolis, MN: The University of Minnesota Press.

Thomson, R. I., & Derwing, T. M. (2015). The effectiveness of pronunciation instruction: A narrative review. *Applied Linguistics, 36,* 326–344.

Weinberger, S. H. (1994). Functional and phonetic constraints on second language phonology. In M. Yavas (Ed.), *First and second language phonology.* San Diego, CA: Singular Publishing Group, Inc.

Wiig, E. H., & Secord, W. (1989). *Test of language competence-expanded edition.* San Antonio, TX: Psychological Corporation, Harcourt–Brace Jovanovich, Inc.

Wong, R. (1987). Learner variables and prepronunciation considerations in teaching pronunciation. In J. Morley (Ed.), *Current perspectives on pronunciation* (pp. 13–28). Washington, DC: TESOL.

Yavas, M. (1994). Final stop devoicing in interlanguage. In M. Yavas (Ed.), *First and second language phonology* (pp. 267–282). San Diego, CA: Singular Publishing Group, Inc.

University Speech-Language-Hearing Disorders Clinic

Street Address

City, State

SPEECH AND LANGUAGE EVALUATION

Client Name: <u>Manuel T.</u> Date of Birth:_____ Date of Testing: _____

Chronological Age: <u>30</u> Primary Area of Concern: <u>L2 Phonology</u>

Language of Testing: <u>English</u>

Clinician: <u>Heather Smith</u> Supervisor: <u>Andrea Jones</u>

I.   Statement of Problem and Background Information

As a speaker of English as a second language, Manuel was concerned about his production of vowel and consonant sounds. In the nine years since he arrived from Peru, he had sought assistance with his pronunciation from a number of different sources. He took a course in English at an ESL institute, a summer university course in voice and diction, and attempted to see a private speech-language pathologist, but was discouraged by the fees. He reports some overall improvement in his vocabulary and his level of confidence in speaking English over the last few years. He still, however, reveals feelings of frustration and anxiety when trying to express himself in English; this occurs primarily at his work site. He feels most uncomfortable using L2 when speaking to strangers and addressing a group or class. Married to a Spanish speaker, and having mostly Spanish-speaking friends, Manuel spends the greater proportion of speaking time using L1. Although generally experiencing good health, Manuel has suffered from bouts of anxiety and depression which have contributed to difficulties concentrating. He has been under the care of a psychiatrist who has prescribed a variety of medications. Manuel has recently completed a BA degree in economic science and is entering an MBA program. He believes that improvement in speaking English will enhance his career potential.

II. Communication Assessment

This section is the primary source of data supporting eventual treatment goals.

Language

A. Content/Form

ORAL LANGUAGE: Based on a conversational speech/language sample, Manuel was found to produce language expected of his age and educational background, with the following L1/L2 differences, attributed to L1. These changes affected auxiliary 'do' ("How _____you phrase it?"), plurals ("many kinds of works"; the kind of works), prepositions ("I got my MBA on January"; "at the first five years"), word order ("There are reasons why is that"). third person singular ("My voice change_____when"; "My word order get_____mixed up"), gerund ("It would be like give_____up"), regular past tense ("I haven't respond_____"), articles ("I don't like the snakes"; "I have a new shoes"), semantics ("The leaves are coming off the trees"; "she's doing a lot of splashes while she's swimming").

WRITTEN LANGUAGE: All the above changes with the addition of differences in subject/verb agreement ("my nervousness do not let me control myself"; "talking with people that is close to me").

STANDARDIZED TESTING: *The Figurative Language Subtest* of the *Test of Language Competence (TLC)* (Wiig & Secord, 1989) was administered to test the client's understanding of figurative language. Received 15 of a possible 36 points (Mean and Standard Deviation for adults (18+) = 30.7 (S.D. 4.9)). He was unable to match the expression for 25% of the items, and interpret the expression for 50% of the items.

B. Use

Exhibited a full range of expected language functions and appropriate conversational conventions (e.g., turn taking, topic maintenance, contingent responses to questions and statements).

Speech-Sound Production

A. PHONETIC: *Compton Phonological Assessment of Foreign Accent* (1983) and the *Sentence Sub-Test* from *Fischer-Logemenn Articulation Test* (1971) were administered to assess phonetic repertoire in the context of spontaneous production of single words, phrases, and reading of phonetically balanced sentences and paragraph. All L2 consonants except for those not sampled (/z /within word, and word final) were within phonetic repertoire though not observed in all L2 positions (e.g., /z/ → [s] word final). Great deal of variability with vowel production especially for /ɪ/, /æ/, /ɔ/, /ʌ/, /ə/,/ɜ/

B. PHONOLOGICAL: Based on a continuous-speech sample, the following dialectal patterns were observed.

CONSONANT PATTERNS:

Devoicing of final consonants

Stopping of /θ/ and /ð/

Interchanges: /dʒ/ → [j]; /j/ → [dʒ]

/d/ → [ð]; /ð/ → [d]

Individual substitutions: /dʒ/ → [d] or [ʒ],   trilled r [r]

Clusters are reduced within words and in word-final positions; some examples are:

Within word	Word Final
/bj/ → [b] vocabulary [vokæb_ulɛri]	/st/ → [s] against [gens_]
/gw/ → [w] LaGuardia [la_wardia]	/lt/ →[l] difficult [difikʌl_]
/gz/ →[z] example[e_zampul]	/dz/ →[s] rewards [riwɔs]
/nʃ/ → [ʃ] internship [inter_ʃip]	/gz/ →[s] eggs [e:s]
financial[faɪnæ_ʃul]	/kst/ →[st] mixed [mɪst]
/ksp/−[sp] explain [e_splen]	/nst/ →[ns] advanced [advans]

VOWEL PATTERNS:

tensing: ɪ→ i; ʊ→u

raising: ɛ→e; a→o;

lowering: ɔ→a; ʌ→a

backing: æ→a or ɑ; ʌ→o or u; ə→ʊɚ or ɛɚ

fronting: o→a or ʌ; ɔ→ a; a→æ

PROSODY: Unstressed L2 syllables of multisyllabic words are not reduced, which gives full-vowel value to these syllables rendering a range of full vowels in the place of schwa (e.g., <u>education</u> [edukeʃon], <u>immigrant</u> [imigrʌnt], <u>institute</u> [institut], <u>composition</u> [kaposiʃon], <u>united</u> [dʒunaɪtɛd], <u>characteristic</u> [karitaristik]

AUDITORY DISCRIMINATION: Nonstandardized testing (Discrimination Task for Consonants) resulted in 6 errors of 35 pairs of consonant contrasts; nonstandardized task for vowels resulted in 4 errors of 22 pairs of vowel contrasts. The consonants in the following syllable pairs were judged to be the same: bale-vale, tin-sin, doze-those, so-though, mat-pat, bat-pat; the vowels in the following pairs were judged to be the same: set-sat, ball-bull, bet-bat; fit-feet was judged to be different.

FLUENCY: Typical rate and rhythm in conversational speech

VOICE: Perceptual judgment of volume, pitch, resonance, quality judged to be appropriate to age and gender during conversation.

III. Associated Behavioral Systems

This section includes factors supporting or negatively impacting communication behaviors; these data provide a primary source for determining procedures.

A. **SENSORIMOTOR**

1. Peripheral Speech Mechanism: The Oral Speech Mechanism Screening Examination-Revised (OSMSE-R; St. Louis & Ruscello, 1987) was administered to determine the structural and functional adequacy of the articulators. All structures and functions appear to be within typical limits except for missing premolars bilaterally; diadochokinetic rates for all syllables were within one standard deviation of the mean for his age

2. Body Stability—Upon observation appeared to be within normal limits

3. Hearing: Screening revealed a 55 dB loss at 4000 Hz in the left ear; all other frequencies screened bilaterally were within normal limit i.

B. **COGNITION:** High achieving academically. No cognitive assessment procedures administered.

C. **PSYCHOSOCIAL:**

1. Reported beginning to learn English at 21 years of age

2. Expressed strong motivation to improve English syntax and pronunciation

3. Reported speaking Spanish primarily at home and with friends; speaks English only at work

4. Reported to be depressed, unfocused and anxious generally, and particularly tense when required to express himself in English

Assessment Summary

Manuel, a 30-year-old speaker of Peruvian-accented English demonstrates moderate dialectal patterns in both phonology and syntax. Consonant patterns comprise segment substitutions and interchanges affecting singletons and clusters; vowel patterns include raising, lowering, tensing, backing, and fronting. L1 syllable stress patterns affect vowel production, accounting primarily for the absence of schwa (replaced by a stressed full vowel). Syntactic L1 influence is exhibited primarily in morpheme use in both spoken and written language. Interpretation and expression of figurative language is also moderately affected as revealed by the TLC. While client appears motivated to modify his productions for social and occupational benefits, major strides are likely to be curtailed by the age beginning L2, the frequency of using L1, and his current psychosocial status.

Recommendations/Referrals

Include recommendations to: (a) initiate treatment or not; (b) determine frequency and duration of treatment; (c) contact allied professional(s) and guide/educated caregiver(s).

Long-Term Goals and Procedural Approach (In Templates)

Clinician Signature: _____   Date:_____

(Printed Name)

Graduate Student Clinician

Supervisor's Signature: _____   Date:_____

(Printed Name, degree, certification)

Speech-Language Pathologist.

Appendix B: Contrastive Analysis Charts

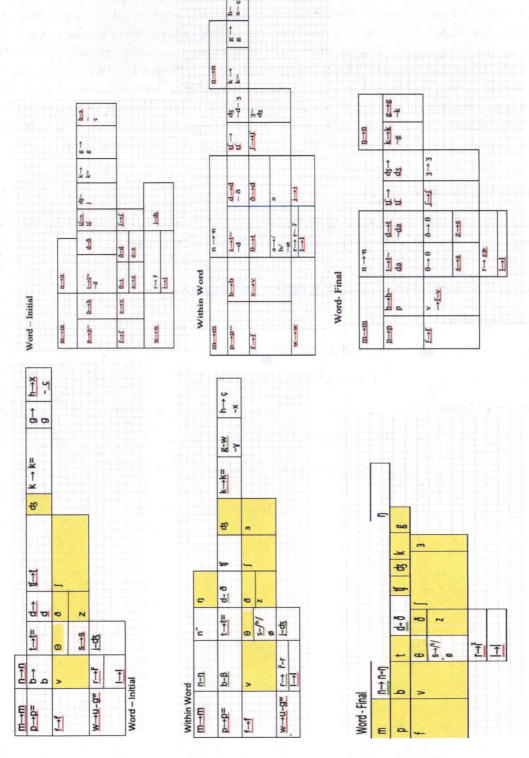

FIGURE B1: English Consonants and (→) Spanish Equivalents; English Consonants and (→) Manuel's Production (Dark Boxes = Sounds Absent)

i		u
ɪ		ʊ
e	ɜ ɝ ə ɚ	o
ɛ	ʌ	ɔ
æ	a	ɑ

FIGURE B2a: English vowels and Spanish equivalents, Dark boxes = Sounds absent in Spanish

ɪ→i		u→ʊ~ʌ
ɪ→i~ɪ		ʊ→u
e→e	ɜ→ ɝ→ɛɜ~ɔ ə→ ɚ→ʊə~ɛə	o→a~ʌ
ɛ→ɛ~e	ʌ→a~o~u~ɔ~æ	ɔ→ɔə~o~a
æ→a~ɑ	a→a~æ~o	ɑ→a

FIGURE B2b: Manuel's productions (with alternating sounds, ~)

chapter 11

School-Age Language-Learning Disabilities and Literacy

READER WILL:

- Define language-learning disabilities
- Define literacy
- Follow intervention planning through three phases for a child with language-learning disabilities

This chapter addresses language-learning disabilities and intervention planning for a 13-year-old boy, Cori, who has been diagnosed as having a language-learning disability. Cori, whose family comes from Nicaragua, attends 6th grade in a Brooklyn, New York, middle school. Cori is bilingual (Spanish/English), although his dominant language is English. He has an older brother, who works as a technician for a well-known computer company, and a younger sister attending school. Cori's parents report that he typically speaks to them in short, single-verb sentences, and avoids engaging in conversations. Teachers report similar language production in response to requests for information in class. Parents indicated, however, that he is more talkative with friends. His most frequent response to questioning is "I don't know," even when asked about familiar experiences. Cori is performing below grade level in many of his subject areas, including math and science, and his greatest difficulty is in the areas of reading, reading comprehension, spelling, and writing. Appendix 11-A presents a summary of results of Cori's speech/language and literacy evaluation.

Language-Learning Disabilities and Literacy

Cori's referral to a speech-language pathologist for assessment and treatment is notable, since the greatest concern of his parents and teachers is Cori's school performance and reading problems. The field of speech-language pathology has broadened over the past decade to incorporate literacy. Literacy refers to the individual's ability to read and to the transmission of knowledge by engaging in various forms of discourse via writing and other symbolic systems of expression (music, art, etc.). These competencies are central to academic success in school, where information is delivered primarily by talking teachers and text.

Distinctions are made in the literature between "literacy as referring to the acts of writing and reading "and literacy" as a way of thinking and speaking" (Langer, 1987; Perfetti, 1984). Langer identifies literacy as "culturally based" and as involving "higher intellectual skills appropriate to the culture, and … learned by children as they interact with families and communities" (Langer, 1987, p. 2).

Another distinction is made between reading with comprehension (e.g., Catts & Hogan, 2003; Kamhi & Catts, 2011) and "reading" as simply the ability to decode print into speech acts (speaking written words without comprehension, e.g., Cowder, 1982). It may be possible to decode print without comprehension (e.g., sounding out a sentence from a foreign language based on knowledge of the new language's graphemic and phonemic system.) However, just as imitation is not evidence of verbal language, decoding by itself is not evidence of reading. Reading, like oral language, signifies the extraction of meaning from a linguistic code. Readers draw upon perception of graphemes and phonological, syntactic, and semantic processes to "make sense of print, to predict what comes next, and to construct meaning" (Goodman, 1986; also Catts & Kamhii, 2011; Perfetti, 1984).

Literacy is the product of an ongoing process of language development and language enrichment, beginning in the home, and extending across the life span. The linguistic, cognitive, sensorimotor, and cultural foundations of literacy are established during the preschool years (see especially Heath [1982]).

Children with language-learning disabilities often appear to be developing appropriately before entering school; problems comprehending and producing language, however, begin to be recognized on entering school. Historically, conflicting accounts appeared in the literature about children who presented with typical intelligence but manifested problems in academic language performance, reading, and related subject areas such as mathematics and language arts. These children were labeled as incorrigible, culturally disadvantaged, aphasic, minimally brain damaged, and passive learners (e.g., Hallahan & Mercer, 2001; Kirk, 1976; Outridge, 1967; Shaywitz, 2003).

In 1981, the National Joint Committee for Learning Disabilities (NJCLD), composed of organizations serving individuals with school-based language/learning problems (including the American Speech and Language Association) defined learning disabilities as follows:

> "Learning disabilities is a generic term that refers to a heterogeneous group of disorders manifested by significant difficulties in the acquisition and use of listening, speaking, reading, writing, reasoning or mathematical abilities. These disorders are intrinsic to the individual and presumed to be due to central nervous system dysfunction. Even though a learning disability may occur concomitantly with other handicapping conditions (e.g., sensory impairment, mental retardation, social and emotional disturbance) or environmental influences (e.g., cultural differences, insufficient-inappropriate instruction, psychogenic factors), it is not the direct result of those conditions or influences." (Hammill, Leigh, McNutt, & Larsen, 1981, p. 336)

This definition of learning disabilities implicates symbolic behavior across a spectrum of modalities (oral, visual, grapho-motor, etc.) and academic domains (reading, mathematics, language arts, etc.). This definition suggests, further, that speech-language intervention for children with learning disabilities addresses access to age- and grade-appropriate curriculum.

Language-learning disabilities, also referred to in the literature as "Specific Language Impairment" (SLI), implicate, specifically, difficulties in the area of verbal language. Other forms of learning disabilities include dyslexia (reading disability), dysgraphia (grapheme producing disability), dyscalculia (difficulty in the area of mathematics, involving number manipulation), and central auditory processing disorder, which also implicates the processing of the sound stream influencing verbal language comprehension and production (U.S. Department of Health and Human Services, National Institute on Deafness and Other Communication Disorders, 2019).

Planning intervention for children with language-learning disabilities begins with a consideration of baseline data within the client's diagnostic report. Planning continues across the long-term, short-term, and session phases delineated earlier in this text. The following details intervention planning for Cori, beginning with the long-term planning phase.

Planning Long-Term Goals

Step 1: Decide What Area(s) of Speech and Language to Target

1A. REVIEW BASELINE DATA (APPENDIX 11-A). Baseline data contained within Cori's diagnostic report (Appendix 11-A) indicate that Cori manifests mild to moderate delays in verbal language and moderate delays in reading and spelling. He engages in discourse using complex sentences with friends and with the clinician. Spontaneous conversation is less frequent and less complex in interactions with family.

Although Cori engages in social discourse, he has difficulty engaging in expository discourse (i.e., explaining) in academic settings, and especially about language-oriented topics (e.g., word definitions, rules of spelling and report writing, editing writing assignments, etc.). He also does not use figurative expressions.

Although Cori does not present with a history of articulation problems, he demonstrates weakness in the area of phonological awareness. This is manifested in difficulty identifying and producing rhyming words in both English and Spanish (he performs better given nonsense syllables). He has difficulty segmenting words by phonemes and consonant clusters; he also has difficulty identifying grapheme–vocalic phoneme correspondences (including /r/ controlled vowels and vowel digraphs) and distinguishing long from short pronunciations of vowels (in English) with reference to graphemic context. As noted earlier, Cori also manifests a spelling disability.

Cori's output is also less complex in the context of standard, norm-referenced assessments, as compared with in naturalistic discourse contexts. This was documented by his below-mean performance on tests of narrative comprehension and production, academic achievement in the areas of reading and spelling, comprehension of figurative language, and verbal reasoning, and metalinguistic skills (figurative language and inferential reasoning about problems presented verbally).

Baseline data also suggest that a major factor contributing to language difficulties is his developmental level in the area of cognition. The cognitive demands of tasks influence his production of causal sentences. He functions primarily at the preoperational level. Eighth-grade curricula in areas including math, science, and social studies address complex causal and temporal relations requiring operational reasoning to fully understand.

Baseline data summarized above (and more completely described in the Appendix) will serve as a guide to the identification of areas of language to address in long-term goals. These data will be examined with reference to developmental taxonomies that will help us identify components of language and their natural course of acquisition.

Step 2. Identify One or More Developmental Taxonomies or Complexity Hierarchies That Define Relevant Components of Language and their Developmental Trajectories

INFORMATION PROCESSING. Information processing paradigms commonly underlie assessment and intervention planning for children with language-learning disabilities; this may be an extension of the influence that information processing paradigms have had on adult language disorders. Historically, the field of language-learning disabilities emerged from adult language disabilities associated with traumatic brain injury and aphasia (Hallahan & Mercer, 2001). As noted earlier, until the 1980s, language-learning disabilities were commonly referred to as "childhood aphasia" or "minimal brain damage" (e.g., Outridge, 1967). A model of information processing proposed by Osherson and Lasnik (1990), offers a useful taxonomy for approaching the assessment and planning of intervention in the case of Cori.

Osherson and Lasnik's (1990) model contains three levels of processing relevant to the regulation of behavior in service to functional language and literacy: perception/sensorimotor, linguistic, metalinguistic/executive. These processing levels are developmental and generative; once attained, they apply to multiple behaviors across multiple contexts.

Both goal and procedure planning are influenced by processing levels implicated in a language disorder. Linguistic and metalinguistic competencies are addressed in long and short-term goal planning. Perception and sensorimotor functioning as well as linguistic and metalinguistic processes are also addressed in procedure planning and, ultimately, in session goals and procedures. Definitions of information processing levels and Cori's performance patterns relevant to each processing level are as follows:

PERCEPTION/SENSORIMOTOR PROCESSING. Perception relevant to language and literacy involves distinguishing phonemes and graphemes from one another and abstracting these linguistic objects from the stream of acoustic or visual stimuli encountered when listening or reading. Cori's difficulty in reading consonant clusters and diphthongs and delays in the area of spatial cognition potentially implicate perception.

Sensorimotor processing involves the use of feedback from goal-directed physical action to regulate behavior. Sensorimotor action is a component of most activities, including articulation, reading and writing, cooking, solving math problems represented by math cubes, engaging in science experiments, etc. In Cori's case, difficulty in establishing grapheme–phoneme correspondences and delays in achieving operational reasoning potentially implicate sensorimotor functioning, especially the use of sensory feedback.

LINGUISTIC PROCESSING. Linguistic processing refers to the regulation of functional speech and language by rules of language content, form, and use. Linguistic "rules" are nonconscious mental procedures that individuals execute to derive meaning from linguistic data (e.g., phonemic, syntactic, pragmatic) or represent meaning linguistically. These rules enable the production and comprehension of language. Delays in the use of complex, multiverb sentences; conversational skills; and narrative production implicate linguistic processing in Cori's case.

METALINGUISTIC AND EXECUTIVE PROCESSING. Metalinguistic processes permit conscious reflection upon (i.e., thinking about) language content, form, and use (e.g., while reading, spelling, writing reports, interpreting figurative language, etc.). Executive processing is reflected in the internal conversations that one engages in to regulate behavior in goal-oriented, problem-solving activities (Singer & Bashir, 1999). Cori's reading and spelling difficulties, lack of participation in expository discourse about linguistic tasks, performance on assessments of phonological awareness, and academic problems implicate both metalinguistic and executive processing. Therefore, taxonomies that explicate the development of linguistic and metalinguistic competencies that underlie functional communication will guide long- and short-term goal planning for Cori.

Discourse and Discourse Genres

Discourse refers to connected speech, as manifested in conversation, acts of persuasion, presentations of various sorts, and storytelling. Children of Cori's age are expected to engage in a variety of discourse types for a variety of reasons. Discourse engages both linguistic and metalinguistic processes. Discourse, however, manifests its own intrinsic organization and, in turn, developmental achievements captured by developmental taxonomies. Four genres of discourse recognized in the literature are central to literacy: expository, conversational, narrative, and argumentative (i.e., hortatory). Each can be characterized according to a sequence of developmental achievements.

EXPOSITORY DISCOURSE. Expository discourse refers to the use of language to convey information (Bliss, 2002; Keil, 2006). Explanations can include definitions; causal and procedural explanations; comparisons; etc. Explaining how to assemble a gaming computer or why the circuit breaker keeps tripping after the setup are examples of expository discourse. Expository discourse incorporates more literate and technical vocabulary as compared with conversational forms of discourse that serve social functions (Nippold, Hesketh, Duthie, & Mansfield, 2005). Representing complex causal and procedural relationships verbally and comprehending complex verbal explanations can pose significant linguistic and cognitive challenges for students with language disorders (Ward-Lonergan, Liles, & Anderson, 1999).

CONVERSATIONAL/SOCIAL DISCOURSE. Conversational discourse is a more interactive and less formal genre (Bliss & McCabe, 2006, Liles, Crystal, & Anderson, 1999). Conversational discourse occurs in social settings with friends and family. An example is talk among a group of high school friends discussing the latest hip-hop phenomenon, movie, or school gossip.

NARRATIVE DISCOURSE. A third discourse genre, narrative discourse, may occur within or apart from conversational discourse. Narration relies on stories (personal, fictional), folklore, or drama as media. Telling stories, enacting plays, relaying folklore are examples of narrative discourse

HORTATORY DISCOURSE. "Hortatory" discourse represents a fourth discourse genre. This type of discourse serves persuasive or argumentative functions, exemplified by debates, sales pitches, spiritual exhortations, etc. This type of discourse invokes logic and often speaks to audiences' emotional and ideological perspectives and is exemplified in debates, lectures, and essays (Levinsohn, 2012).

COGNITIVE DEMANDS AND DISCOURSE. All discourse types require speakers to tap into their cognitive and linguistic resources as they attempt to communicate their ideas in a clear and organized fashion. However, expository discourse tends to emphasize speaking in precise monologues (Berman & Verhoeven, 2002). The need to make explicit reasoning about potentially complex phenomena heightens linguistic complexity and, in turn, performance demands. Expository discourse is also sensitive to topic and context (Nippold, 2010). For example, conversation about an ongoing physical event makes different demands on the speaker than speaking about some aspect of language (e.g., spelling, rules of essay construction, rules of syntax, figurative language forms).

Taxonomies That Represent the Organization and Complexity of Discourse

MACROSTRUCTURE. The organization of the macrostructure of expository and hortatory discourse is captured by the level of information processing referenced, complexity of reasoning and logic employed (Levinsohn, 2012). Piagetian research (e.g., Piaget, 1952, 1976, 1978) best characterizes developmental characteristics of reasoning reflected in expository discourse.

The macrostructure of narrative discourse is depicted in story grammars. Several taxonomies that derive from research on the development of the macrostructure or internal organization of narratives guide goal planning. These taxonomies fall into two categories:

1. One set of taxonomies characterizes primarily fictional stories, culminating in the ability to tell a story that incorporates characters who set goals, encounter problems, and attempt to achieve problem resolutions. These types of stories are stressed in cultures in which book reading to children is a common household routine. Related taxonomies include Berman and Slobin (1994), Lahey (1988), Stein and Glenn (1979), Trabasso, van den Broek, and Suh (1989).

2. A second set of taxonomies characterizes the internal organization of oral narratives (typically, personal narratives, including "high point" narratives). In such stories, the climax incorporates an unusual, hard-to-believe but entertaining personal experience (e.g., You'll never believe what happened to me today; I saw a dragon; really, let me tell you about it … Champion, 2003; Labov & Waletsky, 1967). These types of narratives are most common in families and cultures in which storytelling is more related to family and community experiences and often serves daily living or community information-transmission functions.

Microstructure. The complexity of the microstructure of all forms of discourse, including narrative discourse, is typically assessed with reference to "T-units." T-units are complete sentences (independent clauses), and all subordinate (dependent) clauses included. The complexity of T-units increases as the complexity of morphology and semantic and syntactic organization of constituent clauses increases. T-units, as well as pragmatic devices, such as prosodic patterns, parallel tense, pronoun referencing, and ellipsis, also address narrative cohesion—another component of a narrative's microstructure.

Linguistic taxonomies, such as Bloom and Lahey's taxonomies for simple (SVC) and complex (multiverb) sentences may also be applied to the assessment of individual sentences that comprise the microstructure of stories.

Step 3: Establishing Long-Term and Subordinate Long-Term Goals

Two long-term goals were established addressing two separate areas of language difficulty: Discourse and reading. Each was derived with reference to the three derivation sources reviewed earlier: (a) baseline data, (b) the guiding information processing paradigm, and (c) related taxonomies.

Long-term goal 1. *Cori will engage in a variety of developmentally appropriate discourse types (goal-based causal chains, personal/high point narratives, expository, and hortatory [persuasive])*

Justification. Cori does not engage in two of the narratives types targeted as long-term goals, although each is common in everyday academic and social contexts. Expository and persuasive discourse is encountered throughout the day and across speaking situations. Explaining and persuading occur in everyday social situations (e.g., explaining to mother why Takashi 6ix9ine has talent and persuading her to permit listening) and in academic settings—in interactions with teachers and text. Explaining takes place verbally and in writing (especially given homework), on tests, in book reports, etc. Although Cori produces temporal and causal chain narratives, the complexity of his procedural and causal reasoning in written and verbal explanations is at the pre-operational level. Narratives, furthermore, lack detail (e.g., information about settings, internal responses of characters, complications and problem-solving attempts). More complex procedural and causal content reflecting operational reasoning and more developed story grammars are expected from students across the curriculum.

Argumentation occurs whenever individuals express and defend a position, in social and academic contexts. Argumentation occurs more formally in school settings, where formal and informal discussions and debates on topics of the day are commonly encouraged.

SUBORDINATE LONG-TERM GOAL 1A. *Cori will produce complex sentences coding temporal and conditional causal (if/then) relations in problem-solving contexts involving operational reasoning.*

JUSTIFICATION. Achievement of conditional causal semantic relations and complex temporal semantic relations are longer-term achievements than less complex causal relations. Causal and temporal semantic relations manifest their own developmental trajectory at the linguistic level of processing (Moses, Klein, & Altman, 1989; Nippold, 2016; Piaget, 1952). Problem-solving contexts involving operational reasoning represent common performance demands across middle and high school courses. Cori reasons at the preoperational level.

SUBORDINATE LONG-TERM GOAL 1B. *Cori will use figurative language forms (idioms, metaphors, similes, analogies, riddles, puns) in conversation and in verbal and written narratives.*

JUSTIFICATION. Baseline data indicate that metalinguistics (related to spelling, phonological awareness, narratives) is an area of weakness. Children of Cori's age are expected to approach language in academic settings in an analytical way when reading, writing, spelling, and listening to narratives.

Furthermore, Cori manifests delays in executive functions of language as seen in academic performance and difficulty regulating behavior with reference to instructions, such as "before you do this do that"; such instructions require Cori to use linguistic terms, such as "before" and "after" to guide behavior (e.g., to enact the second part of a command before the first.)

LONG-TERM GOAL 2. *Cori will read grade-appropriate text, including multisyllabic words containing vowel digraphs, fluently.*

JUSTIFICATION. Cori reads below grade level, and has particular difficulty reading multisyllabic words and component digraphs. Establishing complex grapheme–phoneme correspondences and phonological and morphological awareness represent areas of difficulty, and invoke multiple processing levels: Perceptual, linguistic, and metalinguistic.

SUBORDINATE LONG-TERM GOAL 2. *Cori will produce accurate and alternative spellings of multisyllable words, including words that contain vowel digraphs and consonant clusters in academic discourse and written text.*

JUSTIFICATION. Cori is not reading multisyllabic words fluently and has significant difficulties spelling. As noted earlier, Cori manifests weakness in the areas of phonological and morphemic awareness, as well as processing complex grapheme/phoneme patterns. Spelling invokes metalinguistic processes, which can, in turn, facilitate reading.

The following templates (Figures 11.1a and 11.1b) summarize the decisions and information referenced in the derivation of long-term and corresponding subordinate long-term goals for Cori.

Deriving the Long-Term Goal			
Decision	**Guiding Information**		
Areas of Speech/ Language to be Targeted, Referent Taxonomy, and Current Level of Performance	**Area of Speech/Language**	**Referent Taxonomy**	**Current Performance**
	1. Language production and comprehension	Content/Form/Use Story grammars Discourse genres Lahey (1988) Stein and Glenn (1979) Cameron, Wambaugh., Wright, and Nessler, (2006)	Typically speaks in single-verb sentences. Restricted range of complex sentences and connectives with primarily conjunction form. Avoids engaging in conversations. Performing below grade level in narrative comprehension and production, as well as in a number of subject areas.
	2. Literacy	Reading Spelling Shaywitz (2003) Duckworth (2001)	Reads below grade level, difficulty in reading multisyllabic words fluently, difficulties in spelling

Projecting a Prognosis	**Maintaining Factors**	**Severity**	**Current Performance**		
	Cognitive	Mild Mod. Sev.	Preoperational reasoning; difficulty comprehending and using figurative language; difficulty with phonological and morphemic awareness and spelling		
	Sensorimotor	Mild Mod. Sev.	Visual hypotonia		
	Psychosocial	Mild Mod. Sev.			
	Medical	Mild Mod. Sev.			
	Caretaker Attendance	Frequently		Intermittently	Rarely

Time Frame	**Time Allotted**	One year

Long-Term Goals	1. Cori will engage in a variety of developmentally appropriate discourse types: narrative (e.g., goal-based causal chain and personal/high point narratives), expository (procedural and causal) and hortatory (persuasive). 2. Cori will read grade-appropriate text containing multisyllabic words with consonant clusters and digraphs (vocalic and consonantal) fluently in text.

FIGURE 11.1a: Deriving Long-Term Goals

Deriving Subordinate Long-Term Goal(s): Language			
Long-Term Goal: 1. Cori will engage in a variety of developmentally appropriate discourse types (e.g., goal-based causal chain and personal/high point narratives), expository (procedural and causal) and hortatory (persuasive)			
Decision	**Guiding Information**		
Areas of Speech/Language Intrinsic to the Long-Term Goal	**Area of Speech/Language**	**Referent Taxonomy**	**Current Performance Level**
	Microstructure of narrative discourse Complex sentences Cohesive devices	Complex content/form interactions Story grammar (literate and personal narratives) Bloom and Lahey (1978); Lahey (1988); Labov and Waletsky (1967)	Speaks primarily in single-verb sentences, although is able to produce complex conjunction sentences and sentential complements
	Metalinguistics and executive functions	Figurative language and executive functions Nippold and Rudzinski (1993) Nippold (2016)	Difficulty comprehending and using figurative language
Subordinate Long-Term Goals	1a. Cori will produce a range of complex sentence forms coding a variety of content, with appropriate cohesive devices in conversational and narrative discourse, within problem-solving contexts. 1b. Cori will use figurative language forms (idioms, metaphors, similes, analogies, homonyms) in conversation and in verbal and written narratives.		

Deriving Subordinate Long-Term Goal(s): Literacy			
Long-Term Goal: 2. Cori will read grade-appropriate text containing multisyllabic words with consonant clusters and digraphs (vocalic and consonantal) fluently in text			
Decision	**Guiding Information**		
Areas of Speech/Language Intrinsic to the Long-Term Goal	**Area of Speech/Language**	**Referent Taxonomy**	**Current Performance Level**
	Reading	Reading stages Shaywitz (2003)	Reads below grade level (decoding and comprehension)
	Metalinguistics	Spelling Duckworth (2001)	Moderate to severe difficulties with spelling
Subordinate Long-Term Goals	2a. Cori will read multi-syllabic words containing digraphs (vocalic and consonantal) fluently in text. 2b. Cori will produce accurate and alternative spellings of multisyllabic words containing onset and coda consonant clusters, and vowel and consonant digraphs in academic discourse and written text.		

FIGURE 11.1b: Deriving Subordinate Long-Term Goals

Planning a Procedural Approach

Having established long-term goals for Cori, we proceed to think about the procedural approach. The following are the steps leading to that derivation.

Step 1. Identify Approaches to Treatment within Clinical Research with Reference to Long-Term Goals

Long-term goals for Cori target multiple forms of discourse and reading. We will begin by looking at approaches to discourse intervention. These are followed by approaches to the treatment of literacy problems, the focus of the second long-term goal. Approaches to discourse and complex sentence production incorporate primarily two theoretic perspectives about language acquisition: social cognitive and constructivist.

Approaches to Intervention Aimed at Discourse and Complex Sentence Production

SOCIAL COGNITIVE. One approach to the facilitation of narrative discourse influenced by social-cognitive learning theory addresses executive functions; this approach is prompted by the common core curriculum and involves (a) direct instruction on the components of story grammar; (b) children's creation of stories incorporating these components; and (c) analysis of familiar stories (that have been read to children) with reference to story grammar components. This approach is exemplified in the use of graphic organizers (e.g., story maps, Alturki, 2017). Children are presented the components of a good story (i.e., setting, initiating event, problem, attempt, resolution, etc.). Children then fill in the story components (abstracted from a familiar story or parts of newly invented ones. This approach has proved effective with children with language-learning disabilities, including those for whom English is a second language (e.g., Alturki, 2017; Isikdogan & Kargin, 2010).

A second, more linguistically oriented, approach (but still within the social cognitive framework) involves retelling familiar stories from books that have been read or experienced through media, such as television and cinema. Story retells may be accompanied by forms of perceptual support (picture sequences, as in the use of wordless picture books, such as "Frog Where Are You?" [Mayer, 2003]).

CONSTRUCTIVIST. Constructivist approaches to discourse intervention address the reasoning that underlies the kinds of procedural and causal relationships that the child can envision and discuss. As such, constructivist approaches influence narrative, expository, and argumentative discourse, the focus of our first long-term goal for Cori.

Constructivist methodology involves engaging the client in goal-directed, problem-solving activities that challenge operational thinking. Clients are typically provided with concrete materials to manipulate and are encouraged to reflect on their actions and explanations. Often disequilibrium evoked by problems that arise in the course of problem solving spurs clients to modify their behavior, explore and try different approaches to goal achievement and problem solving. The outcome is the growth and reorganization of procedural and causal knowledge about variables implicated in a phenomenon.

Feedback from the manipulation of concrete objects in the context of goal-directed problem-solving activities and reflection underlies, the formation of more complex procedural and causal relations, and more complex levels of reasoning. Reflection upon such feedback can contribute to the emergence of more complex, higher level reasoning and new mental representations, including reasoning about language (metalinguistic), and the use of internal language (executive).

THEORY OF MIND AND CONSTRUCTIVISM. Recognizing that others can have points of view different from one's own and respecting those points of view is necessary for successful engagement in social and argumentative (hortatory) discourse, as well as reading comprehension and enjoyment. Development of theory of mind viewed from a constructivist perspective is facilitated by disequilibrium that may be experienced when the child recognizes that others are expressing points of view in conflict with those familiar to him or her. Engaging in conversations with teachers, peers, and others represents one context in which children encounter disparate points of view; reading is another.

Social-Cognitive Approaches to Reading Intervention, Integrating Constructivist, and Relationship-Based Processes

The second long-term goal addresses Cori's reading difficulties. According to Shaywitz (2003), dyslexia is a phonological disorder, influenced by deficits in phonological awareness. Catts (2018) cautions that reading and spelling problems implicate morphemic awareness as well. As such, interventions for reading and spelling problems typically address word recognition, phonological and morphemic awareness, and reading comprehension.

In discussing intervention practices in previous chapters, we attempted to draw connections between circumscribed treatment approaches and corresponding theories of learning and rehabilitation (e.g., ABA intervention and operant theory). Differences among approaches are sometimes emphasized, and particular approaches to the exclusion of others are recommended. This dichotomous orientation does not work in the area of reading. Reading programs incorporate multiple kinds of procedures, reflecting the integration of processes accounted for by multiple learning theories. As such, the reading programs summarized below reflect the integration of four theoretic orientations: Social cognitive (scaffolding), constructivist, and relationship-based pragmatic.

LEXICAL AND SUBLEXICAL WORD RECOGNITION. Word recognition is a central objective of reading intervention programs. That is because the word is the fundamental unit of meaning and form from the perspective of the reader, as it is from the perspective of the speaker in verbal language. Two routes to word recognition have been identified in the literature: lexical and sublexical (Joubert & Lecours, 2000).

Research by Joubert and Lecours (2000) has revealed that schema-based word recognition (whole word, syllable, morpheme, and grapheme based) maintains both developmental and functional primacy across the life span. Sublexical processes (which correspond with word segmentation by phoneme, grapheme–phoneme correspondence, and sound blending) complement schema-based processes in cases of failure to identify a novel or overly complex word.

Despite the primacy of schema-based word recognition in reading, the ability to segment words by phoneme (with reference to phoneme–grapheme correspondences) is essential for the achievement of reading fluency (Ehri, 1999; Shaywitz, 2003). Developmentally, children first identify holistic visual symbols on signs above their favorite stores, in favorite books read to them, on cereal boxes, etc. Children then enter a phase of learning letters, learning to associate sounds with letters, and figuring out that words are made up of sounds and are different from the things that they signify (Shaywitz, 2003). Children also learn to segment words according to syllabic, morphemic, and graphemic/sound schema intrinsic to their language. Children who do not successfully navigate this final stage may continue to amass a store of sight words, but their memory for words becomes overwhelmed and does not serve fluent reading. Reading interventions address schema construction, typically through clinician-directed metalinguistic word analysis and word comparison exercises. An example is the Wilson Reading Program, which addresses word recognition and grapheme/sound segmentation exercises in the context of English-word syllable structures (closed, vowel-consonant-e, open, "vowel-team", vowel-r, consonant-le). Note that syllable structures in the reading literature are described differently than syllable structure in the literature on the linguistic of verbal language (e.g., onset-rime, peak-coda; Bernhardt & Stemberger, 2000).

ESTABLISHING MENTAL REPRESENTATIONS. Establishing mental representations of graphemes, phonemes, syllables, morphemes, and words is central to the most popular commercial reading programs (e.g., Wilson Language Training Corp (2019), Linda-Mood Bell Learning Processes (2019), Orton-Gillingham (Gillingham & Stillman, 1997), Lively Letters (Telian & Telian-Castagnozzi, 2019). These objectives are addressed primarily through drill in the recognition of site words and the establishment of grapheme–phoneme correspondences in isolation and in the context of meaningful and pseudo words containing variable syllable and graphemic/phonemic/morphemic scheme structures. Within these programs, children practice (a) segmenting or sounding out words or pseudo words segment by segment; (b) recognizing morphemes in words, and (c) reading by analogy across words containing the same morphemic structures. In the Wilson Reading Program, drill includes multimodality sensorimotor exercises (through articulation of phonemes, syllables, and words, tracing graphemes physically on paper or in the air, using manipulables to create letters, etc.).

DIRECT INSTRUCTION. Direct instruction about rules governing the relationships between pronunciation, a sound's graphemic context, grapheme–syllable structure and within word–morpheme correspondences is another feature of commercial reading programs. Direct instruction about rules of language invokes metalinguistic processes, i.e., reflection on linguistic objects and rules of pronunciation.

PERCEPTION. Another approach to the representation and processing of grapheme–phoneme word segments involves efforts to improve auditory and visual processing speeds (implicating speech and grapheme perception). Fast ForWord (Tallal, 1997) is perhaps the best known of a number of computer-based intervention programs that are designed to address problems in these areas (see, also, Mifflin [2019] for another example). Speech and visual perception involve extremely high-speed processing of stimuli. High-speed processing is typically the function of the temporal lobe of the left hemisphere of the central nervous system (more recently attributed to "ventral stream" cortical function), Fridriksson et al. (2016). That function with reference to speech is to evaluate rapidly fluctuating components of transitional wave forms (e.g., formant structures), sound pulses (e.g., voice onset time), and frequency distributions that occur at a rate best measured in milliseconds (i.e., thousandths of a second); Evaluation of such features of sound underlies the detection of phoneme sequences (Raphael, Borden, & Harris, 2011). If the left hemisphere is not up to speed, so to speak, speech comprehension may be affected.

Fast ForWord and derivative computer-based programs involve engaging children in computer-based activities in which children listen to and practice following instructions in which acoustic information presented to the client is manipulated to promote improved processing speeds through rewarded drills and practices.

Visual perception in the process of reading operates similarly, as the eyes scan the written page in the process of word recognition (Wren, 2019) and transform the scan phonologically. A meta-analysis of outcomes of Fast ForWord and similar intervention programs designed to address speed of processing have, however, yielded inconclusive results (Gillam et al., 2008).

Learning the letters, and the sound–letter correspondences through instruction and practice is essentially a scaffolded, social cognitive approach to intervention. Contrastively, discovery based on manipulation (mental and physical) of letters and sounds and words emanates from constructivist processes. Discovering sound and visual patterns in written materials, recognizing that spoken and written words can be segmented, and noticing similarities as well as distinctions among segments represent constructivist components of reading interventions yielding schema recognition. Similarly, experiencing letter construction through multiple sensorimotor modalities (e.g., physical gestures, tracing across sandpaper, bending pipe cleaners, etc.) incorporates the constructivist premise that feedback from goal-directed actions facilitates the construction of mental representations.

SPELLING. A subordinate long-term goal was established for spelling, recognizing that spelling invokes meta-phonology, which contributes to reading as well. Constructivist and social-cognitive approaches to spelling dominate.

Duckworth (2001), a colleague of Piaget's, has made seminal contributions to constructivist educational programs. Duckworth's approach to spelling is one of those contributions. Duckworth advises encouraging children in the classroom to invent as many ways as possible for spelling specific words. Given a set of possible spellings, the educator identifies the acceptable spelling and may provide reasons for its acceptance. According to Duckworth, the process of generating alternative spellings encourages children to reflect on phonemic, morphemic, syllabic and graphemic factors that influence spelling and word construction.

More traditional approaches to spelling involve direct instruction on rules and regularities that guide spelling, including recognition and analysis of 'schemas" based on graphemic/phonological patterns, syllable and morphological structures of words, and exceptions to regular spelling patterns (Reid & Hresko, 1999).

Relationship-Pragmatic Approaches Incorporating Social-Cognitive and Constructivist Processes

Scaffolded reading routines are common to most reading programs. Scaffolding engages linguistic and executive processes, as an "expert" facilitates skill acquisition in "novices" in the context of routines (Ratner & Bruner, 1978). The expert initially draws the learner's attention to relevant objects, events, and information and guides the learner in performing the task at hand by modeling, explaining, and allowing the learner opportunities to perform the task under guidance. Over time, the learner initiates the routines and takes over more and more aspects of the activity.

Scaffolded reading routines occur in some cultures by caregivers who initiate reading routines early in a child's life. Parents who read their children bedtime stories, attend library functions with their children, and teachers who engage children in "circle-time" activities common to preschool programs all scaffold reading.

Not all families, however, read to their children or provide their children early reading experiences (e.g. Heath, 1982). In such cases, children come to school-based reading activities at a disadvantage compared with those children who have experienced early reading routines.

A significant body of research supports the creation of social scaffolded reading routines at home and in the classroom or therapy room. Shaywitz (2003), remarking about the importance of vocabulary building in learning to read, wrote, ". . . being surrounded by books, listening to stories read aloud, talking about the characters and events in the story, . . . all help a child develop her thinking skills and her imagination, build her vocabulary, and become aware of the world around her." Guthrie, McRae, and Klauda (2007), in their Concept-Oriented Reading Instruction (CORI) program, recommend encouraging work in groups and encouraging conversations among readers about books read (see also Kamhii and Catts, 2013). Orton-Gillingham and Lindamood-Bell reading programs direct significant attention to reading comprehension in the context of reading routines.

These relationship-based reading programs also incorporate constructive, learner-oriented components, including (a) giving readers a choice of text, (b) encouraging students to bring personal experiences to bear on interpretations of reading content, (c) acknowledging multiple possible interpretations (as opposed to single right and wrong "main ideas"), and questioning aimed at probing grader's personal response to reading material. Guthrie et al. (2007), like Shaywitz, also advocate integrating reading instruction with concrete experiences related to the reading material; CORI integrates reading and science, including experimentation. Orton-Gillingham and Lindamood-Bell incorporate multisensory experiences related to letter identification (e.g., tracing letters in the air, creating letters from sensory materials such as sand, etc.) and meaning representation through multiple modalities.

Shaywitz (2003) wrote,

> "A kindergarten child's reading program is rounded out by a range of activities that enhance her language skills and her enjoyment of literature. Whether at school or at home, being surrounded by books, listening to stories read aloud, talking about the characters and events in the story, and playing with blocks or puppets all help a child develop her thinking skills and her imagination, build her vocabulary, and become aware of the world around her." (Location 3201)

Heath (1982) emphasized the importance of joint-reading activities in the clinic in cases in which such activities were not common in the home. Scaffolded reading routines are typified by the clinician first reading to the child and then gradually allowing the child to take over as she begins to recognize words, utilize context clues, and analyze phonemic segments to take on unfamiliar vocabulary (see also Ratner & Bruner [1977] for a discussion of the importance of such routines for language development in general).

Approaches to Figurative Language, Metalinguistics

One of Cori's subordinate long-term goals addresses the *use of figurative language forms (idioms, metaphors, similes, analogies, riddles, and puns) in conversation and in verbal and written narratives*. The ability to interpret and use figurative language is a developmental achievement that emerges during the elementary school years (Nippold, 2016; Spector, 1990; Wiig & Secord; 1989). What contributes to its emergence is the ability to consider multiple possibilities and perspectives; this developmental cognitive achievement follows an earlier stage in which children entertain only singular approaches to word meaning, perspective taking, goal achievement, and problem solving (Karmiloff-Smith, 1986a, 1986b).

CONSTRUCTIVIST. Constructivist approaches to facilitating metalinguistic processing promote reflection on events and efforts to envision alternative possibilities (e.g., meaning, procedures, causes, points of view). Curiosity in the context of successful experiences or discomfort and disequilibrium in problematic situations can promote considerations of alternative possibilities (Forman & Hill, 1990; Piaget, 1985). Appreciation and use of figurative language forms come out of the discovery of alternate possibilities.

SOCIAL-COGNITIVE SCAFFOLDING. Scaffolded instruction represents a more typical approach to facilitating metalinguistic competence. Children are instructed directly on meaning of linguistic units that can have both multiple and nonliteral interpretations. In addition, children are taught how to use semantic and syntactic textual cues to discover meaning, for example, appositives, relative clauses, similes, illustrations and examples, etc. (Nippold, 2016).

Inference making about internal states of characters and outcomes of events is facilitated by direct instruction about relevant textual clues and interpretation of those clues. Clues may be in the form of metacognitive and metalinguistic verbs (e.g., knows, predicts, interprets, implies); and factive and nonfactive verbs (knows versus thinks, believes, could, etc.).

Direct instruction may be aimed at recognition of the logical forms of language. Logical forms of language engage logic in meaning derivation. Conjunctions are logical forms: The conjunction "and" placed between two clauses or sentences signifies an additive relation. "But" or "or," on the other hand, signifies contrast and exclusion. "Which," "all," and "some" refer to membership in a group, either engaging in or being excluded from an event.

"If–then" constructions engage syllogistic logic: Two outstanding forms are modus ponens and modus tollens. Syllogistic logic emphasizes the reality-creating quality of language, as used in explaining, coercing, debating, politicking. Syllogistic logic begins with a premise expressed within an "if–then" relation that establishes the basis for inferential reasoning: For example, the statement "If a glass falls on this marble floor, it will break" establishes a basis for being extremely careful handling glass at a party. However, finding a broken glass in a trash can after the party suggests that it was dropped—but one cannot be 100% sure. Another possibility would be that it was intentionally stepped on, maybe as practice by two tipsy guests portraying a Jewish wedding ceremony. But consider the following premise: "If and only if a glass is dropped on a marble floor will it break." Given that linguistically established state of reality, one can now be 100% positive that that broken glass in the trash was actually dropped. Such types of verbal reasoning often elude children with language-learning disabilities (e.g., Leevers & Harris, 2000).

Maintaining Factors

In addition to the learning premises, maintaining factors that have been identified as contributing to speech and language performance may need to be addressed in designing procedures. In Cori's case, cognition is a maintaining factor. Cori's tendency to reason at the preoperational level will need to be considered when we operationalize the procedural approach at the short-term planning phase.

Figures 11.2a and 11.2b illustrate the derivation of the long-term procedural approach.

Short-Term Planning

Short-term goals will flow from long-term goals, as the clinician considers the developmental and functional relations among the goals, the client's present level of functioning, and the associated developmental taxonomies that guided their derivation. The first decision to be made is how to prioritize long-term goals. The client's baseline data (present level of functioning) and the developmental research (i.e., the corresponding developmental taxonomy used to establish goals) will guide this decision.

The first long-term goal targets engagement in multiple types of discourse (narratives, expository, personal, hortatory [i.e., persuasive]). As discussed earlier, Cori presently produces narratives that include, primarily, temporal sequences of personal experiences, and those may include elementary causal content: for example, "My friend Ken got detention for getting into a food fight during lunch." Cori does not produce narratives or engage in discourse (explanatory, argumentative) that reference more complex causal reasoning.

Children of Cori's age and grade level would be expected to engage in more complex discourse (e.g., involving causal chain narratives and expository discourse). In school, such complex language activity is often in situations that invoke correspondingly more complex operational reasoning (the target of the first long-term objective). Such causal relations are often expressed via conditional causal ("if...then") utterances, or in complex sentences that contain comparative components (e.g., If there are unequal weights on either side of a fulcrum you need to have the heavier weight closer to the fulcrum to balance it; you need to equalize the weight." Moses, Klein, & Altman, 1989; Piaget, 1952). A subordinate long-term goal was established to address the production of complex sentences.

Planning the Procedural Approach: Language		
Decision	**Guiding Information and Client-Specific Details**	
Ultimate Behavior to be Acquired	**Long-Term Goals**	1. Cori will engage in a variety of developmentally appropriate discourse types (e.g., goal-based causal chain and personal/high point narratives), expository (procedural and causal) and hortatory (persuasive) 1a. Cori will produce a range of complex sentence forms coding a variety of content, with appropriate cohesive devices in conversational and narrative discourse, within problem-solving contexts. 1b. Cori will use figurative language forms (idioms, metaphors, similes, analogies, homonyms) in conversation and in verbal and written narrative.
Approaches to Intervention	**Types of Evidence**	**Reference**
	Meta-Analysis	
	Experimental	
	Clinical Practice/ Developmental	Piaget (1985); Moses, Klein, and Altman (1989); Moses (1994)
	Theory	
Premises about Language Learning or Rehabilitation Derived from Clinical Research Relevant to Achieving Long-Term Goals	**Theory**	**Premises**
	Constructivism	Feedback from the manipulation of concrete objects and from varying problem-solving procedures in context of goal-directed activities and problem-solving activities underlies the development of more complex procedural and causal relations. Encouraging reflection on figurative language forms in developmentally and culturally appropriate contexts, and encouraging creation of alternative meanings and interpretations of words and phrases promote metalinguistic competence.
	Relationship-Based Pragmatic	Engaging in extended conversation about events of interest facilitates language development.
	Social Cognitive	Modeling the use of figurative language (in multiple contexts, including songs, rap, humor, text) promotes metalinguistic competence.
	Operant	Context in which behavior is embedded and consequences following a target behavior shape the behavior (by strengthening or weakening behavior).
Maintaining Factors that Need to be Addressed	**Maintaining Factors**	**Specific Aspects**
	Cognitive	Reasons at preoperational level
	Sensorimotor	Visual hypotonia
	Psychosocial	
	Medical	

FIGURE 11.2a: Planning the procedural approach for language

Planning the Procedural Approach: Literacy		
Decision	**Guiding Information and Client-Specific Details**	
Ultimate Behavior to be Acquired	**Long-Term Goals**	2. Cori will read grade-appropriate text containing multisyllabic words with consonant clusters and digraphs (vocalic and consonantal) fluently in text. 2a. Cori will read multi-syllabic words containing digraphs (vocalic and consonantal) fluently in text. 2b. Cori will produce accurate and alternative spellings of multi-syllable words containing onset and coda consonant clusters, and vowel and consonant digraphs in academic discourse and written text.
Approaches to Intervention	**Types of Evidence**	**Reference**
	Meta-Analysis	Coleman, Venediktov, Troia, and Wang (2013)
	Experimental	Shaywitz (2005)
	Clinical Practice/ Developmental	Kamhii and Catts (2013) Shaywitz (2003)
	Theory	
	Theory	**Premises**
Premises about Language Learning or Rehabilitation Derived from Clinical Research Relevant to Achieving Long-Term Goals	Constructivism	Encouraging reflection on sound relations (rhymes), syllable segments in words, morphemes facilitates phonological awareness and reading.
	Relationship-Based Pragmatic	Caretaker-child reading routines focused on child's interests facilitate word recognition and reading.
	Social Cognitive	Modeling vocabulary, sound–letter correspondences, graphemic patterns, morphemes within joint-reading routines with age-/grade-appropriate text facilitates word pattern recognition, schema construction, and reading.
Maintaining Factors that Need to be Addressed	**Maintaining Factors**	**Specific Aspects**
	Cognitive	Reasons at preoperational level
	Sensorimotor	Visual hypotonia
	Psychosocial	
	Medical	

FIGURE 11.2b: Planning the procedural approach for literacy

According to Stein and Glenn (1979) and Lahey (1988), temporal chain narratives precede causal chain narratives developmentally. Short-term goals targeting narratives that describe temporally organized procedures in complex problem-solving activities, and narratives that contain conditional causal ("if…then") semantic relations would support expository (explanatory) discourse in academic classroom and textual contexts. Problem-solving activities that promote the consideration of relationships among interacting objects, making of comparisons, and operational reasoning would be especially relevant contexts for addressing such goals.

A second long-term goal addresses Cori's difficulties in reading and spelling. Developmentally, the overall organization of text material (macrostructure) influences reading. That is because comprehension of reading material is influenced by the relationship between the content and form of the reading material, the reader's own interests and experiences, and the kinds of relationships the reader makes spontaneously (e.g., additive, temporal, causal) when he or she thinks about and tells stories. The Lahey (1988) taxonomy that guided long-term planning indicates that repeated action additive chain narratives represent an early developing story grammar that is a prerequisite for the emergence of causal chain narratives. Cori produces temporal chain narratives to convey personal experiences. Targeting fluent reading of additive and temporal chain text incorporating references to familiar routines would make sense as a second short-term goal.

Related to all forms of discourse and reading at Cori's age is the use and comprehension of figurative language forms *(idioms, metaphors, similes, analogies, riddles, puns)*. Figurative language was targeted as another subordinate long-term goal. We will consult corresponding taxonomies (Nippold, 2016; Spector, 1990) with reference to baseline data relevant to figurative language. Similes are among the earliest developing figurative expressions—especially, similes that compare familiar objects (e.g., Shrek was as big as the giant in Jack and the Beanstalk!). Learning to create and interpret puns based on homonymy (i.e., two words that sound the same but have different meanings) represents developmentally early forms of humor (e.g., Spector, 1998). A relevant short-term goal could address the production and interpretation of early developing forms of figurative language, including similes, puns, and riddles.

A final subordinate goal relevant to reading called for Cori to "produce accurate and alternative spellings of multisyllable words containing vowel digraphs." Spelling is a metalinguistic task. Spelling is facilitated by being able to segment words by syllable and by recognizing repeated syllabic patterns across words. Such competency applies to reading as well as spelling (Shaywitz, 2003).

Bound morphemes (prefixes and suffixes) offer readers recognizable patterns. Apel and Lawrence (2011) have emphasized that morphemic awareness complements phonemic awareness as a critical metalinguistic competence central to reading as well as spelling. Morphemes that have syntactic functions (tense, pluralization, nominalization etc.) can be hierarchized with reference to development (e.g., Brown, 1973). Metalinguistic awareness of such morphemes can be hierarchized with reference to the linguistic developmental sequence. As such, a short-term goal will be established in which Cori would segment and spell words with reference to morphology of common suffixes (er, ing, tion, ed, es). Short-term goals and their derivation are presented in Figures 11.3a and 11.3b.

Deriving Short-Term Goals: Language		
Decision	**Guiding Information and Client-Specific Details**	
Long-Term Goal and Corresponding Subordinate Long-Term Goals and Taxonomies Addressed	**Long-Term Goal and/or Subordinate Long-Term Goal(s)** / **Taxonomy**	**Current Performance Level**
	1. Cori will engage in a variety of developmentally appropriate discourse types: narratives (e.g., goal-based causal chain and personal/high point), expository (procedural and causal) and hortatory (persuasive) / Literate narratives, personal/high point narratives, discourse genres, hortatory discourse, executive functions, causal relations, reasoning, and problem solving	Uses primarily single-verb sentences Performing below grade level in subject areas
	1a. Cori will produce a range of complex sentence forms coding a variety of content, with appropriate cohesive devices in conversational and narrative discourse, within problem-solving contexts. / Lahey (1988); Cameron and Wambaugh (2006); Cameron, Wambaugh, Wright, & Nessler (2006); Labov and Waletsky (1967) Levinsohn (2012); Nippold (2016); Piaget (1952,1976, 1978)	
	1b. Cori will use figurative language forms (idioms, metaphors, similes, analogies, homonyms) in conversation and in verbal and written narrative. / Figurative language, humor Nippold (2016); Spector (1990)	Does not use figurative expression
Time Frame	**Time Allotted: 6 months.**	
Short-Term Goal and Rationale	**Long-Term Goal Addressed:** 1. Cori will engage in a variety of developmentally appropriate discourse types: narratives (e.g., goal-based causal chain and personal/high point), expository (procedural and causal), and hortatory (persuasive)	
	Short-Term Goal(s) Cori will produce temporal chain expository (explanatory) narratives describing how to accomplish a task.	
	Rationale with reference to: development/complexity/difficulty Temporal chain procedural narratives develop before causal chain and complex causal explanations.	

FIGURE 11.3a: Deriving short-term goals for language

	Subordinate Long-Term Goal Addressed 1a. Cori will produce a range of complex sentence forms coding a variety of content, with appropriate cohesive devices in conversational and narrative discourse, within problem-solving contexts.
	Short-Term Goal Cori will produce conditional causal complex sentences in problem-solving contexts that promote operational reasoning.
	Rationale with reference to: development/complexity/difficulty Single causal "if/then" sentences anticipating outcomes of causal relations between manipulable objects is an early achievement in the development of ability to produce a narrative explaining complex causal relations.
	Subordinate Long-Term Goal Addressed 1b. Cori will use figurative language forms (idioms, metaphors, similes, analogies, homonyms) in conversation and in verbal and written narratives.
	Short-Term Goal(s) Cori will interpret transparent similes and metaphors and humor/puns based on homonymy that appear in songs and oral and written text.
	Rationale with reference to development/complexity/difficulty Transparent similes and metaphors and puns are early metalinguistic achievements, achieved before opaque figurative expressions.

FIGURE 11.3a CONTINUED: Deriving short-term goals for language

Operationalizing the Procedural Approach

The next short-term planning task for Cori is to operationalize the procedural approach established during long-term planning. Implications drawn from learning premises identified within the procedural approach will guide this process.

The first step of this task is to review short-term goals that correspond to a long-term goal and related subordinate goals. Two short-term goals were established that target *narrative production (procedural, causal) in the context of problem-solving tasks that promote operational reasoning.* Cognition was identified as a maintaining factor. Another short-term goal involved a related subordinate goal—*interpretation of figurative forms—transparent similes and metaphors and humorous puns.*

The next step in operationalizing the procedural approach is to derive implications about characteristics of nonlinguistic and linguistic contexts from an examination of learning premises. A constructivist premise was identified: *Reflection upon feedback from the manipulation of concrete objects and varying procedures in the context of goal-directed problem-solving activities underlies the formation of more complex procedural and causal relations.* This premise

Deriving Short-Term Goals: Literacy			
Decision	**Guiding Information and Client-Specific Details**		
Long-Term Goal and Corresponding Subordinate Long-Term Goals and Taxonomies Addressed	**Long-Term Goal and/or Subordinate Long-Term Goal(s)**	**Taxonomy**	**Current Performance Level**
	2. Cori will read grade-appropriate text containing consonant clusters and multisyllabic words and digraphs fluently.	Reading Shaywitz (2003)	Reads below grade level Difficulty with metalinguistic tasks, including in the area of phonological awareness
	2a. Cori will read multisyllabic words containing consonant clusters and digraphs (vocalic and consonantal) fluently in text.		
	2b. Cori will produce accurate and alternative spellings of multisyllabic words containing onset and coda consonant clusters, and vowel and consonant digraphs in academic discourse and written text.		
Time Frame	**Time Allotted: 6 months**		
Short-Term Goal and Rationale	**Long-Term Goal Addressed:** Cori will read grade-appropriate text containing multisyllabic words with consonant clusters and digraphs (vocalic and consonantal) fluently in text.		
	Short-Term Goal(s) Cori will read familiar, repeated action additive chain narratives (adapted from familiar songs, raps, poetry, ads). Cori will read temporal chain narratives that describe procedures for executing familiar tasks (recipe, familiar routine). Cori will segment and spell words with reference to morphology of suffixes ("tion," "y," "ed," "s"). **Rationale with reference to: development/complexity/difficulty** Repeated action additive chains and temporal chains are earlier developing narratives. Context of familiar routines (songs, recipes) allows for anticipation of vocabulary and word meaning while reading. "tion," "y," "ed," "s" are high-frequency morphemes representing early acquired semantic functions (noun creation, regular past tense, plural).		

FIGURE 11.3b: Deriving short-term goals for literacy

implies that Cori be presented problem-solving tasks that involve the manipulation of concrete objects and that incorporate operational reasoning. This premise also suggests that the clinician allow Cori to address tasks spontaneously, without instructions. However, the premise also indicates that the clinician should engage Cori in conversation about how and why events unfolded (i.e., incorporating procedural and causal questions). The clinician will ask Cori to instruct him or her on how to accomplish the task. The clinician will encourage Cori to try again if Cori fails to accomplish the task. The clinician will accept "wrong" answers to questions but will encourage reflection on problems and contradictions.

With reference to the figurative language goal, the manipulable objects are words, problem-solving procedures are derivation of word meanings, and modeling is the clinician's use of figurative terms. The context would derive from Cori's interests, popular songs, comedy routines, accompanied by text-based written transcriptions. Cori could be prompted to explain what the artist means by that word. The clinician could offer the literal interpretations as opposed to figurative to encourage Cori to correct her.

The final short-term goals addressed reading, the target of the second long-term goal. The first such short-term goal has Cori reading *repeated action additive chain narratives (adapted from familiar songs, raps, poetry, ads) and temporal chain narratives describing procedures for enacting familiar routines (recipe, familiar task instructions)*. Here, the social cognitive premise is that models and scaffolded routines facilitate learning. This premise implies that repeated engagement in daily routines, provided by media (music, ads, etc.) and social experiences, will provide a supportive context for reading interventions.

The second reading-related short-term goal addressed spelling: *Cori will segment and spell words with reference to morphology of suffixes (tion, ing, y, ed, es)*. This objective implicates phonological and morphemic awareness, central to reading (Apel & Lawrence, 2011; Catts & Kamhii, 2013). A constructivist approach to achieving this objective would have Cori searching for patterns in words that reveal relations among words with reference to syllables, and morphemes. Furthermore, social-cognitive theory suggests that providing opportunities in sessions for joint-reading activities in which target patterns are identified and modeled will facilitate reading. Short-term goal templates for Cori are presented in Figures 11.4a and 11.4b.

Operationalizing the Procedural Approach: Language	
Decision	**Guiding Information and Client-Specific Details**
Short-Term Goals to be Addressed	Cori will produce temporal chain expository (explanatory) narratives describing how to accomplish a task in context of problem solving.
	Cori will produce conditional causal complex sentences in problem-solving contexts that promote operational reasoning.
	Cori will interpret (transparent similes and metaphors) and humor/puns based on homonymy that appear in songs, oral, and written text.
Derive Implications for Procedure Planning from Theory-Based Premises	**Constructivist Premise 1**: Feedback from the manipulation of concrete objects in context of goal-directed problem-solving activities, and reflection on feedback, underlie the formation of more complex procedural and causal relations. **Implications**: Therefore, the clinician will operationalize the procedural approach by presenting Cori problem-solving tasks that involve the manipulation of concrete objects and incorporate conservation \(operational reasoning)
	presenting task to Cori, allowing him to address task spontaneously, without instructions. Clinician will engage Cori in conversation about how and why events unfolded (critical exploration).
	Constructivist Premise 2: Varying behavior in process of problem solving facilitates more complex relational knowledge. **Implications**: Therefore, the clinician will operationalize the procedural approach by encouraging Cori to try again if he fails to accomplish the task.
	accepting "wrong" answers to questions and encouraging reflection on and drawing attention to contradictions.
Derive Implications for Procedure Planning from Maintaining Factors	**Maintaining Factors**
	Cognitive: Difficulty reasoning about language. Reasons at preoperational level **Implication**: See implications of constructivism
	Sensorimotor: Visual–motor hypotonia **Implication**: Monitor visual tracking

FIGURE 11.4a: Operationalizing the Procedural Approach for Language

Operationalizing the Procedural Approach: Literacy	
Decision	**Guiding Information and Client-Specific Details**
Short-Term Goals to be Addressed	Cori will read familiar, repeated action additive chain narratives (adapted from familiar songs, raps, poetry, ads) Cori will read temporal chain narratives that describe procedures for executing familiar tasks (recipe, familiar routine) Cori will segment and spell words with reference to morphology of suffixes ("tion," "y," "ed," "s")

Derive Implications for Procedure Planning from Theory-Based Premises	**Constructivist Premise:**
	
	Varying behavior in process of problem solving and reflecting on word structure (syllables, morphemes, sound segments, grapheme–phoneme correspondences, sound relations [rhymes]) facilitates part–whole relations, metalinguistic knowledge, including phonological awareness.
	    Implication: Therefore, the clinician will operationalize the procedural approach by engaging Cori in play with words (as manipulable objects)
	
	    segment words multiple ways (verbally by phoneme, syllable, morpheme) given words represented by manipulables (cubes, written words)
	
	Social-Cognitive Premise:
	Modeling problem-solving procedures facilitates learning
	    Implication: Therefore, the clinician will operationalize the procedural approach by modeling segmentation of words described earlier
	
	Operant premise: Context (behavioral antecedents and consequences) shapes behavior
	    Implication: Therefore, the clinician will operationalize the procedural approach by providing token reinforcers and verbal praise after each trial or group of trials

Derive Implications for Procedure Planning from Maintaining Factors	**Maintaining Factors**
	
	Cognitive: Difficulty with metalinguistics. Reasons at preoperational level. Difficulty considering, trying alternate possible procedures, causes
	    Implication: See constructivist premises and implications.
	
	Sensorimotor Visual–motor hypotonia
	    Implication: Clinician will monitor visual tracking

FIGURE 11.4b: Operationalizing Procedural Approach for Literacy

Session Planning

Session objectives represent acts of learning. They derive from both the short-term goals that they address and the operationalized procedural approach that captures the linguistic and nonlinguistic characteristics of activities that promote learning or rehabilitation. These characteristics are informed by the clinical research and theoretic premises about learning and rehabilitation.

Session objectives are different from long and short-term goals; as acts of learning, session objectives may be skill oriented and not necessarily generative or communicative as are outcomes of longer-term interventions.

Session objectives include details about the linguistic and nonlinguistic context of the target behavior. The linguistic context includes the communication behavior of the clinician or others who might be interacting with the client. The linguistic context also includes characteristics of the speech and language behavior in which the target behavior is embedded. As such, planning session objectives involves careful consideration and regulation of demands that assigned tasks make on the client. The following are the derivations of session objectives for Cori, with reference to corresponding short-term goals, operationalized procedural approaches, and performance demands addressed in the areas of verbal language and reading.

Session Goal Planning with Reference to Verbal Language

Step 1: Prioritize Short-Term Goals

With reference to short-term goals that addressed verbal language, two were prioritized: the production of temporal chain expository (explanatory) narratives describing how to accomplish a task in the context of problem solving and the production of conditional causal complex sentences in problem-solving contexts that promote operational reasoning. With reference to the first short-term goal focusing on temporal chain narratives, the following session goals were created:

EARLY SESSION GOAL. Cori will *produce a temporal chain narrative* describing a recipe for making chocolate chip cookies given *packaged ingredients and measuring tools* 2 times/45 minute session.

LATER SESSION GOAL. Cori will *produce a temporal chain narrative* instructing the clinician *how to position a board on a fulcrum and place unequal weights onto either side of the board to make the board balance.*

With reference to the second short-term goal focusing on conditional causal sentences, the following session goals were created:

EARLY. *Cori will explain why boards balance on a fulcrum given the following situations:* 4 times/45 minute session.

> *a board with two of the same blocks positioned on each side*
> *unequal weights on each side (given that the heavier weight is positioned closer to the fulcrum)* 4 times/45 minute session.

LATER. *Cori will direct the clinician on where to position two blocks of unequal weight and size on each side of a board positioned on a fulcrum in order to balance the board.*

Constructivist learning theory guided creation of the activity. Cori will be presented problem-solving tasks that involve the manipulation of concrete objects and that incorporate conservation (operational reason). The clinician will present a task to Cori, allow him to address the task spontaneously, without instructions. Using the method of critical exploration, the clinician will engage Cori in conversation about how and why events unfolded (i.e., incorporating procedural and causal questions). The clinician will ask Cori to instruct her on how to accomplish the task. The clinician will encourage Cori to try again if he fails to accomplish the task. The clinician will accept "wrong" answers to questions but will encourage reflection on problems and contradictions.

Performance demands controlled include the following:

Cognition

Manipulable objects provide feedback for complex reasoning and representation of complex causal relations

Operational reasoning developmentally more advanced than preoperational

Semantic Relations

Explanations about causal relations are more complex than descriptions of temporal relations.

A third short-term goal addressing figurative expressions (transparent similes and metaphors and humor/pun) was also prioritized—implicating metalinguistic competence: The following are the corresponding session goals that were established:

EARLY. *Cori will interpret the following terms presented in a song lyric following clinician's expressed confusion and literal interpretation:*

> *"Lit," "fire," "shorty," and "woke"*

LATER. Cori will interpret puns based on homonymy in response to the query "Why do you think that joke is supposed to be funny?"

> *What do you call a shoe salesman who cheats you? A real heel!*
> *What do you call a crazy banker who also owns a bakery? A "dough nut."*

Additional Performance Demands Addressed

Interpret familiar single words and homonyms that have literal and figurative meaning before complex syntactic structures (a noun phrase containing a relative clause).

Session Goal Planning with Reference to Reading

Step 1. Prioritize Short-Term Goals

We have now planned session goals addressing the first set of short-term goals involving verbal language. We now turn to the short-term goals that address reading. One was prioritized:

Cori will segment and spell words with reference to morphology of suffixes ("tion," "ing," "y," "ed," "es").

These are the corresponding session goals that were established:

EARLY. *Cori will, by clapping, segment syllables in two- and three-syllable words containing the morphemes "ing" and "tion" read by the clinician; 8/10 trials.*

LATER. *Cori will read high-frequency two-syllable words containing the morphemes "ing" and "tion" (acting, action; staying, station; facing, fiction; running, lotion; racing, diction; 8/10 trials.*

THE DECISION-MAKING PROCESS. The Shaywitz (2003) reading taxonomy indicates that fluent reading incorporates the ability to analyze (i.e., segment) words according to phonology and morphology (also Apel & Lawrence, 2011; Kamhii & Catts, 2013). The short-term goal of *segmenting and spelling words with reference to morphology of suffixes ("tion," "ing," "y," "ed," "es")* addresses these metalinguistic competencies.

Step 2. Regulate Performance Demands

We now extend our consideration of performance demands to phonological and morphological awareness activities. Performance demands addressed include:

How segments are indicated (clapping before verbally).

Segment high-frequency and familiar to low-frequency and novel words

Semantic and syntactic function of morphemes ("ing" as an inflection that creates progressive tense and gerunds) is less complex than, for example, "ify" that could create a verb from an adjective (simple/simplify) or a verb from a noun (dignity/dignify).

COMPARISONS THAT NEED TO BE CONSIDERED. Two words containing the same root + different morphemes less complex than two words containing different roots and different morphemes; for example, acting; action is easier than racing; diction.

RESPONSE MODE. Indicating syllable segments by clapping is less challenging than segmenting verbally while reading.

SEMANTIC/SYNTACTIC FUNCTION(S) OF MORPHEMES. ("ing" as an inflection that creates progressive tense and gerunds, and "tion," which signals "noun" less complex than "ify" that could create a verb from an adjective [simple/simplify] or a verb from a noun [dignity/dignify]).

Step 3. Review Operationalized Procedural Approach (Learning Premises and Implications for Procedures). With Reference to Premises Derived from Constructivist Theory, Clinician Will

Encourage reflection on sound relations (rhymes), syllable segments in words, onset-rime segments within syllables.

Figures 11.5a and 11.5b present session goal templates for Cori.

Deriving Session Goals and Procedures: Language	
Decision	**Guiding Information and Client-Specific Details**
Long-Term Goal and Related Subordinate Goals Addressed by Short–Term Goals	**Long-Term Goal:** 1. Cori will engage in a variety of developmentally appropriate discourse types: narratives (e.g., goal-based causal chain and personal/high point narratives), expository (procedural and causal) and hortatory (persuasive) **Subordinate Goals:** Cori will produce: 1a. A range of complex sentence forms coding a variety of content, with appropriate cohesive devices in conversational and narrative discourse, within problem-solving contexts. 1b. Figurative language forms (idioms, metaphors, similes, analogies, homonyms) in conversation, and in verbal and written narratives
For Each Short-Term Goal, Consider Implications of:	**Short-Term Goals:** 1a. Cori will produce temporal chain procedural narratives to explain how to achieve a task in problem-solving contexts. 1b. Cori will produce conditional causal content/form interactions to describe procedures and outcomes in problem-solving contexts that involve operational reasoning. 1c. Cori will interpret transparent similes and metaphors and humor/puns based on homonymy in songs, oral and written text. **Taxonomies:** Lahey (1988); Cameron, Wambaugh, Wright, and Nessler (2006); Labov and Waletsky (1987); Levinsohn (2012); Nippold (2016); Piaget (1952, 1976, 1978); Nippold (2016); Spector (1990)
Learning and Rehabilitation Premises	<table><tr><td>**Learning Theories**</td><td>**Implications Drawn (in the operationalized approach)**</td></tr><tr><td>**Constructivism**</td><td>Cori will be presented problem-solving tasks that involve the manipulation of concrete objects that incorporate conservation (operational reason). The clinician will present task to Cori, allow him to address task spontaneously, without instructions. Using the method of critical exploration, Clinician will engage Cori in conversation about how and why events unfolded (i.e., incorporating procedural and</td></tr></table>

FIGURE 11.5a: Session goals for language

		causal questions). Clinician will ask Cori to instruct him/her on how to accomplish the task. Clinician will encourage Cori to try again if Cori fails to accomplish the task. Clinician will accept "wrong" answers to question but will encourage reflection on problems, contradictions.
	Social Cognitive	Model figurative language expressions in conversation with Cori.
	Relationship-based Pragmatic	Engage with reference to Cori's interests and experiences; have extended conversations about problem-solving experiences, probing Cori's perspective.
	Operant	Respond positively to Cori's ideas about problem-solving procedures, ideas about causality and meanings of figurative expressions. Do not criticize (e.g. respond "no" to), ideas expressed that appear to be "wrong" (do not match clinician's ideas).
and Maintaining Factors	**Maintaining Factors**	**Implications Drawn (in the operationalized approach)**
	Cognitive	Provide perceptual support and objects to manipulate for feedback.
	Sensorimotor	Monitor visual tracking.

Session goals addressing Short-Term Goal 1a

Early. Cori will *produce a temporal chain narrative* describing a recipe for making chocolate chip cookies given *packaged ingredients and measuring tools* 2 times/45 minute session.

Later. Cori will *produce a temporal chain narrative* instructing the clinician *how to position a board on a fulcrum and place unequal weights onto either side of the board to make the board balance.*

FIGURE 11.5a CONTINUED: Session goals for language

Performance Demands Controlled	Performance Variable Controlled	How the Variable Is Controlled	Aspect of Session Goal Affected
	Developmental sequence of narrative production	Temporal before causal	Target
	Cognitive complexity	Preoperational reasoning before operational reasoning	Linguistic context
	Cognitive complexity	Problem solving involving manipulables before verbal reasoning	Nonlinguistic context

Session goals addressing short-term goal 1b.

Early. Cori will *explain why board balances* on a fulcrum while manipulating a board with two weights positioned on each side.

Later. Cori will *explain using "if…then" complex sentences in response to the clinician's query* "What will happen if I put this here and that there" (while repositioning two blocks of unequal weight and size in various places on each side of a board positioned on a fulcrum in order to balance the board) 8/10 attempts

Performance Demands Controlled	Performance Variable Controlled	How the Variable Is Controlled	Aspect of Session Goal Affected
	Developmental sequence of narrative production	Causal after temporal	Target
	Cognitive complexity	Preoperational reasoning before operational reasoning	Linguistic context
	Cognitive complexity	Problem solving involving manipulables before verbal reasoning	Nonlinguistic context

FIGURE 11.5a CONTINUED: Session goals for language

Session goals addressing short-term goal 1c.

Early. Cori will *interpret* the following terms presented *in a song lyric following clinician's expressed confusion and literal interpretation:*

"Lit," "fire," 'shorty,' and "woke"

Later. Cori will *interpret puns based on homonymy* in response to the query "Why do you think that joke is supposed to be funny?"

What do you call a shoe salesman who cheats you? A real heel!
What do you call a crazy banker who also owns a bakery? A dough nut.

Performance Demands Controlled	Performance Variable Controlled	How the Variable is Controlled	Aspect of Session Goal Affected
	Early session goal linguistic complexity	Interpret familiar single words that have literal and figurative meanings before deriving humor from relations between homonyms	Target
	Familiarity of context	Presented in a song rather than prose	Linguistic context text
	Pragmatic salience	Clinician's confusion promotes reflection	Linguistic context
	Later session goal	Interpret humor with reference to complex semantic and syntactic structures after single words that can have multiple	Linguistic complexity
	Metacognitive complexity	Explanation and Interpretation of pun before production	Target

FIGURE 11.5a CONTINUED: Session goals for language

Deriving Session Goals and Procedures: Literacy	
Decision	**Guiding Information and Client-Specific Details**
Long-Term Goal and Related Subordinate Goals Addressed by Short–Term Goals	**Long-Term Goal:** 2. Cori will read grade-appropriate text containing multisyllabic words with consonant clusters and digraphs (vocalic and consonantal) fluently in text **Subordinate Goals:** 2. Cori will produce accurate and alternative spellings of multisyllable words containing onset and coda consonant clusters, and vowel and consonant digraphs in academic discourse and written text.
For Each Short-Term Goal, Consider Implications of:	**Short-Term Goal:** STG2a. Cori will read temporal chain narratives that describe procedures for executing familiar tasks (recipe, familiar routine) STG2b. Cori will segment and spell words with reference to morphology of suffixes ("tion," "y," "ed," "s") **Taxonomies:** Shaywitz (2003); Duckworth (2001)
Learning and Rehabilitation Premises	 **Learning Theories** **Implications Drawn (in the operationalized approach)**

Learning Theories	Implications Drawn (in the operationalized approach)
Constructivism	Engage Cori in play with words (as manipulable objects) Segment words multiple ways (verbally by phoneme, syllable, morpheme) given words represented by manipulables (cubes, written words)
Social Cognitive	Model segmentation of words described above (constructivism)
Relationship-based pragmatic	Engage with Cori with reference to Cori's interests and experiences
Operant	Provide token reinforcers and verbal praise after each trial or group of trials

and

FIGURE 11.5b: Session Goals for Literacy

Maintaining Factors	Maintaining Factors	Implications Drawn (in the operationalized approach)
	Cognitive	Difficulty with metalinguistics. Reasons at preoperational level. Difficulty considering, trying alternate possible procedures, causes Implication: See constructivist premises and implications above.
	Sensorimotor	Monitor visual tracking
	Psychosocial	
	Medical	

Session Goals Addressing Short-Term Goal 2b

Early. Cori will *indicate syllable segments of words by clapping given two- and three-* syllable words containing the morphemes "*ing*" and "*tion*" read by the clinician 8/10 trials.

Later. *Cori will read pairs of high- and medium-frequency two-syllable words containing the morphemes "ing" and "tion" (acting, action; staying, station; facing, fiction; running, lotion; racing, diction 8/10 trials.)*

FIGURE 11.5b CONTINUED: Session Goals for Literacy

Performance Demands Controlled	Performance Variable Controlled	How the Variable Is Controlled	Aspect of Session Goal Affected
	Response mode	Indicate segments by clapping before verbally segmenting.	Target behavior
	Vocabulary and morphemes	High frequency to low frequency and novel morphemes ("ing" and "tion" are early developing morphemes)	Target behavior
	Linguistic context		
	Linguistic context	Comparing two words containing the same root + different morphemes less complex than two words containing different roots and different morphemes (e.g., acting; action is easier than racing; diction)	Target behavior (Later session goal)

FIGURE 11.5b CONTINUED: Session Goals for Literacy

Summary

In this chapter, we planned intervention for Cori, a child of school age who presented with language-learning disabilities, which included a reading problem. Cori represents but one example of a heterogeneous population of individuals who present with language problems that influence academic and social performance. These individuals are labeled as learning disabled, language learning disabled or as manifesting specific-language impairment, depending on the profession and professional taking the lead in the diagnosis. Language problems may manifest themselves through mathematics, reading, listening to teacher talk, verbal reasoning, and the use of internal language (self-talk) to regulate behavior. Language problems associated with language-learning disabilities do not signify intellectual deficits or any other kind of "deficit." The issue may implicate perception, linguistic organization, and/or metalinguistic and executive processes.

The intervention plan we formulated is one of many potentially workable possibilities. Our plan along with alternative possibilities is the product of a three-phase planning process. Following the central tenets of this process, long-term and short-term goals were functional and generative, guided by research-based developmental taxonomies. Procedure planning, which lead to session goals and procedures, was grounded in clinical research and premises about learning intrinsic to the theoretical foundation of such research. Session goals and procedures were finally established after careful consideration and management of performance demands made on our client by potential target behaviors, and characteristics of the linguistic and nonlinguistic context in which target behaviors were embedded.

REFERENCES

Alturki, N. (2017). The effectiveness of using group story-mapping strategy to improve reading comprehension of students with learning disabilities. *Educational Research and Reviews, 12*, 915–926.

Apel, K., & Lawrence, J. (2011). Contributions of morphological awareness skills to word-level reading and spelling in first-grade children with and without speech sound disorder. *Journal of Speech, Language, and Hearing Research, 54*, 1312–1327.

Berman, R., & Slobin, D. (Eds.) (1994). *Relating events in narrative: A cross linguistic study*. Hillsdale, NJ: Erlbaum.

Berman, R., & Verhoeven, L. (2002). Cross-linguistic perspectives on the development of text-production abilities. *Speech and Written Language & Literacy, 5*, 1–43.

Bernhardt, B., & Stemberger, J. (2000). *Workbook in non-linear phonology for clinical application*. Austin, TX: Pro-ed.

Bliss, L. S. (2002). *Discourse impairments: Assessment and intervention applications*. Boston, MA: Allyn & Bacon.

Bliss, L. S., & McCabe, A. (2006). Comparison of discourse genres: Clinical implications. *Contemporary Issues in Communication Science and Disorders, 33*, 126–137.

Cameron, R. M., Wambaugh, J. L., Wright, S. W., & Nessler, C. L. (2006). Effects of a combined semantic/ phonologic cueing treatment on word retrieval in discourse. *Aphasiology, 20*, 269–285.

Catts, H. W., Fey, M. E., Zhang, X., & Tomblin, J. B. (1999). Language basis of reading disabilities: Evidence from a longitudinal investigation. *Scientific Studies in Reading, 3*, 331–361.

Coleman, J. J., Venediktov, R. A., Troia, G. A., Wang, B. P. (2013). *Impact of literacy interventions on achievement outcomes in children with language-learning disabilities*. ASHA's National Center for Evidence-Based Practice in Communication Disorders.

Duckworth, E. (2001). *"The having of wonderful ideas" and other essays on teaching and learning* (3rd ed.). Cambridge, MA: Harvard University Press.

Ehri, L. C. (1999). Phases of development in learning to read words. In J. Oakhill & R. Beard (Eds.), *Reading development and the teaching of reading: A psychological perspective* (pp. 79–108). Oxford, England: Blackwell Science.

Felton, M., & Kuhn, D. (2001). The development of argumentive discourse skill. *Discourse Processes, 32*, 135–153.

Forman, G. E. & Hill, F. (1990). *Piaget in the preschool*. Montvale, CA: Wellesley.

Fridriksson, J., Yourganov, G., Bonilha, D., Basilakos, A., Den Ouden, D. B., & Rorden, C. (2016). Revealing the dual streams of speech processing. *PNAS, 113*, 15108–15113.

Geschwind, N. (1970). The organization of language and the brain. *New Series, 170*(3961), 940–944.

Goodman, K. (1986). *What's whole in whole language?* Portsmouth, NH: Heinemann.

Gilingham, A., & Stillman, B. (1997). *Gillingham manual: Remedial training for children with specific disability in reading, spelling, and penmanship* (8th ed.). Cambridge, MA: Educators Publishing Service.

Gillam, R., Loeb, D., Hoffman, L., Bohman, T., Champlin, C., Thibodeau, L., … Friel-Patti, S. (2008). The efficacy of fast forward language intervention in school-age children with language impairment: a randomized controlled trial. *Journal of Speech, Language, and Hearing Research, 51*, 97–119.

Guthrie, J. T., McRae, A., & Klauda, S. L. (2007). Contributions of concept-oriented reading instruction to knowledge about interventions for motivations in reading. *Educational Psychologist, 42*, 237–250.

Hallahan, D. P. & Mercer, C. D. (2001). *Learning disabilities: Historical perspectives. Executive summary*. Washington, DC: ERIC.

Hammill, D., Leigh, J. E., McNutt, G. & Larsen, S. C. (1981). A new definition of learning disabilities. *Learning Disability Quarterly, 4*, 336–342.

Heath, S. B. (1982). What no bedtime story means: Narrative skills at home and school. *Language in Society, 11*, 49–76.

Heath, S. B. (1986). Critical factors in literacy development. In S. DeCastella, A. Luke, & K. Egan (Eds.). *Literacy, society, and schooling* (pp. 209–229). New York, NY: Cambridge University Press.

Isikdogan, N., & Kargin, T. (2010). Investigation of the effectiveness of the story-map method on reading comprehension skills among students with mental retardation. *Education Science Theory and Practice, 10*, 1509–1527.

Joubert, S. A., & Lecours, A. R. (2000). The role of sublexical graphemic processing in reading. *Brain and Language, 72*, 1–13.

Kamhi, A. G. & Catts, H. (Eds.) (2013). *Language and reading disabilities* (3rd ed.). New York, NY: Pearson.

Karmiloff-Smith, A. (1986a). From meta-process to conscious access: Evidence from children's metalinguistic and repair data. *Cognition, 23*, 95–147.

Karmiloff-Smith, A. (1986b). Stage/structure versus phase/process in modelling linguistic and cognitive development. In I. Levin (Ed.), *Stage and structure* (pp. 192–212). Norwood, NJ: Ablex.

Keil, F. C. (2006). Explanation and understanding. *Annual Review of Psychology, 57*, 227–254.

Kirk, S. A. (1976). In J. M. Kauffman & D. P. Hallahan (Eds.), *Teaching children with learning disabilities: Personal perspectives* (pp. 239–269). Columbus, OH: Charles E. Merrill.

Labov, W., & Waletzky, J. (1967). Narrative analysis. In J. Helm (Ed.), *Essays on the verbal and visual arts* (pp. 12–44). Seattle, WA: University of Washington Press.

Levinsohn, H.H. (2012). Reasoning styles and types of hortatory discourse. *Journal of translation, 2*, 1–10.

Liles, B. (1993). Narrative discourse in children with language disorders and children with normal language: A critical review of the literature. *Journal of Speech and Hearing Research. 36*, 862–882.

Linda-Mood Bell Learning Processes. (2019). Gander Publishing. Retrieved from www.Granderpublishing.com

Mayer, M. (2003). *Frog where are you?* New York, NY: Dial.

Mifflin, H. (2019). *Earobics (Step 2): Sound foundations for reading and spelling*. Buffalo, NY: Independent Living Aids.

Moses, N. (1994). The development of procedural knowledge in adults engaged in a tractor-trailer task. *Cognitive Development, 9*, 103–130.

Moses, N., Klein, H., & Altman, E. (1990). An approach to assessing and facilitating causal language in learning disabled adults based on Piagetian theory. *Journal of Learning Disabilities, 23*, 220–229.

Nippold, M. (2016). *Later language development: School-age children, adolescents, and young adults* (4th ed.). Austin, TX: Pro-Ed.

Nippold, M. A., Hesketh, L. J., Duthie, J. K., & Mansfield, T. C. (2005). Conversational vs. Expository Discourse. *Journal of Speech, Language, and Hearing Research, 48*(5), 1048–1064.

Nippold, M. A., & Rudzinski, M. (1993). Familiarity and transparency in idiom explanation: A developmental study of children and adolescents. *Journal of Speech and Hearing Research, 36*, 728–737.

Osherson, D. N., & Lasnik, H. (1990). *An invitation to cognitive science* (Vol. 1). Cambridge, MA: MIT.

Outridge, D. (1967). The differential diagnosis of childhood aphasia. *The Slow Learner, 14*, 122–125.

Perfetti, C. A. (1984). Reading acquisition and beyond: Decoding includes cognition. *American Journal of Education, 93*, 40–60.

Pollio, M. R., & Pollio, H. R. (1974). The development of figurative language in children. *Journal of Psycholinguistic Research, 3*, 185–201.

Piaget, J. (1952). *Construction of reality by the child*. New York, NY: Norton.

Piaget, J. (1976). *The grasp of consciousness*. Cambridge, MA: Harvard University Press.

Piaget, J. (1978). *Success and understanding*. Cambridge, MA: Harvard University Press.

Piaget, J. (1985). *The development of thought: The equilibration of cognitive structures*. Chicago, IL: Chicago University Press.

Rantner, N., & Bruner, J. (1978). Games, social exchange and the acquisition of language. *Journal Child Language, 5*, 391–401.

Raphael, L. J., & Borden, G. J., & Harris, K. (2011). *Speech science primer*. Baltimore, MD: Lippincott Williams & Wilkins.

Ratner, N., & Bruner, J. (1977). Games, social exchange, and the acquisition of language. *Journal of Child Language, 5*, 391–401.

Reid, D. K., & Hresko, W. (1999). *A cognitive approach to learning disabilities*. Austin, TX: Pro Ed.

Shaywitz, S. (2003). *Overcoming dyslexia: A new and complete science-based program for reading problems at any level*. New York: NY: Vintage.

Singer, B., & Bashir, A. (1999). What are executive functions and self-regulation and what do they have to do with language-learning disorders? *Journal of Language, Speech and Hearing Services in School, 30*, 265–273.

Spector, C. C. (1990). Linguistic humor comprehension of normal and language impaired adolescents. *Journal of Speech and Hearing Disorders, 55*, 543–551.

Spector, C. C. (2009). As far as words go. Baltimore, MD: Brookes.

Sutton-Smith, B. (2008). Play theory. *American Journal of Play, 1*, 80-123.

Stein, N., & Glenn, C. (1979). An analysis of story comprehension in elementary school children. In R. Freedle (Ed.). *New directions in discourse processing* (Vol. 2, pp. 53–120). Norwood, NJ: Ablex.

Tallal, P. (1997). *Fast ForWord*. Oakland, CA: Scientific Learning.

Telian, N. A. & Telian-Castagnozzi, P. A. (2019). *Lively Letters Instruction Manual* (3rd ed.). Weymouth, MA: Reading with TLC.

Thordardottir, E. (2008). Language-specific effects of task demands on the manifestation of specific language impairment: A comparison of English and Icelandic. *Journal of Speech, Language, and Hearing Research, 51*, 922–937.

Torgesen, J. (1982). The learning disabled child as an inactive learner: Educational implications. *Topics in learning and learning disabilities, 2*, 42–52.

Toregsen, J. K. (1998). Catch them before they fall: Identification and assessment to prevent reading failure in young children. *American Educator*, 1–8.

Trabasso, T., van den Broek, P., & Suh, S. (1989). Logical necessity and transitivity of causal relations in stories. *Discourse Processes, 12*, 1–25.

U.S. Department of Health and Human Services, National Institutes of Health, National Institute on Deafness and Other Communication Disorders. (2019). *NICD fact sheet: Specific language impairment in children*. Retrieved from https://www.nidcd.nih.gov/sites/default/files/Documents/publications/pubs/NIDCD-Fact-Sheet-Specific-Language-Impairment_091217.pdf

Ward-Lonergan, J. M., Liles, B. Z., & Anderson, A. M. (1999). Verbal retelling abilities in adolescents with and without language-learning disabilities for social studies lectures. *Journal of Learning Disabilities, 32*, 213–223.

Westerveld, M. F., & Moran, C. A. (2011). Expository Language Skills of Young School-Age Children. *Language, Speech, and Hearing Services in Schools, 42*, 182–193.

Wiig, E., & Secord, W. (1989). *Test of language competence*. Austin, TX. Pro-Ed.

Wilson Language Training Corp. (2019). *Wilson reading system* (4th ed.).

Wren, S. (2019). *Wren reading framework*. Austin, TX: Southwest Educational Development Laboratory.

BOX 11.1: Popular Reading Programs

Reading Program	Focus	Activities
Lindamood–Bell	"Multisensory." Uses the different senses to help students make connections between sounds, letters, and words and blend sounds into words. Addresses comprehension through use of imagery.	Students are asked to create mental images of what they are reading about. E.g., "Can you picture the lion?" "Can you describe how she's playing with her cubs?"
Orton-Gillingham	Using auditory, visual, and kinesthetic elements, all language skills are taught by having students listen, speak, read, and write. Use of multiple senses encouraged to facilitate mental representation and memory. Sound–symbol associations and linguistic rules are introduced.	Students begin by reading and writing sounds in isolation. Students engage in sensory exercises, such as tracing letters in sand or in the air. Students identify and articulate consonants, vowels, digraphs, blends, and diphthongs. They then proceed to advanced structural elements such as syllable types, roots, and affixes. As students learn new material, they continue to review old material to the level of automaticity. The teacher addresses vocabulary, sentence structure, composition, and reading comprehension.
Wilson	The Wilson Reading System is organized around six syllable types found in English; sounds are taught only as they relate to the syllable being studied. Wilson materials and texts are phonetically controlled, containing word lists, sentences, and paragraphs that incorporate only the elements of word structure taught in or up to the corresponding lesson.	Students learn by hearing sounds, manipulating color-coded sound, syllable and word cards, performing finger tapping exercises, writing down spoken words, reading aloud and repeating what they have read in their own words, and hearing others read as well. Skills and knowledge are reinforced through visual, auditory, kinesthetic, and tactile senses.

Discourse Genre	Stages	Co-developmental Achievements	References

Literate/oral narrative	Literate
	  Additive chains
	    List
	    Repeated action
	    Descriptive
	  Temporal chains
	  Causal chains
	    Automatic
	    Reactive
	    Goal based
	    No obstacle
	    Obstacle
	    Embedded
	    Conjoined
	      Setting
	      Initiating event
	      Problem
	      Attempt
	      Internal response
	      Resolution
		Oral narrative
		  Temporal chain
		  (Personal
		  narrative)
		    High Point
		    Abstract
		Orientation
		    Most
		  reportable event
		    High point
		    Causal
		theory
		    Coda
			Labov and
			  Waletsky (1987)
			Lahey (1988)
			Stein and Glenn
			  (1979)
			Slobin and Berman
			Trebasso (1989)

Expository/ explanatory discourse	Definitional/identifying
	  physical objects by:
	  Subordinate cat.
	  Function
	  Attribute
	  Superordinate cat
	Comparative
	  Subordinate cat.
	  Function
	  Attribute
	  Superordinate cat
	Procedural
	Causal
	  Sensorimotor
	  Preoperational
	  Operational
		Metalinguistic
		  Linguistic areas:
		    Phonological
		  awareness
		    Rhymes
		    Words
		    Syllables
		    Segments
		    Morphemes
		    Syntax
		    Multiple-
		  Meanings
		  Semantic/
		    word
		    meaning
		  basis
		    Syntactic
		  basis
			Nippold, Hesketh,
			  Duthie and
			  Mansfield,
			  (2005)
			Piaget (1952; 1976;
			  1978)
			Moses, Klein,
			  Altman (1990)

(Continued)

Discourse Genre	Stages	Co-developmental Achievements	References

		Analogies
		Similes
		Metaphors
		   Trans-parent
		   Opaque
		   Puns	

Hortatory/ argumentative/ persuasive		Transactive statements Transactive questions Maintain strategy across discourse partners Modify strategy in response to partner's position on topic Rebuttal Corner Add-advance-substantiate	Felton and Kuhn (2001) Levinsohn (2012)

Client: Cori

D.O.B.: C.A.: 13.6

Informants: Ms. M. (Mother), and N.C.

SPEECH-LANGUAGE COMMUNICATION EVALUATION

Statement of Problem

Cori is a 13.6-year-old male who attends eighth grade at the Church Hill School, in Manhattan, New York. He is currently receiving counseling 2× and speech services 1× weekly. Cori was referred to the Downtown Brooklyn Speech-Language and Hearing Clinic by his mother, Ms. M., and father, N.C. Both Ms. M. and N.C. served as reliable informants. Cori was brought to the clinic for evaluation and assessment for his triennial review. Cori's mother expressed concerns about his auditory processing, comprehension, and reading abilities. Cori expressed his own concerns about reading comprehension and "thinking about how to pronounce words I read."

Ms. M. stated that Cori began having noticeable difficulties in preschool and underwent a neuropsychological evaluation in 2006. He was diagnosed with Attention Deficit Disorder (ADD) Inattentive Type, Cognitive Disorder Not Otherwise Specified (NOS), and Visual Hypotonia. In 2008, Cori was diagnosed with oral and fine motor dyspraxia, dyslexia, and dyscalculia (math disorder).

Background Information

Cori lives in Brooklyn, New York, with his mother, a preschool teacher, his father, a corrections officer, an 11-year-old brother, and a 6-year-old sister. Cori indicated that he enjoys music, video games, and playing basketball. He enjoys reading nonfiction novels, preferably those centered on historical events. His favorite subjects are history and math.

Ms. M reported an eventful pregnancy. She was treated for Hyperemesis gravidarum and was hospitalized numerous times due to dehydration. Cori was delivered via normal vaginal delivery as the product of a full-term pregnancy, weighing 6 lb. Ms. M reported that Cori was a colicky infant and difficult to feed. She stated that major sensorimotor milestones were age appropriate (sitting, crawling, walking), but stated he was uncoordinated and "accident-prone" as a toddler. Cori drank independently from an open cup at 7 months and finger-fed himself at 9 months. He was weaned from breast and bottle at 17 months. Ms. M reported that Cori was a picky eater as he refused meats, breads, and pureed foods.

Cori produced typical infant prespeech sounds. He began using single words at 18 months and two-word utterances at 27 months, which Ms. M described as unintelligible and "unclear."

Cori has a history of ear infections and asthma, for which he was prescribed Albuterol and Flovent. Cori is also allergic to soy products, cheese, and pollen. Ms. M also stated that Cori was diagnosed with visual perceptual and visual-motor delays; he received vision treatment for 1 year. Cori has a family history of learning disabilities on his maternal side.

Cori received Early Intervention (EI) services at 17 months (occupational, physical, and speech-language therapy). Physical Therapy was incorporated into Cori's physical education in the second grade.

Results of Communication Assessment

Language: Standardized Testing

The Clinical Evaluation of Language Fundamentals-5 (CELF-5). The CELF-5 was administered to assess the client's receptive and expressive language skills. Results were as follows:

	Raw Score	Scaled Score	Scaled Score Points ±	Confidence Interval (90% level)	Percentile Rank	Percentile Rank CL	Age Equivalent
Following Directions (FD)	20	7	± 2	5 to 9	16	5 to 37	9:0
Formulated Sentences (FS)	46	15	± 2	13 to 17	95	84 to 99	>21: 5
Recalling Sentences (RS)	62	10	± 1	9 to 11	50	37 to 63	13:10

Understanding Spoken Paragraphs (USP)	10	7		± 2	5 to 9	16	5 to 37		
Semantic Relationships (SR)	10	8		± 2	6 to 10	25	9 to 50		9:8

	FS	RS	USP	SR	Sum of scaled scores	Standard score	Standard Score Points ±	Confidence interval (90% Interval)	Percentile Rank	Percentile Rank CI
Core Language Score (CLS)	15	10	7	8	40	100	± 5	95 to 105	50	37 to 63

Performance on the CELF-5 Core Language component of the assessment was within the mean for Cori's age. Cori performed significantly below the mean for his age on items that assessed narrative comprehension and executive functions. The CELF-5 assesses linguistic and executive function/metalinguistic knowledge and skills. Executive function skills involve thinking about language and using language to solve problems and suppress interfering behaviors.

Cori performed significantly above the mean in his ability to produce logically appropriate sentences; he produced semantically and syntactically appropriate two-verb conjunction sentences (when imitating model utterances, and when given the following types of words to use to generate sentences: temporal conjunctions (when, before, until), causal conjunctions (and, because, if). He did not produce complete sentences using contingent conjunctions (until, although, unless). He also simplified perfect tenses (e.g., have eaten → have ate). Narrative comprehension was assessed in context of retelling short stories (expository and causal chain narratives), which were read to Cori; Cori performed below the mean for his age on this section. Cori made inferences and predictions. As stories increased in length, Cori demonstrated some difficulty recalling specific information. As stories got longer, he relied on experience or referred to an action in the story or an association as a main idea. The task required reference to a causal relationship (problem-resolution) as the main idea.

A series of problem-solving tasks were presented verbally; these tasks incorporated temporal, spatial, and seriation elements (e.g., The pencil was in the box). The box was in a bag next to the locker. The pencil was: in the locker, next to the locker, beside the box, etc.). Cori performed one standard deviation below the mean for his age.

Cori manifested difficulty following directions including "before" and "after" instructions that required Cori to enact the second part of the command before the first. The difficulty increased as the length of the instruction increased (e.g., Point to the X and the circle after you point to the big triangle and the little black triangle.). Cori could follow verbal directions concerning number and position of shapes (nouns) with adjective modifiers (e.g., first black triangle, last white circle). It is noteworthy that during testing, Cori recognized a problem within this subtest. The command "point to the last or first" item in a sequence can refer either to the item on the left or right end of the sequence. Cori explicitly requested clarification.

Language: Nonstandard Assessment of Spontaneous Language Production

A nonstandard analysis of Cori's spontaneous production of syntax and semantic relations indicates that expressive language is age appropriate. Cori produces a range of complex sentences with appropriate connectives. Morphology (production of verb tenses, function words) is age appropriate. Cori is able to engage in extended conversation with adults, maintaining contingency in response to statements and questions. He is able to produce extended personal narratives. Pragmatic skills, especially his ability to reflect on his learning challenges, are quite mature.

Phonological Awareness

The Phonological Awareness Test-2 (PAT-2). A nonstandard administration of the PAT-2 was conducted to assess phonological awareness, phoneme–grapheme correspondence, and phonetic decoding skills. The results were as follows:

An item analysis revealed strong phonological awareness skills in the areas of rhyming, segmenting words by syllable, words in sentences, and initial and final phonemes of words.

Cori demonstrated difficulty segmenting phonemes within syllables in single and two-syllable words. He identified phonemes in clusters as the entire cluster and sometimes identified phonemes in syllables as the complete syllable ([pl- op]/*plop*); ([li-və]/*lever*, he demonstrated difficulty identifying medial vowels and diphthongs).

In the area of grapheme–phoneme correspondence, Cori produced phonemes corresponding to the presented grapheme for consonants, long and short vowels, and consonant blends. He manifested difficulty producing phonemes corresponding to r-controlled vowels, vowel digraphs, and diphthongs; e.g., Cori produced [ɔ] for /aɚ/), and [ae] for the digraphs /eI and /aI/ and [ju] for the digraph /ou/. Cori also had difficulty reading nonsense CVCe word forms: he substituted short vowels for long vowels.

Nonstandard assessment of comprehension of figurative language. Cori was also asked to interpret metaphoric lyrics in a popular song (Bastille's *Your Voice is a Weapon*.) Cori manifested good comprehension of the figurative meaning of lyrics presented.

Maintaining Factors

Cognition

Wechsler Individual Achievement Test Second Edition (WIAT-II)

Three subtests of the Wechsler Individual Achievement Test—Second Edition were administered to assess reading and spelling skills. Results were as follows:

	Raw Score	Standard Score	Confidence Interval (90% level)	Percentile Rank	Grade Equivalent	Age Equivalent
Reading Comprehension	70*	71	± 6	27	6.3	9.4
Pseudo-word Decoding	37	89	± 5	23	4.5	10.8
Spelling	26	73	± 6	4	3.5	9.0
*Weighted						

Cori performed between 1 and 2 standard deviations below the mean for his grade level. He manifested difficulty in reading comprehension, especially with reference to causal relations within stories. Greatest difficulty was in the area of spelling. Item analysis revealed that Cori (a) utilized context clues to determine meaning of words, (b)

(c) deleted consonants within consonant clusters, and plural /s/, (d) spelled phonetically when vocabulary rose above grade level, and when spelling required the analysis of word roots. For example, when asked to spell absence, he spelled "apsents." Cori did not identify word roots. He misspelled words containing contractions. He often substituted homonyms (sealing for ceiling), even within linguistic contexts that signaled the meaning of the word to be spelled. When reading aloud, Cori deleted suffixes and inverted words in sentences; he often self-corrected.

Piagetian Tasks

Cori was presented two Piagetian tasks: conservation of volume, and board balance. The purpose was to evaluate reasoning and logical problem-solving given manipulable concrete objects to support reasoning.

The conservation of volume task involved computing the height of a building (number of floors it would need) to contain the same number of $1'' \times 1'' \times 1''$ rooms as a comparison building. The building in question was 1/2 the width and equal length ($H \times 2'' \times 4''$). The comparison building was a $4'' \times 4'' \times 4''$ cube. Cori was offered $1'' \times 1'' \times 1''$ blocks (representing the "rooms" in the buildings), a $4'' \times 4'' \times 4''$ cube (representing the comparison building), and a ruler to determine the height of the building in question. Cori estimated that the narrower building would have to be higher than the comparison building due to the narrower width. However, he unsystematically estimated the height (two additional inches). He did not systematically compensate for the 1/2 loss of width (by doubling the height). He, therefore, did not conserve volume and did not systematically compute the volume of the comparison $4 \times 4 \times 4$ building.

A second task involved board balancing; Cori was challenged to balance a board on a fulcrum. He did so by positioning the center of the board on the fulcrum (with equal lengths of the board extending out from each side of the fulcrum. He was then challenged to balance the board with two additional blocks positioned on top. Cori initially placed one block in the center of the board—on top of the fulcrum. When asked why the board balanced, he explained that the weight was the same on both sides of the board (around the fulcrum). When he was challenged to balance the board with the blocks positioned at the ends of the board, he placed one on top at one end and one under the weighted side as a support. However, he denied the possibility of balancing the board with the two blocks on top on the opposite ends.

These results indicate that Cori tends to focus his attention at one spatial position at a time (i.e., the center or one single end) when reasoning about a problem-solving task involving multiple points of reference. Balancing with weights on opposite sides would have required simultaneous consideration of two points of reference.

Summary and Impressions

Cori is a 13.6-year-old monolingual young man who is an eighth-grade student. He has been diagnosed with ADD Inattentive Type, Cognitive Disorder Not Otherwise Specified (NOS), and Visual Hypotonia. In 2008, he was diagnosed with oral and fine motor dyspraxia, dyslexia, and dyscalculia (math disorder).

Cori was cooperative and engaged throughout the entire assessment. He expressed impressive insight into challenges associated with his learning disabilities. He was able to sustain attention throughout the lengthy testing process.

Cori performed within the mean for his age with reference to combined measures of core language skills (comprehension and production) related to social and academic performance; he manifested difficulty, however, in several areas involving metalinguistic and executive function skills.

Cori had difficulty creating sentences when he was given conjunction adverbs (before, until, when) to include in the sentence and when he was instructed to repeat a sentence containing these items. He also had some difficulty following directions that contained these terms (e.g., "Before you point to a large square point to the small black circle"). Notably, terms such as "before" and "until" often convey both a sense of time or sequence and also indicate the need to wait and reorder behavior. Cori also demonstrated difficulty recalling sentences that contained subordinate clauses and relative clauses. He experienced difficulty in the areas of phonological awareness and establishing phoneme–grapheme correspondences. Cori demonstrated difficulty segmenting single and two-syllable words by individual phonemes, clusters, and syllables. He also demonstrated difficulty identifying word-medial diphthongs or vowels. He manifested difficulty decoding grapheme–phoneme (letter-sound) correspondences related to r-controlled vowels and vowel digraphs and diphthongs.

Cori manifested difficulties in listening comprehension of passages read orally; he performed more than 1.5 standard deviations below the mean for his age on the CELF-5 subtest. When passages were read to him (expository narratives, and causal chains with obstacles), he did not identify causal relations as the main idea. He focused on qualitative and comparative relationships. Cori also experienced difficulty identifying sequential relationships in passive sentences constructions. Given a reading comprehension task in which he could refer back to the passage after being questioned about it, Cori performed at the mean for his age. This suggests that working memory limitations interfere with Cori's linguistic processing capabilities.

Cori manifested significant difficulties spelling. He had difficulty with single consonant letter/sound relationships and consonant cluster/sound relationships. He made errors in initial, medial, and final position of words. Cori spells phonetically and made spelling errors on words that contained contractions.

Cori approached two Piagetian tasks challenging concrete operational reasoning from a preoperational perspective. Cori's performance represents a mild delay in logical and infra-logical reasoning skills. He did not conserve volume when asked to compensate for a change in the dimension of a referent object (a "hotel" on an island).

Cori denied the possibility of balancing a board on a fulcrum with weights placed at extreme ends; he focused on the fulcrum as the point of balance, or on supporting one end of the board. In both the volume and board balancing tasks, Cori tended to focus on one component of the task at a time and not on making comparisons of multiple components. This tendency may have been influenced by visual scanning difficulties related to diagnosed visual–motor hypotonia. Elements of conservation are embedded in many aspects of 8th grade mathematics, as well as subjects such as science and social studies.

Cori manifested a mild delay (one standard deviation below the mean for his age) on a verbal reasoning task involving reasoning about temporal, comparative, exclusionary, and seriation problems presented verbally. Performance declined as the syntactic demands of the task increased.

It is notable that Cori manifests the ability to reflect on his performance and demands of a task. He commented on a problem within the CELF-5 assessment procedures. Cori also demonstrated an ability to analyze figurative language: he explained to the examiner the meaning of metaphors within the lyrics in the Bastille song *Your voice is a weapon*. These skills represent areas of strength in metalinguistic/executive functions. It is also notable that Cori's spontaneous production of syntactic and semantic relations is age appropriate. Pragmatic skills, especially Cori's ability to reflect on his learning challenges, are quite mature.

In sum, results of this speech-language assessment indicate variable delays in the areas of metalinguistics/executive function, phonological awareness, reading comprehension, verbal reasoning and logic, and spelling. Speech/language therapy is recommended (2×45, 1:1).

chapter **12**

Aphasia

Introduction

Aphasia refers to acquired communication disorders that typically occur subsequent to brain injury and can severely limit participation of these individuals in professional, social, and family settings. There are estimated to be up to two million individuals living with aphasia in the United States alone, with 180,000 new cases each year. (https://www.aphasia.org/aphasia-faqs/)

Neurological injuries that lead to aphasia, such as stroke and traumatic brain injury, can affect individuals throughout the lifespan, with older adults being more likely to present with acquired aphasia. It is widely known that there is extensive variability in the severity and type of deficits associated with aphasia as no two brain injuries are identical. Thus, individuals may have particular difficulty with different components of language production and/or comprehension.

Much of the history of aphasiology has examined aphasia through the lens of models of the unimpaired neurocognitive processing system. An individual's deficits are often described with respect to language ability (e.g., expressive vs. receptive impairment), and the nature of the neurological injury (e.g., cortical vs. subcortical) is used to develop a diagnosis. Many of these areas have seen great advances in the 21st century, as our understanding of the neurobiology of language has deepened from traditional frameworks focusing on broad distinctions (e.g., the classical Wernicke–Lichtheim–Geschwind model focusing on the roles of Broca's area, Wernicke's area, and the arcuate fasciculus that connects them; Geschwind, 1970) to frameworks reflecting our current understanding of neural processing across networks of regions such as the dual-stream account of language processing (Fridriksson et al., 2018; Hickok & Poeppel, 2004). At the functional level of description, there has also been a move away from broad clinical categories (such as Broca's vs. Wernicke's aphasia) toward a view of language impairment with respect to the functions that rely on the two processing streams and their interaction and interconnections with sensorimotor and cognitive networks. In this sense, our understanding of aphasia has deepened along with our understanding of the neurobiology of language, and the past two decades have been an exciting time of growth in these areas. Figure 12.1 depicts the Wernicke–Lichtheim–Geschwind language processing model. Figure 12.2 depicts the locations and language-related functions of ventral and dorsal language processing streams, as well as the preliminary and distributed processes (Fridriksson, Yourganov, Bonilha, Den Ouden, & Rorden, 2016; Hickok, 2012; Hickok & Poeppel, 2007).

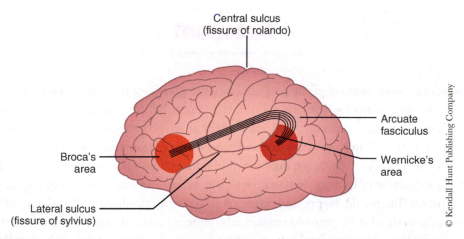

FIGURE 12.1: Depiction of Wernicke–Lichtheim–Geschwind Language Processing Model, In Which Speech and Language Processes and Deficits to Their Processes Are Largely Ascribed to Specific Neural/Lesion Locations

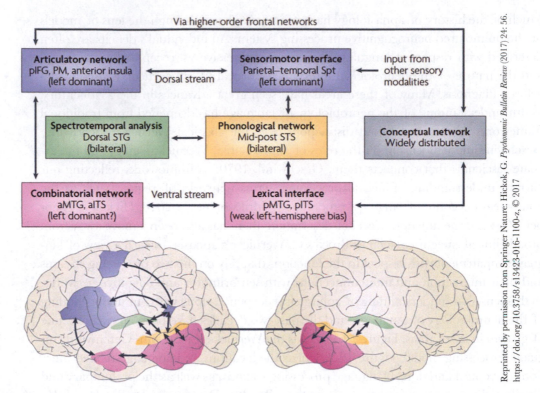

Reprinted by permission from Springer Nature: Hickok, G. *Psychonomic Bulletin Review* (2017) 24: 56. https://doi.org/10.3758/s13423-016-1100-z, © 2017

FIGURE 12.2: Depiction of Dual-Stream Language Processing Model, In Which Speech and Language Processes and Deficits to These Processes Are Attributed to a Broad Cortical Network of Regions (Hickok & Poeppel, 2004)

Assessment

Consideration of both linguistic and nonlinguistic processes is an important component of intervention planning. Insights about factors contributing to a language problem will be achieved during assessment, and will contribute to the generation of a prognosis, and the specification of intervention goals and procedures. Untangling the myriad of possible factors contributing to language disability and rehabilitation potential can be a challenge for the evaluator in cases of aphasia, especially when apraxia accompanies aphasia, as is common. Buchwald, Rapp, and Stone (2007) offer an illustration of differential diagnosis in a study of a 58-year-old woman who suffered a cerebrovascular accident (CVA, left-hemisphere fronto-parietal infarct involving posterior frontal lobe, including Broca's area, pre- and postcentral gyri, and the supramarginal gyrus). The CVA resulted in severely impaired spoken language and a right hemiparesis, with relatively intact comprehension of single words. The language problem was accompanied by articulation difficulties.

One characteristic of this individual's articulation was the insertion of /ə/ between consonants in onset consonant blends (e.g., *bleed* → [bəlid]). The authors asked whether this insertion was (a) a phonemic (linguistic) process, representing epenthesis of the phoneme /ə/ in order to reduce articulatory performance demands (the resulting CV syllable is more natural than CCV), or (b) a sensorimotor (nonlinguistic) error arising from mistiming of articulatory movements (e.g., slowing the consonant transition leading to the presence of inserted vocalic material). Answering this type of question (i.e., "are errors phonological or motoric?") may have implications for establishing a prognosis, as well as establishing intervention goals and procedures.

To address this question, Buchwald et al. (2007) included a variety of measures, such as diadochokinetic tests assessing the articulatory rate (revealing mild-to-moderate slowness) and word-repetition tests assessing the lexical and sublexical factors that might be contributing to articulatory inaccuracy. The lexical factors included word frequency (no effect), followed by word frequency groups organized with reference to other word-level properties, such as stress patterns and number of phonemes (negative results). The sublexical factors that were assessed included complexity and type of onset consonant clusters (which did affect performance). To determine whether the impairment was a central output impairment, the authors also evaluated the effects of syllabic complexity across tasks (e.g., word reading, picture naming, auditory word repetition). The individual's performance was similar in each domain, suggesting that the impairment arises at a central output level required for speech production as opposed to the level of word retrieval (see Goldrick & Rapp, 2007, for a fuller explanation of this logic).

This review of controls implemented in a study of articulation in a client with aphasia illustrates the myriad of variables that could potentially present performance demands or act as maintaining factors in cases of speech and language disorders following CVAs. Additional possibilities arise when assessing language disorders, for example, problems associated with cognition (memory and recall), and the language system itself (disorders intrinsic to morphology and syntax).

Functional Communication

Consistent with our model of intervention planning and the perspective of the American Speech-Language and Hearing Association, functional communication will represent the long-term outcome of intervention in cases of aphasia. One might ask, "what constitutes functional communication in cases of aphasia?"

Functional communication for individuals with aphasia, as for all people, refers to the linguistic expression and comprehension of intentionality and content of mind in personally relevant, real-world contexts. As discussed above, aphasia is a consequence of cerebral-vascular events that can affect speech and/or language in many different ways by virtue of potential damage to many possible cortical areas that are responsible for language-related information processing functions.

Rehabilitation cannot always address each and every impediment to recovery of intact linguistic performance. Rehabilitation does not aim to cure impaired information processing skills, such as word retrieval or short-term memory acuity, or restore grammatically perfect sentence structure, instead, it aims to help clients discover pathways to linguistic expression and comprehension of intentionality and content of mind in real-world contexts. Thus, rehabilitation will incorporate strategies designed to allow the client to compensate for impediments to language performance. These strategies may incorporate contributions from the client's significant others and may also be organized according to a hierarchy of complexity or degree of perceptual support (e.g., see Cameron, Wambaugh, Wright, & Nessler, 2006, for cueing hierarchy). In sum, therapeutic outcomes should:

- Have a meaningful impact on communication and on life

- Be culturally appropriate and personally relevant

- Include training of communication partners to support communication of and communication with the person with aphasia

Intervention Planning for CK

In this chapter, we will plan intervention goals and procedures for CK, a 74-year-old man who presents with aphasia following damage to the auditory dorsal stream—auditory areas in the superior temporal sulcus, motor areas in the left inferior frontal gyrus (parts of Broca's area), and left superior planum temporale region. Language performance was characterized by moderate deficits in repetition (i.e., imitation) and lexical retrieval, with relatively intact comprehension. CK's speech presents with multiple phonemic paraphasias and grammatical errors. These symptoms appear in oral reading as well, which is marked by neologisms and phonemic paraphasias. Nevertheless, CK keeps a notebook, which he uses to write and cue vocabulary that he has trouble recalling. Despite these difficulties, CK presents with a positive, optimistic outlook. His wife of 30 years (a high school English teacher), is a support to him. CK was employed as stagehand in Broadway theater and television.

Initiating intervention during the first three months after stroke is most effective in promoting a positive outcome (Edmonds, Mamito, & Ojeda, 2011). It was during this time period that CK was referred to the clinic by his physicians at New York University Hospital. CK's summary diagnostic report is presented in Appendix A.

Establishing Long-Term Goals

Step 1: Baseline Data.

The first phase in developing a management plan is projection of long-term treatment outcomes. The first step in that process is to review baseline data within diagnostic reports and outcome summaries from past interventions. As is typical for diagnostic reports about clients with CVAs and other speech-language problems, language disability and communication problems rise to the foreground, and strengths and abilities are often assigned secondary status. In the case of CK, paraphasias, word-retrieval problems, and telegraphic speech were highlighted in the diagnostic report. However, upon closer inspection we learn that CK's communication reveals preserved competencies.

CK engages in narrative discourse (personal, autobiographical, and expository). In context of discourse, he establishes identifiable topics, elaborates on topics, and provides contingent information. Within discourse, he references state, temporal, causal, and epistemic semantic relations. He produces primarily single-verb sentences, although he is also capable of producing complex sentences (conjunction and sentences with sentence complements). The following is an example:

CK: Cat is a, the cat in the tree worried about the . . . fell down. The son, probably a father, brother . . . um, helping the . . . And she probably scared because the dog and what can you do? And she went to the fireman, the good people and is thinking and the cat could be ok. Th-th-the girl is bicycle, ladder, and a dog.

They're ok, they'll get it out there. Fireman.

CK lives in Queens, New York, with his wife and has two children and two grandchildren. His interests include traveling, photography, and opera. CK received a Bachelor of Arts degree in Social Sciences from Fordham University. As noted above, he previously worked as a stagehand in New York theater productions and for the New York affiliate of a national television network.

Positive prognostic indicators include his high motivation and engagement in therapy tasks, strong familial support (his wife accompanies him to sessions and is willing to participate), and use of compensatory strategies (e.g., notebook).

Step 2: Relevant Taxonomies

The second step in long-term planning is to identify complexity hierarchies: These hierarchies guide goal planning by illuminating areas of speech, language, and communication to address in therapy and sequences of behavioral objectives to address across intervention. CK can engage in discourse. He enjoys talking about history, his travels, museum visits, and opera. He also attends movies and plays. Supporting his ability to express himself through narrative (personal and literate) and expository discourse would be a functional achievement. Goal setting, therefore, may be guided by hierarchies of discourse functional genres and their macrostructures (e.g., story grammars, logical organization) and microstructures (e.g., content–form interactions, cohesive devices, morphology). Goal setting may also be guided by hierarchies of cues that communication partners may provide

(Cameron et al., 2006, see Appendix B). Box 12-1 presents discourse genres and developmental hierarchies within genres (Bliss & McCabe, 2006; Lahey, 1988; Labov & Waletsky, 1967; Levinsohn, 2006).

BOX 12-1 Discourse Genres, Stages, and Parallel Developmental Achievements

Discourse Genre	Stages	Parallel Developmental Achievements	Reference
Literate narrative	Additive Chains	**Oral narrative**	Labov and Waletsky (1987)
	List	Temporal chain (personal narrative)	Lahey (1988)
	Repeated action	High point	
	Descriptive	Components of high point narratives	Stein and Glenn (1979)
	Temporal chains		Sutton-Smith (2008)
	Causal chains	Abstract	
	Automatic	Orientation	Berman and Slobin (1994)
	Reactive	Most reportable event/ high point	
	Goal-based		Trebasso, van den Broek, and Suh (1989)
	No obstacle	Causal theory	
	Obstacle	Coda	
	Embedded/con-joined		
	Components of causal chains		
	Setting		
	Initiating event		
	Problem		
	Attempt		
	Internal response		
	Resolution		

Expository /explanatory discourse	Definitional/existential	Metalinguistic awareness	Nippold, Hesketh, Duthie, and Mansfield (2005)
	Physical objects	Linguistic objects	
	Subordinate category	Morphemic	Moses, Klein, and Altman (1990)
	Function	Syntactic	
	Attribute	Phonologic	
	Superordinate category	Rhymes	
	Comparative	Words	
	Subordinate category	Syllables	
	Function	Segments	
	Attribute	Multiple meanings	
	Superordinate category	Semantic basis	
		Syntactic basis	
	Procedural	Analogies	
	Causal	Similes	
	Sensorimotor	Metaphors	
	Preoperational	Transparent	
	Operational	Opaque	
		Puns	
Hortatory/argumentative/persuasive		Transactive statements	Felton and Kuhn (2001)
		Transactive questions	
		Maintain strategy across discourse partners	
		Modify strategy in response to partner's position on topic	
		Rebuttal	
		Corner	
		Add–advance–substantiate	

DISCOURSE GENRES AND STORY GRAMMARS. Five discourse genres are identified in Box 12-1: expository, literate, personal, argumentative, and social (Bliss & McCabe, 2006; Labov & Waletsky, 1997; Lahey, 1988). Each form of discourse has its own intrinsic organizational characteristics, and one can identify a hierarchy based on organizational complexity within each discourse genre. *Expository* discourse may be organized according to (a) descriptions of objects or events, (b) comparisons of objects or events, (c) procedures intrinsic to achieving a goal or outcome, and (d) causal explanations (Piaget, 1952, 1976, 1978). *Literate* narratives increase in complexity from additive to temporal to goal-based causal chains with embeddings, conjoined episodes, obstacles and resolutions, and features such as settings, attempts, plans, internal response, and so on (Lahey, 1988; Stein & Glenn, 1979). *Personal* narratives may be simple temporal sequences about events of the day (i.e., a child's response to, "what did you do at school?") or more complex high-point narratives that contain a most reportable experience or event, causal theories and judgments, abstracts, and codas. *Hortatory* discourse serves persuasion and argumentation.

At the macrostructural level, hortatory discourse is organized with reference to a thesis and supporting arguments. Supporting arguments may be situational, motivational, credentialing, or enabling. Supporting arguments may also be more or less self-centered or made to address others' perspectives (e.g., a man attempting to persuade his wife why he should purchase the latest iteration of the iPhone arguing that it has a faster processor and bigger screen—an argument referencing personal interests, versus the argument that the new iPhone would help his wife locate him because it has a new tracking feature that she could access from her phone—a potentially valuable feature from his wife's point of view). Verb tense and aspect and voice represent the microstructure. Social conversation, like narratives, at the microstructural level are organized by utterance cohesion and content–form complexity of constituent sentences (Labov, 1990; Labov & Waletsky, 1967; Lahey, 1988). Narratives, for purposes of analysis, are also organized according to clausal "T Units" or "C Units" (Nippold, Heskith, Duthie, & Mansfield, 2005).

VOCABULARY, WORD KNOWLEDGE, AND SYNTAX. Two problem areas associated with aphasia involve vocabulary and syntax. Impediments to vocabulary production are seen in paraphasias—word generation problems that may be semantic in nature (e.g., producing the word, "crocodile" when the intent is to remark on an attractive "crocus") or phonologic (e.g., pronouncing "crocodile" as "clockodile"). Impediments are also seen in word-retrieval problems—long pauses when the word simply does not come to mind, although the intent to produce the word and the associated idea is there.

In the realm of syntax, the speaker may be only capable of producing one word at a time, or may be verbal, but producing telegraphic speech (omitting function words, such as prepositions, auxiliaries, tense marker, articles) and speech streams that contain paraphasias or other unintelligible utterances.

When planning treatment, it is useful to recognize that vocabulary and syntax interact. In fact, to know a word is to know its phonologic form, its meaning, and how the word interacts with syntax to form sentences (Bloom, Lahey, Hood, Lifter, & Fiess, 1980; Chomsky, & Lasnik, 1977). Having knowledge of such relationships will inform selection of interventions targets (e.g., vocabulary and the linguistic context of target words). Appendix 12-B illustrates how knowledge of specific verbs includes knowing the syntactic properties of complements that make grammatical sentences containing the specific verb, and complements that do not.

Edmonds, Mammino, and Ojeda (2011) have developed a network strengthening treatment for aphasia. This treatment targets verbs and the related thematic roles that nouns serve as subjects and complements of verbs (i.e., receive case from the verb or from the associated inflections). For example, Edmonds et al. target the verb "measure" and accompanying nouns by presenting the client with the sentence, "The carpenter is measuring the lumber." Edmonds et al. found that this approach generalized to untrained verbs and facilitated sentence production and the retrieval of nouns among aphasics with no more than moderate apraxia and expressive language disorder.

In a similar vein, Thompson and Shapiro (2005) presented individuals with agrammatic Broca's aphasia, sentences selected for their lexical and syntactic properties (verb-complement structure). Findings included improvement in comprehension and production of both trained and untrained structures. Generalization occurred for sentences that were linguistically related to those trained. Improvements in spontaneous discourse were also charted. Thompson & Shapiro also found that generalization was enhanced when the direction of treatment is from more to less complex structures, consistent with the complexity account of treatment efficacy (CATE, Thompson, Shapiro, Kiran, & Sobecks, 2003).

CUEING AND SCAFFOLDING. CK has devised several strategies aimed at supporting his attempts at communication. These strategies include picture use, drawing, and writing, which serve to provide perceptual support for his messages. Along these lines, Cameron, Wambaugh, Wright, and Nessler (2006) have developed a cueing system to facilitate language and communication in individuals with aphasia. We may employ this cueing hierarchy in our planning for CK. This cueing hierarchy is presented in Appendix B.

The cueing hierarchy extends from minimal cueing (the provision of single-word or single-sound prompts relevant to an intended communication) to a maximal "heavily loaded" semantic cue delivered within a sentence-completion prompt. Because CK's own cueing and perceptual support strategies are proving effective, the incorporation of cueing within the communication context (delivered outside of the therapy room by his wife and other regular communication partners) could prove an effective compensatory strategy.

An analogy may be drawn between "cueing" as an intervention strategy and the use of modeling and expansion techniques in scaffolded learning routines (Ratner & Bruner, 1978). Bloom's (1995) principle of "relevance" applies as well. This principle holds that communications about an individual's intent and content of mind are most accessible for language development. Utilized most effectively, cueing is directed to the client to facilitate communication about that client's content of mind and intended message. The conversational partner discerns the intent of the speaker (in this case, the individual with aphasia). Intent may be signaled by a comment the individual makes, the focus of the individual's attention, gestures, or other acts of engagement and communication. The partner then either expands upon the individual's initial communication attempt or anticipates and provides the appropriate and relevant cue.

For example, if the cueing level is completion of a semantically loaded sentence and the speaker's intent is to obtain a slice of lemon-meringue pie from a bakery shelf containing various types of fruit pies, the cue might be: "That lemon pie looks good! I would like_____ ("a piece," "some lemon pie")." Or if the neighbor's dog is barking, "That dog is barking, tell him to_____ ("stop barking," "be quiet," "shush")."

ASSISTIVE DEVICES. Related to cueing is the potential use of an assistive communication device that may facilitate cueing or even provide speech generation. The value of such intervention strategies and assistive devices is suggested by additional information in the diagnostic report that sensorimotor problems may be masking linguistic competence. It is notable that reading comprehension is characterized as "intact," but oral reading of sentences and paragraphs is marked by the same linguistic characteristics as oral language. This suggests that the interface between sensorimotor functions and language is impaired, but the perception-language-cognitive interface is not affected or at least less affected by the CVA. An assistive device may help CK overcome these obstacles to functional communication.

Aided AAC approaches present their own challenges, however and involve the use of "external representations of meaning," requiring a different subset of language and cognitive skills to execute messages as compared to natural speech production. AAC devices represent extensions of sensorimotor modalities that have been employed by language, which until the onset of aphasia have allowed the individual the ability to communicate effortlessly through speech, gesture, manual signs, and so on (Beukleman & Mirenda, 2013). Use of AAC strategies require the individual to locate vocabulary within an external device in order to successfully relay content of mind. Communication partners must also be trained to assist the individual with aphasia when using the AAC system, such as implementation of cueing strategies and operational requirements of the system (Beukleman & Mirenda, 2013).

AAC systems are presently being incorporated into computer devices (Loncke, 2014). The Lingraphica™ model is an AAC device specifically designed for individuals with aphasia. Besides assisting in daily communication routines, Lingraphica™ offers options for an individual to participate in therapy sessions remotely with a clinician through their TalkPath™ therapy services. In addition, the Lingraphica™ device allows the client to use the voice output as auditory feedback for cueing and recasting communication attempts.

Functional Communication and Taxonomies in Cases of More Severe Forms of Aphasia

Before considering the maintaining factors implicated in CK's performance, we will consider the significance of functional communication in more severe forms of aphasia and the potential taxonomies that could guide intervention planning.

As has been explained earlier, CK presented with language characteristics of conductive aphasia—a milder form of language disabilities that often accompany CVAs. In conductive aphasia, comprehension is relatively intact, and individuals can recognize difficulties that they are experiencing expressing themselves. There are cases of aphasia in which comprehension and production of language are more severely affected, across both verbal and nonverbal modalities (e.g., reading, writing). In some cases, such as Wernicke's "fluent aphasia," self-recognition of the disability may be impaired. The individual retains the ability to speak, albeit often unintelligibly. Yet comprehension of speech may be severely dysfunctional, so the individual is not aware of the problem. In Broca's "nonfluent aphasia," on the other hand, speech comprehension may be relatively functional but expression (word, phrase, and sentence generation) limited. In such cases, linguistic competencies that we have been referring to as accounting for the generativity of functional communication may no longer be accessible. Yet, cognition in terms of intentionality and content of mind remains. In such cases, how do we conceptualize long-term objectives, which have been characterized as fundamentally generative outcomes of intervention?

In any generative hierarchy of linguistic achievements, intentionality, itself, stands as the foundation of functional communication. Intentionality refers to having an objective and an idea and a desire to reveal that idea to others. Related to intentionality, the functions of intentional communication captured in pragmatic taxonomies are themselves generative: for example, comment, request, respond to request and commands, protest, obtain, or direct attention (i.e., notice) are among the most prominent (Halliday, 1975, 1993). In the area of content–form interactions, communications that are the most functional are those that capture the messages most central to the individual's daily routines, significant others, and personal desires.

Additionally, as has been emphasized throughout this chapter, intervention should center around activities and routines that are identified by the client as most significant to himself or herself in everyday real-life settings. Chapey et al, 2000; Martin

(1981a;1981b), Examples of meaningful goals aimed at facilitating life-participation for a 62-year-old farmer with limited expressive language ability offered by Hinkley (2018) included ordering farm supplies and conversing with his wife at dinner time.

Step 3: Maintaining Factors

Projecting a long-term prognosis of an ultimate language outcome includes considering what additional behavioral systems are either supporting rehabilitation or getting in the way of communication. In CK's case, his psychosocial state is a significant plus. He is motivated, engaged, and appears to maintain a positive outlook.

Cognition, a second potential maintaining factor, appears to be intact judging from the brief story told by CK. He is mindful of the emotional state (fearful) of the main character, and is expressing causal relations in context of a goal-based causal chain story. Word-retrieval problems and paraphasias, however, may indicate cognitive involvement (accessing meaning-based representations, monitoring language produced for pronoun-referent gender agreement) or impairments in linguistic organization (confusing/failing to distinguish "she" from "he" at the phonologic or morphologic level). We plan to integrate cueing employing a variety of modalities and devices.

In considering the use of cueing, difficulties with repetition (i.e., imitation) of verbal stimuli associated with conductive aphasia have to be kept in mind. CK manifests difficulty with repetition of increasingly complex phrases. Such difficulties typically emanate from problems in phonologic processing associated with conduction aphasia (Davis, 2007). As such, cues employed in discourse with CK will be designed to minimize demands on verbal imitation (at least during the earlier phases of intervention). Such cueing strategies will support sentence completion rather than direct utterance repetition. The following are long-term goals and related subordinate long-term goals.

Long-Term Goal and Related Subordinate Goals

Long-term goal. CK will engage in a variety of discourse genres with support of assistive devices and conversational partners.

Subordinate goals

1a. CK will produce context-appropriate vocabulary (e.g., verbs, nouns) in context of discourse with support of assistive devices and conversational partners.

1b. CK will increase the range of language functions relevant to maintaining conversations and repairing miscommunications.

1c. CK's wife will employ cueing and response strategies to initiate, extend, and reward conversations with CK.

Figures 12.3a and 12.3b illustrate the derivation of long-term and subordinate long-term goals.

Deriving the Long-Term Goal				
Decision	**Guiding Information**			
	Content–form narrative production	Lahey (1988)	Produces personal, temporal and automatic causal chain narratives	
		Stein and Glenn (1979)		
		Bliss and McCabe (2006)	Produces primarily single-verb sentences	
			Produces complex sentences (two-verb) utterances coding state, temporal, causal, epistemic, and object specification	
			Telegraphic speech (syntax)	
Projecting a prognosis	**Maintaining factors**	**Severity**	**Current performance**	
	Cognitive	Mild Mod. Sev.	BA in Social Sciences; worked as stagehand	
	Sensorimotor	Mild Mod. Sev.	Right hemiplegia	
	Psychosocial	Mild Mod. Sev.	Wife; two children; interests include traveling, photography, and opera	
	Medical	Mild Mod. Sev.		
	Caretaker attendance	Frequently	Intermittently	Rarely
Time frame	Time allotted	One year		
Long-term goals	CK will engage in a variety of discourse genres with support of assistive devices and conversational partners.			

FIGURE 12.3a: Long-Term Goals

Deriving Subordinate Long-Term Goal(s)			
Long-Term Goal: CK will engage in a variety of discourse genres with support of assistive devices and conversational partners			
Decision	**Guiding Information**		
Areas of speech/language intrinsic to the long-term goal	**Area of Speech/Language**	**Referent Taxonomy**	**Current Performance Level**
	Vocabulary	Hierarchy constructed based on (a) familiarity with terms, (b) Dolch frequency, (c) grammatical category, and (d) phonologic complexity (number of syllables, syllable structure, phonemic segments)	Semantic paraphasias and neologisms Uses general, nonspecific terms
	Language use	Cueing: Cameron et al. (2006) Theory of mind: Nippold (2016) Functions: Lahey (1988)	Language functions are limited to asking questions, attempts to initiate conversations about personal events, requests for clarification Usually one conversational turn Responses are contingent, with perceptual support
Subordinate long-term goals	1a. CK will produce context-appropriate vocabulary (verbs, nouns) in context of discourse with support of assistive devices and conversational partners. 1b. CK will increase the range of language functions relevant to maintaining conversations and repairing miscommunications. 1c. CK's wife will employ cueing and response strategies to initiate, extend, and reward conversations with CK.		

FIGURE 12.3b: Subordinate Long-Term Goals

Planning the Procedural Approach

After establishing the long-term goals, we search for approaches to intervention as a basis for deriving intervention procedures. Procedures are derived from the literature describing approaches to intervention and evidence of efficacy, along with the theoretic premises about rehabilitation processes intrinsic to clinical research.

The following are the steps on planning a procedural approach to achieving CK's long-term goals.

Step 1: Review of the Literature Relevant to Achieving the Long-Term Goals.

Long-term goals are communication based. We envision a participation-focused (as opposed to impairment focused) intervention. Those that have been shown to be effective include Supported Conversation for Adults with Aphasia (SCA; Kagan, Black, Duchan, Simmons-Mackie, & Square, 2001), Promoting Aphasics' Communicative Competence (PACE, Davis, 2007; Davis & Wilcox, 1985), Constraint-Induced Aphasia Therapy (Meinzer, Thomas, Daniela, Taub, & Rockstroh, 2007); principled task decomposition (Fredericksen & White, 1989); visual action therapy (Helm Estabrooks, Albert, & Nicholas, 2013; Helm-Estabrooks, Fitzpatrick, & Barres, 1982); and melodic intonation therapy (Sarno, Silverman & Sands, 1970; Sparks, Helm, & Albert, 1974; Sparks & Holland, 1970).

SCA (KAGAN ET AL., 2001). The supported conversation approach reflects premises of both relationship-based pragmatic theory and social cognitive theories of rehabilitation. The idea is that individuals need to engage in conversational discourse, they need acknowledgement and confirmation from their communication partner that their message was successfully conveyed, and scaffolded support from communication partners facilitates engagement and ultimately rehabilitation.

SCA emphasizes (a) the need for multimodal communication, (b) partner training, and (c) opportunities for social interaction. Underlying principles of SCA include:

1. Functional communication can be facilitated/improved by teaching strategies to communication partners.

2. Communication includes social interaction and the exchange of information and ideas; opportunities for social interaction are emphasized (Kagan, Black, Duchan, Simmons-Mackie, & Square, 2001).

PACE. In this treatment approach, the individual with aphasia and the clinician take turns as the message sender or receiver. Picture prompts for conversational messages are hidden from the listener (similar to a barrier task), and the speaker uses his or her choice of modalities for conveying messages (Davis & Wilcox, 1981).

CONSTRAINT-INDUCED. Constraint-induced programs (Meinzer et al., 2007) represent a second client-centered intervention approach with one significant difference from the PACE approach. In constraint-induced interventions, clients are prevented from using nonverbal modes of communication. But in conversational settings, clients produce sentences, from structurally simple to complex, following an intensive intervention schedule (multiple sessions weekly). The theoretic basis of constraint-induced intervention is that the act of speech and language production stimulates neurologic function and language recovery.

Pierce, Menahemic, Falcov, O'Hallaran, and Toghler (2017) addressed outcomes following two intensive client-centered treatment approaches: multimodal and constraint-induced. Findings indicated that both interventions are effective; the issue raised was what role intensity as compared to treatment type played in recovery of language function.

With reference to the significantly different orientation of intensive client-centered programs and deficit-based programs, Wilssens et al. (2015) conducted a comparative investigation of the effectiveness of Constraint-Induced Aphasia Therapy (CIAT) and BOX in an individualized drill-based lexical-semantic treatment focusing on semantic analyses of words (i.e., matching words that have similar meanings and word retrieval, Visch-Brink & Bajema, 2001).

Findings revealed improvements in language function in all participants following treatment. The CIAT group's improvements were most evident on language production tasks. The BOX group improved significantly in language comprehension (e.g., semantic word association) tasks, but not production.

It is notable that constraint-induced, multimodal, and deficit-focused interventions are applied across aphasia types (i.e., fluent, nonfluent, and conductive). Similar outcomes across aphasia types have also been reported (Pierce, Menahemic, Falcov, O'Hallaran, & Toghler, 2017); Robey (1998), in a meta-analysis of the effectiveness of aphasia treatments, concluded the following: Language disorders in aphasia are heterogeneous in nature. Interventions vary in goal and procedure. Two variables are supported by evidence of positive outcomes: (a) early initiation of intervention relative to stroke and (b) intensity of intervention.

PRINCIPLED TASK DECOMPOSITION (FREDERICKSEN & WHITE, 1989). Principled task decomposition focuses on delimited activities or routines that are important to the client's day-to-day happiness—for example, ordering in a restaurant. Multiple approaches to communication that will allow the client to achieve the goals that are identified, and then order according to performance demand. For example, there are multiple ways to get food in a restaurant: (a) have someone else order for you, (b) say what you want, (c) point to what you want, or (d) use a device to communicate what you want. Baseline data about the client's present communication status and prognosis are considered in identifying the strategy to target. In this case, pointing poses the minimal performance demand. Verbally requesting (especially in cases of restricted expressive abilities) presents the greatest performance demand. An assistive device provides support for verbalizing, modulating the performance demand.

An additional issue to consider is whether the strategy interferes with achievement of another desired goal. Having someone else request interferes with independence, a potentially critical objective for most individuals.

VISUAL ACTION THERAPY. Visual action therapy incorporates the production of gestures to represent objects. Given that the fundamental objectives of any intervention for aphasia is the communication of intentionality to another and an optimal degree of independence, multiple modalities may be employed as means for conveying messages. The criterion for success is comprehension and acknowledgement of one's message by the communication partner. In more severe cases of aphasia, gesture may be the most available, which is the least stressful means of communication. Gestures may also serve as a self-produced support for verbal forms of communication.

MELODIC INTONATION THERAPY, PROSODY AND MUSIC. Several approaches to intervention for aphasia attempt to recruit right-hemispheric function to compensate for damage following CVA's affecting left-hemisphere function. Perhaps the most prominent is melodic intonation therapy (Sarno, Silverman, & Sands, 1970; Sparks & Holland, 1976). Following this approach, the clinician instructs the client to apply a simple intonation-prosodic-stress pattern, mimicking Standard English sentence intonation and prosody to the production of sentences. This approach has proven to be effective with individuals with good comprehension but moderate difficulties in expression. The approach incorporates in a four-level hierarchy of instruction:

Level 1. Clinician hums a melody pattern (3/4 whole note range). Client taps rhythm and stress of the melody with his hand.

Level 2. (a) Clinician intones sentence and client taps as at level 1. (b) Clinician intones sentence again and the client attempts to imitate in unison; this step may be repeated. (c) Client imitates in unison again while clinician fades the model. (d) Clinician models sentences with intonation; client imitates after the model sentence is produced by clinician. (e) Clinician requests, using melodic intonation, that the client produce sentence independently.

Level 3. Level 2d and 2e procedures are repeated, culminating in a final step in which clinician intones a request for information related to sentence that was imitated.

Level 4. Earlier model, delay, reproduce, and questioning steps are repeated and intensified. Level 4 procedures culminate in the clinician's asking additional and more tangential questions referencing the imitated message.

Sparkes and Holland, 1976 caution about the use of familiar melodies borrowed from popular music to facilitate language production in aphasia. Familiar melodies may invoke the lyrics of the particular songs. As such, familiar melodies may lead to interference with the production of the intended message.

INTERVENTION PROCEDURES FOR USE OF ASSISTIVE COMMUNICATION DEVICES. CK presently uses external methods to represent content of mind (e.g., drawing, writing, pictures, and a notebook). In addition, CK's high motivation and engagement in therapy tasks, as well as his strong family support, are positive factors that would indicate successful use of an AAC system. The AAC system intervention can be planned according to a classification system initially developed by Garrett and Beukelman (1995), which presents a hierarchy ranging from individuals who can use AAC systems independently to those who are more successful using AAC with partner supports. Within these categories, AAC intervention varies according to the individual's participation levels, communication needs, as well as cognitive and linguistic skills. According to this classification system, CK may function initially as a "transitional communicator"; he will use an external symbolic system with support from a communication partner. Specifically, when CK is experiencing problems communicating a message using the device or verbally, he may benefit from partner cues indicating possible vocabulary options within the AAC system. In addition, CK may benefit from partner support in identifying cues, indicating that an attempted verbal message has failed. For example, CK may not realize his verbal message failed until a partner indicates "I am not understanding."

Several intervention strategies can be suggested for CK initially as a "transitional communicator." Because CK is motivated to engage in narrative discourse, he may benefit from use of visual scenes to organize narrative information and to depict possible comments and questions he can use to interact with others regarding the topic (Beukleman & Mirenda, 2013). As a low-tech or manual AAC option, photographs from personal events can be chosen and messages or phrases that promote conversation can be written next to the photograph. CK can be encouraged to point to the phrases or messages at appropriate times during conversation. In addition, many speech-generating devices or AAC apps for tablet-based computers (i.e., Apple iPad) offer the option to utilize visual scenes, which contain messages the individual can "speak" by touching various hotspot locations in the scene that are programmed with messages. Evidence has shown that visual scene displays help individuals convey personal stories and participate in reciprocal conversation by providing semantic and organizational supports (Beukleman & Mirenda, 2013). Additional therapy strategies may also include use of role-playing to practice use of an AAC system in simulated life activities such as ordering at a restaurant. It is suggested with "transitional communicators" that cues are not given unless it is clear that the communicator is having difficulty communicating without further support (Beukleman & Mirenda, 2013).

Communication partners must be trained to implement the necessary cues in order to support CK in use of AAC strategies. Training for communication partners is critical for the successful use of an AAC system by an individual with complex communication impairments (Loncke, 2014). Training must involve teaching the cueing strategy/system to the communication partner (including relatives and co-residents), to assist the individual with aphasia to communicate with the AAC system successfully. Involvement of the spouse, life partner, or other immediate family members in therapy sessions can provide an opportunity for training to learn the cues and strategies most effective in assisting the individual using AAC (Loncke, 2014).

META-ANALYSES OF EVIDENCE SUPPORTING INTERVENTION PROCEDURES: Robey (2008), in a meta-analysis of efficacy of interventions for aphasia, concluded the following: Language disorders in aphasia are heterogeneous in nature. Interventions vary in goal and procedure. Two variables are supported by evidence of positive outcomes: (a) early initiation of intervention relative to stroke and (b) intensity of intervention. Cherney, Patterson, Raymer, Frymark, and Schooling (2008), in a second meta-analysis focusing on constraint-induced language production techniques (requiring the client to produce and practice sentence production), found that among a variety of approaches studied, only constraint-induced methods were supported by experimental research. This study also reinforced the precept that intensity (session frequency and length) of intervention is related to positive outcomes.

Step 2: Identify Theoretic Premises about Rehabilitation Intrinsic to Procedural Approaches

The performance-based procedural approaches identified above are built upon the premises of relationship-based pragmatic, social cognitive, and operant theories. Each theory is relationship based, reflecting the premise that communication skills develop within circles of communication based on the expression of cognitive and emotional intent. Each theory also reflects a social cognitive orientation toward scaffolding (with the communication partner cueing, modeling) and operant premise that efforts to communication are best maintained in context of feedback from others' signaling and rewarding success.

Step 3: Identify Maintaining Factors that will need to be Addressed in the Planning of Session Procedures

As discussed above, sensorimotor and cognitive maintaining factors will need to be considered in procedure planning.

Figure 12.4 presents the procedural approach.

Planning the Procedural Approach		
Decision	**Guiding Information**	
Ultimate behaviors to be acquired	**Long-term goals and corresponding subordinate long-term goal(s)**	**Long-term goal** CK will engage in a variety of discourse genres with support of assistive devices and conversational partners. **Subordinate goals** 1a. CK will produce context-appropriate vocabulary (verbs, nouns) in context of discourse with support of assistive devices and conversational partners. 1b. CK will increase the range of language functions relevant to maintaining conversations and repairing miscommunications. 1c. CK's wife will employ cueing and response strategies to initiate, extend, and reward conversations with CK.
Approaches to intervention	**Types of Evidence**	**Reference**
	Meta-analysis	
	Experimental	
	Descriptive/clinical practice	1. Supported Conversation for Aphasia (SCA, Kagan et al., 2001) 2. Promoting Aphasics' Communicative Competence (PACE, Davis, 2000, 2005; Davis & Wilcox, 1985), principled task decomposition (Fredericksen & White, 1989) 3. Visual action therapy (Helm-Estabrooks, Albert, and Nicholas, (2013); Helm-Estabrooks, Fitzpatrick, & Barres, 1982)
Premises about language learning or rehabilitation from clinical research relevant to achieving long-term goals	**Theory**	
	Theory	**Premises**
	Constructivism	
	Relationship-based pragmatic	Communication skills develop within circles of communication based on the expression of cognitive and emotional intent to a communication partner, and that partner providing feedback acknowledging the speaker's intent
	Social cognitive	Scaffolding performance by an expert (significant other) involving modeling, cueing, explicating facilitates rehabilitation
	Operant	Communication is best maintained in context of feedback from others signaling and rewarding success
Maintaining factors that need to be addressed	**Maintaining Factors**	**Current Performance**
	Cognitive	
	Sensorimotor	Right hemiplegia, mild apraxia, high-frequency hearing loss
	Cognition	Difficulties with word retrieval, semantic paraphasias, topic maintenance

FIGURE 12.4: Planning the Procedural Approach

Short-Term Planning

Step 1: Review long-term Goal, Related Subordinate Goals, and Associated Guiding Taxonomies.

We now turn to short-term planning. The first step in short-term goal planning is to review long-term goals. Short-term goals are steps toward the achievement of long-term outcomes. Also, complexity hierarchies/taxonomies that guided long-term planning are consulted to assure that short-term goals are continuous and consonant with long-term goals. The long-term goal established for CK as follows:

1. CK will engage in a variety of discourse genres with support of assistive devices and conversational partners.

Subordinate

1a. CK will produce context-appropriate vocabulary (verbs, nouns) in context of discourse with support of assistive devices and conversational partners.

1b. CK will increase the range of language functions relevant to maintaining conversations and repairing miscommunications.

1c. CK's wife will employ cueing and response strategies to initiate, extend, and reward conversations with CK.

Taxonomies guiding these objectives were proposed by Nippold et al. (2015, on discourse genres), Piaget (1952, 1976, 1978; on causal content of expository discourse with reference to Piagetian cognitive stages), and Cameron et al. (2006; on cueing hierarchy).

Short-Term Goals

CK will extend conversation in context of expository discourse (comparative and temporal chain) in response to a sentence cue.

CK will produce context-appropriate vocabulary in context of expository discourse in response to sentence cues and self-cueing with assistive devices.

CK will verbally confirm listener's comprehension.

CK's wife will present loaded-content sentence prompts to initiate conversation and will confirm comprehension of CK's intended message by restating the message.

Justification

Taxonomy. A complexity hierarchy was envisioned with reference to three variables: (a) discourse genres, (b) complexity of the semantic relations intrinsic to the discourse genre (see Box 12-1), and (c) cueing hierarchy (degree of similarity between the cue and the intended utterance). Expository discourse ranges from low to high complexity, depending on the intrinsic organization of the content—semantic relations constituting the discourse. Descriptions of common familiar objects and object functions represent the low-end of complexity (analogous to descriptive, additive chains; Stein & Glenn, 1979; Lahey, 1988). Temporal sequences of procedures enacted to accomplish a familiar task represent intermediate level of organization, whereas cause and effect relations represent more complex discourse—with complexity increasing in line with the complexity of reasoning invoked by the task. Figure 12.5 illustrates the derivation of short-term goals.

Operationalized Procedural Approach

At the long-term planning phase, the procedural approach envisioned was guided by premises derived from three theories of rehabilitation: relationship-based pragmatic, social cognitive, and operant. The following are those premises and implications for establishing session goals and designing session procedures for CK.

Premise 1: Social Cognitive

1. Scaffolding speech and language by providing models, verbally expanding upon individual's intended message, and offering verbal instructions to aid problem-solving (especially in the use of assistive devices) facilitates rehabilitation.

IMPLICATIONS: Acts of intentional communication will be cued (comments addressing CK's intended communication topic) by communication partners in context of conversation (especially expository discourse).

Comments by communication partners relevant to CK's intended communication topic, including cues, will elaborate on CK's productions and will offer a linguistic model.

Premises 2a and 2b: Relationship-Based Pragmatic

2a. Rehabilitation of speech and language is facilitated in real communication with significant others in which the speaker is free to express his or her intent and the communication partner acknowledges understanding of the speaker's message. 2b. Therapy is most effective when delivered by the client's significant others.

IMPLICATIONS: Engage communication partners in therapy sessions. Teach communication partners supportive conversational techniques. Arrange for programming of assistive device. Demonstrate use of assistive device.

Deriving Short-Term Goals			
Decision	**Guiding Information and Client-Specific Details**		
Long-term goal and corresponding subordinate long-term goals and taxonomies addressed	**Long-Term Goal and/or Subordinate Long-Term Goal(s)**	**Taxonomy**	**Current Performance Level**
	CK will engage in a variety of discourse genres with support of assistive devices and conversational partners	Cameron, Wambaugh, Wright, and Nessler (2006)	Produces personal, temporal, and automatic causal chain narratives Produces primarily single-verb sentences Produces complex sentences (two-verb) utterances coding state, temporal, causal, epistemic, and object specification Telegraphic speech (syntax)
	1a. CK will produce context-appropriate vocabulary (verbs, nouns) in context of discourse with support of assistive devices and conversational partners. 1b. CK will increase the range of language functions relevant to maintaining conversations and repairing miscommunications. 1c. CK's wife will employ cueing and response strategies to initiate, extend, and reward conversations with CK.	Hierarchy of familiarity and complexity with reference to CK's experiences, phonologic complexity of word (syllable structure), and word frequency data https://www.wordfrequency.info/free.asp?s=y Nippold (2016) Westby & Robinson (2014) Lahey (1988)	Semantic paraphasias and neologisms Uses general, nonspecific terms Language functions are limited to asking questions, attempts to initiate conversations about personal events, requests for clarification Usually one conversational turn Responses are contingent, with perceptual support

FIGURE 12.5: Short-Term Goals

Time frame	Time allotted: six months
Short-term goals and rationale	**Long-term goal addressed:** CK will engage in a variety of discourse genres with support of assistive devices and conversational partners.
	Short-term goal CK will engage in expository discourse (comparative and temporal chains) by extending conversation. **Rationale with reference to development/complexity/difficulty** CK attempts to initiate expository discourse where he attempts to describe his interests. Efforts are often frustrated by his linguistic limitations.
	Subordinate long-term goal addressed 1a. CK will produce context-appropriate vocabulary (verbs, nouns) in context of discourse with support of assistive devices and conversational partners.
	Short-term goal CK will produce context-appropriate vocabulary in context of expository discourse in response to sentence cues and self-cueing with assistive devices. **Rationale with reference to development/complexity/difficulty** Sentence cues and self-cueing, with an assistive device, provides perceptual support for specific vocabulary.
	Subordinate long-term goal addressed 1b. CK will increase the range of language functions relevant to maintaining conversations and repairing miscommunications.
	Short-term goal CK will acknowledge and verbally confirm listener's comprehension. **Rationale with reference to development/complexity/difficulty** Referencing listener's perspective is an important step in the social and cognitive areas in support of successful communication.
	Subordinate long-term goal addressed 1c. CK's wife will employ cueing and response strategies to initiate, extend, and reward conversations with CK.
	Short-term goal(s) CK's wife will present *loaded-content* sentence cues to initiate conversation and acknowledge CK's messages by restating the message. **Rationale with reference to development/complexity/difficulty** Having complete sentences that model intended message provides perceptual support; having one's message acknowledged is a rewarding consequence, which supports extended conversation.

FIGURE 12.5 CONTINUED: Short-Term Goals

Premise 3: Operant

Reinforcing consequences (feedback) will increase the frequency of targeted behavior (i.e., communication attempts).

IMPLICATIONS: CK's acts of communication will be acknowledged by the communication partner.

Operationalizing the procedural approach also takes into account maintaining factors, and requires that the clinician envision implications for intervention to mitigate or augment the role that nonlinguistic behavioral systems may be having on language functions. In CK's case, cognition is a maintaining factor. The implication for session goal and procedure planning is as follows:

Clinician and CK's wife will provide cues as linguistic support for CK's communication efforts. This addresses word retrieval, working and short-term memory, and recall. CK will use assistive device to cue oneself. Cues also address sensorimotor elements of language production by providing a model of articulatory gestures, syllable and word structures, morphemes, and morpheme sequences necessary to produce language.

Figure 12.6 illustrates the operationalized procedural approach.

Session Planning

Session planning differs from long- and short-term planning by virtue of the functions that treatment sessions serve and the role of context in goal and procedure planning. Treatment sessions address the process of rehabilitation, including the linguistic and nonlinguistic context in which treatment is embedded, whereas long- and short-term goals represent the outcomes of treatment.

Step 1: Distinguish and Consider, Individually, Each Set of Short-term Goals Derived from each Long-term Goal and Related Subordinate Goals

Short-term goals derived from different long-term goals are considered separately when planning session goals. This is because procedural approaches that drive session planning are derived with reference to individual long-term goals. Planning for different long-term goals and addressing different aspects of speech and language may yield different procedural approaches. In CK's case, only one long-term goal was set, accompanied by several subordinated goals. Therefore, one set of short-term goals will be considered during the planning of session goals. The long-term outcomes that were projected are as follows:

Operationalizing the Procedural Approach	
Decision	**Guiding Information and Client-Specific Details**
Short-term goals to be addressed	1a. CK will engage in expository discourse (comparative and temporal chains) by extending conversation. 1b. CK will produce context-appropriate vocabulary in context of expository discourse (comparative and temporal chain) in response to sentence cues and self-cueing with assistive devices. 1c. CK's wife will present *loaded-content* sentence cues to initiate conversation and acknowledge CK's messages by restating the message.
Clinical research: evidence-based procedures	Supported Conversation for Aphasia (SCA, Kagan et al., 2001) Promoting Aphasics' Communicative Competence (PACE, Davis, 2000, 2005; Davis & Wilcox, 1985) Principled Task Decomposition (Fredericksen & White, 1989) Visual Action Therapy (Helms Estabrooks, 2013; Helm-Estabrooks, Fitzpatrick, & Barres, 1982)

Derive implications for procedure planning from theory-based premises	**Relationship-based/pragmatic premise:**
	Communication skills develop within circles of communication based on the expression of cognitive and emotional intent to a communication partner, and that partner providing feedback acknowledging the speaker's intent.
	    Implication: Therefore, the clinician will operationalize the procedural approach by creating interest-based activities promoting conversation based on client's interests and experiences and present intent; Including spouse in intervention (to cue, respond to, and affirm successful communication)
	
	Operant premise:
	Efforts to communication are best maintained in context of feedback from others, signaling and rewarding success.
	    Implication: Therefore, the clinician will operationalize the procedural approach by providing feedback to signal comprehension of client's intent during discourse
	
	Instructing spouse on how to provide feedback to signal comprehension of client's intent during discourse; incorporate practice during session

FIGURE 12.6: Operationalized Procedural Approach

	Social cognitive premise:
	Scaffolding performance by an expert (significant other) involving modeling, cueing, and other forms of perceptual support
	Implication: Therefore, the clinician will operationalize the procedural approach by providing sentence-completion models relevant to client's intended message, modeling context-appropriate vocabulary, reducing extent of cueing as client progresses; clinician will also provide instructions and model use of assistive device
Derive implications for procedure planning from maintaining factors	**Maintaining factors**
	Sensorimotor: Mild apraxia, right hemiplegia, high-frequency hearing loss
	Implication: Model vocabulary as perceptual support for articulation and to facilitate intelligibility of message to others; incorporate assistive device for modeling and to augment messages when not comprehended by others
	Cognition: Difficulties with word retrieval, semantic paraphasias, topic maintenance
	Implication: Cueing strategies will be employed

FIGURE 12.6 CONTINUED: Operationalized Procedural Approach

Long-term goal

1. CK will engage in a variety of discourse genres with support of assistive devices and conversational partners.

Subordinate goals

1a. CK will produce context-appropriate vocabulary (verbs, nouns) in context of discourse with support of assistive devices and conversational partners.

1b. CK will increase the range of language functions relevant to maintaining conversations and repairing miscommunications.

1c. CK's wife will employ cueing and response strategies to initiate, extend, and reward conversations with CK.

Short-Term Goals

CK will extend conversation in context of expository discourse (comparative and temporal chain) in response to a sentence cue.

CK will produce context-appropriate vocabulary in context of expository discourse, after a model and by self-curing using an assistive device.

CK will verbally confirm listener's comprehension.

CK's wife will present loaded-content sentence prompts to initiate conversations and will confirm comprehension of CK's intended message by restating the message.

Step 2. Prioritize Short-term Goals

The set of short-term goals established for CK interact in a way that allows all to be addressable within the same time period. The initial goal targeting conversation within expository discourse ought to contain topic relevant vocabulary and, ideally, proactive communications about messaging intelligibility by CK to his listener.

Step 3. Inspect the Operationalized Procedural Approach

In reflecting on premises of relevant theories of rehabilitation and maintaining factors, implications were drawn about the kinds of activities and clinical interactions that will help CK achieve his short- and long-term targets.

Based on the implications derived from premises of rehabilitation, session goals will be written for CK's daily communication partners as well as for CK himself. Communication partners will learn cueing strategies modeled by the clinician that address CK's intended communication topic, strategies for elaborating on CK's productions modeled by the clinician, as well as procedures for providing linguistic models and acknowledging CK's intended messages. These strategies that will be employed by the clinician and caretaker reflect social cognitive, relationship-based, and operant premises. Session activities will address topics of interest to CK, chances for CK to express his intent and what is on his mind, and for communication partners to be accommodating and provide feedback relevant to CK's intended messages, communication successes, and requests to be alerted when communication efforts are not comprehended.

Step 4. Identify and Regulate Performance Demands

Performance demands emanate from (a) complexity of speech and language production or comprehension targeted in the session goal, less to more complex linguistic structures are planned as targets; (b) familiarity and source (CK or clinician) of message content, messages addressing more to less familiar topics are planned as targets ; (c) presence and nature of cues, models, and other forms of perceptual support and scaffolding, more explicit cues and other forms of perceptual support (manipulable objects, pictures) before less support are planned within the linguistic and nonlinguistic context; (d) familiarity, frequency, and phonologic complexity of vocabulary items, more familiar and less complex vocabulary will be introduced before less familiar and more complex, as linguistic context and target.

Considering all of the variables identified above, the following early and later session goals were designed for CK:

Deriving Session Goals and Procedures	
Decision	**Guiding Information and Client-Specific Details**
Long-term goal and related subordinate goals addressed by short-term goals	**Long-term goal** CK will engage in a variety of discourse genres with support of assistive devices and conversational partners. **Subordinate long-term goals** 1a. CK will produce context-appropriate vocabulary (verbs, nouns) in context of discourse with support of assistive devices and conversational partners. 1b. CK will increase the range of language functions relevant to maintaining conversations and repairing miscommunications. 1c. CK's wife will employ cueing and response strategies to initiate, extend and reward conversations with CK.
For each short-term goal, consider implications of:	**Short-term goals** 1a. CK will engage in expository discourse (comparative and temporal chains) by extending conversation. 1b. CK will produce context-appropriate vocabulary in context of expository discourse (comparative and temporal chain) in response to sentence cues and self-cueing with assistive devices. 1c. CK's wife will present *loaded-content* sentence cues to initiate conversation and acknowledge CK's messages by restating the message. **Taxonomies** Bloom and Lahey (1978); Lahey (1988) Stein and Glenn (1979) Bliss and McCabe (2006) Westby and Robinson (2014) Nippold (2016)

FIGURE 12.7: Session Goals

Learning and rehabilitation premises	Learning Theories	Implications Drawn (in the Operationalized Approach): Clinician Will:
	Social cognitive	Provide CK sentence-completion models relevant to client's intended message, modeling context-appropriate vocabulary, reducing extent of cueing as CK progresses
	Relationship-based pragmatic	Create interest-based activities promoting conversation based on client's interests and experiences and present intent Include spouse in intervention (to cue, respond to "checks," and affirm successful communication)
	Operant	Provide feedback to signal comprehension of client's intent during discourse Instruct spouse on how to provide feedback to signal comprehension of client's intent during discourse; incorporate practice during session

and Maintaining factors	Maintaining Factors	Implications Drawn (in the Operationalized Approach)
	Sensorimotor	Provide models of vocabulary with cue provided
	Cognition	Cueing to address difficulties with word retrieval, semantic paraphasias, topic maintenance
	Psychosocial	Acknowledge message articulated by CK

FIGURE 12.7 CONTINUED: Session Goals

Performance demands controlled	Performance Variable Controlled	How the Variable Is Controlled	Aspect of Session Goal Affected
	Semantic/syntactic complexity	Cue single-verb sentence before 3+ constituent multi-verb sentence	Target for CK Target for wife, Linguistic context of target
	Familiarity of message content	Familiar conversational topics before novel topic	Linguistic and nonlinguistic context
	Perceptual support	Cue level 2 after cue level 1 Presence of pictures and audio/visual excerpts before no visual cues Presence of pictures and written vocabulary items on an assistive device	Linguistic and nonlinguistic context
	Familiarity, frequency, and phonologic complexity of vocabulary items	More familiar, frequent, and directly related to topic before less familiar and infrequent, or figurative	Linguistic context and target behavior

FIGURE 12.7 CONTINUED: Session Goals

Early Session Goals

CK will complete *three 3+constituent sentences, coordinating attribution and existence* (one attribute of the opera, Aida and composer Verdi), *given a sentence completion cue.* Example: (Verdi was a great composer, Aida is . . . ["a great opera"] Verdi's operas were tragic, Aida is . . . ["a tragic opera"]; Verdi's operas were big. Aida is ["a big opera"] . . .).

CK's wife will *repeat the sentence* referring to the opera, Aida, spoken by CK (acknowledging his message).

Later Session Goals

CK will *extend the conversation initiated by his wife* on *Notre Dame*. Example, "It's lucky that" . . . by producing a three-constituent sentence that completes a relative clause [e.g., "nobody was in Notre Dame"]).

CK will *initiate a second circle of communication* about *Notre Dame*. CK will *use the word "cathedral"* by *activating a visual representation on the assistive device* and *self-cueing* use of *the phrase "beautiful cathedral"* (e.g., "It was a beautiful Cathedral."). Figure 12.7 illustrates the derivation of session goals and procedures on the Moses-Klein SLIP template.

Summary

In this chapter, our intervention planning model was applied to a second adult with aphasia, CK. The first, Mr. B, appeared in Part 1 of this textbook. Illustrated in the process was that across the lifespan and across disparate communication problems, generative functional communication is always the intended long-term outcome of intervention. Goal planning is always guided by research-based linguistically relevant complexity hierarchies, which we also refer to as taxonomies. Procedure and session goal planning are always guided by clinical research and theoretic principles defining speech and language acquisition and rehabilitation processes intrinsic to that research.

REFERENCES

Berman, R. A., & Slobin, D. I. (1994). *Relating events in narrative: A cross-linguistic developmental study*. Hillsdale, NJ: Laurence Erlbaum.

Beukleman, D. R., & Mirenda, P. (2013). *Augmentative and alternative communication: supporting children and adults with complex communication needs* (4th ed.). Baltimore, MD: Paul H. Brookes Publishing Co.

Bliss, L. S., & McCabe, A. (2006). Comparison of discourse genres: Clinical implications. *Contemporary Issues in Communication Science and Disorders, 33*, 126–137.

Bloom, L. (1995). The transition from infancy to language: Acquiring the power of expression. Cambridge: Cambridge University Press.

Bloom, L., Lahey, M., Hood, L., Lifter, K., & Fiess, K. (1980). Complex sentences: Acquisition of syntactic connectives and the semantic relations they encode. *Journal of Child Language, 7*, 235–262.

Buchwald, A. B., Rapp, B., & Stone, M. (2007). Insertion of discrete phonological units. An articulatory and acoustic investigation of aphasic speech. *Language and Cognitive Processes, 22*, 910–948.

Cameron, R. M., Wambaugh, J. L., Wright, S. W., & Nessler, C. L. (2006). Effects of a combined semantic/phonologic cueing treatment on word retrieval in discourse *Aphasiology, 20*, 269–285.

Chapey, R., Duchan, J. F., Elman, R. J., Garcia, L. J., Kagan, A., Lyon, J. G., & Simmons-Mackie, N. (2000). Life participation approach: A statement of value for the future. *ASHA Leader, 5*, 2–4.

Cherney, L. R., Patterson, J. P., Raymer, A., Frymark, T., & Schooling, T. (2008). Evidence-based systematic review: Effects of intensity of treatment and constraint-induced language therapy for individuals with stroke-induced aphasia. *Journal of Speech, Language, and Hearing Research, 51*, 1282–1299.

Chomsky, N., & Lasnik, H. (1977). Filters and control. *Linguistic Inquiry, 8*, 425–504.

Davis, G. A. (2007). *Aphasiology: Disorders and clinical practice* (2nd ed.). Needham Heights, MA: Allyn & Bacon.

Davis, G. A., & Wilcox, M. J. (1981). Incorporating parameters of natural conversation in aphasia treatment: PACE therapy. In R. Chapey (Ed.), *Language intervention strategies in adult aphasia* (pp. 169–193). Baltimore, MD: Williams & Wilkins.

Edmonds, L. A., Nadeau, S., & Kiran, S. (2009). Effect of Verb Network Strengthening Treatment (VNeST) on lexical retrieval of content words in sentences in persons with aphasia. *Aphasiology, 23*, 402–424.

Edmonds, L. A., Mammino, K., & Ojeda, J. (2011). *American Journal of Speech-Language Pathology Supplement*. Select Papers from the 43rd Clinical Aphasiology Conference by University of Florida—Health Sciences Ctr Library, Lisa Edmonds. Retrieved from http://ajslp.pubs.asha.org/

Felton, M., & Kuhn, D. (2001). The development of argumentive discourse skill. *Discourse Processes, 32*, 135–153.

Fredericksen, J. R., & White, B. W. (1989). Principled task decomposition. *Acta Psychologica, 71*, 89–146.

Friederici, A. (2012). The cortical language circuit: From auditory perception to sentence comprehension. *Trends in Cognitive Sciences, 16*, 262–267.

Fridriksson, J., Yourganov, G., Bonilha, B., Den Ouden, C., & Rorden, A. B. (2016). Revealing the dual streams of speech processing. *PNAS, 113*, 11508–11513.

Fridriksson, J., den Ouden, D.-B., Hillis, A. E., Hickok, G., Rorden, A. B., Yourganov, G., & Bonilha, L. (2018). Anatomy of aphasia revisited. *Brain, 141*, 848–862.

Garrett, K., & Beukelman, D. (1995). Changes in the interaction patterns of an individual with severe aphasia given three types of partner support. *Clinical Aphasiology, 23*, 237–251.

Geschwind, N. (1970). The organization of language and the brain. *New Series, 170*(3961), 940–944.

Halliday, M. A. K. (1975). *Learning how to mean: Explorations in the development of language*. London: Edward Arnold. (New York: Elsevier, 1977)

Halliday, M. A. K. (1993). Toward and language based theory of learning. *Linguistics and Education, 5*, 93–116.

Helm-Estabrooks, N., Albert, M., & Nicholas, M. (2013). *The manual of aphasia and aphasia therapy* (3rd ed.). Austin, TX: Pro-Ed.

Helm-Estabrooks, N., Fitzpatrick, P. M., & Barres, B. (1982). Visual action therapy for global aphasia. *Journal Speech Hearing Disorders, 47*, 385–389.

Hickok, G. (2012). The cortical organization of speech processing: Feedback control and predictive coding the context of a dual-stream model. *Journal of Communication Disorders, 45*, 393–402. doi:10.1016/j.jcomdis.2012.06.004

Hickok, G., & Poeppel, D. (2004). Dorsal and ventral streams: A framework for understanding aspects of the functional anatomy of language. *Cognition, 92*, 67–99.

Hickok, G., & Poeppel, D. (2007). The cortical organization of speech processing. *National Review of Neuroscience, 8*, 393–402.

Hinkley, J. (2018). The best fit: Selecting a targeted aphasia intervention. *American Speech-Language and Hearing Association* (WEB 16301.)

Kagan, A., Black, S. E., Duchan, J. F., Simmons-Mackie, N., & Square, P. (2001). Training volunteers as conversation partners using "supported conversation for adults with aphasia" (SCA): A controlled trial. *Journal of Speech, Language and Hearing Research, 44*, 624–638.

Labov, W., & Waletzky, J. (1967). Narrative analysis. In J. Helm (Ed.), *Essays on the verbal and visual arts* (pp. 12–44). Seattle: University of Washington Press.

Lahey, M. (1988). *Language disorders and language development*. New York: MacMillan.

Levinsohn, H. H. (2012). Reasoning styles and types of hortatory discourse. *Journal of translation, 2*, 1–10.

Loncke, F. (2014). *Augmentative and alternative communication: Models and applications for educators, speech-language pathologists, psychologists, caregivers, and users*. San Diego, CA: Plural Publishing.

Martin, A. D. (1981a). Therapy with the jargonaphasic. In J. Brown (Ed.), *Jargonaphasia* (pp. 305–326). New York: Academic Press.

Martin, A. D. (1981b). An examination of Wepman's thought centered therapy. In R. Chapey (Ed.), *Language interventions strategies in aphasia and related neurogenic communication disorders* (pp. 141–154). Baltimore, MD: Williams & Wilkins.

Meinzer, M., Thomas, E., Daniela, D., Taub, E., & Rockstroh, B. (2007). Extending the Constraint-Induced Movement Therapy (CIMT) approach to cognitive functions: Constraint-Induced Aphasia Therapy (CIAT) of chronic aphasia. *Neurorehabilitation, 22*, 311–318.

Moses, N., Klein, H., & Altman, E. (1990). An approach to assessing and facilitating causal language in learning disabled adults based on Piagetian theory. *Journal of Learning Disabilities, 23*, 220–229.

Nippold, M. A., Hesketh, L. J., Duthie, J. K., & Mansfield, T. C. (2005). Conversational vs. expository discourse. *Journal of Speech, Language, and Hearing Research, 48*, 1048–1064.

Nippold, M. (2016). *Later Language Development: School-age Children, Adolescents, and Young Adults*. (4th ed.) Austin, TX: Pro-Ed.

Piaget, J. (1952). *Construction of reality by the child*. New York: Norton.

Piaget, J. (1976). *The grasp of consciousness*. Cambridge, MA: Harvard University Press.

Piaget, J. (1978). *Success and understanding*. Cambridge, MA: Harvard University Press.

Pierce, Menahemic, Falcov, O'Hallaran, Toghler (2017).

Ratner, N., & Bruner, J. (1978). Games, social exchange and the acquisition of language. *Journal Child Language, 5*, 391–401.

Robey, R. R. (1998). A meta-analysis of clinical outcomes in the treatment of aphasia. *Journal of Speech, Language, and Hearing Research, 41*, 172–187.

Sarno, M., Silverman, M., & Sands, E. (1970). Speech therapy and recovery in severe aphasia. *Journal of Speech and Hearing Research, 13*, 607–623.

Sparks, R. W., & Holland, A. L. (1976). Method: Melodic intonation therapy for aphasia. *Journal of Speech and Hearing Disorders, 46*, 287–297.

Sparks, R. W., Helm, N., & Albert, M. (1974). Aphasia rehabilitation resulting from melodic intonation therapy. *Cortex, 16*, 303–316.

Stein, N., & Glenn, C. (1979). An analysis of story comprehension in elementary school children. In R. Freedle (Ed.), *New directions in discourse processing* (Vol. 2, pp. 53–120). Norwood, NJ: Ablex.

Thompson, C. K., & Shapiro, L. (2005). Treating agrammatic aphasia within a linguistic framework: Treatment of underlying forms. *Aphasiology, 10/11*, 1021–1036.

Thompson, C. K., Shapiro, L. P., Kiran, S., & Sobecks, J. (2003). The role of syntactic complexity in treatment of sentence deficits in agrammatic aphasia: The complexity account of treatment efficacy (CATE). *Journal of Speech, Language, and Hearing Research, 46*, 591–607.

Tippett, D. C., Niparko, J. K., & Hills, A. E.(2014). Aphasia: Current concepts in theory and practice. *Journal of Neurology and Transl Neuroscience, 2*, 1042.

Trabasso, T., van den Broek, P., & Suh, S. (1989). Logical necessity and transitivity of causal relations in stories. *Discourse Processes, 12*, 1–25.

Webster, J., & Whitworth, A. (2012). Treating verbs in aphasia: Exploring the impact of therapy at the single word and sentence levels. *International Journal of Language & Communication Disorders, 47*, 619–636.

Westby, C., & Robinson, L. (2014). A Developmental perspective for promoting theory of mind. *Topics in Language Disorders, 34*, 362–382.

Wilssens, I., Vandenborre, D., Van Dun, K., Verhoeven, J., Visch-Brink, E., & Marien, P. (2015). *American Journal of Speech-Language Pathology, 24*, 281–294.

World Health Organization. (2001). *International classification of functioning, disability and health*. Geneva, Switzerland.

Appendix 12-A

CK Diagnostic Report Summary

Name: <u>CK</u>   Date of Birth: <u>11/29/43</u>   Date of Testing: <u>5/30/18</u>

Chronological Age: <u>74</u>   Diagnosis & ICD-10: <u>Conduction Aphasia, R47.01</u>

Language of Testing: <u>English</u>

I. Statement of Problem

CK is a 74-year-old English-speaking male receiving services at the Anytown Speech-Language Hearing Clinic following a conduction aphasia diagnosis. He was diagnosed with mild-to-moderate conduction aphasia after sustaining a left cerebrovascular accident (CVA). CK attends a 50-minute individualized session once per week as well as a 50-minute aphasia group session once per week.

II. Background History

Medical history. CK was admitted to a New York City hospital after exhibiting symptoms of a CVA (e.g., difficulty speaking and right-sided hemiparesis) on December 23, 2018. Following his left CVA, he was diagnosed with conduction aphasia (i.e., damage to auditory dorsal stream—auditory areas in the superior temporal sulcus, motor areas in the left inferior frontal gyrus [parts of Broca's area], and left superior planum temporale).

After discharge from the hospital, CK was admitted to the NYU Rusk Rehabilitation Center for outpatient services before attending the Anytown Clinic. He currently takes the following medications: tamsulosin (urinary retention), Plavix and aspirin (blood thinners), Toprol (beta-blocker), losartan (high blood pressure), and rosuvastatin (high cholesterol).

Communication. According to previous clinical documentation, CK presents with a conduction aphasia characterized by moderate deficits in repetition and lexical retrieval, with relatively intact comprehension. His speech presents with multiple phonemic and semantic paraphasias, neologisms, and grammatical errors. These same speech characteristics manifest themselves during oral reading.

Sensorimotor. CK exhibited right-sided weakness after his CVA. He experiences high-frequency hearing loss at 4000 Hz in both ears. Visual acuity is within normal limits.

Cognitive. CK manifests deficits with topic maintenance, turn-taking, and arithmetic skills.

Psychosocial. CK lives in Woodside, Queens, with his wife. He has two children and two grandchildren. His interests include traveling, photography, and opera. CK received a Bachelor of Arts degree in Social Sciences from Fordham University. He previously worked as a stagehand.

Additional services. CK receives no additional services (i.e., physical therapy).

III. Results of Communication Assessment

Behavioral Observations during Assessment

CK arrived at the Anytown Clinic on time by himself and was conversing with other clients in the lobby when greeted by the clinician. CK ambulated independently to the clinic room. He maintained a positive demeanor throughout the session as evidenced by initiation of conversation with the clinician and excitement to share pictures of his family. CK used writing and drawing as compensatory strategies to convey information for future reference, including information about where his children live. He was attentive and actively participated in all assessment tasks. He occasionally demonstrated shifts in attention when providing additional information on an image seen during the assessment but was easily redirected to continue the task.

Language

Content–Form Interactions: Expressive form–content interactions were assessed with reference to nonstandard discourse-level productions.

CK spoke autobiographically; stories comprised primarily single-verb sentences. The following is an excerpt from a story about CK's father in response to the clinician's query about persons who have influenced CK:

"My father. I think so.

Yes because he wanted, was very esprick (strict)

He went"

Clinician: Not sure where he went

"Eszhvavior" (Referring to his own high school—CK attended Fordham University, his father attended New Jersey Institute of Technology).

"All, we had dressings and midisins and stuff

You had Latin and Greek and other things going on

I like it. I was a rebel."

(He continues, shifting topic to facing the draft intermingled with his father's profession)

"I don't know why. I wanted to—my relative, he, I want the navy

For some, I want the navy. Two persons, They were brother.

A lot of people." (Here, CK returns to his father). "She was very good,

Because he was very honets (honest) wanted a lawyers but he wanted an engineer. . ."

CK produced the following narrative, given a picture illustration of the events described in the narrative.

"Cat is a, the cat in the tree worried about the . . . fell down.

The son, probably a father, brother . . . um, helping the. . .

And she probably scared because the dog and what can you do?

And she went to the fireman, the good people and XXXX is thinking and the cat could be ok.

Th-th-the girl is bicycle, ladder, and a dog. They're ok, they'll get it out there.

Fireman."

As illustrated in the narratives above, CK produces one word to three-constituent utterances during conversations. Within narratives, he references state, temporal, causal, and epistemic semantic relations. He produces primarily single-verb sentences, although he is also capable of producing complex conjunction sentences and sentences expressing epistemic relations with sentence complements.

CK's expressive language is characterized by word-finding difficulties, occasional grammatical errors, and abrupt shifts in topic (e.g. "The girl is . . . bicycle, ladder, and a dog."). In conversation, CK sometimes references pictures he keeps in a notebook or writes a word he is having trouble recalling verbally. CK sometimes self-corrected paraphasias: for example, he produced the word "father" for "brother," then stated, "brother." Utterances are usually contingent on the linguistic context, both intrapersonally and interpersonally. He stated (e.g., "Idida" signifying the opera [Aida] in response to the clinician's query about what he likes to do). Responses contained phonemic and semantic paraphasias (e.g., he referred to strawberries, bananas, and apples as "vegetables," and "can" for "cup"). CK wrote names of three operas in response to the clinician's query about other operas he enjoys.

Overall, CK demonstrated moderate deficits in expressive language characterized by anomia, paraphasias, and difficulties with repetition of increasingly complex phrases.

Receptive language skills were also assessed using structured, nonstandardized tasks. Tasks targeted comprehension of wh-questions (e.g., what, who, where) and ability to follow functional motor commands. When CK was asked what day of the week it was, he responded with "W," suggesting a deficit in lexical retrieval.

Standardized assessment

During the word–sentence repetition task, CK was able to repeat single words (nouns). He required multiple repetitions to imitate productions of numerical values (e.g., 23, 50 dollars) and sentences (He only reproduced nouns.). He benefitted from the clinician reducing her rate of speech and writing out the phrase. CK provided associative information about image stimuli during moments of anomia. For example, when shown an image of a windmill, CK noted the object was "in Holland" before producing the correct word.

CK completed 3 out of 3 (100%) motor commands (temporal, sequential).

Receptive language was also assessed throughout the session using clinical observation.

During the formal writing assessment, CK demonstrated moments of confusion when he was asked to write numbers. For example, when the clinician prompted CK to "write the numbers one through ten," CK moved in closer, signaling his need for a repetition or clarification of the directions. CK benefitted from the clinician providing incremental steps for this task (i.e., Write the number one, now write the next number). CK contingently responded to the clinician's questions during conversational discourse and during administration of the Eating Assessment Tool (EAT-10). Overall, CK demonstrated mild impairments in receptive language characterized by occasional misunderstanding of complex sentences, and requests to enact a temporal procedural sequence.

Language Use

Parameters of language use including eye contact, turn-taking, topic maintenance, and topic initiation were informally assessed throughout the session. CK maintained appropriate eye contact throughout the session and initiated conversation with the clinician. During conversation, CK asked follow-up questions to the clinician demonstrating appropriate turn-taking skills. He occasionally demonstrated inappropriate shifts in topic, such as during the picture description task in which he would begin describing one aspect of the image and shift mid-sentence to another topic present in the image. In the autobiographical narrative presented above, CK shifts from talking about himself to referencing his father, without referencing the focus of his comments (he does not always reference pronouns and sometimes confuses gender (using "she" and then "he" to refer to his father).

Literacy

Reading and writing skills were formally assessed through administration of subtests from the Boston Diagnostic Aphasia Examination, 3rd Edition (BDAE-3). CK's raw scores on the *Reading* subtest (with cues) are presented in Table 12-1. Standard scores and percentiles were not calculated due to cueing.

In *oral word reading* task, CK produced the following phonemic paraphasias: "purkle" for purple, "four" for forty-five, and "sever" for seashore. Overall, CK demonstrates moderate impairments in oral reading skills, characterized by phonemic paraphasias, while reading words, phrases, and sentences aloud. His reading comprehension, however, is intact.

In context of the *mechanics of writing* task, CK occasionally had difficulty with the directions of the task and needed further clarification from the clinician. For example, when asked to write the letter "t," CK wrote the word "tee" and required extra clarification to produce just the individual letter. He had increased difficulty writing numbers to dictation and needed multiple repetitions for each prompt (Table 12-2).

TABLE 12-1: Reading Subtest of the BDAE-3

Subtest	Raw Score
Matching across Cases and scripts	4/4
Number matching	4/4
Picture-word match	3/4
Basic oral word reading	6/15
Oral reading of sentences	2/5
Comprehension of orally read sentences	3/3
Reading comprehension –sentences and paragraphs	4/4

TABLE 12-2: CK's Scores on the Writing Subtest of the BDAE-3

Subtest	Raw Scores
Mechanics of writing (well-formedness of letters)	14/14
Mechanics of writing (correctness of letter choice)	21/21
Mechanics of writing (motor facility)	14/14
Primer word vocabulary	2/4
Regular phonics	2/2
Common irregular forms	3/3
Written picture naming	3/4

During the *primer word vocabulary* task, CK modified words by adding or subtracting morphemes coding for number and tense (e.g., produced "cats" for cat, "running" for run). Overall, CK demonstrated difficulty writing numbers to dictation, as evidenced by the need for additional repetitions or simplified prompts. CK's writing is characterized by well-formed, legible letters with appropriate spacing and spelling.

Speech-Sound Production

CK exhibited multiple phonemic paraphasias during speech; these were characteristics related to lexical retrieval and phonological processing difficulties following conduction aphasia. Articulation was within functional limits.

Fluency

Parameters of fluency including repetitions, prolongations, and blocks were assessed by clinical observation. CK occasionally repeated words during conversation and the picture description task; however, these characteristics were due to his difficulties with lexical retrieval and not related to a fluency disorder.

Voice

Aspects of voice including pitch, loudness, voice quality, respiratory effort, and resonance were within normal limits, based on clinical judgment.

IV. Associated Behavioral Systems

Sensorimotor

ORAL PERIPHERAL SPEECH-MECHANISM EXAMINATION. Speech structures were observed to be symmetrical, steady, and intact at rest. Strength, tone, range of motion, and coordination of the articulators were determined to be within functional limits.

Swallowing. Swallowing function was assessed through administration of the EAT-10. CK received a score of 1 out of 40 on the assessment, indicating no difficulties with a safe and efficient swallow. CK commented affirmatively in response to the statement, "The pleasure of eating is affected by my swallowing." He explained further that he cannot eat foods he used to enjoy, such as steak. CK did not demonstrate signs of airway protection deficits or inadequate management of oral secretions. No signs of coughing or choking while swallowing were noted. Therefore, it was determined that swallowing is within functional limits.

GROSS AND FINE MOTOR FUNCTIONS. Gross and fine motor functions were informally assessed throughout the session using clinical observation. CK's gross motor function was clinically judged to be within normal limits as evidenced by independent ambulation with a normal gait and appropriate posture while seated throughout the session. He also demonstrated normal fine motor function through correct grasp of a writing instrument during writing tasks.

HEARING AND VISION. CK responded appropriately to all visual and auditory stimuli throughout the session. During structured tasks, CK often moved forward in his seat, indicating a need for repetition of a prompt. However, this was clinically judged to be due to deficits in receptive and expressive language and not an auditory concern.

Cognition

During a picture description task, CK demonstrated possible difficulties with selective attention or inhibition of stimuli as evidenced by shifts in topic mid-sentence. Despite this, he remained attentive during all assessment tasks and contingently responded to all test materials. Long-term memory was assessed through biographical questions about children/grandchildren's names, his hometown, and so on. CK correctly identified all information during these tasks and through conversation at the beginning of the session.

Visual memory was assessed through a structured task requiring CK to memorize several images depicted on a sheet of paper and later identifying which images he saw. CK accurately identified the two images he had previously seen. Executive function skills were within functional limits in context of daily routines. For example, when first being seated in the clinic room, CK noticed he was missing his notebook and went to the lobby to search for it.

CK has difficulties with numerical values when presented orally.

Psychosocial

CK maintained a positive demeanor throughout the session and demonstrated positive social interactions with the clinician, supervisor, and other clients in the lobby. He engaged the clinician in conversation and demonstrated high motivation to complete all session tasks. He enjoyed speaking about his family as evidenced by showing pictures. It was determined that CK has strong familial support and regularly visits with his children and grandchildren.

Assessment Summary

CK is a 74-year-old male who was seen for a speech-language assessment to determine current communicative skills and inform treatment planning for the upcoming semester. He presents with a mild-to-moderate conduction aphasia following a CVA.

CK's expressive language is moderately impaired and is marked by instances of anomia, phonemic paraphasias, and difficulties with repetition of phrases of increasing complexity. He has notable difficulty with repetition of numbers and conversion of orally presented numerical values into written values.

CK's receptive language skills are mildly impaired due to difficulty comprehending abstract, multistep commands. CK demonstrates moderately impaired oral reading due to the presence of paraphasias and repetition while reading aloud; however, his reading comprehension is within normal limits. Language use, fluency, voice, and motor speech production are all clinically judged to be within functional limits. CK demonstrates occasional inattention characterized by abrupt shifts in topic. Besides this, cognitive function is intact as well. Positive prognostic indicators include his high motivation and engagement in therapy tasks, strong familial support, and use of compensatory strategies (e.g., notebook).

Appendix 12-B

Semantic/Phonologic Cueing Hierarchy

(Cameron, Wambaught, Wright, & Nessler, 2006)

1. Wh-question using the context of the story presented to elicit the targeted intended utterance (IU), verbal feedback provided for correct or incorrect response (7- to 8-second response time allowed—same for following steps).

2. Semantically nonspecific sentence completion cue presented, IU requested, verbal feedback provided for correct or incorrect responses (e.g., writing "She started _____.").

3. Semantically loaded sentence completion cue presented, IU requested, verbal feedback provided for correct or incorrect responses (e.g., writing "She picked up her pen and started _____.").

4. Semantically loaded sentence completion and first sound cue presented, IU requested, verbal feedback provided for correct or incorrect responses (e.g., writing "She picked up her pen and started /r/_____.").

5. Verbal model of target IU presented, repetition of target IU requested.

6. Integral stimulation presented to elicit target IU (maximum of five verbal models).

7. Next IU presented if integral stimulation does not elicit the target.

Appendix 12-C

Illustration of Relations between Syntax and Word Knowledge: Interaction between Selected Content Categories of Verbs and Complement Types Allowed and Disallowed in English

Content Category of Verb	Type of Complement Allowed (in English)	Type of Complement Prohibited	Example
Action	Noun phrase		The dog **ate** the bone
		Sentence	The dog **ate** that she went home
Locative action	Prepositional phrase		She **sat** on the chair
		Noun phrase	She **sat** the chair
Epistemic	Noun phrase		I **know** Harriet
	Sentence		I **know** that you are going to visit Harriet
Some state verbs	Noun phrase		She **wants** pizza
	Infinitive verb phrase		She **wants** to eat pizza
	Infinitive verb phrase with a phonologically realized subject		She wants **Mary** to eat Pizza
Some other state verbs	Infinitive verb phrase without a phonologically realized subject		Mary **has** to go home
		Infinitive verb phrase with a phonologically realized subject	Mary **has** Sharon to go home